Louisiana Rocks!

Louisiana Rocks!

The True Genesis of Rock & Roll

Tom Aswell

PELICAN PUBLISHING COMPANY
GRETNA 2010

Library of Congress Cataloging-in-Publication Data

Aswell, Tom.
  Louisiana rocks! : the true genesis of rock and roll / by Tom
Aswell.
      p. cm.
  Includes bibliographical references and index.
  ISBN 978-1-58980-677-1 (hardcover : alk. paper) 1. Popular
music—Louisiana—History and criticism. I. Title.
  ML3477.7.L8A89 2009
  781.6409763—dc22
                                    2009017023

Printed in the United States of America
Published by Pelican Publishing Company, Inc.
1000 Burmaster Street, Gretna, Louisiana 70053

Contents

Preface

The origins for this book date back to 1980 and an impulsive call to singer John Fred. I had an idea for a project on which I would need help—both logistical and financial—to pull off successfully. John, a native of Baton Rouge, had scored a number 1 hit with *Judy in Disguise (With Glasses)* in January 1968. The song sold five million copies and was sandwiched between two other songs that charted for him, *Shirley* and *Hey, Hey Bunny*.

The first time I saw him was in 1968. My wife and I were in a pizza parlor just off the Louisiana Tech University campus in Ruston. He had just completed a concert at Tech and he and his Playboy Band entered the restaurant and took a table next to us. His real name was John Fred Gourrier and twelve years later, finding him listed in the phone book, I called him with my proposal. "I think it's a great idea," he said. "Why don't you come by my house and we can talk about it?"

He greeted me at his front door and after exchanging pleasantries, led me into his living room where I made my pitch for what I knew would be an ambitious project: a videotape of Louisiana rock and roll stars. He listened intently before speaking. "I think this is a great project," he said. "Do you have any idea how popular Louisiana singers are in the United Kingdom? They love Louisiana artists in England." The late 1970s and early '80s, however, was a period of high interest rates, runaway inflation, and accompanying recession. Stagflation, the pundits called it. The Louisiana oil patch had dried up, and the state was broke. Economic reality prevailed, dooming our project to failure. Suddenly, John snapped his fingers. "A book!" he blurted. "Tom, you're a writer. Why don't you write a book?"

I promised him I would think about it but took no action for nearly a quarter of a century. Life takes strange twists, however. On April 15, 2005, John Fred Gourrier died in New Orleans' Tulane Medical Center. His health deteriorating, he had undergone a kidney transplant in the fall of 2004 but developed complications that took his life.

I never knew John Fred as well as I would have liked. We worked together on the project for just a few weeks— and only sporadically at that. Still, his death was a defining moment for me. I made a determination the day that I learned of his death that I would delay no longer. I immediately began researching Louisiana's musical history, thinking I would have two or three dozen singers to write about. Three years later, I was still conducting research and interviews. Those two or three dozen singers soon grew to almost three hundred personalities.

As I digested document upon document, read book after book, listened to CD after CD, and watched DVD after DVD, I accumulated an ever-growing list of artists who, like John Fred, are no longer living. Most of those died too young. I started a log. Since I first approached John Fred in 1980, ninety-one singers, musicians, disc jockeys, and recording executives with connections to Louisiana have died. Sixty-four of those deaths occurred before John's own. Since April 15, 2005, and the publication of this book, another twenty-seven have died.

Each was a tragic loss and with each passing we lose another irreplaceable part of the whole. The chasm that separates us from our past continues to grow deeper and wider. Their music was Louisiana's gift to the world. This is my attempt to preserve that legacy by documenting the contributions made in a unique time by many unique people. Their achievements are far too important to allow their stories to die with them.

Six of the first ten inductees into the Rock and Roll Hall of Fame had direct ties to the state. Louisiana members, with their year of induction, include: Fats Domino of New Orleans and Jerry Lee Lewis of Ferriday, 1986, the inaugural year of the hall; the Coasters, whose Will Jones of Shreveport was a member, 1987; Lead Belly of Mooringsport, 1988; Louis Armstrong of New Orleans, 1990; Dave Bartholomew of Edgard, 1991; Professor Longhair of Bogalusa, 1992; Mahalia Jackson of New Orleans, 1997; Jelly Roll Morton of New Orleans, Lloyd Price of Kenner, and Allen Toussaint of New Orleans, 1998; Earl Palmer of New Orleans, 2000; James Burton of Minden, 2001; Floyd Cramer of Campti, 2003; Buddy Guy of Lettsworth and Percy Sledge of Baton Rouge, 2005; Little Walter and the Ventures (Gerry McGee of Eunice was a member of the Ventures), 2008; and D.J. Fontana, 2009. Inductees not from Louisiana but who recorded in Louisiana or have strong Louisiana connections include Elvis Presley, Sam Cooke, Little Richard, and Ray Charles, 1986; Big Joe Turner and Hank Williams, 1987; Johnny Cash, 1992; John Fogerty of Creedence Clearwater Revival and Etta James, 1993; Janis Joplin, 1995; Stephen Stills of Crosby, Stills and Nash, 1997; and Paul Simon, 2001.

Efforts are ongoing to enshrine zydeco musician Clifton Chenier, pianists Lonnie Johnson and Dr. John, the Neville Brothers, and New Orleans recording executive Cosimo Matassa.

Louisiana singers, session artists, writers, producers, and studios sold more than a billion records, mostly from the early 1950s through the mid-'60s. Of the 500 Songs That Shaped Rock and Roll, as designated by the Rock and Roll Hall of Fame, forty-eight have direct Louisiana ties. Thirty are on the list of 365 Songs of the Century, as compiled by the Recording Industry Association of America and the National Endowment for the Arts.

There were others, many others, and each played an important role, but it was John Fred who made the suggestion that a book be written about his contemporaries. It was he who was so keenly aware of the impact his peers had on American pop culture. He spent most of his life promoting Louisiana music and musicians, even hosting a radio oldies show in his final years until he was no longer able to do so.

He died with a love of Louisiana music in his heart and so it is with pride and humility that I dedicate this book to the memory of John Fred Gourrier.

Acknowledgments

There is a theory, first alluded to by Hungarian author Frigyes Karinthy, that each of us is connected to every other being on the planet by no more than six steps, or six degrees of separation. After laboring over this work for four years, interviewing performers, producers, recording executives, and songwriters, I am convinced that in the music business, the degrees of separation are reduced to a maximum of two. There are so many Louisiana musicians who have recorded with, played behind, produced, and toured with other singers, players, and producers that it is virtually impossible not to make a direct connection to any American musician of any genre by the simple act of interviewing a handful of Louisiana's own artists.

That was the daunting task I discovered soon after I undertook this project. Talk to five or six musicians and suddenly there's a link with hundreds of others as the list expands exponentially. Thus the task of reining me in fell to others who had to find a way to curb my enthusiasm. Judith Howard, Stephanie Deselle, Mary Stagg, and my wife, Betty, spent untold hours with red ink pens poring over manuscript drafts. I will always be indebted to them. Scores of entertainers gave freely of their time for interviews that I know were inconvenient and a bother. But still they gave. Mike Shepherd harassed me day and night with new information and stacks of photographs as well as miles of video. Mike, director of the Louisiana Music Hall of

Fame, is special in his love for and promotion of Louisiana's wonderful musical legacy. Louisiana needs his enthusiasm and dedication to preserving the musical heritage that has given the world so much pleasure.

I have already cited the editorial contributions of my wife, Betty, but she has done so much more. She has tolerated my dreams and aspirations for forty-one years. More than that, she has fed me, clothed me, scolded me, and encouraged me as the situation dictated, all while doting over three daughters and seven grandchildren. She's my rock.

I would like to thank Pelican Publishing Company for seeing the value of a work such as this. I offer a special note of appreciation to Pelican editor in chief Nina Kooij, who has been patient with my questions and who has been tolerant of my general ignorance of the publishing industry. To Lindsey Reynolds, Pelican assistant editor, fell the yeoman's task of correcting, editing, and revising my copy to conform to Pelican's exacting standards. I can never thank her enough for her untiring work. Others at Pelican who deserve special thanks are Katie Szadziewicz, who has been of immense assistance in promoting this work, and Scott Campbell, who scheduled book signings all over the state.

Finally, a special thanks to Adrian Erwin who designed and set up my Web page.

Introduction

"If Music be the food of love, play on."
—William Shakespeare, *Twelfth Night*

Memphis and Sun Records gave us Elvis Presley and Jerry Lee Lewis. Their music provided the impetus that thrust rock and roll into the national consciousness in the mid-1950s, begetting what many saw as a cataclysmic cultural explosion. The alien, raucous new music aroused teenagers, plunged parental despair to new depths, and provoked preachers to call the wrath of God down upon its purveyors. Yet, farther to the south, the eclectic compilation of Louisiana musical talent—from New Orleans rhythm-and-blues to swamp pop to Cajun/zydeco to blues to Shreveport rockabilly—had ignited the fuse years before.

Some cite the origin of rock and roll as 1955's *Rock around the Clock* by Bill Haley and His Comets. Sales, spurred by its use in the 1954 movie soundtrack *The Blackboard Jungle* and later in the television series *Happy Days*, eventually reached twenty-five million records. In 1949, however, six years before *Rock around the Clock* was a hit, Fats Domino recorded a song in his hometown of New Orleans called *The Fat Man,* which some historians argue was the first rock and roll song.[1] That same year Hank Williams, Sr., residing in Bossier City while performing as a regular on the *Louisiana Hayride,* recorded *Lovesick Blues.*[2] The song was a radical break from traditional country and opened the door for the rockabilly sound that would soon follow.

Earlier still, in 1947, Roy Brown recorded *Good Rockin' Tonight* in the same New Orleans studio Domino would later use.[3] It was covered by R&B singer Wynonie Harris later that year and Elvis recorded his own cover of the song for Sun in 1954. So why weren't Roy Brown or Fats Domino credited with creating this new sound that would turn the music world on its ear? The answer is simple and tinged with pathos: white stations didn't play "colored" music. Elvis would knock down the barriers a decade later, but even he had difficulty getting air play for his first record.

Instead, we heard Pat Boone's saccharin covers of Little Richard's *Tutti Frutti* and *Long Tall Sally* and Fats Domino's *Ain't That a Shame*. Gale Storm offered her version of Smiley Lewis's *I Hear You Knocking*, and Ricky Nelson gave us his takes of Domino's *I'm Walking* and *I'm in Love Again*. There were two benefits of the white covers. First, they tipped off millions of unsuspecting teenagers to the existence of the bawdier, rawer, more risqué R&B music. That, in turn, helped open the doors for other black artists waiting in the wings. Second, for every Pat Boone, Gale Storm, and Ricky Nelson copy sold, black artists like Dave Bartholomew, Fats Domino, and Little Richard reaped lucrative royalties as the songs' composers.

New Orleans and Shreveport radio stations were exceptions to the precept that this rebellious, impertinent music be ignored. Because a few stations dared defy convention, R&B artists received valuable exposure in the Deep South. The resultant changes brought about over a scant fifteen years revolutionized popular music forever. The music's appeal was such that future rockabilly star Buddy Holly found it necessary to sneak out of his Lubbock, Texas, home to listen to Shreveport's 50,000-watt KWKH on his parents' car radio to circumvent a household R&B ban.

Change came slowly. In 1958, the National Academy of Recording Arts and Sciences inexplicably disregarded the contributions of genuine R&B artists. Nominees for the first Grammy award for best rhythm-and-blues performance that year included Nat "King" Cole, Harry Belafonte, Perez Prado, Earl Grant, and the Champs,[4] artists about as closely identified with R&B as a Louisiana nutria is akin to a thoroughbred racehorse. The Champs won for *Tequila*. Fats Domino, Little Richard, Huey "Piano" Smith, Ray Charles, Lloyd Price, and Sam Cooke were simply ignored. Those six combined for thirteen top 10 R&B hits in '57 and '58, eleven of which were in the top 5 on the *Billboard* charts.[5]

As late as 1963, certain songs by certain artists remained taboo. Ray Charles followed *I Can't Stop Loving You* with another country hit. His ramped-up cover of the Jimmie Davis classic *You Are My Sunshine* reached number 1 on the R&B and number 7 on the pop charts in December of 1962. The management of Ruston's KRUS gave its blessing to the album's flip side, a cover of Hank Williams' *Your Cheatin' Heart*, which went to number 29 pop and number 23 on the R&B charts. To ensure that deejays played the correct side, management took a knife and cut a giant X across the *Sunshine* tracks.

An important musical and cultural upheaval began in the late 1940s. As it continued through the early '60s in Louisiana, it played a major role in the rock and roll explosion that loomed on the horizon for America and the rest of the world. Five distinct musical styles developed in Louisiana during this period. Shreveport's *Louisiana Hayride* in the northwest corner of the state launched the careers of Hank Williams, Elvis Presley, Johnny Cash, and others as country morphed into rockabilly.[6] New Orleans, as far as it could be culturally and geographically from Shreveport, dominated the charts with blues and R&B. Fats Domino, Lloyd Price, Little Richard, Guitar Slim, and Professor Longhair headed an extensive list of musical prodigies. In the south Louisiana prairies, fiddles, accordions, and washboards coalesced with guitars, drums, and pianos to create both Cajun and zydeco music. Buckwheat Zydeco, Rockin' Dopsie, Rockin' Sidney, Doug Kershaw, Rod Bernard, and Clifton Chenier held sway over the Acadiana music scene. Zydeco, Cajun, rockabilly, R&B, and blues came together to produce another genre called swamp pop, spotlighting G.G. Shinn,

Van Broussard, Clint West, Joe Barry, Jay Chevalier, and T.K. Hulin, among others. Each style drew inspiration from the others. In the process, the contributions made to rock and roll by Louisiana artists were extraordinary.

The period from the late 1940s to the early 1960s was unique in Louisiana. Singers, songwriters, sidemen, producers, and disc jockeys converged with independent recording studios, record labels, and distributors to give us a cultural phenomenon that likely will never be duplicated. The corporatization of the recording industry weakened the undercapitalized independent recording studios at the expense of artist development, effectively slamming the door on aspiring talent. Artist creativity and development at the local level, if not killed outright, were at least critically wounded. Radio station consolidation, the result of a profit-driven mindset, resulted in the shrinkage of station playlists and was merely the final nail in the coffin.

Somehow, though, in one wonderfully coordinated musical revolution, in one state, in one era, it all came together. From New Orleans to Shreveport to Baton Rouge to Lake Charles, from the Dew Drop Inn in New Orleans to the *Louisiana Hayride* in Shreveport to the bayou dives and the plains honky-tonks, Louisiana was a siren's song for every picker, singer, piano player, promoter, and record producer. The allure was so tempting, so irresistible, that future stars were pulled unresisting into the vortex.

So begins the story of the true genesis of rock and roll.

1

The Birth of Rock and Roll: Cosimo Matassa and J&M Studio

He didn't own a record label. He wasn't even a recording producer, but the failure to elect Cosimo Matassa (April 13, 1926-) to the Rock and Roll Hall of Fame is the single biggest omission since the hall's first induction ceremonies in 1986. He was, after all, every bit as responsible for the advent of rock and roll as Elvis Presley, Buddy Holly, or Bill Haley. In fact, it is no stretch to speculate that had there been no Cosimo Matassa, the world may never have heard of Elvis, Fats Domino, Lloyd Price, Little Richard, or many others. He certainly earned the right to be listed alongside Berry Gordy, Alan Freed, Phil Spector, Tom Donahue, Paul Ackerman, Milt Gabler, and Dick Clark among the hall's inductees.

Since the genre was born in his New Orleans studio in 1947 and nurtured there until it gained its footing in Shreveport and Memphis, from where it spread across the land like so much kudzu, it would seem only logical to recognize him as the Godfather of Rock and Roll. He deserves much of the credit for the 450 gold records, 600 top 10, and 1,150 top 100 songs with direct ties to Louisiana. The Louisiana Music Commission once compiled a list of 101 reasons why Matassa should be in the Rock and Roll Hall of Fame.[1]

The 101 reasons listed by the Music Commission consisted mainly of the impressive string of hits turned out by his studio, including songs by Little Richard, Ray Charles, Fats Domino, Big Joe Turner, Roy Brown, Professor Longhair, Shirley and

Lee, Smiley Lewis, Jimmy Clanton, Irma Thomas, Johnny Adams, Frankie Ford, Guitar Slim, the Meters, Ray Charles, the Spiders, Lloyd Price, Huey "Piano" Smith, Clarence "Frogman" Henry, Bennie Spellman, Art and Aaron Neville, Ernie K-Doe, Joe Barry, and Robert Parker, among others. Another reason was his decision to provide a place in his studio where Vernon Winslow (Dr. Daddy-O) could broadcast his radio show as an alternative to having to take the freight elevator to the radio studio in the upper floor of a whites-only New Orleans hotel.

In late 1999, New Orleans and Louisiana paid proper homage to the building from which so many rock and roll and R&B hits sprang in the golden era of 1947 to 1956. Matassa's recording studio, J&M Studio, located at 838-840 North Rampart Street, was designated a historic landmark by the city and state on December 10, 1999, the fiftieth anniversary of the studio's first recording session with Fats Domino and Dave Bartholomew.[2] The building is a Laundromat today, but inside, the walls are lined with photographs of a who's who of R&B performers who at one time or another recorded at the quaint old studio. The official landmark brass plaque that adorns the exterior of the building reads:

First Recording Studio of Cosimo Matassa
Built Circa 1835 with Galleries Likely Added in the 1850s
In 1944, J&M Amusements Acquired the Building, and
Cosimo Matassa Soon Opened J&M Recording Studio.
Oscar "Papa" Celestin, Danny Barker, and the Dukes of
Dixieland recorded jazz here.
The "New Orleans Sound" developed from pioneering
rhythm & blues and rock & roll recordings made here
between 1947 and 1956 by Paul Gayten, Annie Laurie, Roy
Brown, Professor Longhair, Dave Bartholomew, Fats Domino,
Guitar Slim, Shirley & Lee, Lloyd Price, Jerry Lee Lewis,
Little Richard, Ray Charles and others.

"I never intended on being in the recording business," Matassa says as he settles into a chair in his cluttered office above Matassa's Market. The crowded family grocery store is tucked away from the tourist traffic in the New Orleans French Quarter at the corner of Dauphine and St. Phillip Streets. Matassa, born in New Orleans, pursued chemistry as a major at Tulane University. In late 1943, World War II was raging when he told his father he wanted to drop out of school. Certain that he would be drafted when he turned eighteen in April of the approaching year, he said he wanted to kick back a few months.

"Well, I wasn't drafted because of some physical problems," he recounts, "and I found out I wasn't cut out to be a chemist. My father was old-school Italian and he told me it was either go back to school or go to work, so I went to work." He got a job with J&M Services, a jukebox business, and in a few years, found the demand for used records from the jukeboxes was such that he bought the business. "When the war ended, I opened a combination appliance and record store at the corner of Rampart and Dauphine." Matassa continues, "When I realized the demand for records was more than for appliances, I soon dropped the appliances and concentrated on records."

Matassa eventually converted a small room in the back of the record store to a recording studio so that people could make a record for their personal use. "That was in 1945," he says. "The recording studio soon became a commercial enterprise because of the interest it generated." Matassa had only a direct-to-disc recording system in those days, prehistoric by today's digitalized standards. "There were no tape recorders, so if a singer or musician messed up, we had to discard the entire acetate disc and start over," he explains. The system dictated that performers complete their songs within a specified time because the disc would cut off automatically, usually in less than three minutes. "We kept that system for several years before I was able to purchase a tape recorder," he recalls. In many recording sessions, Matassa was forced to do a lot of microphone sharing because of the limitations of his equipment.

"We were never state-of-the-art," he says. He would, for example, move a boom-mounted microphone from the drummer to the saxophone for the sax solo and then back to the drummer.

"Roy Brown's *Good Rockin' Tonight* was a direct-to-disc recording," says Matassa. There was also Guitar Slim's *The Things That I Used to Do*. "Ray Charles not only played piano on that song, but he directed it too. In those days, we had to go all the way through, mistakes and all, and at the end, he [Ray] would address each of the musicians and tell them where they messed up, and he was never wrong. He also played piano for Fats Domino, and he did two half-sessions for Atlantic Records in my studio."

Unlike most black artists of that day, Ray Charles did not stay at the Dew Drop Inn, the epicenter of New Orleans black entertainment in the early 1950s, choosing instead to stay at the Foster Hotel just up the street. "The movie *Ray* was an excellent movie," Matassa says, "but it short-changed New Orleans. Ray based himself out of New Orleans for three years early in his career. He spent three years of his life in New Orleans, but it's never once mentioned in the movie."[3]

World War II liberated the music business because it scattered recording personnel all over the United States, which meant independent studios, pressing plants, and distributors started popping up in places they had never been before. It seemed for a while that nearly every town of any size had a recording studio. That encouraged the development of local talent that otherwise would never have been able to obtain exposure. The trifecta of local talent, independent studios eager to record the talent, and local radio stations willing to play the records cracked the heretofore impenetrable monopoly enjoyed by the major recording companies. Between 1955 and 1959, the U.S. market share of the four major record companies (RCA, Columbia, and Decca were joined by Capitol by that time) had plummeted from 78 percent to 44 percent. By 2005, the "new" big four (EMI-Capitol, Warner, SonyBMG, and Universal) had regained a 70 percent market share.[4]

Matassa says demographics worked against many black artists in the early days of rock and R&B, but his studio opened doors previously shut to New Orleans artists. "We didn't intentionally seek out black artists in those days. I grew up in the French Quarter where blacks and whites lived side by side. We didn't have black neighbors or white neighbors; they were just neighbors. We were integrated long before it became a social issue. The place had vitality. Many residents were new immigrants and many more were black. We were integrated—we just didn't know it."

Today, Matassa is unhappy with developments in the music business. The practice of sampling another singer's or group's lyrics in a song is a trend that upsets him. So, too, do the explicit lyrics that have found their way into music. "Go back and listen to some of the old blues songs and compare them to today's rap," he suggests. "Blues singers had implied sex in their songs. Take *Big Legged Woman*, for example. There's not a dirty word in that entire song, but you know exactly what the singer's saying, what he's implying: raw sex. Same with Big Joe Turner's *Shake, Rattle and Roll*. Rap music, for some reason, finds it necessary to be graphic, to interject all the four-letter words you can think of—and then some."

The heyday of the independent studio is far behind Matassa, and he ended up losing about $200,000 before getting out of the business. Still, he says, he'd do it again if the opportunity arose. "We had a lot of fun back then. We were just one big family. All the artists played and sang backup for each other. Most people think Fats Domino played his own piano but he didn't always. Huey 'Piano' Smith did the piano work on many of Fats' records. He also did the piano intro on Smiley Lewis's *I Hear You Knockin'*. We were always looking for that 'sweet spot' in the studio where it would all come together." J&M charged fifteen

Cosimo Matassa started it all in his tiny J&M Recording Studio on New Orleans' North Rampart Street in 1947. Sixty years later, he was inducted into the Louisiana Music Hall of Fame. (Courtesy of Louisiana Music Hall of Fame)

dollars per hour for recording sessions, and musicians were paid not by Matassa but by the record labels. Union scale for musicians was $41.25 for a four-song session.

"I've known people who worked all their lives at a job they hated so they could provide for their families. I was fortunate enough to make a good living at a job I loved. I think we just matured ourselves out of business." In a moment of candor, he reveals the fate that befell many of the independents. "One thing about the music business is that the only thing harder to get than that first hit is the second hit. You have a lot of one-hit wonders out there. That's not good because the independent recording studios back then were paid by the distributors, but they paid us for the first hit from proceeds derived from the second hit, and they'd pay us for the second hit from revenues generated by the third hit, and so on. In my case, I went too long between hits."[5]

In a July 16, 2009, story in *USA Today*, Matassa lamented the fact that the music business never developed and flourished in New Orleans. "If you went to a bank about real estate, they'd say, 'See Mr. Jones.' If it was for oil, 'See Mr. Smith.' For music, it was, 'Get out of here before I call the police.'" Despite the financial setbacks that spelled the end for his studio, Matassa has no regrets. Well, perhaps one: he never had the opportunity to record Mahalia Jackson.

He describes New Orleans as having a "deep pool of talent" and retains fond memories of the musicians who paraded through his studios in a near endless procession for more than two decades. Little Richard, for example, was "wild, but extremely talented." There was Ray Charles's incredible memory for detail during recording sessions. Dr. John's talent was evident even while he was still in high school, and Professor Longhair was unique, but regrettably his talents lay dormant during years he worked as a janitor and did not play. Allen Toussaint was simply "a genius."

Still, one has to wonder how far any of those artists

would have gone in their careers if Cosimo Matassa had never installed that cramped, antiquated recording studio in the rear of his father's store back in 1945.

2

The Groundbreakers

Decades before anyone had ever heard of rock and roll, six musical pioneers laid the foundation upon which scores of Louisiana musicians would build careers in the years to come. Their contributions came in the fields of gospel, jazz, barrelhouse blues, country music, folk, and blues. They came from jail, from brothels, from churches, and even from schoolhouses. Individually and collectively, their influence on modern music was profound and continues more than a century after most of them were born. Country morphed into rockabilly. Gospel and barrelhouse blues combined to produce boogie-woogie and rhythm-and-blues while folk and blues have stood the test of time on their own merits. Others who followed saw how these early performers pulled themselves out of poverty with their musical talents; thus encouraged, a veritable flood of talent surged onto the national entertainment scene.

Lead Belly

Lead Belly (January 15, 20, 21, or 29, 1885, 1888, or 1889-December 6, 1949) was born Huddie Ledbetter in Mooringsport, Louisiana, just outside Shreveport.[1] Possessing a legendary quick temper, he was arrested and convicted of murder in Texas in 1917 and sentenced to twenty years' imprisonment. One story had him serenading the Texas governor for a pardon. Other versions say he was simply released early on good behavior in 1925. Five years

25

Early publicity photo of Huddie "Lead Belly" Ledbetter, a native of Mooringsport, Louisiana, near Shreveport.

later, he was back in prison for attempted murder, this time in the Louisiana State Penitentiary at Angola. It was while in prison that he earned his nickname as both a play on his surname and for his physical toughness.

Folklorist John Lomax and his son Alan discovered Lead Belly in 1933 while searching for singing talent in the nation's prisons. Louisiana governor Oscar K. Allen signed his release and Lead Belly was again a free man. Upon his release, Lead Belly worked as Lomax's driver. They drove to New York, where he signed his first recording contract with American Record Corp. He achieved little commercial success with that record company because label executives insisted that Lead Belly sing blues instead of folk music, to which he was better suited.[2]

In 1940, following yet another jail sentence, he found the folk music scene exploding in popularity and befriended Woody Guthrie and Pete Seeger. Seeger, who attempted to conceal his Harvard upbringing by wearing faded jeans, stood in stark contrast to Lead Belly, who always wore a clean white shirt, starched collar, well-pressed suit, and shoes that were always shined. While in New York, Lead Belly recorded his best-known songs: *Rock Island Line, The Midnight Special,* and *Goodnight, Irene.*[3]

By 1948, he was starting to feel the early effects of the disease that would shortly take his life. He began a tour of Europe in May 1949 but numbness in his legs and right hand persisted. He was diagnosed with amyotrophic lateral sclerosis (ALS), Lou Gehrig's disease. He died just over six months later, on December 6, and was buried in the Shiloh Baptist Church Cemetery eight miles west of Blanchard, Louisiana, near Shreveport.

Six months after his death, Seeger and his group, the Weavers, took Lead Belly's *Goodnight, Irene* to the number 1 position on the pop charts. Frank Sinatra, Ernest Tubb, and Red Foley each recorded covers of the song. The Lonnie Donegan Skiffle Group reached the top 10 in both the U.S. and in England with *Rock Island Line.* Johnny Cash had a top 40 country hit with it in 1970. Johnny Rivers had a number 20 *Billboard* hit of *The Midnight Special* in 1965 and Creedence Clearwater Revival later recorded it as well. Jimmie Rodgers had a number 3 hit in 1957 with *Kisses Sweeter Than Wine,* a song that Lead Belly had adapted from the Irish folk song *Drimmer's Cow.* The Highwaymen had a number 13 hit with Lead Belly's *Cotton Fields* in 1962. *In New Orleans*, however, was the biggest hit of any of his songs by another artist. The Animals changed the name to *House of the Rising Sun* and it became a number 1 hit for three weeks in 1964 and earned the British group a gold record.[4] Kurt Cobain covered *Where Did You Sleep Last Night* in 1993 to close Nirvana's *MTV Unplugged* special, and the Rolling Stones adapted *The Bourgeois Blues* for their song *When the Whip Comes Down.* Others who have covered Lead Belly songs include the Grateful Dead, Gene Autry, Led Zeppelin, Jerry Garcia, and Rod Stewart.

Three of Lead Belly's songs are among the Rock and Roll Hall of Fame's 500 Songs That Shaped Rock and Roll: the Animals' *House of the Rising Sun,* Lonnie Donegan's *Rock Island Line,* and his own version of *The Midnight Special*.

Lead Belly was inducted into the Rock and Roll Hall of Fame in 1988.[5]

Jelly Roll Morton

Jelly Roll Morton (1890-1941), born Ferdinand Lamothe, grew up in New Orleans and began learning piano at age ten. Two years later, he was working in the brothels of Storyville as a piano player. From 1904 to 1917, he roamed the South as an itinerant pianist, working clubs in Louisiana, Mississippi, Alabama, and Florida. Keeping New Orleans as his base, he traveled to St. Louis and Kansas City, eventually making his way to the West Coast and then to Chicago. There he established himself as a piano talent and made several classic recordings for RCA Victor and other labels.[6]

Some of his better-known recordings include not only original compositions but pieces written by other famous composers. They include *Cannon Ball Blues*, *Wolverine Blues*, *King Porter Stomp*, *Black Bottom Stomp*, *Beale Street Blues*, *Shreveport Stomp*, *Mournful Serenade*, *Red Hot Pepper*, *Tiger Rag*, *My Melancholy Baby*, *I Ain't Got Nobody*, *Honeysuckle Rose*, *Tin Roof Blues*, and his signature *Jelly Roll Blues*.

By the 1930s, Jelly Roll had fallen on such hard times that he somehow lost the diamond from his front tooth. He played dives in Washington, D.C., eventually managing a jazz club where he played occasionally. In 1938, folklorist Alan Lomax documented his life in a series of interviews about early jazz for the Library of Congress. Morton blamed his encroaching ill health on a voodoo spell.[7]

Alonzo "Lonnie" Johnson

A blues and jazz singing pioneer and guitarist, Alonzo "Lonnie" Johnson (February 8, 1894-June 16, 1970) probably owed his life to a 1917 tour of England with a musical revue. On his return to New Orleans in 1919, he found that most of his family had died in the influenza pandemic. He somehow avoided the disease while overseas.

He is credited with taking the guitar from a supportive role to a featured instrument with his innovative solos. Blues singer B.B. King said Johnson played licks that no one else, including King himself, has been able to duplicate. "The man was way ahead of his time," King told writer Dean Alger. Though Johnson had more than two dozen recordings, few, if any, are recognized as standards today. Instead, he is remembered for his brilliant guitar techniques.

He worked throughout the 1920s with a variety of bands and musicians, including Eddie Lang, Duke Ellington, and Louis Armstrong. Johnson's career, however, was a rollercoaster ride that occasionally found him working menial jobs between his great musical accomplishments. He died in Ontario, Canada, from injuries received in a 1969 auto accident. He was posthumously inducted into the Louisiana Blues Hall of Fame in 1997. By bringing jazz, pop, and blues together, he extended his influence to Sun Records artists Elvis Presley and Jerry Lee Lewis.[8]

Jimmie Davis

Jimmie Davis (September 11, 1899-November 5, 2000), born in the now-deserted Jackson Parish town of Beech Springs, became one of the most successful singers of both country and gospel music and twice served as governor of Louisiana. His most famous song, 1939's *You Are My Sunshine*, was covered by dozens of artists, including Bing Crosby, Aretha Franklin, Gene Autry, Johnny and the Hurricanes, Mitch Ryder, and Ray Charles. It was named the official state song of Louisiana in 1977. It won a Grammy Hall of Fame Award in 1999, and that same year was named one of the Songs of the Century by the Recording Industry Association of America.

Despite growing up in poverty (he shared a bed with several siblings until he was nine years old), Davis worked as a street musician to pay his way through Louisiana College in Pineville. Upon obtaining his master's degree in education from Louisiana State University, he landed a teaching job at the all-female Dodd College in Shreveport and earned extra money singing on a local radio station.

Early on, he had a penchant for risqué songs and like Jimmie Rodgers, he made frequent use of double entendres in his lyrics. When a talent scout heard him, he was signed to a recording contract and had his first major hit with *Nobody's Darling but Mine*. He followed that with *It Makes No Difference Now.*

By the late 1930s Davis had entered politics. He was elected Shreveport's commissioner of public safety before winning a seat on the Louisiana Public Service Commission. In 1943, he was elected governor. Even then, his singing career continued with his number 1 hit *There's a New Moon Over My Shoulder*. He traveled to Hollywood to make a handful of B westerns, playing himself in the 1947 movie based on his own life story, *Louisiana*.[10] In 1959, Davis won his second term as governor,

Jimmie Davis sits at his desk in the State Capitol in Baton Rouge during his second term as governor (1960-1964). (Courtesy of Louisiana Music Hall of Fame)

during which he began to record gospel music almost exclusively, achieving a hit with *Suppertime*. During his two administrations, he established a state retirement system and funding for more than $100 million in public improvements while leaving the state with a $38 million surplus. He built the Sunshine Bridge over the Mississippi River, the Toledo Bend Reservoir, and a new Governor's Mansion, all criticized at the time but later acknowledged as beneficial to the state. He also coordinated pay periods of state employees who sometimes received paychecks a week late.[11]

Leaving office in 1964, at age 65, he continued to record for the next thirty years. He was elected to the Nashville Songwriters Hall of Fame in 1971 and to the Country Music Hall of Fame in 1972. He died at his home at the age of 101 and is buried in the Davis Family Cemetery in Quitman. He is the only politician elected to the Country Music Hall of Fame, the Nashville Songwriters Hall of Fame, and the Gospel Music Hall of Fame.[12]

Louis Armstrong

Digging through garbage cans in search of edible food during the early years of the twentieth century might not be the preferred image of a young Louis Armstrong (August 1, 1901-July 6, 1971). Born in one of the poorest sections of New Orleans, he developed street smarts and a dirty mouth at an early age. Had he not fired a pistol on New Years' Eve and been sent to the Jones Home for Colored Waifs at the age of thirteen, he likely would never have grown up to become one of the greatest jazz musicians of all time. It was there that he was introduced to the cornet.

A year later he was scratching out a living in places like the Come Clean Dance Hall, the Funky Butt Hall, and the Mahogany Hall. He worked in the infamous Storyville district as a musician and as a pimp. He abandoned the seamier side of life when one of his girls stabbed him.[13]

In 1922, Armstrong headed north to Chicago, where he hooked up with Joe "King" Oliver's Creole Jazz Band. In 1935 he hired as his manager Joe Glaser, rumored to be connected to the Mob run by Al Capone. Taking care of the business details, Glaser proved to be a capable manager and freed Armstrong up to concentrate on his music. Glaser remained his manager until Armstrong's death in 1969.[14]

In May of 1964, Armstrong bumped the Beatles out of the number 1 position on the *Billboard* Hot 100 with *Hello, Dolly!* and in 1968 he had another number 1 hit with *What a Wonderful World*. Both songs were indicative of his transition from playing the horn to performing vocals, a move necessitated by failing health following a 1959 heart attack.

Satchmo died in his sleep at his Queens, New York, home. His funeral attracted over twenty-five thousand mourners. Honorary pallbearers were Gov. Nelson Rockefeller, Mayor John Lindsay, Bing Crosby, Ella Fitzgerald, Guy Lombardo, Duke Ellington, Dizzy Gillespie, Pearl Bailey, Count Basie, Harry James, Frank Sinatra, Ed Sullivan, Earl Wilson, Alan King, Johnny Carson, David Frost, Merv Griffin, Dick Cavett, and Bobby Hackett.[15]

Statue of Louis Armstrong, who progressed from a street-wandering orphan to become one of the world's foremost musicians. (Courtesy of Louisiana Music Hall of Fame)

Armstrong was inducted into the Rock and Roll Hall of Fame as an Early Influence. His *West End Blues* was chosen as one of *Billboard*'s 500 Songs That Shaped Rock and Roll.[16]

Mahalia Jackson

The daughter of a Baptist preacher, Mahalia Jackson (October 26, 1911 or 1912-January 27, 1972) was born in New Orleans. After her mother died when she was five, Mahalia was raised by family members until she moved to Chicago in 1928.

She married Isaac "Ike" Hockenhull in 1936. He encouraged Mahalia to pursue a professional singing career in lieu of singing in the Greater Salem Baptist Church choir. She won an audition but turned down an offer from Decca Records and Louis Armstrong. It wasn't until she teamed up with Chicago gospel music icon Thomas Dorsey in 1929 that her singing career took off. Her signature performance of Dorsey's *Precious Lord, Take My Hand* became one of the most requested songs at her concerts.[17]

Her recording of *Move on up a Little Higher* sold more than eight million copies in 1946 and was named on *Billboard*'s 500 Songs That Shaped Rock and Roll. In addition, her recording of *He's Got the Whole World in His Hands* climbed to number 69 in 1958. In 1950, she was the first gospel singer to appear in concert at Carnegie Hall and in 1958, at the Newport Jazz Festival. She sang at Pres. John F. Kennedy's inauguration and at the funeral of Dr. Martin Luther King.[18] She consistently brought movie theater patrons to tears when she sang *Trouble of the World* during the funeral of the Annie Johnson character in the movie *Imitation of Life*. She died of a heart attack in Chicago.

3

The Birth of R&B

"Rock and roll was not a marriage of rhythm-and-blues and country and western. That's white publicity. Rock and roll was just a white imitation, a white adaptation of Negro rhythm-and-blues."

—Louis Jordan

Marriage, imitation, or adaptation—it really doesn't matter. In those early pioneer days of rock and roll in Louisiana, particularly New Orleans, there were few racial lines drawn. There was one common language: music. The top singers in New Orleans were black while Cosimo Matassa, the man who put the city's music on the map, was white. The songs offered up by Ricky Nelson and Pat Boone as alternatives to Fats Domino and Little Richard were not imitation or adaptation. Those were simply corporate-inspired, polite, white covers of black music recorded because it was thought that white kids wouldn't listen to black music. The corporate suits couldn't have been more wrong. Instead of overshadowing Fats, Boone's cover of *Ain't That a Shame* sparked a renewed interest in Domino's earthier version of the song. Domino, who wore a diamond ring on each finger, was performing in a New Orleans club several years after the release of the cover when he learned that Boone was in the audience. Calling Boone up to the stage, he held his hand up and pointed to the most prominent of his sparkling, diamond-adorned rings. "This man bought me this ring with this song." The two then performed *Ain't That a Shame* together.[1]

Long before New Orleans became synonymous with hit records, the city was a hotbed of live entertainment in bars and dancehalls. Besides attracting nationally acclaimed artists, these venues provided a platform where local

Abandoned and neglected today, the Dew Drop Inn on LaSalle Street in New Orleans was once one of the most active African-American entertainment venues in the nation.

performers were given free rein to develop their unique styles. Although instrumental in springboarding Louisiana music to prominence, the Pelican Club, the Tijuana, the Gypsy Tea Room, the Astoria, Lincoln Beach, and the Golden Cadillac are gone now, as is the Dew Drop Inn.[2]

For a quarter century, from 1945 to 1970, the Dew Drop Inn, located at 2836 LaSalle Street in uptown New Orleans, attracted the elite among the nation's black entertainers. The story of the Dew Drop, however, is really the story of one man, Frank G. Painia (June 4, 1911-July 1972). Painia was a barber who attained only a seventh-grade education. He moved to New Orleans with his family in 1934 and became a partner in a barbershop on LaSalle Street. A couple of years later, Painia opened his own shop across the street, on the corner of LaSalle and Sixth.

He soon purchased a bar and grocery store just two doors away and renovated the building to accommodate his barbershop and a restaurant, which was added to the barroom that he named the Groove Room. He renamed the complex the Dew Drop Inn and opened in April of 1939. Just two short years later, the United States would enter World War II, raging in Europe. At the time great numbers of people were in transit, but the city lacked a quality place for blacks to stay. Taking advantage of the room shortage, Painia built a hotel next door, expanding the Dew Drop into two buildings.

Because New Orleans had no nightclub suitable for the nation's top black entertainers, the decision to offer live entertainment was easy. Painia first experimented with local entertainment in the lounge. Finding a demand for live music, he began searching for big name performers even as workers were putting the finishing touches on the latest addition to the Dew Drop.

By October of 1945, the *Louisiana Weekly* was calling the Dew Drop the "swankiest nightclub" in New Orleans. Featuring two shows nightly on weekends and an amateur contest on Fridays, the Dew Drop lived up to its reputation. For the cover charge of seventy-five cents, one could catch such acts as Big Joe Turner, Ivory Joe Hunter, Jackie Wilson, Clarence "Gatemouth" Brown, comedians, jugglers, shake dancers, and female impersonators. The Dew Drop always had a house band. In the 1940s it was either Dave Bartholomew or Edgar Blanchard and the Gondoliers. By today's standards, the club wasn't much in the way of opulence, holding only two hundred to three hundred people. It had plain wooden tables and chairs, but the tables had clean, white tablecloths, and everyone who worked there wore a fresh uniform.[3]

Painia was also a good promoter who was not above doing whatever was necessary to attract customers to his club. Deacon John Moore, who entertained regularly at the Dew Drop, paid a nostalgic visit to the deserted club in January 2007. Staring pensively at the long-neglected building, he suddenly laughed at one of the thousands of memories that must have been rushing through his mind. "You know,

Frank used to slip a few dollars to taxi drivers to get them to pick up tourists and bring 'em to the Dew Drop," he said. "He got a lot of crowds that way."

That was not without risks, however. One person who visited the club was actor Robert Mitchum. "He didn't know nothin' about segregation in those days, but he soon learned," John recalled. "He was arrested on a charge of mingling."[4]

The Dew Drop jump-started the careers of many New Orleans musicians. Young musicians Earl King, Huey Smith, and Allen Toussaint got their starts there. Toussaint called the Dew Drop a musician's haven, adding that local musicians would plan their evenings around stops at the Dew Drop. When bands got ready to go to Houma or Vacherie, they would meet at the Dew Drop. When they returned from a gig, they would go inside the club and jam. There were musicians around the Dew Drop twenty-four hours a day. The Dew Drop hit its stride in the 1950s, as performers like Ray Charles, James Brown, and Little Richard became regulars on LaSalle Street. Little Richard later immortalized the club when he recorded a song called *Dew Drop Inn*.

Another figure associated with the Dew Drop for nearly two decades was Patsy Valdalia, a transvestite singer/emcee known as the "Toast of New Orleans." R&B artist Tommy Ridgley once described Patsy as a great emcee. Employing the feminine reference when speaking of Valdalia, Ridgley said she was one of the reasons for the great after-hours jam sessions at the club that often lasted until nine o'clock the next morning.

The Dew Drop Inn's salad years moved nonstop into the 1960s as Painia continued to vary his floor shows to meet his audiences' tastes. When soul became the latest trend, the Dew Drop hosted Sam Cooke, the Ike and Tina Turner Revue, Joe Tex, Otis Redding, and Solomon Burke. Burke said musicians had no better friend than Painia. Artists knew that if they got in a jam, if they could get to New Orleans, Frank Painia would help them out, Burke explained. Painia would feed them and board them until they got back on their feet. According to Burke, if Painia couldn't use an artist at the Dew Drop, he'd get on the phone and try and get him work somewhere else. Painia, in fact, worked as a booking agent for many of the artists who performed at the Dew Drop Inn, including Ray Charles and Guitar Slim.[5]

Nothing lasts forever, not even the glory years for the Dew Drop. While the Dew Drop was attracting big stars, many of them soon began experiencing difficulty collecting from Painia. "It got so bad that a couple of times, the musicians' union had to collect the money for the performers," said Deacon John, president of New Orleans Local 174-496 of the American Federation of Musicians. "Finally, it just came down to having Frank not deal with the performers at all. The union would collect from him and pay the performers," he said.[6]

Ironically, desegregation sped the demise of the Dew Drop. Blacks finally were able to go to Bourbon Street or patronize other local music establishments. That meant a lot of customers left the Dew Drop for unexplored worlds. "Yeah," said Deacon John, "that's exactly what happened. A lot of black people decided they was going to the Blue Room [in the Monteleone Hotel] to exercise their new-found rights." Painia's failing health exacerbated the onset of financial problems for the club.

The Dew Drop's Groove Room closed down by the late 1960s, and the hotel was expanded to take its place. Live music continued in the front bar, but the impressive floor shows ceased to exist. The weekly ads that once ran in the *Louisiana Weekly* shrunk to a mere column in width and appeared only sporadically. Still, as late as the summer of 1967, Big Joe Turner performed at the Dew Drop.

Frank Painia was sick by this time and died from cancer in July 1972. After his death, the barbershop, restaurant, and bar were leased to new occupants as Painia's wife, Feddie, struggled to keep the hotel open. By the mid-1970s, the building had fallen into disrepair and was listed for sale on several occasions.[7]

Today the Dew Drop sits quietly on LaSalle Street, its

Deacon John Moore, a veteran of the New Orleans music scene, played many gigs at the Dew Drop Inn during its heyday.

façade neglected and in need of major renovations. A sign proclaims the home of the Dew Drop Inn to anyone who might care. Painia's grandson Kenneth Jackson tried for a time to keep the hotel open while cutting hair in his grandfather's establishment before he, too, finally gave up and closed the shop. He says occasionally someone would come by from out of town and ask for Frank Painia. Now, both Jackson and the barbershop are gone, the only reminder being a lonely light bulb atop a glass tube that once held a rotating barber pole.

Deacon John, standing in a cold, drizzling January rain nearly a year and a half after Hurricane Katrina emptied the Magnolia Housing Project, across a nearly deserted LaSalle Street, turned for one last look at the Dew Drop Inn. Somehow, the missing "L" in the word "lounge" only underscored the old building's state of disrepair. "Man, there were some good times here," he said. "I could tell you stories for hours on end. Some of 'em would have to be off the record, but what stories I could tell . . ."[8]

Isidore "Tuts" Washington

In 1984, Isidore "Tuts" Washington (January 24, 1907-August 5, 1984) became the toughest act to follow in the history of entertainment. A master of barrelhouse blues in New Orleans bars and brothels long before the term "rhythm-and-blues" became part of the American vocabulary, he was a musical icon in a city teeming with music.

Washington taught himself to play piano at the age of ten and by his teens he was playing in the city's top Dixieland bands. He secured a comfortable living with a steady gig at the Pontchartrain Hotel's Bayou Room. All the while, he was passing on his knowledge to future stars James Booker, Roy Byrd (Professor Longhair), Fats Domino, and Smiley Lewis. It was with Lewis, in fact, that Washington achieved his greatest professional success. The two played together from the late 1940s until their breakup in 1952. Washington claimed to have written much of Lewis's early material.

Washington moved to St. Louis in the early 1950s but was back in New Orleans by the end of the decade. It wasn't until 1983, at age seventy-six, that he finally acquiesced to recording his first—and only—solo album, *New Orleans Piano*

Professor. On August 5, 1984, he pulled off an all-time coup for a performer. Upon completion of a performance at the New Orleans World's Fair, Tuts Washington stood, acknowledged the thunderous accolades of an appreciative audience, and fell dead on the stage. He was seventy-seven years old. It was the kind of exit of which performers dream and Hollywood movie scripts are made. And it was vintage New Orleans.[9]

Champion Jack Dupree

He had only one song that made the R&B charts during his long and storied career. Still, Champion Jack Dupree (July 4, 1910-January 12, 1992) was a masterful piano player in the mold of Jelly Roll Morton, Tuts Washington, James Booker, and Professor Longhair. Born William Thomas Dupree, he lost his parents in a mysterious house fire while still an infant and was sent to the city's Colored Waifs Home for Boys. He received his introduction to the piano from "Drive 'Em Down" Willie Hall and Roy Byrd (Professor Longhair) during this time. He also learned to box as a youth.[10]

Dupree moved north in 1930. While in Detroit, he met boxer Joe Louis, who rekindled his interest in the sport. He fought in 107 bouts and won the Indiana state lightweight championship, earning the nickname "Champion Jack." By 1940 he was out of boxing.

Returning to the piano, he signed a recording contract with Okeh Records. In 1942, however, he was drafted into the U.S. Navy, was captured by the Japanese, and spent two years as a POW. Following the war he moved to New York and, using a variety of aliases, recorded for no fewer than twenty-one different record labels. He recorded under names like Meat Head Johnson, Lightnin' Jr., and Brother Blues.[11]

Dupree recorded a song called *Junker Blues,* a common theme that was subsequently recorded by Professor Longhair (*Tipitina*), Fats Domino (*The Fat Man*), and Lloyd Price (*Lawdy Miss Clawdy*) under three different titles. His 1958 classic album, *Blues from the Gutter,* was about drug use, prostitution, and the seamier side of life. Following the release of *Blues from the Gutter*, he moved to Europe and over the next thirty years lived in Switzerland, France, England, Denmark, and Germany and recorded several albums, including the superb *Blues at Montreaux* on Atco Records, an album that featured King Curtis on saxophone.[12]

In 1990, thirty-two years after leaving America, Dupree returned to New Orleans to appear at the New Orleans Jazz and Heritage Festival. It was his first visit to his hometown since 1954. He stole the show. Following his Jazz Fest performance, he remained in the city long enough to record *Back Home in New Orleans*. The album was backed by a lineup of legendary New Orleans musicians. He returned for an encore performance at Jazz Fest in 1991 and played the Chicago Blues Festival that same year. Back in the studio, he recorded two more albums, *Forever & Ever* and, perhaps prophetically, *One Last Time*. He died in Hanover, Germany, of complications from cancer.[13]

Professor Longhair

If there is one individual whose name is synonymous with New Orleans R&B piano, it is Professor Longhair (December 19, 1918-January 30, 1980). "Fess" served as an inspiration for Huey "Piano" Smith, Fats Domino, Allen Toussaint, and John Rebennack (Dr. John). Moreover, Elvis Presley's biographer Albert Goldman said that Longhair also influenced Presley's early Sun Records sessions. Dr. John once quit a regular gig in order to play one night with the Professor. A strong friendship developed between the two and Dr. John later produced Longhair's 1959 remake of *Go to the Mardi Gras* for Ron Records. This version has become the standard that is played extensively every year in New Orleans during Carnival.

Longhair's revered status, so late in coming, continues long after his death. Yet Fess once was so indigent that he swept floors for a record store in New Orleans, a considerable—and ironic—comedown. Born Henry Roeland Byrd in Bogalusa,

Louisiana, he moved with his mother and brother to New Orleans as a boy and grew up tap-dancing on Bourbon Street for change.[14]

Having never played the instrument before, he found an abandoned piano in an alley. Discovering that many of the keys did not work, he developed a style of playing that depended on his knowing which keys were good and which did not work. He would jump the bad keys. "Some of the guys said I was cross-chording," he said years later. "Whatever it was, I was getting to the right keys. With these good pianos, it's simple for me to do what I was doing then."[15]

A characteristic of his playing style involved kicking the front of the piano with his shoe. He kicked holes in more than one instrument while performing. Once, when he went on stage to play Fats Domino's solid white baby grand, Domino jumped onto the stage and placed a piece of plywood in front of the professor's feet.

Professor Longhair is best known for his recordings of *Mardi Gras in New Orleans, Big Chief,* and *Tipitina.* The latter song inspired the name of the foremost nightclub for live music in New Orleans. The club, opened in January 1977, had a special juice bar with a piano where Longhair, a partner, played on a regular basis. With Fess as a mainstay, the club grew in popularity, as did Longhair's reputation and standing. A visit by Paul McCartney and other musical dignitaries only added to the Longhair mystique.

Many early rock and roll artists, particularly black artists, were cheated out of millions of dollars in royalties, and Fess was no exception. Following his collaboration with Earl King on the 1965 release of *Big Chief* he abandoned his music career, reviving it in 1971, the second year of the New Orleans Jazz and Heritage Festival. His return to the stage was nothing short of spectacular. The entire festival came to a standstill as the audience, food vendors, and even musicians playing on other stages stopped what they were doing to listen and watch the Professor in rapt admiration. It was a defining moment in Jazz Fest history.[16]

In the years after that dramatic comeback show, Professor Longhair would embark on his first European tour and follow that with his first national tour of the U.S. He signed a record deal with Alligator Records and released several albums. Recognized as the patron saint of Jazz Fest, he performed the festival's finale from 1972 to 1979. He was featured on the PBS concert series with Dr. John, Earl King, and the Meters. He completed his final album, *Crawfish Fiesta*, at the age of sixty-two. Considered his finest effort, it was scheduled for release on January 31, 1980.

On January 30, the eve of the album's release, Longhair came home and went straight to bed after talking to his wife. "Then I heard him cough," she said. He made no other sound, and she knew instinctively he was gone. The second line that followed his coffin to the Gentilly cemetery stretched an unprecedented ten blocks, making it one of, if not *the* longest jazz funeral procession in the city's history. More tributes followed his death. In 1987 he received a Grammy for his early Atlantic recordings, released as *House Party New Orleans Style,* and in 1992, he was inducted into the Rock and Roll Hall of Fame.[17] On May 25, 1997, the National Association of Independent Record Distributors and Manufacturers (NAIRD) inducted him into its hall of fame. The induction coincided with the release of a new album, *Fess Gumbo*.[18]

Roy Brown

Roy Brown (September 10, 1925-May 25, 1981) has never received the recognition he deserves. With *Good Rocking Tonight*—which became an instant hit—he recorded the very first song to reference "rocking" and put Cosimo Matassa's studio on the map with its first hit record. Not only did it establish New Orleans as the epicenter of a new genre of popular music, it paved the way for Fats Domino, Lloyd Price, Little Richard, and Big Joe Turner.

Brown offered *Good Rockin' Tonight* to Wynonie Harris during the latter's performance in New Orleans in March

1947, but Harris, already an established star, brushed off Brown. Rather than slink away at the rebuff, Brown waited until intermission and then sang the song himself—with Harris's band. Brown approached his songs with the same emotion that would later be emulated by Bobby "Blue" Bland, B.B. King, Little Milton, Johnny Ace, and Jackie Wilson. He would influence Little Richard and rockabilly artists Elvis Presley and Buddy Holly.[19]

Born in New Orleans, Roy moved with his family to the St. Landry Parish town of Eunice while he was still very young. His mother died when he was fourteen and he and his father moved to Houston, where he attended high school. After a flirtation with boxing, he turned his attention to singing. His favorite artist was Bing Crosby. When he entered his first amateur show, he won with a performance of (I've Got Spurs That) Jingle, Jangle, Jingle. That was all the encouragement he needed to start singing—and winning—in every contest he could find. While singing in a Houston club, he was heard by visiting Shreveport club owner Billy Riley, who offered him the then-extraordinary sum of $125 a week. It was during his nine-month tenure at Riley's Palace Park in Shreveport that he shifted his focus from songs like Stardust to blues numbers, even though he professed to favor contemporary music.

After the Shreveport club burned to the ground, Roy moved on to Galveston, Texas, where he worked at Club Grenada and simultaneously at radio station KGBC, where he claimed to have written Good Rockin' Tonight. Schoolteacher and part-time piano player Joel Harris claimed that he wrote the song and gave it to Brown. Either way, Brown added the song to his repertoire and it soon became the most requested song at Club Grenada.[20]

In March of 1947, Brown left Galveston suddenly and returned to New Orleans. Upon his arrival, dead broke, he learned that Wynonie Harris was appearing at the Dew Drop Inn. He scribbled the lyrics to Good Rockin' Tonight on a paper bag, hoping to entice Harris into buying the song.

After Harris snubbed him, Harris's band let Roy perform the song at intermission and a band member suggested that he record it. Four days later, after Brown had written three more songs—*Lollipop Mama, Miss Fanny Brown,* and *Long about Midnight*—he was in Cosimo Matassa's studio for his first recording session for J&M. Because Matassa was experiencing problems with one of the microphones, Brown had to bend down low and sing into the piano microphone for the entire four-song session.

The song hit the R&B charts by July and Brown soon was back in the studio to record twenty-two more songs by the end of 1947. Eight of those were released, including *Miss Fanny Brown* and *Mighty, Mighty Man.* The next step was to put Brown and his band, the Mighty Men, on the road. They earned as much as twenty-five hundred dollars per night, performing choreographed dance steps. Wynonie Harris, meanwhile, had a change of heart and rushed into the studio to record *Good Rockin' Tonight* and fairly or unfairly, it was his, not Brown's original version that the Rock and Roll Hall of Fame chose as one of its 500 Songs That Shaped Rock and Roll. Between late 1949 and mid-1951, Brown had six records make the national R&B top 10.[21]

In 1953, at the peak of his career, Brown discovered his personal manager Jack Pearl, King Records president Syd Nathan, and Ben Bart, his booking agent at Universal Attractions, had been defrauding him by using two different contracts to book his performances. Only the contract that quoted a smaller guarantee than the promoter was paid was shown to Brown. The difference was pocketed by the co-conspirators.

When Brown reported Pearl to the musicians' union, Universal Attractions retaliated by booking Brown at opposing ends of the country simultaneously, making it impossible for him to keep his commitments. Laden with a no-show reputation, Brown dropped Universal and began booking himself across the South, paying promotion costs from his own pocket.

By 1954, Elvis Presley's cover of *Good Rockin' Tonight* signaled changes about to take place in the music industry that would have a profound effect on Brown's career. Though he would continue to tour with Ray Charles, Joe Turner, Etta James, and Larry Williams, he would have only one more major hit. *Let the Four Winds Blow* was little more than an audition tape, and Dave Bartholomew, the man who signed Brown for Imperial, felt it was out of time and tempo. However, Imperial released it and it sold a million copies, climbing to number 29 during its fifteen-week stay on *Billboard*'s Hot 100. Imperial nevertheless declined to renew Brown's contract because Brown revealed he was being audited by the IRS; Imperial didn't want IRS agents prying into their books as well.[22]

Brown settled in San Fernando, California, but his last public performance was in New Orleans. His 1981 Jazz Fest appearance ended a twenty-year absence from the city. It was a triumphant return that dredged up memories of Brown in his heyday. A month later, two days after realizing his long-held dream of seeing his daughter graduate from college, he suffered a fatal heart attack.[23]

Fats Domino

The Associated Press, Fox News, and CNN reported on September 1, 2005, that rock and roll pioneer Fats Domino (February 26, 1928-) was missing and feared dead in the wake of Hurricane Katrina.[24] He was later rescued from his flooded home in New Orleans' Lower Ninth Ward, however, and taken to the triage unit on the Louisiana State University campus in Baton Rouge.[25] He returned home on October 15 to find a large, hand-lettered sign painted on his balcony. "R.I.P. Fats," it said, "You will be missed."

Domino is one of the most enduring—and endearing—icons of rock and roll. Without a single number 1 song on the pop charts, Fats quietly became the top male R&B artist of the 1950s. He placed forty-six songs on the R&B charts during the '50s, nine of which went to number 1

Fats Domino had to be rescued from the second floor of his Cavin Avenue home in New Orleans' 9th Ward following the flooding of Hurricane Katrina.

The sign on the fence in front of Fats Domino's publishing company reads, "No Bulldozing." His publishing company is adjacent to his home.

while another nine reached number 2. Of those forty-six hits, thirty-one crossed over onto the pop charts, a record second only to Elvis's.[26]

Fats, with 65 million record sales in the 1950s, outsold Chuck Berry, Little Richard, James Brown, Ray Charles, and every other rock pioneer of that decade, except Elvis. When Chuck Berry's *School Day* moved into the number 1 spot on the R&B charts on April 13, 1957, it bumped Fats from the top position he'd held for twenty-seven straight weeks. The streak began on October 6, 1956, when *Blueberry Hill* took over the number 1 spot, followed by *Blue Monday*, which in turn was followed on March 23, 1957, by *I'm Walkin'*. On March 9, 1957, Domino's presence was such that he had four songs on the *Billboard* Hot 100 chart: *Blue Monday*, number 10; *I'm Walkin'*, number 35; *Blueberry Hill*, number 43; and *What's the Reason I'm Not Pleasing You*, number 83.

New Orleans became the epicenter of R&B music when *I'm Walkin'* moved into the number 1 position on the R&B charts, joined by Little Richard's *Lucille* and Lloyd Price's *Just Because* among the R&B top 5. Overall, Domino had sixty-six songs to make the pop charts—one more than the Beatles. His record sales exceed 110 million and include twenty-three gold records. Paul McCartney has said Domino's *Ain't That a Shame* is one of his ten favorite songs.[27] National Public Radio cited *Ain't That a Shame* as one of the 100 greatest American songs of the twentieth century. The song was inducted into the Grammy Hall of Fame.

Domino was one of eight children in a home where French was the first language. He learned piano from older brother-in-law Harrison Verrett and made his first public performance at the age of ten. He soon was playing regular gigs at local honky-tonks for three dollars a week.[28] His career was jeopardized when at age fourteen, he nearly lost his fingers in an accident at the bedspring manufacturing plant where he worked. Told he would never play again, he persevered. By 1949 he was performing at the Hideaway

Club when trumpeter Dave Bartholomew brought Imperial Records founder Lew Chudd to the club to see Fats. Chudd quickly signed Domino to a recording contract.[29]

Bartholomew, who cowrote, arranged, and produced forty of Domino's hit songs and whose band played on his recordings, helped him rewrite the first song he heard Fats perform. On December 10, 1949, Bartholomew and Domino entered Cosimo Matassa's J&M Studio on North Rampart and recorded *The Fat Man*. The song was originally recorded as *Junker Blues* by New Orleans singer Champion Jack Dupree. With Herbert Hardesty featured on tenor saxophone, the song peaked at number 2 on the R&B charts in February 1950. It sold an estimated one million records. Fats followed *The Fat Man* with *Every Night about This Time,* which climbed to number 5 in November of 1950. It was his first song to make use of piano triplets. *Goin' Home* became his first number 1 R&B hit in April of 1952.[30]

While backing up artists like Joe Turner and Lloyd Price (that's Fats playing piano on Price's number 1 R&B hit *Lawdy Miss Clawdy*), he continued writing with Bartholomew. In 1955, *Ain't That a Shame* hit number 1 on the R&B charts and remained on the chart for twenty-six weeks.[31] The best, however, was still to come. Over the next two years, Domino would record eight gold records, beginning with *I'm in Love Again* and *My Blue Heaven,* which reached numbers 3 and 19, respectively, on the *Billboard* Hot 100 in June of 1956. Those were followed in August by *When My Dreamboat Comes Home*, which climbed to number 14. Then, in December 1956, his biggest selling record, *Blueberry Hill*, peaked at number 2 behind Guy Mitchell's *Singing the Blues.*[32]

Ironically, the song for which Fats may be best known proved to be most troubling in recording. He was never able to record *Blueberry Hill* in a single take. Though he was enthusiastic about doing the 1940 Glenn Miller song, Fats did not know the lyrics and no one in the studio that day could come up with the sheet music. He continually stumbled over the words, and the studio ended up splicing together the best parts of several takes, a rare practice at that point in recording history.[33] Moreover, Fats played the wrong chords and band members improvised a riff during the bridge. It took all day to record and still Bartholomew was unhappy with the results, intended for the "B" side to *Honey Chile*, the song Domino performed in the movie *Shake, Rattle and Rock!* Lew Chudd released the record over Bartholomew's stringent objection that the song was "no damn good." Chudd called him back two weeks later and joked that they were cutting nothing but no-good records in the future because *Blueberry Hill* had already sold three million copies.[34]

The hits continued with other songwriters as well. Baton Rouge warehouse worker Roy Hayes gave Bartholomew a song he had written and Domino's version of *I'm Gonna Be a Wheel Someday* reached number 17 on the charts in September 1959. Earlier that year, a teenager was told by his father to get a job or get out of the house, so the young man wrote *Be My Guest.* With Fats' talent, the song peaked at number 8 in December 1959. Thus began the songwriting career of Tommy Boyce, who later teamed with Bobby Hart to form Boyce and Hart. Bobby Charles Guidry of Abbeville wrote *Walkin' to New Orleans*, which was the first Fats Domino song to feature a string section and his last top 10 song, peaking at number 6 in August 1960.[35]

Fats passed on one of Bartholomew's compositions to Smiley Lewis because he thought *I Hear You Knocking* would be the song to put his friend over the top. Instead, Gale Storm covered the song and took it to number 2 on the *Billboard* Hot 100 and to number 15 on the R&B charts in December 1955. Lewis, meanwhile, peaked at number 2 on the R&B charts but failed to crack the pop charts. Fats also turned down *You Talk Too Much,* a song written by his brother-in-law, so Joe Jones could record it.[36]

Domino cast a long shadow with his music. *Going to the River* was the first R&B song ever heard by Bobby Charles

Guidry, John Fred, and Buddy Holly. *I'm in Love Again* was the first rock and roll song that George Harrison ever heard, and *Ain't That a Shame* was the first song John Lennon learned to play. So great was his influence on the Beatles, they even serenaded Fats in a trailer behind Tad Gormley Stadium just prior to their 1964 New Orleans concert. They started singing *I'm in Love Again*, and of course Fats joined in. The ultimate tribute, however, came when Lennon and McCartney wrote *Lady Madonna* in homage to Domino's playing style. Fats returned the gesture in 1968 when he covered the song and it became his final top 100 hit.[37]

Fats Domino and Friends: Immortal Keyboards of Rock & Roll became the most watched special in Cinemax history in 1988. Recorded live at Storyville in New Orleans (now Jimmy Buffett's Margaritaville), the show featured Fats, Paul Schaffer, Ron Wood, Ray Charles, Jerry Lee Lewis, and Baton Rouge bass player Harold Cowart.[38] Prior to that, he starred in *Fats Domino Live!* Recorded in Los Angeles in 1985, it was not released on video until 1992.

After taping the show, Fats decided that he would no longer leave New Orleans. He disliked touring and claimed he couldn't find food he liked anywhere else. He made an exception when he appeared in an all-white suit for his 1986 induction into the inaugural class of the Rock and Roll Hall of Fame. Even at the time of his highest honor, he had the presence of mind to say he wished Elvis, Buddy Holly, and Sam Cooke were present.[39]

In keeping with his resolve to stay in New Orleans, Domino failed to attend the twenty-ninth annual Grammy Awards in 1987 to accept a Lifetime Achievement Award. In 1988, he appeared in the video *Legends of Rock 'n' Roll* with James Brown, Jerry Lee Lewis, Ray Charles, B.B. King, and Little Richard. In 1995, the Rhythm & Blues Foundation presented him with the Ray Charles Lifetime Achievement Award in Los Angeles and in 1998 both he and Dave Bartholomew were inducted into the Songwriters Hall of Fame at the National Academy of Popular Music's twenty-ninth annual ceremony in New York City.[40] Also in 1998, he declined an invitation from the White House to accept a National Medal of Arts from Pres. Bill Clinton, sending his daughter Antoinette in his stead.[41]

In 1996, Domino's *Blueberry Hill*, which entered the Grammy Hall of Fame in 1987, was rated number 13 among the Top 40 Jukebox Singles of All Time by the Amusement & Music Operators Association in America. The National Endowment for the Arts and the Recording Industry Association of America in 2001 named it number 18 among the Songs of the Century.[42]

The first indication to the world that Fats had not perished in the flooding that left much of New Orleans submerged came when his daughter saw a *New Orleans Times-Picayune* photograph of her father being rescued from his home at the corner of Caffin Avenue and St. Claude on August 30, 2005. His rescue prompted an outpouring of well wishes by internet bloggers. He returned home to discover that only three of his twenty-three gold records—*Rose Mary* (recorded in 1953 in honor of his wife, Rosemary), *I'm Walkin'*, and *Blue Monday*—were found. Domino said, "Well, somebody got the rest of them."[43]

One of his prized possessions lost in the post-Katrina flooding—besides his gold records—was a black and white photo of him and Elvis Presley. The photo was found when Domino returned to his home after the hurricane, but it was unsalvageable.[44] Though they were professional competitors in the '50s, Domino never considered Elvis his rival. When the two performed simultaneously in Las Vegas, Elvis often would sneak down to catch Domino's late shows.

During short breaks in the recovery search of his two adjacent houses (he lived in one and operated his publishing company from the other), Domino took the time to pose with well-wishers. By March 2006, workers from the Louisiana State Museum, clad in white hazmat suits, had sifted through his mold-covered home and pulled out a Wurlitzer keyboard and two pianos, a black Steinway baby grand used for writing and practicing and a white Steinway baby grand. The latter and the keyboard were returned to the family, but Domino consented to donating the black Steinway to a special state museum Katrina exhibit in New Orleans. Covered in mud and asbestos for six months, the piano was taken to Houston, where its four thousand parts had to be individually cleaned in restoration efforts. Corroded and broken screws had to be replaced, as did every bit of felt in the dampers. Workers were pleased that they were able to get two of the piano strings to play. Other strings broke during the flooding and some were so taut that when snapped, they became embedded in the sides of the instrument. The piano, as well as photos, rescue signs, and oral histories, became part of the permanent Katrina exhibit in 2008.[45]

The perfect ending to the Katrina saga would have been for Fats to bowl over an appreciative audience at the 2006 New Orleans Jazz Fest. Sadly, it was not to be. Scheduled to close the event on May 7, Fats was forced to bow out and check into a hospital instead. Upon leaving the hospital, however, he made a detour to Jazz Fest long enough to apologize to a disappointed crowd. Waving and tipping his cap from the stage, he stepped to the microphone. "I'm sorry I'm not able to perform," he said. "I love you all and always will. Thank you very much."[46]

New Orleans' *OffBeat* magazine honored Domino at its twelfth annual Best of the Beat music awards on January 27, 2007, at the House of Blues. After New Orleans mayor Ray Nagin presented Fats with a proclamation designating January 27 as Fats Domino Day, the Lil' Band o' Gold, made up of C.C. Adcock, Warren Storm, David Egan, and Kenny Bill Stinson, accompanied by five saxophones led by Herb Hardesty, played a series of Domino's songs. The Fats Domino Tribute was presented by Bernard Productions as a benefit for New Orleans Musicians' Hurricane Relief Fund.[47]

The Recording Industry Association of America (RIAA) on August 13, 2007, formally recognized Fats with its

Fats Domino is congratulated by Mike Shepherd, director of the Louisiana Music Hall of Fame, upon the singer's induction. (Courtesy of Louisiana Music Hall of Fame)

American Music Legend award, only the second artist to be so recognized. The first was Johnny Cash a decade earlier.[48] The RIAA also took advantage of the occasion to replace twenty of Domino's gold records. The presentations were made in a French Quarter nightclub before about a hundred family members and close friends, including Irma Thomas, Charmaine Neville, Jean Knight, Eddie Bo, Cosimo Matassa, and Deacon John Moore.[49]

Among the gold records replaced by the RIAA were *Going to the River, Blue Monday, Valley of Tears, Blueberry Hill, I'm in Love Again, Ain't That a Shame, Poor Me, Whole Lotta Loving,* and *I Want to Walk You Home.* The two-year delay in replacing the gold records was attributed to the necessity of historians locating Domino's long-lost sales records.

To ensure authenticity, historians also had to track down original 78-rpm recordings so that they could be dipped in gold and printed with Domino's name and the song titles. Jennifer Ballantyne, spokeswoman for Capitol/EMI, the recording label that assisted with the project, said that everything, down to the record labels and framing, was replicated. That was certainly better than Marvin Gaye's discovery that one of the gold records presented to him by Motown Records was in reality a Supremes album that had been dipped in gold paint.[50]

In September 2007, Vanguard Records released *Goin' Home: A Tribute to Fats Domino*, a two-CD set featuring Paul McCartney, Elton John, Robert Plant, Norah Jones, Bonnie Raitt, and Lenny Kravitz performing covers of his songs.[51]

Big Joe Turner

Big Joe Turner (May 18, 1911-November 24, 1985) was from Kansas City but lived and performed in New Orleans, during which time some of his finest recordings were done at Cosimo Matassa's Rampart Street studio. It took awhile for him to make the transition from blues to rock and roll, but when he did, he did it with a flourish. In the late 1940s, Turner recorded for a number of labels: RPM, Down Beat/Swing Time, MGM, Freedom, and Imperial.[52] In 1951, he signed with Ahmet Ertegun's Atlantic label and began recording in New Orleans. Besides Lee Allen on sax, another member of his session band was a young Fats Domino.[53]

Matassa, owner of J&M Studio, said that Atlantic was often forced to record Turner in New Orleans. "I think he lived here for some time and he was always performing somewhere along the Gulf Coast," Matassa remembers. "Sometimes Ahmet Ertegun and Jerry Wexler of Atlantic Records came down for the sessions, but a lot of times Big Joe would just go into the studio and record himself." Matassa says Turner "was one of those guys who sang so powerfully and had a real emotional sound that really struck a nerve when you listened to him."[54]

It didn't take Turner long to hit big with *Chain of Love*, which stayed at number 2 on the R&B charts for four weeks. He followed that with *The Chill Is On*, which reached number 3 on the R&B charts. In 1952, he hit the charts again with *Sweet Sixteen*. His first number 1 hit was *Honey Hush* in 1953, later covered by Johnny Burnette and Jerry Lee Lewis, among others. It remained at the top of the R&B charts until it was dislodged by Guitar Slim's *The Things That I Used to Do*. Turner followed *Honey Hush* in December of 1953 with his biggest hit of all, *Shake, Rattle and Roll*, which again put Turner at the very top of the R&B charts.[55]

Turner's version of *Shake, Rattle and Roll* remained on the R&B charts for more than six months, but like many R&B singers of the early 1950s, he would see his biggest hit covered by a white artist. Bill Haley and the Comets' version hit the charts in October of 1954, nine months before their bigger, better-known hit, *Rock Around the Clock*.[56] During his recording session of April 28, 1954, Haley told a reporter that the lyrics to the song had been rewritten. "We stay clear of anything suggestive," he said, apparently in reference to the line "you wear low dresses/ the sun comes shining through," which was expunged from his version. The lyrics "I'm like a one-eyed cat/peeping in a seafood store" may have seemed innocuous enough, but in the black vernacular of the day, the seafood store was synonymous with a vagina, so it didn't take much imagination to understand what the one-eyed cat suggested. Those lines were left intact by the unsuspecting Haley.[57]

The two men became close friends, often fishing together and even toured together. Turner was gracious enough to allow Haley to perform the song as if it were his own while Turner sang his other hits.[58] Turner may have had the last laugh whenever Haley unwittingly repeated the one-eyed cat/seafood store line in live performances and again when the Rock and Roll Hall of Fame named Turner's version as one of 500 Songs That Shaped Rock and Roll. He was inducted into the Rock and Roll Hall of Fame in 1987.

Lloyd Price

Lloyd Price (March 9, 1933-) became one of the earliest architects of rock and roll when Dave Bartholomew signed him to a contract with Specialty Records. On March 3, 1952, he entered Cosimo Matassa's J&M Studio and with Fats Domino playing the piano, recorded *Lawdy Miss Clawdy*.[59] Based on a commercial jingle he'd written earlier, the song shot to the top of the R&B charts for seven weeks that year. It was included by the Rock and Roll Hall of Fame as one of 500 Songs That Shaped Rock and Roll and would be covered by Elvis Costello, the Buckinghams, Fats Domino, Little Richard, Larry Williams, Johnny Rivers, Ronnie Hawkins, Conway Twitty, Mickey Gilley, Paul McCartney, John Lennon, and Elvis Presley. Presley also performed it during his 1968 NBC comeback special.[60]

Price grew up in the New Orleans suburb of Kenner. Influenced early on by Louis Jordan, Roy Milton, and Amos Milburn, he formed his own band with younger brother Leo (who later wrote *Send Me Some Lovin'* for Little Richard). Price was nineteen when he entered the studio to record for the first time as Specialty Records owner Art Rupe looked on. Session producer Dave Bartholomew was unhappy with pianist Salvador Doucette and was having considerable difficulty getting *Lawdy Miss Clawdy* the way he wanted it. As if on cue, Fats Domino drove up in his new black Cadillac to pay a social call on Matassa and Bartholomew.[61]

Bartholomew asked Fats to sit in on the session. He at first refused, saying his contract with Imperial Records forbade his participation in a session for another label without Imperial owner Lew Chudd's approval. After Domino had been lubricated with liquor, however, he declared that he was going to have some fun. With that, Fats played the song through once, adding his own piano introduction and solo. Cosimo started the tape rolling and *Lawdy Miss Clawdy* was recorded, featuring the surreptitious rolling piano triplets of the top R&B artist in America. Participating incognito, Fats was paid the princely sum of $54.50, union scale for session musicians.[62]

Price had four more R&B top 10 songs in 1952 and 1953: *Oooh, Oooh, Oooh* (number 4), *Restless Heart* (number 5), *Tell Me Pretty Baby* (number 8), and *Ain't That A Shame* (number 4). When he was drafted into the army in 1953, his string of hits was momentarily interrupted. Five years to the day from his *Lawdy Miss Clawdy* recording session, on March 3, 1957, he recorded *Just Because* for the ABC-Paramount label. The song hit number 3 on the R&B charts and even crossed over to number 29 on the pop charts.[63]

During his three-year army hitch, he fronted a large dance band that featured mostly swing music for G.I. audiences. The experience gave him the inspiration to combine the full sound of an orchestra with the bouncy rhythm-and-blues tempo. His idea proved to be a hard sell, however, because of the pack mentality of record executives who believed that rock and roll had to be performed by small combos. Price persisted and on songs like *Stagger Lee* a vocal group augmented his shouting style and a big band, as envisioned when he left the army, filled out the sound for the recording.

Recorded in 1959, *Stagger Lee* topped both the R&B and pop charts for four weeks. On the heels of *Stagger Lee,* he hit number 4 on the R&B chart and number 23 on the pop charts with *Where Were You (On Our Wedding Day)*. *Personality* hit number 1 on the R&B chart and number 2 on the *Billboard* Hot 100. *I'm Gonna Get Married* reached numbers 1 and 3, respectively, on the R&B and pop charts. *Come into My Heart* was a number 3 hit on the R&B charts and reached number 20 on the pop charts.[64]

When he performed *Stagger Lee* on Dick Clark's *American*

Bandstand, Clark insisted that the lyrics be cleaned up to present a wholesome sound that would be acceptable to mainstream America. The "two men gambling" line became "two men arguing," thanks to a determined campaign by the Legion of Decency that also resulted in the lines referring to the killing and the barroom being deleted. In 1960, he again broke into the R&B top 10 with *Question,* but the rapid pace of his hits was unquestionably slowing.[65] His last top 20 song was a remake of Errol Garner's *Misty*, released on his own Double-L label. It reached number 11 on the R&B chart. [66]

Price was also an astute businessman. He was a nightclub owner, recording executive, songwriter, producer, bandleader, booking agent, and promoter. He helped launch the recording career of Wilson Pickett on his Double-L label. He started a second record label, Turntable, and opened a nightclub that bore the same name.

When his business partner, Harold Logan, was murdered in 1969, Price moved to Africa, where he invested in various ventures. He teamed with Don King to promote a music festival in Zaire. The extravaganza drew 120,000 people who came out to see James Brown, B.B. King, Etta James, Bill Withers, the Spinners, and others. Price and King also promoted fights between Muhammad Ali and George Foreman in Zaire and between Ali and Joe Frazier in Manila.[67]

Price returned to America in the early 1980s, but for the most part, he stayed away from performing until he was lured into joining a European tour with Jerry Lee Lewis, Little Richard, and Gary "U.S." Bonds. On March 18, 1994, Price received the Pioneer Award at the sixth annual Rhythm & Blues Foundation ceremonies in Los Angeles and on January 12, 1998, he was inducted into the Rock and Roll Hall of Fame. He lives in New York State.[68]

Guitar Slim

Specialty Records faced a major dilemma when Lloyd Price, its biggest star, was drafted into the army in 1953.

The label's distributor and promotion man Johnny Vincent quickly filled the void when he signed Eddie Jones, a.k.a. Guitar Slim (December 10, 1926-February 7, 1959). Jones was born in Greenwood, Mississippi. His mother died when he was five and he was sent to Hollandale, Mississippi, to be reared by his grandmother. While there, he earned his living working in the cotton fields and plowing behind a mule.[69]

He spent his free time soaking up music in the Hollandale honky-tonks. Introduced to the guitar by bandleader Willie Warren, Eddie was heavily influenced by the playing of T-Bone Walker and Clarence "Gatemouth" Brown. He even adopted Gatemouth's *Boogie Rambler* as his theme song. He started working clubs in the New Orleans area in the late 1940s and recorded for Imperial in 1951 and for JB Records in Nashville in 1952 before signing with Johnny Vincent and Specialty the following year.[70]

Eddie Jones was an outrageously flamboyant performer who dyed his hair to match his shoes and wore specially tailored, brightly colored suits when performing. Taking the name Guitar Slim, he began experimenting in distorted overtones a full decade before Jimi Hendrix. Wearing his loud suits and flaunting his dyed shoes and hair, he would come onto the stage with more than three hundred feet of microphone wire connected to his guitar. Invariably, at some point in his performances, he would climb onto a valet's shoulders, and the two would walk through the crowd, out the front doors, and across the street, never missing a beat. Motorists would often come to a complete stop to gawk at the wildly dressed black man sitting on his valet's shoulders and playing a guitar. Inside, the band would occasionally incur Slim's wrath by unplugging his guitar from the amp and playing a completely different number as a prank while he was outside.[71]

New Orleans songwriter-pianist Al Reed said Guitar Slim had a greater impact on the electric sound than any other guitarist. Once, Slim and Fats Domino were scheduled to engage in a "Battle of the Blues" at the Monroe Civic

Auditorium. Fats was scheduled to go on last because he had several hit records. Before the show, Slim warned Fats that he was going to run him off the stage.

The auditorium was packed and true to his word, Slim had the crowd going wild. Slim walked off the stage with his guitar, slipped out the back door of the auditorium, and got into a car, still playing. No one knew where Slim had gone. When Fats came on, he told the people, "Ain't gonna be no battle tonight." Instead, Fats played his regular show. By 1951, record companies were starting to hear about this unique guitar player from New Orleans. Imperial produced four songs by Guitar Slim at Cosimo Matassa's studio, but the songs went nowhere. But 1952's *Feelin' Sad*, with Huey Smith on piano and David Lastie on sax, took off.

Slim stayed upstairs at the Dew Drop Inn when he was in New Orleans and police often were called in to quiet him down when he cranked up his guitar as early as seven or eight in the morning, belting out music that could be heard blocks away. Earl King said Slim's room was always in disarray. At any given time, there might be seven or eight women in his room and songs were written in eyebrow pencil on pieces of paper tacked to the wall.[72]

On October 16, 1953, Guitar Slim entered Matassa's J&M Studio to record what would become the biggest record of his career, *The Things That I Used to Do*. By then, Johnny Vincent had signed Slim to a contract with Specialty, and Vincent's first duty in preparation for the recording session was to get Ray Charles out of jail so that he could arrange the session and play piano. The Rock and Roll Hall of Fame included *The Things That I Used to Do* in its 500 Songs That Shaped Rock and Roll.

Cosimo Matassa remembered the session in an interview half a century later. "That session took all day because Slim was such a perfectionist," he said. Ray Charles not only did the arrangements and played piano, but he also was the producer for the entire session. Johnny Vincent was there, but he was more or less just a cheerleader. Ray became producer by default. He kept the reins on Slim as best he could because Slim had a habit of jumping meter and singing off-mike.[73] Though the session required twenty-four hours to get an acceptable take, Ray was patient and eventually got what he wanted. The exhausted musicians were obviously gratified when it was finally over. As the last bars of the song are played, an exultant Ray Charles is clearly heard in the background as he yells, "Yeah!"

Vincent sent the tapes of the session to Specialty president Art Rupe in Los Angeles, who called the song "the worst piece of shit I've ever heard." He told Vincent he was going to release the song but if it didn't sell, Vincent should look for another job. It shot to number 1 for six weeks and remained on the R&B charts for twenty-one weeks, selling more than a million copies. It was the biggest-selling R&B record of 1954.[74]

There was some minor fallout from the session regarding Ray Charles's participation, especially when the song became such a big hit. When Atlantic executives learned that Ray was on Slim's session, they were upset, but in those days Ray Charles was a hustler's hustler, and because he was Atlantic's biggest star, the incident eventually blew over.[75]

Dew Drop Inn owner Frank Painia took on the responsibility of booking Slim and even bought him a new Olds Rocket 88, which Slim promptly rammed into a parked bulldozer while drunk. His injuries were minor but he was forced to miss a couple of concert dates. Pania took a big chance and sent Earl King in his place. It was a calculated risk since few outside New Orleans had ever seen Slim in the flesh. King, who could play and sound like Slim, pulled off the ruse. At one date, when he launched into *The Things That I Used to Do*, the crowd went crazy and started throwing money onto the stage. Later, when King toured with his own hit song, he played at one of the same clubs. The promoter did a double take and said, "Hey, you look familiar." Back in New Orleans, the first person he saw was Slim, who was out of the hospital but still in a hospital gown. He was carrying a guitar under one arm and an amp under the other. He set upon King, threatening King with lawsuits and even death if King had hurt his reputation.

One of Slim's first stops on his northern tour was the Apollo Theater, where he shared the bill with the Spiders, who were headlining the show. When it came time for Slim's brief set to end, the curtain was closed on him. Slim, though, wasn't through performing, so he simply stepped in front of the curtain and continued playing.

While he was a dedicated performer, Slim did let one thing get in the way of his career: alcohol. Despite warnings by his doctors about his chronic drinking, Slim refused to stop. By 1958, he was sick and weakening fast. Heavy drinking and a different woman nearly every night had taken its toll, and there were times when he was unable to travel. During those times he was forced to remain at his home in Thibodaux. Earl King visited him there once and found 100-proof alcohol bottles all over his room. King, perhaps only half-joking, said Slim drank a pint of gin and chased it with a fifth of black port everyday.

In February 1959, Slim and his band were in Rochester, New York, when he took the stage. Breathing difficulty cut short his first song. The next night he completed his show in Newark, New Jersey, but collapsed after the show and had to be carried to his hotel room. He was thought to be drunk but a doctor was unable to revive him and within hours, on February 7, he died from bronchial pneumonia. He was thirty-two. His death was largely overlooked by the media and the public because it occurred only four days following the plane crash that claimed the lives of Buddy Holly, Richie Valens, and the Big Bopper. His body was returned to Thibodaux and buried along with his guitar in an unmarked grave, leaving the world to wonder just how great he might have been had he lived. Earl King rated him on a par with B.B. King, Ray Charles, and Slim's own role model, Clarence "Gatemouth" Brown.[76]

Ray Charles

He had songs on the *Billboard* charts in an unprecedented six consecutive decades, won twelve Grammy awards, and remains the only artist to have a number 1 *Billboard* hit in five different musical genres. Ray Charles (September 23, 1930-June 10, 2004) melded gospel with blues to give the world R&B and change the face of rock and roll in the same way Elvis would blend country with R&B to create rockabilly. In 2004, *Rolling Stone* magazine ranked him number 10 on its list of The Immortals: The Greatest Artists of All Time.[77]

Born Ray Charles Robinson in Albany, Georgia, Ray Charles saw his brother drown at age five, was blind by age six, and attended the St. Augustine School for the Deaf and the Blind in Florida. His musical odyssey began when, in order to get as far as possible from Florida and still remain in the United States, he went to Seattle in 1947. He met Quincy Jones there and launched his musical career. He shortened his name to Ray Charles to avoid confusion with boxer Sugar Ray Robinson.[78]

Charles didn't establish his singing and playing style until he moved to New Orleans.[79] Working out of Cosimo Matassa's J&M Studio in 1952 through 1954, he spent much of his time with Guitar Slim. Charles occasionally sat in on piano for Fats Domino sessions when Fats was not available to lay down the piano track.[80] Ray experimented briefly with "going to church" with his music, a new technique that involved the infusion of a gospel sound into his blues for what would eventually come to be defined as soul music. It was during his residency at the Hotel Foster on LaSalle Street that he developed the style that would immortalize his music.[81]

Atlantic Records purchased Charles' contract from Swing Time Records for twenty-five hundred dollars in 1952.[82] His first New Orleans recording session for Atlantic occurred at Matassa's studio on August 18, 1953. Ertegun and Wexler flew in from New York for the session, quickly eschewing Cosimo's house band of Red Tyler, Earl Palmer, Lee Allen, and Ernest McLean. In their stead, the Gondoliers were called in. The Gondoliers featured Edgar Blanchard on guitar, Auguste "Dimes" Dupont and Warren Hebrand on saxophone, Frank Fields on bass, and Alonzo Stewart on drums. They had backed Atlantic artist Big Joe Turner on his number 1 hit *Honey Hush* just four months earlier.[83]

It was also in New Orleans that Charles sank deeper into heroin addiction. He earned good money playing sessions and sold out gigs in and around New Orleans, but he needed every dollar to score dope in the projects on Sixth Street. Musician-songwriter Bill Sinegal said a man named Cheatham kept Charles supplied with marijuana and heroin for ten dollars a cap. Sinegal recalled that there were times when he saw an overdosed Ray walking down LaSalle Street with ice cream in both hands. The ice cream was his way of keeping his temperature down, and Cheatham would keep Ray moving so he wouldn't die, Sinegal said.

Even as Charles battled the effects of an addiction, one would never suspect he was blind. Each day, Sinegal said, Charles would walk the one-block distance from the Hotel Foster to the Dew Drop Inn. He would cross Sixth Street, enter the front door of the Dew Drop, and sit down for his daily meal of red beans and rice as the other musicians watched, wondering how he did it. His method was to listen to the sound of his shoes on the sidewalk and if he heard an echo, he knew he was near a wall. If not, he was in an open area or doorway.

In addition to his ability to get around with no assistance, Charles also was a skilled gambler. Sinegal called him a skilled blackjack player who played with cards pinpricked in Braille. He seldom lost, Sinegal said, and one of his favorite victims was R&B performer Bobby Marchan.[84]

Larry McKinley, a disc jockey at WMRY in New Orleans, reminisced about his friendship with Charles in a 2007 interview. "Ray carried a reel-to-reel tape recorder around with him," he said. "I used to really look forward to his returning to New Orleans from the road. He had a little compartment on the back of that recorder where the wire was stored, but he also kept some 'special' cigarettes in there. We'd always get together and smoke those little cigarettes," he laughed. McKinley said on another occasion Charles returned to New Orleans from Atlanta saying that he had a new song he wanted McKinley to hear. "He played a song called *What'd I Say* and after hearing it one time, I told him, 'Ray, you got yourself a hit there.'"[85]

The last recording session Ray did for Atlantic in New Orleans was in December of 1954. Frank Painia, owner of the Dew Drop Inn and Charles' booking agent, personally picked the musicians for the session and once more Wexler and Ertegun flew in to supervise. Warren Bell, Sr., who played alto sax on the date, called it a "bootleg session," meaning it was not booked through the local musicians' union. Whether Wexler and Ertegun didn't want the union to know Ray was recording or they simply lacked sufficient time to file the proper paperwork remains unclear. Either way, they couldn't use Matassa's facilities, so the session was held at the WDSU radio station studio in the French Quarter. This session produced *Mess Around, Don't You Know,* and *It Should've Been Me,* as well as *Along About Midnight, Nobody Cares, Ray's Blues,* and *Mr. Charles Blues.*

Wexler and Ertegun loved *Don't You Know* but were not enamored with the other songs. Their first impulse was to discard them as too progressive for the blues sound they were seeking. Indeed, the songs sounded as though there were a dozen horns playing instead of the five actually used. In fact, *Nobody Cares* wasn't released for two years and only then as a B side. The other songs weren't released until 1962 as part of *The Genius Sings the Blues* album— after Charles had left Atlantic. When the New Orleans musicians' union learned about the secret session, it fined the participating musicians fifty dollars each, more than they had been paid by Atlantic.[86]

During the 1954 Christmas season, barely a month before *I Got a Woman* reached number 1 on the R&B

charts, Charles was booked for a New Year's Eve show in Houston. While there, he met and fell in love with Della Bea Howard. He returned to New Orleans long enough to gather his belongings, bid farewell to his fellow performers, and head back to Texas, where he and Bea were married. It was his second marriage. By the time he married Bea Howard, he had recorded *I Got a Woman*—not in New Orleans, but at a small radio station in Atlanta, Georgia—and his career was primed to carry him to new heights, making him one of the biggest names in popular music.[87]

Charles was remarkably insightful about music and how it is marketed. He said shortly before his death in 2004 that artists with very little talent are packaged and marketed by the record companies to sound like whoever had the last hit. He lamented what he described as a dearth in original talent, saying everything and everyone sounds the same. There was a time, he said, when the voices and stylings of singers like Ella Fitzgerald, Frank Sinatra, Aretha Franklin, Gladys Knight, or Nat King Cole were instantly identifiable.

More than an accomplished singer and piano player, Charles was also a gifted composer and arranger. He learned to read music in Braille and to play by ear while attending St. Augustine School for the Deaf and the Blind in Florida, an accomplishment he said helped him develop an unerring memory. He said he could sit at his desk and write an entire arrangement in his head and never touch the piano. He would dictate the notes to a sighted person: what kind of notes, where they were located on the scale, and for what instrument. Because he played the piano, he knew the chords and the structure and knew the sound he wanted; he claimed he could hear it in his head. As he composed, he knew what he would have the reed section doing, what he would have the trumpet section doing, how the different instruments and sounds would work together. To write an arrangement, he said, it was essential to remember all those things. He said he never wrote or arranged anything he was unhappy with later. There was no reason for it to come out any differently than the way it sounded in his head, he said.[88]

Cosimo Matassa agrees. "I was constantly amazed at his memory. He had perfect pitch and a wonderful ear, and he had an equally wonderful memory. In those days, we didn't stop a song when someone messed up. We had to go all the way through, mistakes and all, and at the end, he would address each of the session musicians and tell them, 'You were flat, you were sharp, you came in too early, you came in too late.' And he was never wrong. He was absolutely marvelous."[89]

On January 23, 1986, Ray Charles joined Chuck Berry, James Brown, Sam Cooke, Fats Domino, the Everly Brothers, Buddy Holly, Jerry Lee Lewis, Little Richard, and Elvis Presley as inaugural inductees into the Rock and Roll Hall of Fame. Three of his songs, *Hallelujah, I Love Her So*; *I Got a Woman*; and *What'd I Say*, were included by the Rock and Roll Hall of Fame among the 500 Songs That Shaped Rock and Roll.[90]

The Spiders

New Orleans R&B is known for its solo artists, but the Spiders, formed in the late 1940s, rank among the Crescent City's premier vocal groups. Beginning as a gospel group calling themselves the Zion City Harmonizers, they later became the Delta Southernaires and made a few recordings and radio appearances from 1952 to 1953. Encouraged by studio head Cosimo Matassa, the group made the switch to R&B and signed with Imperial in late 1953. Newly christened as the Spiders, the group included brothers Hayward "Chuck" Carbo and Leonard "Chick" Carbo. Chick was a bass singer who split lead vocals with his brother. Other members were Joe Maxon, Matthew West, and Oliver Howard.

Their first single, *I Didn't Want to Do It,* went to number 3 on the R&B charts in early 1954, and other sides like *You're the One, Tears Begin to Flow,* and the ribald *I'm Slippin' In* were also hits, making the Spiders a hot concert draw. Maxon and West both left the group in 1955 and were replaced by Bill Moore and Issacher Gordon. The Spiders' string of R&B top 10 hits continued that year with *21* (number 9) and *Witchcraft* (number 5), written by Dave Bartholomew, who produced the group's 1954-1956 recordings. *Witchcraft* was their second top 5 hit and their biggest overall seller. It was later covered by Elvis Presley.[91]

Imperial began grooming Chuck Carbo for a solo career in 1956, a move that created tension within the group. By the end of the year, Chick Carbo had signed with Atlantic Records as a solo artist, a development that effectively brought an end to the Spiders as a group. Chuck cut a few singles for the Imperial, Rex, and Ace labels after going solo and Chick had several releases for Atlantic, Vee-Jay, and Instant. Ironically, neither of the Carbo brothers scored any significant chart hits, although Chuck had a local hit with his cover of Jeannie and Jimmy Cheatham's *Meet Me with Your Black Drawers On*. It was reprised on *Drawers Trouble,* a 1993 comeback album that united Chuck Carbo with pianists Dr. John Rebennack and Edward Frank. Chuck Carbo has not stopped performing entirely, although he made his living as a lumber truck driver when gigs got scarce. Chick died in 1998.[92] Chuck died on July 11, 2008.

Shirley and Lee

Born just ten days apart, Shirley Pixley Goodman (June 19, 1936-July 5, 2005) and Leonard Lee (June 29, 1936-October 23, 1976) were only fourteen when they recorded their first of several hits for Eddie Mesner's Los Angeles-based Aladdin Records, but it was only through a serendipitous stroke of luck that they were even discovered. Shirley and Lee, along with about two dozen classmates from Joseph Clark High School, began hanging around Cosimo Matassa's J&M Studio after school in 1950, hoping to convince him to record them. They persisted and Matassa, more from exasperation than anything else, charged them two dollars to make a tape. Drummer Earl Palmer and saxophonist Lee Allen were in the studio at the time and they helped the

kids out by playing backup to *I'm Gone,* a song that ran
an interminable fifteen verses. Matassa pressed a demo 78
from the master tape and slapped a sticker with the song
title on it and gave it to the kids.

Mesner happened to be in town at that time to record
Lloyd Price and Matassa needed a tape. Matassa grabbed a
used tape, explaining that the recording was just a bunch
of kids who came in to bug him. Mesner, who was always
on the lookout for talent, asked to hear the tape before
Matassa erased it. Hearing Goodman's distinctively high-
pitched voice, Mesner asked who she and how he could find
her. Matassa tried to discourage him but Mesner persisted.
When Matassa later approached Shirley with news of
Mesner's interest, Goodman said the teens thought they
were in trouble. After all, the man before her, just a few
months before, had been trying to chase them away.

Eddie Mesner wanted to team Shirley with a male voice,
so all the boys who were on the tape were auditioned and
Leonard Lee was selected for the contrast of his deep,
bluesy voice. Still, the deal was not finalized until Shirley's
grandmother was convinced to allow her to record. At first
she refused, but when Mesner gave her a thousand dollars—
more than some people made in a year in those days—she
relented. The pair was then hustled back into the studio
for their first professional recording session. Because of
the contrast between Lee's booming baritone and Shirley's
high-pitched voice, the two never sang in harmony. Instead
they relied on a technique that had one singer responding
to the other.

I'm Gone was first released locally and when New
Orleanians bought every available copy, the song was
released nationally and shot to number 2, remaining on
the R&B charts for eleven weeks. A booking agency, Circle
Artists, scurried to get the two on the road for concerts, but
Goodman's grandmother ran the booking agent off when
he offered her five hundred dollars. Mesner told the agent
to offer her a thousand. He did and she signed the consent

form for them to tour with the condition that an adult always travel with them. Circle Artists alternated paying Goodman's mother and grandmother to travel with her until she married. Before the tour kicked off, Shirley and Lee did a show at the San Jacinto Club with Bartholomew's band. Big Mama Thornton of *Hound Dog* fame opened for them before a packed house.

I'm Gone launched a unique string of hit songs by Shirley and Lee chronicling the ups and downs of a youthful love affair that quickly identified them as "Sweethearts of the Blues." Follow-up releases revealed evolving chapters of the Shirley and Lee romance. Fans eagerly purchased each release to keep up with the story line. The second release was *Shirley, Come Back to Me,* followed by *Shirley's Back, Two Happy People, Lee Goofed,* and *Confessin'.*

The public eventually tired of the teenage love saga so Shirley and Lee moved on. In May of 1955 they released *Feel So Good*, which broke into the R&B charts on August 27 and remained there for twenty-five weeks, peaking at number 2. *Feel So Good* featured vocal backing by the Spiders. A year later, they released a bouncing song called *Let the Good Times Roll* that burst onto the R&B charts on July 28, 1956, for the first of nineteen weeks and skyrocketed to number 1. It crossed over onto the pop charts in October, climbing to number 19 and remaining on the charts for twenty weeks. *I Feel Good* reached number 3 on the R&B charts in November 1956 and in December reached number 38 on the pop charts. A remake of *Let the Good Times Roll* in 1960 on the Warwick label again cracked the top 100 for five weeks, peaking at number 48.[93]

Despite the song's popularity, many disc jockeys refused to play *Let the Good Times Roll* because they thought the lyrics were too suggestive. In *Let the Good Times Roll*, it was Shirley's expressed desire to "rock all night long" and Lee's response that he had what it took "to thrill your soul" that the deejays found offensive. However, the ban only served to make teenagers more determined to purchase the record.[94]

Their tours kept the duo busy almost every night. With only one day off per month for a couple of years, touring was especially trying in the '50s because black artists were not allowed to stay in most hotels. They often slept on the tour bus and found it necessary to send out for food. Once, when playing Little Rock during the 1956 riots, the band was forced to abandon its instruments and luggage to escape the auditorium in helicopters.

When Aladdin Records was purchased by Imperial in the early 1960s the Sweethearts of the Blues finally broke up. Shirley moved to California in 1974 and worked as a switchboard operator for *Playboy* magazine.[95] She made a brief comeback with a song called *Shame, Shame, Shame*, written by Sylvia Robinson, who was part of the highly successful Mickey and Sylvia duet of *Love Is Strange* fame. *Shame, Shame, Shame* did extremely well in the R&B charts, where it remained for fifteen weeks, climbing all the way to number 1, and the *Billboard* Hot 100 for sixteen weeks, peaking at number 12.[96]

James "Sugar Boy" Crawford

If there ever was a singer whose life and career were dogged by misfortune, it would be James "Sugar Boy" Crawford (October 12, 1934-). Born in New Orleans, Crawford is still considered by many of his contemporaries to be one of the best singers to come out of the Crescent City.

Leonard Chess of Chess Records in Chicago was in New Orleans in 1954 and heard Crawford and his band. Shortly afterward, Chess released *I Don't Know What I'll Do,* an audition demo he had recorded of Sugar Boy and his group while in town. The record credited Sugar Boy Crawford and the Cane Cutters. Crawford signed a recording contract at his next recording session at Cosimo Matassa's studio. From that session came *Jock-a-Mo,* one of the first records to draw on the New Orleans Mardi Gras. The song became a Carnival season standard in New Orleans and continued to sell throughout 1954. Highlighted by a searing horn break, it was designated a *Cash Box* magazine pick of the week.[97]

Crawford said *Jock-a-Mo* originated from two songs he had heard the local Mardi Gras Indians sing. Other sources attribute the origins of the song to the chanting of slaves in the old Congo Square area of New Orleans. In 1965 the Dixie Cups recorded *Jock-a-Mo* under the name *Iko-Iko.* Crawford maintains he never received any royalties from them. Composer credits do not list Crawford.

By late 1954, Crawford and his band had become a regular attraction at the all-white Carousel Club in Port Allen, across the Mississippi River from Baton Rouge. The Carousel run lasted two years before Crawford and the band returned to New Orleans in order to be near Matassa's recording studio. By then, he had left Chess and signed with Imperial Records and for the first time, he recorded with Matassa's house band instead of his own band. His first effort was *Morning Star,* which did well in the New Orleans area. By 1958, Imperial had dropped most of its New Orleans black artists, including Crawford, in favor of concentrating on its white singers like Ricky Nelson. In 1959, with the backing of Baton Rouge's John Fred and His Playboy Band, he cut *Danny Boy* for S.J. Montalbano's Montel label in Baton Rouge.[98]

Tragedy ended his singing career and nearly cost him his life in 1963. Freedom marches were being held across the South and tensions were running high when he was pulled over in Monroe while en route to a show. Police dragged him from his vehicle and pistol-whipped him. He spent three weeks in a Monroe hospital before he was transferred to New Orleans, where he remained paralyzed for nearly a year. The beating caused a blood clot in his brain and he was unable to see, hear, or walk. Surgery was performed and a plate inserted in his head before he began his slow and painful recovery.

Crawford turned his back on secular music and focused instead on his faith. He enrolled in trade school and became a building engineer specializing in boiler maintenance and repair. He still listens to R&B music but he objects to the environment in which R&B is performed. He did lend his voice, however, as backup vocals for his grandson Davell Crawford's debut album, *Let Them Talk*.[99]

Little Richard

There are not enough superlatives to describe the impact Richard Wayne Penniman, a.k.a. Little Richard (December 5, 1932-) had—and continues to have—on rock and roll music. Elvis is credited with introducing the black sound to white audiences, but Little Richard did more than anyone else to break down those barriers. He brought white kids over to black radio stations to hear and feel a sound that was exciting, authentic, and unlike anything they had ever heard before.

During the early 1950s, Little Richard languished as a dishwasher in the Greyhound bus station restaurant in his hometown of Macon, Georgia. In 1955, New Orleans singer Lloyd Price suggested to his Georgia friend that he send a demo tape to Specialty owner Art Rupe. Rupe liked what he heard and lost no time in flying Specialty A&R man Robert "Bumps" Blackwell into New Orleans to set up a recording session at Cosimo Matassa's studio. Some of the city's top musicians were brought in: drummer Earl Palmer, sax players Lee Allen and Alvin "Red" Tyler, guitarists Edgar Blanchard and Justin Adams, bassist Frank Fields, and pianist Huey "Piano" Smith.[100]

The session began on September 14, 1955, and went poorly for more than two days. Without his piano, Richard was subdued, even boring. Blackwell wanted something raw and edgy, something like the Ray Charles hit *I Got a Woman*, which was then heating up the air waves. Frustrated, Blackwell adjourned with Little Richard and the other players for lunch at the Dew Drop Inn.[101] One story has Richard, seeing the piano on the stage, leaping to the bandstand and launching into "A-wop-bop-a-loo-bop-a-lop-bam-boom." What followed was a raunchy rendition of

Tutti Frutti, a song with homosexual overtones that he had been using in his shows. Blackwell rushed everyone back to the studio for the few remaining hours for which they were booked. The song was unacceptable in its present state, so he chased down a local songwriter, Dorothy Labostrie, to clean up the lyrics. But Richard, the son of a minister, was unwilling to recite the lyrics to the female songwriter, who was equally unwilling to hear them. Blackwell persisted, using the argument that each of them could use the money. Finally, with Richard facing the wall, he sang the lyrics a few times, enough for Labostrie to get a feel for the song and write substitute lyrics.[102]

Labostrie remembered it differently in an interview with author Jeff Hannusch for his book *I Hear You Knockin'.* She says she was listening to the radio on September 3, 1955, when she heard that Bumps Blackwell was looking for songwriters. According to the account recorded in Hannusch's book, Labostrie practically broke Cosimo's door down the next day. Little Richard was sitting at the piano and it was the first time she ever laid eyes on him. She asked to hear his voice and then sat down and put *Tutti Frutti* down on paper in fifteen minutes. Little Richard, on many occasions, has said he wrote the song and that he was cheated out of songwriter's royalties. Little Richard did not write *Tutti Frutti*, Labostrie insists. She says she once lived on Galvez Street and she and a girlfriend often went to the drugstore to buy ice cream. Inspired by the store's new ice-cream flavor, tutti frutti, she kept the idea for a song in the back of her mind until she got to the studio that day.[103]

No matter which version is accurate, Huey Smith was excused from the session and Richard took over the piano. Combining the passion of gospel and New Orleans R&B with the stylings of the local session artists, *Tutti Frutti* became the first of a string of Little Richard hits recorded in New Orleans for Specialty Records.[104] It reached number 2 on the R&B chart and number 17 on the pop charts, selling over five hundred thousand copies. Others to follow included *Long Tall*

Little Richard performs at his induction into the Louisiana Music Hall of Fame. (Courtesy of Louisiana Music Hall of Fame)

Sally (his biggest hit, topping the R&B chart for eight weeks and reaching number 6 on *Billboard*'s Hot 100), *Slippin' and Slidin'* (number 1 on R&B and number 17 on the pop chart), *Rip It Up, Ready Teddy, Heeby-Jeebies, The Girl Can't Help It* (which would become the title track to the Jayne Mansfield movie), *Lucille* (number 1 and 21 on the R&B and pop charts, respectively), *Send Me Some Lovin'* (number 2 on the R&B chart), *Keep a Knockin'* (number 2 R&B and number 8 pop), *Good Golly, Miss Molly* (number 4 R&B and number 10 pop), and *Jenny, Jenny* (number 2 and number 10).[105]

Cosimo Matassa remembered Little Richard's recording sessions at his J&M Studio. "The sessions were always real high energy just because Richard was that kind of guy," he said. Bumps Blackwell would come to town to produce the sessions for Art Rupe at Specialty. There were always several good takes on Little Richard songs because the musicians wanted to get the best take possible for Bumps, who was a perfectionist, and for Richard. The two always thought they could do better, so the sessions often were extended.[106]

When playing white clubs, Richard required his band members to wear pancake makeup so as to seem homosexual. The band hated the makeup, he said in a *TV Guide* interview in 2000, but it was necessary or they would not have been allowed in the white clubs lest they be perceived as a threat to the white girls.[107]

Then, just as abruptly as he had burst upon the scene, Little Richard walked away. The flamboyant performer who took to the stage in sequined costumes, mascara, lipstick, and a six-inch pompadour to attack his piano and shake the rafters in his quivering falsetto gave it all up, though it was a temporary hiatus, on October 13, 1957, the fifth date of a two-week tour of Australia with Gene Vincent and Eddie Cochran. He unexpectedly turned his back on the life of a rock and roll star; threw his diamond rings, valued at eight thousand dollars, into the Sydney harbor; and enrolled in Oakwood Bible College in Huntsville, Alabama, to become a Seventh Day Adventist minister.

His exodus from rock and roll lasted five years and on October 8, 1962, he launched his comeback tour in Europe. Opening for him at the Star Club in Hamburg was an as yet undiscovered group calling themselves the Beatles. A year later, he again toured Europe with another unknown group, the Rolling Stones, providing the opening act. In 1964, the Beatles released their own version of *Long Tall Sally.* Richard next appeared with Chuck Berry, Gene Vincent, Bo Diddley, and Louisiana natives Fats Domino and Jerry Lee Lewis at a rock and roll revival show in Toronto. In September 1972, he was reunited with the core session artists from his historic New Orleans '50s sessions when his album *The Second Coming* was released.

Along the way, he employed two chauffeurs who would go on to stellar careers in show business. The first was Peter Grant, later Led Zeppelin's manager, and the second was a Specialty Records employee whom the company assigned to drive Richard. His name was Sonny Bono.[108]

In 1986, he began a series of live concerts, recording

projects, television appearances, film soundtracks, and commercials. His unique version of the children's tune *Itsy Bitsy Spider* was included on the Disney Records' benefit album *For Our Children.* The album went gold, reaping millions of dollars for the Pediatric AIDS Foundation. He followed that with the Disney album *Shake It All About*, which featured children's songs in his unique style. He also appeared on the children's shows *Mother Goose Rock 'n' Rhyme* and *Sesame Street.*[109]

On January 23, 1986, Little Richard was one of the first ten inductees into the Rock and Roll Hall of Fame. That same year, he was featured in the movie *Down and Out in Beverly Hills.* He was honored with his own star on the Hollywood Walk of Fame in 1990 and following that, he returned to his hometown of Macon, Georgia, for the dedication of Little Richard Penniman Boulevard. In 1993, he received the Lifetime Achievement Award from the National Academy of Recording Arts and Sciences at the thirty-fifth annual Grammy Awards. The following year he received a Lifetime Achievement Award from the Rhythm & Blues Foundation. In 1997, he was presented the American Music Awards Distinguished Award of Merit in recognition of his contributions to music history. He was inducted into the NAACP Image Awards Hall of Fame and in 2003 he was inducted into the Songwriters Hall of Fame.[110]

Smiley Lewis

Born Overton Amos Lemons in the southwest Louisiana town of DeQuincy, near the Texas border, he was reared by a white family in the Irish Channel area of New Orleans. Smiley Lewis (July 5, 1913-October 7, 1966), as he would become known, was exposed to the musical heritage of New Orleans during his teens. By the mid-1930s, he was playing guitar in the Thomas Jefferson Band, which featured Tuts Washington on piano, while working days driving trucks and shoeing horses. It was about that time that Lemons began calling himself by his sobriquet.

In March 1950, Dave Bartholomew with Imperial Records decided to take a chance on Smiley, whom he thought was a good blues singer. Accompanied by Bartholomew's horn section, Smiley recorded *Tee-Nah-Nah* in Cosimo Matassa's studio. The song had been given to Lewis by Tuts Washington, who said it was a song sung by inmates at the Louisiana State Penitentiary at Angola. It was a regional hit, thanks to the promotional efforts of local disc jockey Dr. Daddy-O, who accommodated Lewis when the singer brought him an acetate disc of the song and asked him to play it.

The success of the record put Lewis in demand and he was booked for shows in Louisiana, Oklahoma, Texas, Tennessee, Florida, Georgia, Alabama, and Mississippi. Other records were released by Imperial and its subsidiary label, Colony, but none met with the success of *Tee-Nah-Nah* until *The Bells Are Ringing* reached number 10 on the R&B charts for two weeks in 1952. He recorded *Blue Monday* in 1954, but it was Fats Domino who would score the hit with his version of the song two years later.

In 1955, with the increasing popularity of R&B music, Smiley Lewis had his biggest hit with *I Hear You Knocking*. With Huey "Piano" Smith's piano jump-starting the song, it shot to number 2 on the R&B charts. From May to December of 1955, the number 1 and number 2 positions on the R&B charts were held by New Orleans artists: Shirley and Lee (*Feel So Good*), Little Richard (*Tutti Frutti*), Fats Domino (*Ain't That a Shame*), and Lewis (*I Hear You Knocking*).[111]

Lewis, it seemed, was in the right place at the right time, but just as Fats had done with *Blue Monday*, Gale Storm recorded a cover of *I Hear You Knocking* and her sanitized version, not Lewis's, reached number 2 on *Billboard*'s Hot 100. In 1958, Elvis Presley covered Lewis's 1956 version of *One Night* after scrubbing the lyrics to make them more acceptable to white audiences and then, in 1961, Fats Domino released his own version of *I Hear You Knocking*. Others' success with his songs, along with his own lack of another big hit, left Lewis a frustrated, bitter man. When

Imperial finally cut him loose, he was reduced to opening for Irma Thomas and Ernie K-Doe. In 1970, Dave Edmunds had another hit with *I Hear You Knocking*, but this time, Lewis wasn't around to hear it.[112]

Suffering from stomach cancer in 1965, he attempted a remake of *The Bells Are Ringing,* but his once-booming voice was so weak he could record only one side; producer Allen Toussaint covered the B side with an instrumental. Soon after the aborted session, Lewis entered Charity Hospital. Tuts Washington performed a benefit in the hospital to solicit blood donors. Lewis tried to play with Washington and the other musicians but was unable to perform.

After leaving the hospital, Lewis ran into Earl King on a New Orleans street. King would not have recognized the fellow musician had Smiley not stopped him. King said Smiley, who once weighed 240 pounds, appeared to weigh less than a hundred pounds. He didn't even recognize Lewis's voice. Fats Domino visited Lewis at his home and the two prayed together before Domino left for a show in Chicago. Keeping a promise he made to his dying friend, Domino called him from Chicago. It was the last time the two talked. Another major benefit show was organized by Benny Spellman and Dave Bartholomew. The show was scheduled for La Ray's Club on Dryades Street on October 10, 1966, but Smiley Lewis died three days before the show.[113]

Sam Cooke

Sam Cooke (January 22, 1931-December 11, 1964) was born in Clarksdale, Mississippi, and died tragically just short of his thirty-fourth birthday. He would use New Orleans and Cosimo Matassa's J&M Studio to help launch a career that would carry him to the heights of popularity as one of the pioneers of soul music. Cooke grew up with gospel music and began his professional career at age nineteen as lead singer for the Soul Stirrers, a five-man gospel group.[114]

The Soul Stirrers first recorded for Aladdin Records

but in 1948 switched to Specialty Records, headed by Art Rupe. Rupe had dispatched Little Richard to record at Matassa's studio in 1955, and a year later, Cooke followed. J&M Studio recorded the customary four songs during Cooke's first session: *Lovable, Forever, I Don't Want to Cry,* and *That's All I Need to Know.* Participating as backups to Cooke were drummer Earl Palmer, pianist Warren Myles, and saxophonist Red Tyler. Only one of the four songs charted. *Forever* reached number 60 on *Billboard*'s Hot 100 in January of 1958. Cooke returned to New Orleans on a regular basis and on December 12, 1956, recorded *I'll Come Running Back to You* during a session produced by Bumps Blackwell. The song reached number 1 on the R&B charts in December 1957 and number 18 on *Billboard*'s Hot 100 in January 1958.[115]

In all, Cooke had thirty-nine songs in *Billboard*'s Hot 100. Five of those made the top 10, earning him a handful of gold records, and *You Send Me* was a number 1 song for three weeks in late 1957, selling nearly two million records. On *Billboard*'s R&B charts, *You Send Me, Twistin' the Night Away* (1962), and *Another Saturday Night* (1963) were all number 1 hits. Of the 500 Songs That Shaped Rock and Roll, Cooke had three: *A Change Is Gonna Come, Bring It on Home to Me,* and *You Send Me.*[116] Among the Louisiana musicians who backed Cooke on many of his recordings were Fats Domino, Lloyd Price, Guitar Slim, Dave Bartholomew, Red Tyler, Snooks Eaglin, Allen Toussaint, and Percy Mayfield.

During the civil rights struggles of the turbulent 1960s, he wrote and recorded one of the most poignant ballads of the era. *A Change Is Gonna Come* was written as a response to Bob Dylan's *Blowin' in the Wind.* The song never got higher than number 31 on *Billboard*'s Hot 100, though it did climb to number 11 on the R&B charts in February 1965. *Shake* peaked at number 7 on the pop charts and number 2 on the R&B charts the same month. Cooke didn't live to see either song become a hit.[117]

On December 11, 1964, Cooke was at a party in Los Angeles when he met twenty-two-year-old Elisa Boyer. Together, they left a nightclub and drove to the Hacienda Motel in South Central Los Angeles where they registered as Mr. and Mrs. Sam Cooke. When Boyer left the room with most of his clothing, Cooke, wearing only one shoe and a jacket, broke into the office of manager Bertha Franklin and found Boyer hiding there. Franklin shot Cooke three times with a .22-caliber pistol. Dying, Cooke lunged at Franklin and then collapsed. Franklin claimed that Cooke had tried to rape Boyer and then turned on her. The shooting was ruled a justifiable homicide.[118]

Cooke was inducted as a charter member of the Rock and Roll Hall of Fame in 1986.[119]

Earl King

He is responsible for one of the most recognizable Carnival songs ever recorded, but outside his native New Orleans, few have ever heard of Earl Silas Johnson, a.k.a. Earl King (February 6, 1934-April 17, 2003). King worked as a guitarist, vocalist, songwriter, arranger, sideman, and producer. His songs were covered by Fats Domino, Jimi Hendrix, Stevie Ray Vaughan, Professor Longhair, Johnny Adams, and the Meters.[120]

King grew up in the Irish Channel section of New Orleans. His father, a blues pianist and close friend of Tuts Washington, died when Earl was still young and King was reared by his mother, a large woman affectionately known as "Big Chief." The boy was surrounded by the music of the city and the influence of those who shaped it. He first heard the guitar stylings of Smiley Lewis coming from a neighborhood bar as he walked past. Years later, his memories of that day—and the pungent smell of marijuana that had hung in the air—were still vivid. His first professional job was as backup vocalist for Huey "Piano" Smith. King emulated Eddie Jones, a.k.a. Guitar Slim, and even purchased his first guitar from Slim.

It was in 1954, when producer Johnny Vincent signed

him to a contract with Specialty Records, that King obtained his professional name. King previously had recorded for the Savoy label as Earl Johnson and it was Specialty's intent to promote his records under the name King Earl. The record pressing plant, however, reversed the name and it would remain Earl King thereafter.[121]

The following year, King switched labels and joined Vincent's new Ace Records label. His debut release, *Those Lonely, Lonely Nights*, sold 100,000 copies along the Gulf Coast and went to number 7 on the R&B charts in August 1955, remaining on the charts for eleven weeks. It was successful enough for the Buffalo Booking Agency of Houston to put him on tour with Clarence "Gatemouth" Brown and Smiley Lewis.

A gifted songwriter, King claimed to have arranged and produced for Jimmy Clanton, Huey "Piano" Smith, and Benny Spellman, but that was disputed by Ace owner Johnny Vincent. King left Ace after becoming dissatisfied over royalties he felt were being withheld from him, a claim also denied by Vincent.

In 1959, while on tour with Sam Cooke, Dakota Stanton, and Dave Bartholomew, King opened each show with his composition *Come On (Let the Good Times Roll)*. Bartholomew, A&R man for Imperial Records, remembered the song when they returned to New Orleans and brought King into Matassa's studio to record it. Imperial gave King the opportunity to branch out, to be creative. Working for Bartholomew proved to be beneficial for King, who said Bartholomew was receptive to production ideas and listened to suggestions. The two also began to use different musicians in the studio.[122]

King finally broke into *Billboard*'s R&B singles chart in 1962—with the B side of a record. The A track, *Always a First Time*, was intended to be the hit, but *Trick Bag*, featuring outstanding vocal interjections by Benny Spellman, found popularity. *Trick Bag* climbed to number 17 on the R&B charts.[123]

Then the rumors started. They were only whispers

and murmurs at first, but disturbing nonetheless, that Lew Chudd was preparing to sell Imperial. Fats Domino apparently recognized what was coming as he prepared to find another record company. The rumors proved true when Chudd sold Imperial to Liberty Records. The sale effectively slammed the door on the golden era of New Orleans rhythm-and-blues.[124]

Payola—or the refusal to pay payola, bribe money to disc jockeys in exchange for promoting records—doomed King as a recording artist. Cosimo Matassa formed Dover Records in a last-ditch effort to pull the New Orleans recording scene together. When Matassa refused to pay disc jockeys to play his records, however, they countered by refusing to play them. Everything from Dover went straight into the trash can and with no outlet, record sales for King and other New Orleans artists were nonexistent.

Still, King managed to pull off one more coup in 1964 when he wrote *Big Chief,* a song about his mother, in an effort to help Professor Longhair. Dr. John joined him in the studio on piano. Also present were the Meters as King sang and provided the song's enchanting whistling. Earl laid the vocal and whistling tracks as a demo, which Longhair was supposed to repeat later in his own unique voice. The song was released with King's vocal tracks intact, though Longhair was credited. It became one of the most popular Mardi Gras songs ever, reviving Professor Longhair's career in the process.

Two decades passed before Earl King was heard from again, but in 1986 he was joined by New England's Roomful of Blues band for the release of *Glazed* on New Orleans' Black Top label. The album received a Grammy nomination and featured a cover photo of a New Orleans Tastee Donut shop, where King usually conducted all his business dealings. King died of complications from diabetes.[125]

Bobby Mitchell

Bobby Mitchell (August 16, 1935-May 17, 1989) was the

second oldest of seventeen children in a family that depended mainly on fishing the Mississippi River for its livelihood. Mitchell cut and sold wood as his contribution to the family's income. At age ten, he got a job making deliveries for a liquor store after school. While hanging around the store between deliveries, he first started singing, collecting nickels and dimes from passersby. By seventeen, he had fallen under the influence of R&B singer Roy Brown and formed his own band, the Louisiana Groovers.

The band was discovered by producer Dave Bartholomew, A&R man for Imperial Records. The group's initial record was *I'm Crying*. The song did well in Cincinnati and Houston, but the band, because of the young ages of its members, was unable to promote the song with personal appearances. Mitchell recorded *Try Rock 'n' Roll* in 1956 and it jumped to number 14 on the R&B charts, putting him in demand for shows as far away as New York and Los Angeles.

In 1957, Bartholomew received *I'm Gonna Be a Wheel Someday,* written by Baton Rouge native Roy Hayes. With Mitchell, the song was a strong regional hit. Two years later, Fats Domino covered it and it peaked at number 17. For Mitchell, though, it also was a strong hit in Philadelphia, earning him bookings in that city where promoters and disc jockeys were surprised to find that he was black, not white.[126]

Mitchell was one of the casualties when Imperial dropped all its New Orleans artists except Fats Domino in 1958. He signed with several smaller labels but was unable to generate a major hit. His road career was ended by a heart attack in 1960. He finally received royalties on his Imperial Records with the reissue of the *I'm Gonna Be a Wheel Someday* LP. He died in New Orleans of complications from diabetes, kidney failure, and two more heart attacks.[127]

Huey "Piano" Smith

Huey "Piano" Smith (January 26, 1934-) followed in the huge footsteps of Professor Longhair and Fats Domino, and his pounding piano style provided the

backing for a score of Crescent City singers, helping
to establish the New Orleans sound as a major force
in popular music. Besides being a pianist, he was also
a prominent bandleader of the Clowns, songwriter, and
occasional comedian.

Born and raised in the New Orleans Garden District,
Smith started playing piano at fifteen and soon backed Earl
King, Shirley and Lee, and Guitar Slim. His heavy left-hand
rhythm set his playing apart, but his style was nevertheless
reminiscent of Professor Longhair's. He became a favorite
session pianist for Cosimo Matassa's J&M Studio, playing
on records by Smiley Lewis (banging out the rollicking
piano intro on *I Hear You Knocking*), Lloyd Price, and
Little Richard.[128] For Guitar Slim's recording of *The Things
That I Used to Do*, Smith was dropped from the session in
favor of Ray Charles. Still, Smith and Guitar Slim remained
close friends until Slim's death in 1959.

When Johnny Vincent left Specialty Records in 1955 to
start his Ace Records in Jackson, Mississippi, he convinced
Smith and Earl King to come to Jackson for his new label's

*Huey "Piano" Smith performs at an early New Orleans Jazz
Fest. (Courtesy of Louisiana Music Hall of Fame)*

first recording session. Smith's piano is prominent in King's *Those Lonely, Lonely Nights*, which was the label's first hit.

Smith's own *Rockin' Pneumonia and the Boogie-Woogie Flu* could not crack *Billboard's* top 40 until Baton Rouge's Johnny Rivers covered the song in 1972 and propelled it to number 6. Smith's original reached number 5 on the R&B charts in late 1957 but climbed only as high as number 52 on the pop charts because white disc jockeys refused to play it. Still, the Rock and Roll Hall of Fame saw fit to include Smith's version among the 500 Songs That Shaped Rock and Roll.[129]

The disc jockeys could not ignore his follow-up record. The call-and-response lyrics of *Don't You Just Know It* were hypnotic, and listeners often found themselves singing along involuntarily. Backed by *High Blood Pressure,* the record soared to number 9 on *Billboard's* Hot 100 and number 4 on the R&B charts in early 1958, giving Smith his only gold record. Smith preferred playing the piano to singing, so he recruited female impersonator Bobby Marchan as the Clowns' lead singer for all his records.

Smith recorded the instrumental tracks for what he thought would be his next big hit for Ace and Johnny Vincent. Vincent, however, had other ideas. He had scored successes with Eddie Bo and Smith, but in August of 1958, Vincent found in Jimmy Clanton what he needed: a good-looking white singer he could pit against Elvis. Clanton, of Baton Rouge, became a national sensation with his number 4 hit that year, *Just a Dream*. The song, plus the singer's great looks, were just the combination Vincent wanted and gave him the inspiration to try the same magic with another white singer. Frankie Ford, of the New Orleans suburb of Gretna, was brought into the studio to overdub the vocal to *Sea Cruise,* the instrumental that Smith had recorded. It was released under Ford's name, but the label did say, "with Huey 'Piano' Smith and Orch." It also gave writing credits to Smith. Smith could only watch with a sense of what might have been as the song climbed to number 14.

Shortly after he cut *Sea Cruise,* Smith was approached

by Joe Caronna, the New Orleans distributor for Ace Records who just happened to be Ford's manager. Caronna told Smith that Vincent had decided to replace Smith's *Sea Cruise* vocals with Frankie Ford's, adding that Vincent thought if Smith could sell a million copies of *Sea Cruise*, then a white boy could sell ten million. Smith pleaded with Caronna but Caronna said the decision was final.

According to Smith, Ford recorded the song in Matassa's studio late at night behind closed doors. Claiming he bore no animosity toward Ford, Smith nevertheless said the experience taught him the type of person Vincent was. Disgusted, Smith walked away from the music industry in the late 1960s and went into the gardening business. In 1980, he and his wife, Margrette, became involved with the Jehovah's Witnesses and moved to Baton Rouge.[130] He declined a request for an interview, saying he no longer discusses his career as a rock and roll musician.[131]

Bobby Marchan

Most people assume that the lead singer for Huey "Piano" Smith and His Clowns was Smith. Though Smith wrote and played piano, he was never comfortable as a singer. It was Bobby Marchan (April 30, 1930-December 5, 1999) who fronted the Clowns, though he was never credited as soloist on any of the band's records.[132]

Born Oscar James Gibson in Youngstown, Ohio, Marchan became enthralled at an early age with female impersonators and while still a teenager began performing in drag as a comedian and singer. He organized the Powder Box Revue in 1953. A troupe of female impersonators, the revue was booked at New Orleans' Dew Drop Inn for several weeks. Marchan found the city so much to his liking that he decided to stay. He rented a room at the Dew Drop and in 1954 became master of ceremonies at Club Tijuana.[133]

He was working at the club when Eddie Mesner signed him to a recording contract with Aladdin Records. He recorded *Have Mercy* at Cosimo Matassa's studio for Aladdin but was

Bobby Marchan was a female impersonator before joining Huey "Piano" Smith and His Clowns as lead singer. (Courtesy of Louisiana Music Hall of Fame)

dropped and picked up by Dot, for whom he recorded a follow-up, *Just a Little Ol' Wine.*

One night in 1956, Johnny Vincent, owner of Ace Records, dropped by the club. Thinking Marchan was a woman, Vincent said he liked the peformer's singing. Wanting to record the singer, Vincent gave him two hundred dollars and Marchan signed a contract. A few days later Marchan showed up at Matassa's studio still in drag. Present at the studio were Matassa, Vincent, Huey Smith, and several session musicians. Everyone was in on the charade, laughing at the way Vincent kept treating Marchan as if he were a woman. When Huey finally told Vincent the truth, Marchan said the executive almost had a heart attack.[134]

After scoring a regional hit for Ace Records with *Chickee Wah-Wah,* Marchan joined Smith to form Huey "Piano" Smith and His Clowns but left the band in early 1959. Resuming his drag career, he finally achieved the solo stardom he had always sought when he recorded *There Is Something on Your*

Mind for Fire Records. The song climbed to number 1 on the R&B charts. Marchan continued performing as a female impersonator until cancer and the subsequent removal of a kidney forced him to cut back on his appearances. He died of complications from liver cancer.[135]

Larry Williams

When Little Richard began what would become a five-year hiatus from rock and roll on October 1, 1957, Specialty Records had only one of his songs in the can. *Good Golly, Miss Molly* reached number 4 on the R&B charts and number 10 on the *Billboard* Hot 100 in May of 1958. Before Little Richard's departure, Art Rupe had signed New Orleans native Larry Williams (May 10, 1935-January 7, 1980) to a recording contract. It was Williams who was expected to fill the void left by the flamboyant star.

Williams moved to California as a teenager but returned to New Orleans in 1954 when he was nineteen and met Price, who hired Williams as his valet. Price introduced him to producer Robert "Bumps" Blackwell, which led to a recording contract with Specialty. With Little Richard's departure, Rupe and Specialty were desperate to find a high-energy replacement and Williams was groomed to step into his predecessor's shoes.[136]

Specialty got lucky with Williams even before Little Richard left. His cover of Lloyd Price's *Just Because*, with backing from Little Richard's band, climbed to number 11 on the R&B charts in the spring of 1957. *Short Fat Fannie* soared to number 1 on the R&B charts and number 5 on the pop charts in June of 1957. Barely a month after Little Richard left to enroll in seminary, Williams scored again with *Bony Maronie*, which reached number 4 on the R&B charts and number 14 on the pop charts. *Dizzy Miss Lizzie* reached number 69 on the pop charts in April 1958. After that, Williams had only a couple more minor hits.[137] Despite his failure to score major hits in the U.S., his songs became popular in England and the Beatles had hits by covering three of his songs, *Dizzy Miss*

Lizzie, Slow Down, and *Bad Boy. Bony Maronie* was listed as one of the 500 Songs That Shaped Rock and Roll.

The drought of hits for Williams was exacerbated by his arrest in 1959 for selling narcotics. If the lack of record sales had not been provocation enough, the arrest convinced Specialty to drop him from the record label. Williams moved from label to label after that, recording for Chess, Mercury, Decca, and Island. He teamed up with Johnny "Guitar" Watson and in 1967 the duo had a top 40 hit with *Mercy, Mercy, Mercy.*[138]

Williams, who had a long history of criminal activity that predated his recording career, was killed in his Los Angeles home by a gunshot wound to his head. Medical examiners ruled his death a suicide, though rumors persisted that he was murdered because of his involvement in drugs and prostitution.[139]

Clarence "Frogman" Henry

The 1956 song *Ain't Got No Home* launched the career of Clarence "Frogman" Henry (March 19, 1937-) but the song that inspired his unique stage name was not his biggest hit. Born in the New Orleans suburb of Algiers, Henry learned to play both piano and trombone. It was while performing in the early-morning hours in a club that he first came up with the idea behind *Ain't Got No Home.* The crowd's response was favorable enough that Paul Gayten, New Orleans A&R man for Chess Records, rushed him into Cosimo Matassa's studio in September of 1956 to record the song under the supervision of producer Allen Toussaint.[140]

The novelty song reached number 3 on the R&B charts and number 20 on *Billboard*'s Hot 100. Featuring Henry's range of vocal stylings, and a voice he refers to as the frog, it prompted local disc jockey Poppa Stoppa to tag the nineteen-year-old singer with the "Frogman" nickname that he would carry throughout his career. Argo Records, a subsidiary of Chess, issued his first album, which gave Henry the opportunity to record with Nashville saxophone legend

Clarence "Frogman" Henry performs during his induction into the Louisiana Music Hall of Fame in 2006. (Courtesy of Louisiana Music Hall of Fame)

Boots Randolph and Shreveport pianist Floyd Cramer.

Henry appeared destined to become another one-hit wonder when he had trouble scoring a follow-up hit. But then in 1961 he recorded *(I Don't Know Why) But I Do*, written by Abbeville native Bobby Charles Guidry. *But I Do*, arranged by Toussaint, became Henry's biggest hit, reaching number 4 on *Billboard* Hot 100 and remaining on the charts for sixteen weeks.[141] It received new life when it was included in the soundtrack of the 1994 movie *Forrest Gump*. Henry followed that song in short order with the Mills Brothers standard *You Always Hurt the One You Love*, which peaked at number 12 and remained on the charts for ten weeks.[142]

After switching to the Parrot label, Henry recorded *Have You Ever Been Lonely?*, which just missed breaking into the Hot 100 chart. Following that, in 1964, he opened eighteen concerts in the U.S. and Canada for the Beatles. For the next two decades, he played in clubs on Bourbon Street. He continues to perform at the annual New Orleans Jazz and Heritage Festival.[143] He received the Living Legend Award in 2002 and in 2007 he was inducted into the Louisiana Music Hall of Fame. He has also received the New Orleans Big Easy Entertainment Award for Music Heritage and has been named a Louis Armstrong Cultural Ambassador to New Orleans.[144]

Bill Justis

Before Duane Eddy burst onto the music scene with the bass string guitar reverberations of the instrumental *Rebel Rouser,* there was Bill Justis (October 14, 1927-July 14, 1982). Sid Manker's guitar, enhanced by studio echo effects, provided a pounding backup to the wailing Justis tenor sax on *Raunchy.* The song climbed all the way to number 2 in late 1957. Remaining on the charts for twenty weeks, it was the biggest instrumental success in the history of Sun Records and is generally acknowledged as the first instrumental rock and roll hit.[145]

Justis grew up in Memphis before enrolling in Tulane University where he studied music while playing trumpet in jazz and dance bands in and around New Orleans.[146] Sam Phillips hired him as the musical director for Sun Records in 1957. At the age of thirty, Justis was the "old man" of Sun Studio. He had little interest in this new music called rock and roll until he learned how lucrative it had become. With Manker, he wrote the primitive instrumental that made him a rock star.

Justis managed only one other top 100 hit, *College Man,* but his music career was far from finished. He simply moved to the other side of the microphone, spending the remainder of his career as an arranger, musical director, and A&R man. It was in the latter capacity that he discovered Charlie Rich singing Frank Sinatra lounge songs at the Sharecropper Club in Memphis and redirected his efforts toward rock and roll. The result was *Lonely Weekends,* a big hit for Sun Records that climbed to number 22 and remained on the charts for twenty-one weeks.[147]

His career at Sun came to an abrupt end on a night in March of 1959 when Justis was working in the studio trying to record Charlie Rich. Night sessions were common at Sun and on this particular night, like many before it, Justis and Jack Clement, studio musician, producer, and songwriter, were running a recording session when Sam Phillips and some of his friends dropped by the studio. Justis tolerated their boisterous behavior as long as he could before ordering his boss out of the studio so he could continue his work. Phillips, enraged at being upstaged in front of his friends, fired Justis on the spot and then fired Clement for laughing at the two combatants. Justis said the firings were good breaks for the two men "because we started making money after that."[148]

He went on to arrange songs for Patsy Cline, Dean Martin, Kenny Rogers, the Dixiebelles, and Tom Jones and produced *Rockin' Little Angel,* a number 22 *Billboard* hit for Ray Smith in 1960. In 1972, he scored his first movie, *Dear Dead Delilah* and in 1977 scored the Burt Reynolds-Jackie Gleason movie *Smokey and the Bandit.* A year later, he reunited with Reynolds for *Hooper.* He died of cancer in 1982.[149]

Edgar "Big Boy" Myles

Edgar "Big Boy" Myles (1933-1984) was a member of James "Sugar Boy" Crawford's band. He was a trombone player and one of three vocalists for the group when it was signed by Dave Bartholomew to a recording contract with Aladdin Records in 1952. When Crawford showed up with a sore throat for the group's first four-song recording session at Cosimo Matassa's studio on November 23, 1952, Myles was called upon to perform vocals. Two of the four titles were released in December of 1952. The record with *No One to Love Me* and *Early Sunday Morning* garnered few sales but today is considered a collector's item.

While still contracted to Aladdin, Crawford and Myles recorded for Chess Records in 1953 and Leonard Chess released *Overboard* and *I Don't Know What I'll Do* before the two men were signed to a Chess contract. Two more records were released on Chess after they signed. All were credited to Sugar Boy and the Cane Cutters. Among the songs they recorded for Chess was *Jock-a-Mo*, the classic Carnival song. Although it did not make the R&B charts, it too is considered a classic today.

In 1955, Bumps Blackwell signed Myles to a recording contract with Specialty Records but even with the backing of Lee Allen, Red Tyler, Edgar Blanchard, and Earl Palmer, he failed to generate any sales. Clyde McPhatter's cover of their song *Just to Hold My Hand* reached number 26 on the Hot 100 and number 6 on the R&B charts in the spring of 1957. Likewise, his Ace Records release of *New Orleans* failed to make a ripple, but the cover by Gary "U.S." Bonds peaked at number 6 on the *Billboard* Hot 100 and number 5 on the R&B charts in late 1960.

In 1961, Myles departed New Orleans and promptly disappeared into obscurity until his death in 1984 in New York City.[150]

Frankie Ford

Frankie Ford (August 4, 1939-), born Frank Guzzo, has ridden his biggest hit, *Sea Cruise*, which reached number 14 in the spring of 1959, to a rewarding career in his hometown of Gretna, Louisiana. None of his other four charted songs climbed higher than number 72. Ace Records owner Johnny Vincent, seizing upon teenagers' infatuation with hot rod cars, suggested the name change.

Ford began his music career at age five, performing on the Original Amateur Hour, hosted by Ted Mack, and appearing locally with Sophie Tucker, Ted Lewis, and Carmen Miranda. His early piano influences include Ray Charles, Professor Longhair, Clarence "Frogman" Henry, Fats Domino, and Huey "Piano" Smith. It was Smith's *Sea Cruise* that thrust him into the national spotlight at the age of nineteen.

On his way home from a Philadelphia show, Ford was contacted by Vincent, who told him to come straight to the studio to record. Smith, who had already laid down the instrumental tracks for the song, was involved in a dispute with Bobby Marchan, according to one version of the story. The disagreement with the Clowns' lead singer allegedly blocked efforts to record *Sea Cruise,* so Ford was asked to sing it because he sounded enough like Marchan to pull it off. The technique of dubbing the vocal over Smith's instrumental was also employed for *Roberta,* which was intended as the A side of the record, and for the follow-up release, *Alimony,* which cracked the Hot 100 at number 97.

Ford said he entered the studio never having heard *Sea Cruise.* The first song cut during the session was *Roberta.* Then, with Ford on one of two microphones and the Clowns on the other, *Sea Cruise* was recorded with Smith's piano setting the tempo for the horns and Ford's vocal. Once Vincent got the version he wanted, he sped up the tape until Ford sounded more like Marchan. Initially, the song

Frankie Ford performs Sea Cruise *during his induction into the Louisiana Music Hall of Fame in 2006. (Courtesy of Louisiana Music Hall of Fame)*

was a minor hit in New Orleans and then faded somewhat. Then it suddenly caught fire nationally and climbed all the way to number 14 on *Billboard*'s Hot 100 in April of 1959, remaining on the charts for seventeen weeks.

Ford was featured on the Bravo cable channel's *Music from New Orleans* in 1997. The show also featured Jean Knight, Tommy Ridgley, and Oliver Morgan. He also appeared in the 1978 Paramount Pictures film *American Hot Wax. Sea Cruise* has been used in radio and TV commercials for Diet Coke, Sprite, and Coors Light beer and is featured on the soundtracks of several movies, including *My American Cousin, Stewardess School,* and *Ski Patrol,* as well as the TV shows *Lifestyles of the Rich and Famous* and *Quantum Leap*.

Imperial subsequently signed Ford away from Ace. He again took adantage of a legal dispute involving a New Orleans singer. Joe Jones had cut *You Talk Too Much* for both the Roulette and Ric record labels. Court injunctions kept Jones' version off the shelves so Ford slipped in with his version of the song. Because of the injunctions, buyers could purchase only Ford's release. He said he made more money off *You Talk Too Much* than he did from *Sea Cruise.* When Jones' version was finally released, it surpassed Ford's and climbed to number 3.

When he returned to New Orleans in late 1965, Ford found a changed music scene. Hurricane Betsy had scattered the city's musicians and Imperial had sold out, leaving him without a recording label. The British Invasion had replaced suddenly obsolete horns with guitars, and activity had all but ceased at Cosimo Matassa's J&M Studio. With no recording contract, Ford turned to Bourbon Street, where he found a profitable living playing local clubs. He has since been inducted into the Louisiana Music Hall of Fame.[151]

James C. Booker III

He was born in Charity Hospital in New Orleans and died there forty-four years later. In between, James C. Booker III (December 17, 1939-November 8, 1983) came to be considered as one of the premier—and most tragic—New Orleans pianists of his era.

Sent to Bay St. Louis, Mississippi, at an early age to live with an aunt, both he and his sister Betty Jean took piano lessons. Booker's studies were interrupted at age ten when a speeding ambulance struck him, causing a severe leg fracture. The accident left him with a permanent limp and introduced him to morphine.

He returned to New Orleans to live with his mother and enrolled at Xavier Preparatory School with fellow musician Allen Toussaint, who remembered Booker as a class leader in math, Spanish, and music. During that time, his sister Betty Jean hosted a live Sunday morning gospel show on radio station WMRY. Through her Booker met disc jockey Ernie the Whip. The radio personality gave him an audition that led to a regular Saturday afternoon radio show playing blues and gospel.

When Tuts Washington, a friend of Booker's mother and grandmother, would visit, young Booker would watch and listen as he played. Later, he started sneaking into the joints to watch Washington play. An ex-boyfriend of Booker's sister Betty Jean, pianist Edward Franks, arranged an audition for the young pianist with Dave Bartholomew, which led to an Imperial recording contract and session work at Cosimo Matassa's studio. Matassa recalled that Booker "sounded more like Fats than Fats did" and that Booker actually played piano on some of Fats' tracks.

On weekends Booker traveled with Shirley and Lee, Earl King, and Smiley Lewis, and upon graduation from Xavier Prep in 1957, he joined Joe Tex and traveled with his band all over the South. After he returned to New Orleans, Earl King said Booker began acting foolishly and one night King finally got so weary of his drug-addled behavior that he put Booker out of his car. King also described Booker and Little Richard riding around together in Little Richard's robin's-egg blue Cadillac, driving up and down Canal Street and acting flamboyantly.

Booker was hired in 1958 by Bobby Marchan to work with Huey Smith and the Clowns. The following year, he enrolled in music at Southern University in Baton Rouge, hoping that college might help him overcome his drug habit. He dropped out of school two months from graduation to join Dee Clark's band as an organist. The band broke up in Houston and Booker worked with Roy Hamilton, B.B. King, Little Richard, Dr. John, and Wilson Pickett. He also sat in on recording sessions with Aretha Franklin, Lloyd Price, the Grateful Dead, the Doobie Brothers, Ringo Starr, and Fats Domino.

In 1970, he was arrested outside the Dew Drop Inn and sentenced to two years at Louisiana State Penitentiary in Angola for possession of heroin. He was paroled after six months, with Joe Tex signing the parole papers. He made his way to New York, Pennsylvania, and finally to California, where he recorded with Charles Brown and with T-Bone Walker on Walker's last album, *Very Rare.* Then it was on to Cincinnati, where he performed sessions for King Records.

When he finally reappeared in New Orleans in 1975, he had a patch covering the absence of his left eye. Details of how he lost his eye varied.[152] One version was offered by Dr. John, who said Booker lost the eye after pulling a scam on record producers for whom the two had written arrangements. He said Booker somehow conned the producers into paying for their services three times and was pushing his luck with a fourth attempt. The intended victims of the con caught on and had Booker beaten so badly that he lost the eye. Booker was alleged to have said that if he had lost his other eye as well, he might have been able to play as well as Ray Charles or Art Tatum.[153]

Booker, besides being a hopeless drug addict, repeatedly upstaged band members and also was flagrant with his homosexuality. Often, he propositioned those assigned to share his room or worse, brought men he picked up on the road to the room he shared with horrified roommates.

Whether throwing up on the piano, stumbling behind a bar

to vomit, teaching piano to Harry Connick, Jr., speculating about UFO conspiracies, or entering Jazz Fest in a rented white Bentley, James Booker never did things in a small way. During the 1981 New Orleans Jazz and Heritage Festival, he played a show-stopping performance before three thousand people on the riverboat *S.S. President*, ending his set with a medley of *A Taste of Honey* and *Malaguena*. When finished, he stood and bowed in acknowledgement of the standing ovation and exited. Two days later, he was committed to the psychiatric ward of Charity Hospital after police found him wandering the French Quarter babbling incoherently. The three-piece suit he'd worn on the *President* was encrusted with his own dried vomit.

In October 1982, a three-day studio session was scheduled for Booker at Ultrasonic Studio in New Orleans for his *Classified* album. A week before the session, Booker suffered a seizure and was rushed to a hospital. The session was rescheduled several times before Booker finally got a medical clearance—though he was cautioned that his liver was virtually nonfunctional and that another drink might be his last. The first day of his recording session he refused to play the material he was provided. The second day was even worse, as Booker withdrew to a corner of the studio and sat staring at the wall. On the final day, Booker inexplicably came to life, showing up an hour before the other musicians. The recording engineer had barely turned on the tape machine before he recorded some of his most outstanding piano solos. He cut four songs before the band even set up. Once they joined in, the entire album was on tape in only four hours.

In October 1983, he appeared on a local cable television show. On October 31, he made his final public appearance, playing before five paying customers at the Maple Leaf Club. He failed to show up for his scheduled November 7 gig at the club. The next morning, he took a lethal dose of cocaine at a local bar. He was driven to Charity Hospital and placed in a wheelchair. Left in a hallway, he remained unattended until he was discovered by an orderly, already dead. There were few friends to mourn him; his wake and funeral were sparsely attended. The tributes were even fewer and, for the most part, empty and less than sincere.[154]

Irma Thomas

Irma Thomas (February 18, 1941-) lost all her possessions in the aftermath of Hurricane Katrina when the levees breached, flooding much of New Orleans. Out of town at the time, Thomas was performing at Antone's in Austin, Texas. Because her whereabouts were unknown when the storm hit, she was initially reported as missing.

Watching the storm's carnage on television in Austin, Thomas and her manager-husband, Emile Jackson, were devastated to see an almost submerged street sign in her New Orleans East neighborhood. Antone's management, realizing she would not be leaving Austin for the time being, invited her to play an additional night. The following day, she and Jackson flew to Alexandria and drove to Baton Rouge. They eventually settled in Gonzales with Jackson's aunt while their New Orleans home was undergoing renovations.

Soon after moving in with her husband's aunt, she performed benefits for Katrina victims with Bruce Springsteen, Elvis Costello, and Dr. John and also appeared in the hurricane relief concert at Madison Square Garden a few weeks after Katrina. She sang with Bonnie Raitt and Allen Toussaint for the grand finale of the 2006 Grammy Awards.[155]

Born Irma Lee in Ponchatoula, about an hour northwest of New Orleans, she lived for a time with her father's family in nearby Greensburg before moving with her parents to New Orleans. Pregnant at age fourteen and forced to marry the child's father, she had a second baby before the marriage disintegrated. With a failed marriage and two children at age sixteen, she started waiting tables at what would become the Pimlico Club, on the corner of South Broad and Eve Street. At seventeen, she married Andrew Thomas. Two more children followed, all before she was twenty. When

Irma Thomas, the Soul Queen of New Orleans. (Courtesy of Louisiana Music Hall of Fame)

her second marriage failed, she kept the name Thomas.

Meanwhile, she was gaining a reputation as a talented singer and was sitting in with Tommy Ridgley and the Untouchables at the club. Originally, the club catered to whites and blacks, each race accorded separate entrances. The whites entered from the front and the blacks from the rear of the building. Eventually the venue was converted into what in those days was called a "colored" club. Now the Pimlico Club, it began offering live entertainment Wednesday through Sunday nights. Thomas was making four dollars per night, plus tips, to wait tables. Eventually, patrons started asking for the "singing waitress." That upset her boss, who felt he was paying her to wait tables, not entertain.[156]

When she was fired for her singing, Ridgley took her to Ron Records where she cut her first record, *You Can Have My Husband (But Don't Mess with My Man)*, which climbed to number 22 on the *Billboard* R&B chart in May of 1960. A dispute over royalties ensued, and she signed with Minit

Records, where she worked with Allen Toussaint, recording *It's Raining, Ruler of My Heart,* and *I Done Got Over.* Minit Records, along with Thomas's recording contract, was later obtained by Imperial.

While in New Orleans, Otis Redding heard her sing *Ruler of My Heart,* reworked the lyrics slightly, and released his own version, *Pain in My Heart,* which reached number 11 on the *Billboard* R&B chart in November of 1963 and number 61 on the pop charts in February of 1964. In March 1964, she had her biggest hit with *I Wish Someone Would Care*—and its B side, *Break-a-way*—which climbed to number 17. She was at a low point in her life when she wrote *I Wish Someone Would Care,* a song from her heart. Her second marriage was coming apart over her husband's objections to her singing career and she really wanted someone to stand beside her and support her during a difficult time. She believes the song sold so well because it was an authentic expression of her emotions.

In December 1964, the Rolling Stones had a number 6 hit when they covered *Time Is on My Side*, a song Thomas first recorded. The song later surfaced on a television ad for a diet drink but was sung by neither Thomas nor the Stones. Since the commercial used a generic version of the song, rather than Thomas's own, she was not able to collect royalties for the its use. Arguably, one of her best recordings was a cover of Nat King Cole's *Looking Back,* a song that never charted.

Her career took a downward turn during her tenures with Imperial and then Chess Records and in January 1970, she moved to California, first to Oakland and then to Los Angeles. She sold auto parts in both cities during the day and took nightclub gigs when and where she could. She also recorded for several small labels. Looking back at that period in her life, she now feels she should have gotten better management. "Rock and roll was still in its infancy back then and there were a lot of unsophisticated performers who didn't know how to take care of themselves," she said.

"At the same time, there were a lot of smooth operators just waiting to prey on us. A lot of artists lost a lot of money to record companies, managers, and booking agents."[157]

In 1976, she moved back to New Orleans and to her surprise, found that she was still popular in her hometown as a live performer. The following year she married Emile Jackson, who took over as her manager, and she became a regular performer at the New Orleans Jazz and Heritage Festival. She and Jackson set about rejuvenating her career, even opening a nightclub, the Lion's Den, on Gravier Street near Broad. (The Lion's Den was damaged by Hurricane Katrina, and Thomas has no plans to reopen.) She played at the opening ceremonies for Harrah's New Orleans Casino and at the city's Essence Music Festival. She has toured in Japan, Germany, Switzerland, France, the Netherlands, Italy, and Greece.[158]

Thomas has won two W.C. Handy Blues Awards even though she didn't know she had been nominated either time—she considers herself an R&B singer, not blues in the classic sense—and she has received two Grammy nominations in contemporary blues. All those awards were lost in the Katrina flooding. Philosophical about her misfortune, she is grateful to be alive and to have the opportunity to make more music.[159]

Recorded at the Dockside Studio in Maurice, Louisiana, only months following Katrina, *After the Rain* would seem to be a requiem for victims of the devastating hurricane. Actually, the songs for the album were selected before Katrina. Nevertheless she won her only Grammy in 2007 for Best Contemporary Blues Album. Her reaction to winning the Grammy was vintage Irma. "I wanted to thank New Orleans," she said. "The city believed in me for forty-nine years and it finally paid off."[160]

Danny White

Danny White (July 6, 1932-January 5, 1996) was one of the most popular live performers in New Orleans but success somehow managed to evade him in the studio. Born Joseph Daniel White in New Orleans' Charity Hospital, he was the youngest of seven children. Though he grew up around music in the Holly Grove and Seventh Ward sections of New Orleans, he did not make his professional debut until he was a twenty-year-old marine at Camp Pendleton, California.

In 1962, after he and his band, the Cavaliers, had consistently packed the house for seven years in clubs on Bourbon Street, he signed with Frisco Records, a new label in New Orleans. His initial effort was produced by Wardell Quezergue. *Kiss Tomorrow Goodbye*, backed with *The Little Bitty Things*, did not chart but was still a commercial success for White. In 1964, he did even better with Earl King's composition *Loan Me a Handkerchief.* Also recorded for Frisco, it was leased by ABC-Paramount and while it, too, was a regional success, it failed to crack the charts. White moved production of his next recording efforts to Memphis. There, he recorded at Royal Studios under the direction of two new songwriters, David Porter and Isaac Hayes.[161]

By 1964, White's career was in a free fall. The sweeping change in musical tastes was displacing horns and pianos in favor of guitars and drums. This created a ripple effect, resulting in fewer live shows for White and others. In 1969, he moved to the other side of the studio glass when he began managing the Meters, a group that had previously backed him on his recordings. He also made his last record that year, *Natural Soul Brother*, backed with *One Way Love Affair.* Produced by Allen Toussaint, the song didn't catch on until it was rediscovered years later by collectors. By the early 1970s, White had retired from music and moved to the Washington, D.C. area.[162]

Johnny Adams

Johnny Adams (January 5, 1932-September 14, 1998) was originally a gospel singer before crossing over to secular music with *A Losing Battle,* which climbed to number 27 on the R&B charts in June of 1962. Born Laten John Adams in New Orleans, he was called "the Tan Canary" for his light skin and beautiful voice. The oldest of ten children, he dropped out of school at age fifteen and began singing with gospel groups.[163]

New Orleans recording executive Cosimo Matassa says Adams had an angelic voice and greater range of expression than Aaron Neville. Matassa feels Adams was a victim of bad timing; about the time he began his singing career he, like so many other American artists, was victimized by the British Invasion. "We weren't doing much in the record world by that time," he recalls.

Adams decided to pursue an R&B singing career after his upstairs neighbor, songwriter Dorothy Labostrie, overheard him singing in his bathtub. His rendition of *Precious Lord, Take My Hand* convinced Labostrie to have him signed by the local Ric label. Eighteen-year-old John Rebennack (Dr. John) produced Adams' first recording session, which resulted in *I Won't Cry*. The song was a regional hit and eventually reached number 41 on the R&B charts in 1959.[164]

Berry Gordy once attempted to sign Adams to his Motown label but Ric president Joe Ruffino threatened a lawsuit and the deal with Gordy fell through. He eventually was signed to the SSS label by Shreveport native Shelby Singleton, who had Adams lend his stylings to create a country-soul sound. A brief stint with Atlantic Records proved unproductive, and Adams ended up with Rounder Records, where he stayed for the remainder of his career. Considered one of the more versatile singers, he was equally comfortable with soul, R&B, ballads, jazz, or country, and he once said he could even sing bluegrass.[165]

Hits by Adams included *A Losing Battle* (written by Rebennack and a number 27 hit on the R&B charts), *Release Me* (number 34 R&B and number 82 on the pop charts), *After All the Good Is Gone* (number 75 R&B), and *I Can't Be All Bad* (number 45 R&B and number 89 pop). His biggest hit was 1969's *Reconsider Me* (number 8 R&B and number 28 pop), written by Shreveport's Margaret Lewis.[166]

Adams died in Baton Rouge's Our Lady of the Lake Hospital following a lengthy battle with cancer.[167]

Roosevelt Nettles

Roosevelt Nettles has resided in Phoenix, Arizona, since his 1962 self-imposed exile from the New Orleans music scene. One of eight children, he grew up in New Orleans and sang professionally as a teenager in Mobile, Alabama. He first performed with the Flames, a doo-wop group. Joining the U.S. Air Force in 1958, he formed another nonrecording doo-wop group, the Enchanters.

It was while serving as a member of the Special Forces that Nettles discovered Arizona. He was stationed near Phoenix and fell in love with the state, making it his permanent home after his military tour ended in 1962. He sang regularly at the Stage Seven club there. Disc jockey Lucky Lawrence liked his music and got him the opportunity to cut *Mathilda* (originally by Cookie and the Cupcakes) for Mascot Records. Chess Records purchased the song, backed it with *Drifting Heart,* and reissued the record, which had some success in his home state of Louisiana.

Nettles and Chess could not come to terms on a follow-up record and the association ended. He then cut *Gotcha on My Mind*. His last recording, *You've Let a Fortune Go* backed with *Sorry for Me*, was released on Capitol Records.

He opened for Ike and Tina Turner, Sam Cooke, and the Righteous Brothers until he retired from music altogether in 1966. He works today as a chef, a skill he learned in the service.[168]

Joe Jones

It took three separate attempts, but Joe Jones (August 12, 1926-November 27, 2005) finally succeeded in generating a hit song with *You Talk Too Much*, recorded for Ric Records in 1960. As it turned out, it was to be the only hit for Jones or for the fledgling New Orleans record label. It climbed to number 3 on the *Billboard* Hot 100 and number 9 on the R&B charts in November of that year.

Jones had cut his first record for Capitol Records in 1954 after serving as a valet, pianist, and arranger for blues musician B.B. King.[169] The one-time Juilliard School student also toured briefly with Shirley and Lee. He moved to the Herald label in 1957 and to Roulette a year later. Fats Domino's brother-in-law, pianist Reggie Hall, wrote *You Talk Too Much* and Domino passed it on to Jones, who performed it during his nightclub act for several months before he recorded it.[170]

The record's release and ensuing tour occurred about the time Fidel Castro started to make headlines following his successful coup in Cuba. Responding to Castro's marathon harangues, the band decided to send a copy of the record to the dictator as a not-so-subtle message. To their surprise, while Jones and his band were in Chicago a Castro lieutenant acknowledged receipt of the record. They took the story to *Jet* magazine and received some free publicity.

After Ric's release of *You Talk Too Much,* Roulette discovered that it owned an earlier recording of the same song by Jones. Executives of the two labels, in order to avoid a protracted legal battle over rights to the song, decided on an amicable settlement and Roulette purchased the rights from Ric. Jones never had another major hit and eventually settled into producing and management. In 1964, he met with some success with other New Orleans artists, including Alvin "Shine" Robinson and the all-girl trio the Dixie Cups. But *You Talk Too Much* apparently proved to be a self-fulfilling prophecy for Jones, who was described by John Rebennack as having a knack for talking his way into deals but an inability to see projects through. He moved to Los Angeles in 1973 and became an advocate for the rights of fellow R&B acts after receiving little in royalties from *You Talk Too Much.*[171]

At one point Jones was sued by Cosimo Matassa, who claimed that the singer was in possession of music owned by Matassa. Jones showed up in court with a contract ostensibly signed by Matassa giving Jones rights to the music. The only problem was that Matassa's first name was signed "Cosmo." "He misspelled my name," says Matassa, who won a judgment but never collected from Jones, who was insolvent.[172]

Jones died in Los Angeles following quadruple bypass surgery at the age of seventy-nine.

Jessie Hill

Jessie Hill (December 9, 1932-September 17, 1996) was a gifted drummer, singer, and songwriter. Born in New Orleans and reared in the Ninth Ward, he formed the House Rockers with the Lastie brothers, Melvin on trumpet and David on saxophone.[173] After playing country and western bars and touring the country with a drag troupe led by Bobby Marchan, band members went their separate ways. Hill returned to New Orleans to play drums behind Professor Longhair. He then rejoined Marchan as a member of the Clowns before forming a new version of the House Rockers in 1958.[174]

In 1959, Hill and his band recorded a demo of the classic call-and-response song *Ooh Poo Pah Doo* that half a century later remains a New Orleans R&B classic. Hill tried to sell the song to Joe Ruffino's Ric and Ron record labels. Ruffino wasn't interested but recommended him to Joe Banashak and his Minit label. Banashak was sufficiently impressed to book session time at Cosimo Matassa's J&M Studio and the result was the first of many Allen Toussaint production credits. The song was said to have originated with a local pianist known as Big Four, a regrettably nameless alcoholic who played the club Shy Guy's Place for drinks and tips.[175]

The song earned Hill a gold record, selling eight hundred thousand copies on its way to becoming a Mardi Gras favorite. It climbed to number 28 and remained on the pop charts for sixteen weeks. It remained on the R&B charts for eleven weeks, climbing to number 3.[176] Unfortunately for Hill, at a time when he should have been on top of the world, everything fell apart. He took the House Rockers on a national tour that was to have culminated at New York

City's Apollo Theater but the other band members became so upset at his haphazard accounting methods that the band split up in disharmony prior to a scheduled performance in Washington, D.C. He had one other Top 100 effort, *Whip It on Me*, which spent only one week on the pop charts at number 91 in July of 1960.

A year later, Hill discovered obscure New Orleans vocalist Barbara George, who would record only one hit, before he moved to California. There he teamed up with fellow Louisianans Harold Battiste, Dave Dixon, and John Rebennack. Rebennack convinced him to put his singing career on hold in favor of songwriting. It turned out to be the right decision and in the ensuing years, his songs were recorded by Ike and Tina Turner, Sonny and Cher, and Aretha Franklin. He wrote more than 150 songs and even wrote songs with Willie Nelson.

Chronic drinking problems led to financial difficulties. Following a disagreement with Battiste, he quit his songwriting job, only to be arrested and jailed for an accumulation of traffic violation warrants. While he was in Los Angeles County Jail, his car and all his songwriting materials were stolen. He eventually found his way back to New Orleans in 1977 but was unable to secure any singing dates or songwriting jobs. He was reduced to driving a taxi, his own black Cadillac, which he named the "Poo Cab," but his drinking and narcotics abuse soon led to another collection of DUI infractions and eventually he lost his cabbie's license. The few live performances he did manage to secure were hastily assembled affairs with pickup bands that quickly turned into disasters. Soon he was homeless. Several benefits were held for him but they did nothing to revive his sagging career or personal life. He eventually died of heart and kidney failure. He was buried beneath a plywood marker in Holt Cemetery in New Orleans.[177]

Lawrence "Prince La La" Nelson
Lawrence Nelson, a.k.a. Prince La La, (1936-1963)

died of a heroin overdose at age twenty-seven. His death prompted longtime Ninth Ward friend Oliver "Who Shot the La La" Morgan to memorialize him in song (*Who Shot the La La*).[178]

Nelson was born into a musical family. His brother was guitarist Walter "Papoose" Nelson, who played on most of Fats Domino's recordings and who, on February 28, 1962, also died of a heroin overdose. His father, Walter Nelson, played guitar for R&B singer Smiley Lewis. A sister, Dorothy, was married to Jessie Hill.

It was Hill who was responsible for Nelson's becoming a recording artist. Hill wanted new discovery Barbara George to sing Nelson's song *She Put the Hurt on Me* and played a demo of the song with Nelson's vocal for George and Harold Battiste to hear. Battiste, who was just getting his new A.F.O. record label started, decided instead to have Nelson record the song as the label's first release.[179]

She Put the Hurt on Me reached number 14 on the R&B charts and was credited to Prince La La. "La La" was Nelson's nickname and "Prince" was a tie-in to the African prince costume adopted by Nelson in his publicity photos. The costume, drawn from African and Mardi Gras traditions as much as from Nelson's eccentric mannerisms, would influence John Rebennack, who took on a similar guise for himself in creating his Dr. John, the Night Tripper, persona.[180]

Oliver "Who Shot the La La" Morgan

Oliver "Who Shot the La La" Morgan (1933-August 7, 2007) was never convinced that Lawrence "Prince La La" Nelson's death was accidental, believing instead that his friend's supplier had laced his heroin with poison as revenge for a debt or some other perceived wrong. In 1964, the year following Nelson's death, Morgan recorded *Who Shot the La La?*, which became a national hit. Deacon John Moore speculated at Morgan's funeral in 2007 that the "shot" in the song's title and lyrics may have been referring to a "hot shot," heroin to which poison has been added.

Morgan grew up in New Orleans' Ninth Ward. His home, like so many others, was destroyed by Hurricane Katrina and he and his wife, Sylvia, were evacuated to Atlanta, where he still resided at the time of his death. Among the three hundred attendees at his funeral were Fats Domino, Allen Toussaint, Clarence "Frogman" Henry, Charmaine Neville, Deacon John Moore, and Ernie K-Doe's widow, Antoinette Dorsey.[181]

Al "Carnival Time" Johnson

It was in December 1959 that Alvin Lee Johnson (1940-) entered Cosimo Matassa's recording studio. He emerged from the studio on Governor Nicholls Street with what would become a belated hit song and a new name, Al "Carnival Time" Johnson. Joe Ruffino produced the recording session for his Ric label.[182] *Carnival Time* eventually joined Professor Longhair's *Go to the Mardi Gras* and *Big Chief* and the Hawkettes' *Mardi Gras Mambo* as classics of the New Orleans Mardi Gras season. All four songs are rereleased annually in response to ongoing demand from Carnival-goers.

Even after a half-century, Johnson remains dissatisfied with *Carnival Time.* Because of its unique arrangement, studio musicians insisted that the timing was wrong, and Johnson feels they never got the song completely right. But the song's lyrics, which make sense only to those familiar with the annual Mardi Gras tradition, were right enough to catch on and become a Carnival standard.

Initially, in 1960, *Carnival Time* was obliterated on the charts by Jessie Hill's *Ooh Poo Pah Doo*. It wasn't until Johnson was drafted and subsequently stationed at Fort Bliss, Texas, that he began to hear stories from family and friends that *Carnival Time* was hot back home. He returned to New Orleans at the end of 1964 to find the local music scene decimated by the advent of Beatlemania. Ruffino had died while Johnson was in the army and a protracted legal fight ensued over royalties and rights to the song that left him

Al "Carnival Time" Johnson performs his Mardi Gras hit Carnival Time *at his induction into the Louisiana Music Hall of Fame. (Courtesy of Louisiana Music Hall of Fame)*

jaded with the music business. He returned to performing, however, after finally being awarded full rights to his hit in 1999. In 2005, he reigned as king of Krewe du Vieux and has been inducted into the Louisiana Music Hall of Fame.[183]

Barbara George

If the adage about one's fifteen minutes of fame applies to anyone, Barbara George (August 16, 1943-August 10, 2006) would qualify. Born Barbara Ann, George grew up in the notorious Desire Projects. She got a glimpse of fame with her hit *I Know (You Don't Love Me No More),* but a career plagued by squandered promise and poor business and personal decisions relegated her to rock trivia status.[184]

Bassist Chuck Badie teamed with Alvin "Red" Tyler, Harold Battiste, and others to form the short-lived A.F.O. record label in 1961. Discovered by Jessie Hill, George and her mediocre voice didn't impress A.F.O., but the decision was made to release the record nonetheless. Battiste apparently said that if he had seen her in a club, he wouldn't have given her a second thought. But Jessie and Melvin Lastie convinced him to record her in June of 1961.

Badie's driving bass, Marcel Richardson's piano, and producer Lastie's unique cornet solo combined to overshadow George's unpolished voice. In fact, Lastie's cornet, in lieu of the usual sax solo, was considered a master stroke that led to the song's success. *I Know* entered the R&B charts in November of 1961 and the pop charts in January of 1962 and remained on both charts for nineteen weeks, reaching number 1 on the R&B charts and number 3 on the *Billboard* Hot 100. The magic was never recaptured, though two other songs, *You Talk about Love* (number 46) and *Send for Me* (number 96) also cracked the Hot 100 for her.

George, who was six months pregnant when she recorded *I Know,* played the Apollo Theater in New York after the song became a hit.[185] A promoter named Juggy Murray bought her a Cadillac, a fur coat, and jewelry in an attempt to sign her to his Sue Records. He neglected to tell her that the items were not really gifts, as they were funded by her own royalties. Murray convinced her to buy out her contract with Battiste and sign with his label.

Unable to repeat her success, George developed a drug problem and allowed dealers to use her car to run their drugs. Things went from bad to worse when they pulled an armed robbery and she was sent to the Louisiana State

Prison for Women near Baton Rouge. Upon her release, she moved to Chauvin in Terrebonne Parish to live with her mother. She joined the church and struggled to beat her addictions.[186]

Despite her personal troubles, George maintained a close friendship with Ernie K-Doe and sang *I Know* at his funeral in 2001, the last time she sang a secular song in public. She died five years later and was buried on what would have been her sixty-fourth birthday.[187]

Ernie K-Doe

Ernest Kador, Jr. (February 22, 1936-July 5, 2001) was once quoted as saying, "I'm not sure, but I'm almost positive that all music came from New Orleans." Better known by his professional name, Ernie K-Doe, he is best remembered for one song. Though he broke into the Top 100 four more times, *Mother-in-Law*, a number 1 hit, is the signature song that catapulted him to fame in 1961. K-Doe stumbled upon the novelty song in a studio trash can after its composer, Allen Toussaint, had thrown it away. It first entered the charts in May and remained there for fourteen weeks.

With *Mother-in-Law* jokes always popular, the song was a natural. Add to that Benny Spellman's rich baritone repeating the title line and Allen Toussaint on piano, and the song had all the ingredients to make it a hit. It was just what Joe Banashak needed to give his fledgling Minit Records a much-needed hit.[188]

An earlier effort, *Hello, My Lover,* was a regional success, selling almost one hundred thousand copies, but the song was released under the name Ernie Kador. "There were several disc jockeys all over the country who had interests in record labels and we'd send each other our records," says New Orleans disc jockey Larry McKinley, who was both K-Doe's manager and a partner in Minit Records. "We'd plug each other's records and that's how a lot of songs became hits. I got a lot of calls from deejay friends asking how to pronounce Kador's last name. I told them, 'Don't worry, it

Ernie K-Doe performs at the New Orleans Jazz and Heritage Festival. (Courtesy of Louisiana Music Hall of Fame)

won't be a problem on his next record.'"

The next record was *Mother-in-Law*. The artist's name was changed to Ernie K-Doe and the singer earned a gold record. It also fueled a long-running feud between K-Doe and Benny Spellman over song royalties.[189] Whether the feud was acrimonious or in jest depends on who does the telling. Irma Thomas does not believe the trash talking ever progressed beyond good-natured kidding. McKinley, however, says the dispute was very real. "They were really angry and they really fought. I know, I was K-Doe's manager and he was my meal ticket. I was the one who pulled them apart. Spellman was about 180 pounds and K-Doe was strong but was only about 160. Spellman had K-Doe down on the floor in a neck lock and K-Doe was screaming, 'Get up and fight like a man!'"[190]

Though *Mother-in-Law* was one of the biggest songs in the history of New Orleans R&B, its success angered New Orleans disc jockeys. Minit founder Joe Banashak had a distribution agreement with Lew Chudd of Imperial

Records in California whereby Chudd would distribute the Minit label nationally. When *Mother-in-Law* went gold, *Billboard* published a photograph showing Chudd giving the award to a West Coast disc jockey in appreciation for helping to earn the record. That offended the New Orleans radio personalities, particularly McKinley, because they had introduced the record, just as they had historically promoted all new records by local artists. Banashak said the photo created some ill feelings for him as well.[191]

The success of *Mother-in-Law* also produced its amusing moments. Across the street from Banashak's Minit Records was a Cadillac dealership where K-Doe was employed as a janitor before recording his historic song—and for a short time afterwards. Following the song's release but before K-Doe was aware of the full extent of its success, the singer was working on the dealership's showroom floor. Sitting at the wheel of a shiny new Cadillac convertible as he cleaned and polished the dashboard, he suddenly laid down his dust rag, took the wheel, and leaned back, pretending to drive the vehicle. Spotted by the dealership's owner, he was summarily fired for his temerity.

Broke and unemployed, he called on Banashak, who was visiting with Baton Rouge recording executive S. J. Montalbano, who remembers the exchange over forty years later. "K-Doe walked in and said, 'Mr. Banashak, they just fired me across the street and I wonder if you could loan me some money for lunch.'

"Joe had just received K-Doe's first royalty check and he leaned back in his chair and said, 'Ernie, I'm not gonna loan you any money, but this came for you today and it should cover your lunch.' He reached across the desk and handed K-Doe a check for twenty-four thousand dollars. It was the most money K-Doe had ever seen. Without a word, K-Doe turned and walked back across the street to his former employer. Strutting into the dealership, he said in a loud voice, 'You remember firing me for sittin' in that [expletive] Caddy? Well I'm *buying* that [expletive] car! I'm buying it and I want you to open them [expletive] double doors 'cause I'm driving it out of here. Thrusting his check at a dumbstruck salesman, he said, "Here's a [expletive] check. You can mail me my change!"[192]

In May of 1961, he again broke into *Billboard's* Hot 100 with *Te-Ta-Te-Ta-Ta.* It remained on the charts for five weeks, peaking at number 53. *I Cried My Last Tear* and *A Certain Girl* both put him back on the charts in December of 1961, reaching numbers 69 and 71, respectively. The former was on the charts for five weeks and the latter for four. His only other entry into *Billboard's* Hot 100 was in February of 1962 when *Popeye Joe* appeared for one week at number 99. *Tain't It the Truth*, which captured the unique magic and feel of New Orleans rhythm-and-blues, was relegated to regional status.[193]

After that brief fling with national fame, K-Doe's career floundered and he was unable to record another hit. Beginning in the 1970s, he sank into a decade of alcoholism that reached its depths when he was forced to sing on street corners for spare change. He resurfaced in 1982 as host of a local radio show. His unabashed self-aggrandizement enhanced his on-air antics, gaining him a new generation of admirers. In 1994, he met his future wife, Antoinette Fox, who helped him turn his life around. He opened his own club on Claiborne Avenue, calling it appropriately, the Mother-in-Law Lounge. He performed there frequently, often accompanying his own songs on the jukebox. He was inducted into the New Orleans Music Hall of Fame in 1995, and in 1997 the Rhythm & Blues Foundation Pioneer Award was bestowed upon him in Manhattan. His career now resurrected, he proclaimed himself Emperor of the World.

He died from kidney and liver failure.[194]

Chris Kenner

Chris Kenner (December 25, 1929-January 25, 1976) began his singing career as a member of a spiritual group, and his first recording efforts met with general indifference on the part of music buyers. But when Imperial Records signed him in 1958, he wrote and recorded *Sick and Tired,* which was a hit for Fats Domino later that same year.

When Joe Banashak founded Instant Records in 1961, it was Kenner who got the infant record label off and running with *I Like It Like That.* The song was a novelty tune that Kenner had worked on for some time before putting it on tape. Two years after Kenner had initially recorded the song, Banashak stopped by Instant Records arranger Allen Toussaint's home. Toussaint played some old tapes for Banashak, who liked Kenner's song and asked his host to find the singer. Toussaint rushed Kenner into Cosimo Matassa's studio to record it professionally. Four years later, the Dave Clark Five had a number 7 hit with their cover of it.

Kenner's version of the song got off to a slow start but suddenly caught on and soared to number 2, remaining on the charts for seventeen weeks. Recognized as the Best Rock 'n' Roll Record of 1961 at that year's Grammy awards, it also earned Kenner a Grammy for Best Writer of the Year. The success of *I Like It Like That* led to tours with Jackie Wilson, Roy Hamilton, Laverne Baker, the Coasters, and Gladys Knight. Capitalizing on the New Orleans *Pop-Eye* dance craze, Kenner had a local hit with *Something You Got* for Instant Records, but the effort failed to produce a major national hit and Kenner's stock quickly declined.

Then, in 1963, he wrote and recorded *Land of 1,000 Dances.* With Allen Toussaint on piano and utilizing a driving gospel style, he rattled off a laundry list of popular dances of the day in a bouncing melody that was nearly impossible not to sing along with. In exchange for recording it, composer credit and half the royalties were given to Fats Domino even though he had nothing to do with writing the song. Fats' version was a failure. Kenner's was the bigger success but reached only as high as number 77. In 1965 it was a huge hit, however, for Cannibal and the Headhunters (number 30, fourteen weeks on the charts), who inserted the "Na na na na na" line in it when lead singer Frankie

Garcia forgot the lyrics,[195] and for Wilson Pickett (number 6, eleven weeks on *Billboard*'s Hot 100) in 1966. It was also recorded by Tom Jones, the J. Geils Band, Tina Turner, and Rufus Thomas, providing Kenner songwriter royalties for the remainder of his life.[196]

In 1968, Kenner was sentenced to prison for statutory rape of a minor. He died of a heart attack one month to the day after his forty-sixth birthday.

Lee Dorsey

Whether trying his hand at a boxing career, working as an auto body shop repairman, or singing, Lee Dorsey (December 24, 1924-December 1, 1986) went at each endeavor full bore, successfully, and with characteristic enthusiasm. Known at various times in his career as "Kid Chocolate," "Mr. TNT," and "Cadillac Shorty," he moved with his family to Portland, Oregon, at the age of ten and served in the navy during World War II. Following the war, he boxed under the name "Kid Chocolate" and retired undefeated in the featherweight and lightweight divisions. Moving back to New Orleans in 1955, he worked in an auto body shop owned by disc jockey Ernie the Whip. He sang as he worked to make his day go faster. When independent producer Reynaud Richard heard him, he gave Dorsey a fifty-dollar advance and told him to come to Cosimo Matassa's studio on Governor Nicholls Street.

Two recording sessions produced a song called *Lottie-Mo*. Released on the Valiant (later Instant) label, the song landed him a spot on *American Bandstand*. *Lottie-Mo* also caught the attention of producer Allen Toussaint. When Toussaint and Marshall Sehorn formed their partnership in Sansu Enterprises, it was Dorsey who helped launch the new record label. *Ride Your Pony,* a song leased to Amy, a subsidiary of Bell Records, for distribution, made *Billboard*'s Hot 100 in August of 1965. It reached number 28 and remained on the charts for nine weeks.[197]

Dorsey's professional singing career started four years

Lee Dorsey. (Courtesy of Louisiana Music Hall of Fame)

earlier, in 1961, when he recorded *Ya Ya* for Fury Records. It went to number 7 and sold more than a million records, earning the diminutive singer—he was barely five feet tall—a gold record. The song broke into *Billboard*'s Hot 100 in November and remained on the charts for thirteen weeks. *Ya Ya* was also included in the soundtrack of the 2000 Ben Stiller-Robert De Niro movie *Meet the Parents.*

Dorsey followed *Ya Ya* with *Do-Re-Mi,* which sold four hundred thousand copies and reached number 27 on *Billboard*'s Hot 100.[198] It cracked the charts in January 1962 and remained for nine weeks. Though *Ya Ya* was his biggest commercial success, Dorsey is probably best remembered for his second-biggest hit, *Working in the Coal Mine.* The song, with its familiar *clink,* signifying the sound of a miner's hammer striking metal as he worked in the mine, was released on Amy/Bell Records. It broke into *Billboard*'s Hot 100 in September of 1966 and remained on the charts for twelve weeks, peaking at number 8.

Working in a Coalmine was recorded in Cosimo Matassa's J&M Studio. "Funny thing about that song," Matassa says, "was we didn't have the luxury of falling back on canned or prerecorded sound effects to overdub later. We recorded on a single track, so everything had to be done right there in the studio in real time, to borrow a computer term. We had to have someone standing there as the band played, striking two pieces of metal together to simulate the sound of a hammer hitting metal."[199]

Dorsey died of emphysema in New Orleans.[200]

Benny Spellman

Benny Spellman (December 11, 1931-) was not initially drawn to music; his first love was football. While attending Southern University in Baton Rouge on a football scholarship, the Pensacola, Florida, native began singing with a local jazz group led by Alvin Batiste. His musical career was interrupted by an army tour of duty and afterwards, he returned to Pensacola.

It was by pure chance that Spellman ran into Huey "Piano" Smith and the Clowns at a show in Florida in 1959. The band had wrecked its truck on the way to the show, and Spellman volunteered to drive them back to New Orleans. Smith subsequently invited Spellman to join the Clowns, so he remained in New Orleans. While there, he renewed a friendship with guitarist and Dew Drop Inn bandleader Edgar Blanchard, who coaxed Spellman onto the stage to perform. Club owner Frank Painia was impressed with Spellman's voice and offered him residency at the Dew Drop.

The timing was perfect for Spellman because R&B was flourishing in New Orleans. He signed a contract with Joe Banashak's new Minit Records label, but his first efforts went unnoticed. He made ends meet by serving as a studio session backup singer. He was in the studio when Ernie K-Doe recorded *Mother-in-Law*. Allen Toussaint, the producer and piano player on the song, was dissatisfied with the sound of the song and turned to Spellman and his baritone voice for help.[201]

Spellman soon hit *Billboard*'s Hot 100 with his own double-sided hit, *Lipstick Traces (On a Cigarette)* backed with *Fortune Teller*, which reached number 80 in June of 1962 and remained on the charts for six weeks. Both songs were compositions of Toussaint's. Several groups, including the Rolling Stones, later covered *Fortune Teller,* and the O'Jays covered *Lipstick Traces.* Nothing else ever clicked for Spellman and he finally left the music business in 1968, choosing to become a salesman for Miller Brewing Company in his hometown. His one attempt at a comeback in the late 1980s was cut short by a stroke.[202]

Willie Tee Turbinton

Wilson Turbinton, more readily known as Willie Tee (February 6, 1944-September 11, 2007), is one of the better New Orleans musicians to never achieve commercial success. He did record one minor hit in 1965, *Teasin' You* backed with *Walking up a One Way Street.* Recorded on the NOLA label and distributed by Atlantic, it climbed to number 12 on the R&B charts.

In 1960, he and his brother Earl, a saxophonist, formed their first group, the Seminoles. In high school, his music teacher, Harold Battiste, added Willie to his jazz combo, the A.F.O. Band. Willie Tee recorded *Always Accused* in 1962 as his debut A.F.O. release. Though the song was not a hit, it did establish the merger of R&B with jazz, a genre that became his signature. He subsequently moved to Capitol Records and eventually to United Artists.[203]

Though never a major recording artist, he did become a beach music favorite in North and South Carolina and Virginia. In the late 1960s, Willie Tee and the Souls performed at the Apollo Theater in Harlem. At the urging of Cannonball Adderley, Willie Tee recorded an instrumental album. The album was never released, but the master tapes were rediscovered in Capitol Records' vaults decades later.[204] He contributed to Dr. John's 2004 album *N'Awlinz: Dis Dat or d'Udda* and appeared briefly in the Oscar-winning movie *Ray*.

New York's Tuff City Records reissued many of his early recordings, which became source material for rappers Sean "Diddy" Combs (*Concentrate*), Houston's Geto Boys (*Smoke My Peace Pipe*), and New Orleans' Lil' Wayne (*Moment of Truth*).

Willie Tee Turbinton. (Courtesy of Louisiana Music Hall of Fame)

Wilson "Willie Tee" Turbinton died from colon cancer in New Orleans only four weeks after his brother Earl died of lung cancer.[205]

The Neville Family

The first family of music in New Orleans has to be the Nevilles—brothers Art, Charles, Aaron, and Cyril. Their father, Big Arthur; Charles's daughter Charmaine; and Aaron's son Ivan (a member of Keith Richards' backup band in the 1980s), round out three generations of the musical family.

Big Arthur, the family patriarch, set the bar. Though he never sang professionally, he had a rich singing voice and was a fan of Nat "King" Cole, George Gershwin, and Cole Porter.[206]

Keyboardist Art, the oldest of the four brothers, tasted success early. Still in high school in 1953, he formed a band called the Hawkettes and in 1954 recorded *Mardi Gras Mambo* for Chess. In 1962, he recorded the soulful ballad *All These Things,* a regional hit for him and an even bigger one for Joe Stampley and the Uniques, whose cover version for Paula Records reached number 97 in July 1966.[207]

Charles, the second oldest of the brothers, relocated to New York City, where his saxophone skills earned him regular gigs with several artists, including B.B. King. He moved back to Louisiana but was arrested on marijuana possession charges and served a three-year sentence in the Louisiana State Penitentiary before eventually joining younger brothers Aaron and Cyril in 1975 to back their uncle, George "Big Chief Jolly" Landry, leader of the Wild Tchoupitoulas, on a recording for the Mardi Gras Indians.[208]

The Neville brothers followed a circuitous route before coming together in 1976 as a musical group. Before that, in 1967, Art recruited George Porter, Jr., Joseph "Zigaboo" Modeliste, and Leo Nocentelli to form the Meters.

The youngest of the four brothers, Cyril, learned drums from Clarence "Juny Boy" Brown, Fats Domino's drummer. Aaron Neville's wife, Joel, was the one who recognized his singing potential and nurtured his vocal talent. Cyril later teamed with Aaron to form a band called the Soul Machine. In 1975, while working a gig in New York with brothers Aaron and Charles, Cyril got a call from their mother. The Rolling Stones, she said, wanted the Meters, led by brother Art, to open for their North American and European tours—over 75 dates in all—and Art wanted Cyril to front the Meters.[209] Cyril joined the Meters as a percussionist and vocalist, and the group subsequently toured with the Rolling Stones and served as the studio band for Dr. John, Paul McCartney and Wings, Robert Palmer, Patti LaBelle, Lee Dorsey, and Allen Toussaint, among others.[210]

In 1977, all four brothers finally united to form the Neville Brothers. After several critically acclaimed albums that were less than commercially successful, they made the charts with 1989's *Yellow Moon*.[211]

With all the accolades that have come the way of Art, Charles, and Cyril Neville, as well as the Meters, the most visible of the four brothers—and arguably the most successful—is Aaron (January 21, 1941). Though he has stated that he has never received royalty payments for it, he

The Neville Brothers. (Photo by Jay Blakesberg)

had a number 2 pop hit in January 1967. *Tell It Like It Is* also peaked at number 1 on the R&B charts in December 1966 and made Aaron the first of the Nevilles to make the national charts. The song was named by the Rock and Roll Hall of Fame as one of 500 Songs That Shaped Rock and Roll. Par-Lo, his record label, however, went broke before he was paid. Still, the success of the song propelled him to tour nationally.

Aaron's early musical influences were his father, Big

Arthur, and older brother Art. He developed his style by listening to 1950s doo-wop groups like the Flamingos, Clovers, and Spaniels. He also admired Julie London, but he especially liked the yodeling cowboys of his youth. Specifically, Gene Autry influenced Neville's unique vibrato.

Aaron wrote and sang the title song to the classic Neville Brothers album *Yellow Moon*. Though he liked Julie London well enough to cover her song *Cry Me a River*, his favorite female vocalist is Linda Ronstadt, with whom he won two Grammy Awards for Best Pop Duo with *Don't Know Much* (1989) and *All My Life* (1990). He has said there is no one he would rather sing with and credits her with the resurrection of his solo career. He also collaborated with Ronstadt on their duet album *Cry Like a Rainstorm, Howl Like the Wind* in 1989 and *Warm Your Heart*, a solo album produced by Ronstadt and George Massenburg in 1991.

In addition to the awards he received for his work with Ronstadt, Aaron won two other Grammy Awards: 1989's Best Pop Chant (he was percussionist and vocalist) for *Healing Chant* and 1994's Best Country Collaboration with Vocals with Trisha Yearwood for *I Fall to Pieces*. He has been nominated for fourteen additional Grammy Awards in country and western, pop, gospel, and R&B. He also was named Best Male Singer for two consecutive years in the *Rolling Stone* critics' poll.[212]

On August 29, 2005, his home in New Orleans was destroyed by the floodwaters from Hurricane Katrina. He was on tour in New York at the time and could only watch helplessly as eight feet of water inundated his home, destroying gold and platinum records and other mementos from a career that covered five decades. His family managed to retrieve his four Grammy Awards, one of which was broken. A victim of asthma, he was advised by his doctor not to return to the Big Easy. With no other choice, he made Nashville his new home.[213]

On September 2, only four days after the hurricane, he performed Randy Newman's *Louisiana 1927,* a song about the massive flooding that devastated south Louisiana in the first part of the twentieth century, during NBC's "A Concert for Hurricane Relief." Following Katrina he devoted several months to benefit concerts. He recognizes that his profile and that of his brothers was raised by the storm. People all over the world see them as the face of New Orleans and want to hear them play and to be assured that life goes on, he has said.[214]

Life goes on indeed. On September 18, 2005, only three weeks after Katrina, Aaron sang the national anthem at the New Orleans Saints' home opener, played in LSU's Tiger Stadium in Baton Rouge. On December 16, he appeared as a guest on *The Tonight Show* with Jay Leno and on February 5, 2006, accompanied by fellow New Orleans native Dr. John, he sang the national anthem for the Super Bowl in Detroit.[215] He continues to perform and appears regularly at the New Orleans Jazzfest.

The Dixie Cups

Besides his hit with *You Talk Too Much*, Joe Jones's major contribution to the New Orleans music legacy was the discovery of a group called the Dixie Cups. The trio consisted of two sisters, Barbara Ann (1943-) and Rosa Lee Hawkins (1944-), and a cousin, Joan Marie Johnson (1945-). In 1964 they traveled with Jones to New York, where they were signed by the songwriting team of Jerry Leiber and Mike Stoller for their new record label, Red Bird. They were still enrolled in school when they recorded *Chapel of Love*. It supplanted the Beatles' *Love Me Do* as the number 1 song on both the pop and R&B charts in June.[216] The song remained on both charts for thirteen weeks.[217] Leiber hated the song but it was nevertheless chosen as one of the 500 Songs That Shaped Rock and Roll.[218] Its success helped launch the Red Bird record label and probably helped it sign another female group from New York City, the Shangri-Las.

For a brief moment, the Dixie Cups were the premier girl group in America—until the Supremes reached the number

The Dixie Cups at their induction into the Louisiana Music Hall of Fame. (Courtesy of Louisiana Music Hall of Fame)

1 position on both charts two months later with their first hit, *Where Did Our Love Go.* They went on to dominate the charts on behalf of the distaff side of the pop music family.[219]

Chapel of Love was written by Phil Spector, Ellie Greenwich, and Jeff Barry and was intended for either the Ronettes or the Crystals. Spector, in fact, had the Crystals record the song, but it was never released as a single. However, he did later release a version of the song on a Ronettes album. The Dixie Cups followed up two months after their first single with *People Say,* which climbed to number 12 on the pop and R&B charts. They next released *You Should Have Seen the Way He Looked at Me,* which peaked at number 39 in November of 1964, and *Little Bell,* which made it to number 51.

In May of 1965, they had perhaps their most creative hit and the one most closely identified with New Orleans. The three had just completed a recording session and were clowning around in the studio, tapping on ashtrays with drumsticks and singing a call-and-response Mardi Gras Indian chant

Barbara remembered hearing her mother sing. They didn't realize that Leiber and Stoller had the tapes running. They later overdubbed bass and percussion and *Iko-Iko*, their last hit, climbed to number 20 on both the pop and R&B charts. Allen Toussaint has said the expression Iko-Iko means, "You can kiss my a—." James "Sugar Boy" Crawford, who claims to have written *Jock-a-Mo*, from which *Iko-Iko* was taken, said he never had any idea what the words meant.[220]

The initial successes of the Dixie Cups and the Shangri-Las were not sufficient to sustain Red Bird Records and with its demise in 1966, the Dixie Cups signed with ABC-Paramount. No hits resulted and they left New York in 1974 to return to New Orleans. Once back home, Rosa Lee and Barbara Ann began successful modeling careers. When they later started performing again at events like Jazz Fest, their cousin Joan Marie Johnson declined to join them and was replaced by Dale Mickle.

The Dixie Cups were Rhythm & Blues Foundation nominees in 2002, and the foundation honored them the following year with its Pioneer Award. They have been inducted into the Louisiana Music Hall of Fame.[221]

Robert Parker

He had only one major hit as a solo artist, but Robert Parker (October 14, 1930-) was an integral part of the New Orleans music scene for many years, figuring prominently in the nurturing of the Crescent City's rhythm-and-blues tradition. He decided early on that he wanted to play saxophone even though his mother played piano, and Professor Longhair gave him his first break while he was still a teenager. Music was a passion shared by all his friends—Huey "Piano" Smith, Sugar Boy Crawford, Big Boy Miles, and Danny White. Whenever musicians like Fats Domino, Professor Longhair, or Dave Bartholomew needed musicians for a recording session or a gig, they would come to Parker's neighborhood in search of him or his friends.

Parker was a regular patron at Professor Longhair's

Sunday evening sessions at the Caldonia Inn. When Longhair needed a sax player for a Tuesday night show in Gretna, across the Mississippi River from New Orleans, he hired Parker. That led to a 1949 recording session with the Professor at which the first version of *Mardi Gras in New Orleans* was recorded.

Parker's next job was a five-year stint as leader of the Tijuana Club's house band, a period during which he was known for walking out into the audience while playing and lying on his back under the tables while playing. Though the Tijuana was a small club, it attracted top talent like Little Richard, Gatemouth Brown, Guitar Slim, and Bobby Marchan. Marchan at the time was the club's emcee and performed in drag, a common practice of the day. Dave Bartholomew of Imperial Records and Eddie Mesner of Aladdin Records also were Tijuana regulars.

It was while working at the Tijuana that Parker signed with booking agent Percy Stovall and put together his own band, Robert Parker and the Royals. They were hired to back Roy Brown, Big Joe Turner, Wynonie Harris, Solomon Burke, Charles Brown, and Amos Milburn. Playing cities from Texas to Florida, band members made twenty-five dollars a night on the road and ten dollars a night when performing in New Orleans. At the same time, Parker began getting calls for studio work from Chess and Specialty.

One of his first recording sessions was backing Huey "Piano" Smith on *Don't You Know Yockamo*, and he joined Smith's band the Clowns for an extended tour. He also played on Al Johnson's recording of *Carnival Time*, Irma Thomas's *Don't Mess with My Man*, and records by Johnny Adams, Chris Kenner, Ernie K-Doe, Fats Domino, Frankie Ford, Joe Tex, and Eddie Bo. His first solo recording, courtesy of Ron Records A&R man Eddie Bo, was an upbeat song, *All Night Long*, in 1959. Parker had worked shows with Bo, who in turn used Parker in studio recording sessions he produced.

Two occurences gave his career as a soloist a major

Robert "Barefootin'" Parker performing his hit Barefootin' *for the Louisiana Music Hall of Fame following his induction. (Courtesy of Louisiana Music Hall of Fame)*

boost. Stovall booked Parker and his band for a show at the Tuskegee Institute in Alabama. When he started singing, the girls removed their shoes and piled them in front of the bandstand, an inconsequential gesture that nevertheless rooted itself in the back of Parker's mind. The other event was a show he played in Miami. A comedian opened the show. When Parker came onstage, the comic shouted to the audience, "Everybody get on your feet; you make me nervous when you're in your seat."

When Parker started writing *Barefootin'*, he used the comic's jest as his opening line. He took the completed song to Wardell Quezergue, the A&R man for NOLA Records. Quezergue's partners did not like the song, so it remained unreleased for almost a year. It probably would never have been released had local disc jockey Hank Sample not heard the record in 1966. Sample owned a record store and liked what he heard of the demo. He prevailed on NOLA executives to press some copies of the song and he placed the records on sale at his store. It became an instant hit.[222]

NOLA cut a deal with Cosimo Matassa, who arranged for distribution through Dover Records, and *Barefootin'* began a steady climb up both the pop and R&B charts.[223] It peaked at number 2 on the R&B charts and number 7 on the pop charts, remaining for seventeen weeks. Parker, who had been supplementing his income as an orderly at Charity Hospital, quit his job and signed with Queen's Booking Agency, which scheduled him at the Apollo Theater. His first performance was less than inspiring, but when he removed his shoes during the second show's performance of his new hit song, the crowd went wild. After that, he would only perform the song shoeless.

The deal between NOLA and Dover would eventually sour. NOLA owed Matassa seventy thousand dollars in studio costs when the IRS shut NOLA's doors, leaving both Dover and Matassa holding the bag. It also left Parker with a bitter taste in his mouth, as he believed that some of the NOLA executives got greedy. He was certain that *Barefootin'* sold over a million copies, but he never got a gold record.

Parker soon found himself back in New Orleans playing in Clarence "Frogman" Henry's band on Bourbon Street and doing oldies shows. In 1983, *Barefootin'* was used in a TV commercial for the cleaning agent Spic and Span and the song was rereleased in England. In 1994, Parker and his wife moved upriver from New Orleans to Sunshine in St. James Parish, where he began driving a school bus. In 1999, Harrah's New Orleans Casino used *Where the Action Is*, the flip side of *Barefootin'*, in its radio and television commercials. Parker's version of the song was not used, however, because the casino opted for a recording by Denham Springs' Luther Kent. Still, Parker garnered songwriting royalties from its use. Inducted into the Louisiana Music Hall of Fame, he also performed several times at the New Orleans Jazz and Heritage Festival.[224]

Margie Joseph

New Orleans disc jockey Larry McKinley was usually in the right place at the right time, whether it was his half-interest in Minit Records, serving as Ernie K-Doe's manager, or marrying singer Margie Joseph (January 1, 1950-).[225] Joseph, born in Pascagoula, Mississippi, moved with her family to New Orleans in 1968.[226] It was while attending Dillard University that she met McKinley, who was immediately taken with her soulfully powerful voice. He assisted in landing her a job performing with Cannonball Adderley, which in turn led to a recording contract with Okeh Records, a subsidiary of Columbia Records.

Her debut recording session was held at the Sound Studio in Muscle Shoals, Alabama, but those first efforts failed to generate any activity. In 1969, she moved to Volt Records when Okeh folded. Her initial effort at Volt, *Your Sweet Loving,* cracked the R&B top 50. She followed with a seven-minute cover of the Supremes' *Stop! In the Name of Love,* which helped make *Margie Joseph Makes a New Impression* her only album to reach the R&B top 10.

Frustrated at being unable to regain her popularity with her album *Stay* on the Ichiban label, and with her marriage to McKinley over, she quit the music business in 1988 and worked in education and community service over the next seventeen years. In 2005, she ended her retirement by recording her first gospel album, *Latter Rain.* She now devotes all her musical efforts to Christian and gospel recordings.[227]

Randy Newman

He wasn't born in New Orleans—or Louisiana, for that matter—but Randy Newman (November 28, 1943-), whose father was a U.S. Army captain stationed in Sicily during World War II, spent most of his childhood summers in New Orleans. It was the rich culture of the city that shaped his writing and singing.[228] Only weeks after he was born, Newman moved with his mother from Los Angeles to New Orleans to live with her family. Though influenced by Bob

Dylan and Arthur Alexander, his music owes more to New Orleans artists, especially Fats Domino and Ray Charles.

His best-known album, *Good Old Boys,* addresses the sensitive issue of racism in the Deep South. Many misunderstood his use of the "N word" in *Rednecks,* but the lyrics were biting satire, a critical commentary on an outdated racist system. Generally, it was those who refused to recognize that fact who were most offended by the song. *Louisiana 1927*, on the same album, is a song about the widespread destruction inflicted on south Louisiana by the horrific flood of 1927. Two cuts on the *Good Old Boys* album, *Kingfish* and *Every Man a King,* are about the colorful—and controversial—Louisiana governor Huey P. Long.

Even *Naked Man* has ties to New Orleans. Newman's inspiration for the song came from an attorney friend in New Orleans who defended a man accused of stealing a woman's purse while naked. His somewhat unlikely alibi was that he was in bed with a married woman when her husband came home. He jumped from her bedroom window unclothed and was running down the street when he met another naked man carrying a purse. The second man, he said, handed him the purse with no comment and disappeared into the darkness, leaving the defendant with the burden of explaining not only his nakedness, but also the purse.[229]

In 1971, Newman wrote the soundtrack for the Norman Lear movie *Cold Turkey,* about an entire town that launches a campaign to quit smoking.[230] Meanwhile, his reputation as a songwriter was enhanced when Judy Collins, Dusty Springfield, and Peggy Lee recorded his songs. Three Dog Night scored a number 1 hit with his *Mama Told Me Not to Come* in 1970. That same year, Harry Nilsson recorded an entire album of his compositions, *Nilsson Sings Newman.* He wrote the soundtrack for *The Natural* and he was nominated for two Academy Awards for his soundtrack for the movie *Ragtime.* Newman also received an Oscar nomination in 1996 for *You've Got a Friend in Me* from the Disney animated film *Toy Story*, and fans of the USA

Network series *Monk* are treated to the theme song he penned opening each episode.

Like *Rednecks,* 1977's *Short People* was misinterpreted and predictably, it offended many listeners who failed to understand what he was trying to say. The resulting controversy propelled the song to number 2 by January of 1978, and it held that position for three weeks and remained on the charts for twenty weeks. His recording of *Sail Away* was one of 500 Songs That Shaped Rock and Roll.[231]

King Floyd

King Floyd (February 13, 1945-March 6, 2006), remembered for his hit *Groove Me,* sold more than five million records in the first ten years of his career and then disappeared from public view. He was born in the Crescent City and reared in Kenner.[232] He got his start singing on street corners at age eleven and secured his first paying gig in Bourbon Street's Sho-Bar Club in 1961 through the aid of blues singer Mr. Google Eyes.

In 1963, he moved to New York City and signed with the Shaw Booking Agency. Inspired to write by R&B singer Barbara Lynn, he moved to Los Angeles, where he wrote *Groove Me* while working in an East Los Angeles box factory.[233] There he met New Orleans native and composer/arranger Harold Battiste. Battiste and a Los Angeles disc jockey helped him secure a recording contract with Original Sound, which in 1965 issued *Walkin' and Talkin'.* Floyd was barely eking out a living while working with Battiste so he returned to New Orleans in 1969 and accepted a job with the post office.[234]

In New Orleans, he met producer Wardell Quezergue, who then worked for Malaco Records. On May 17, 1970, they traveled to the Malaco studio in Jackson, Mississippi, to cut *Groove Me.* On the way, Floyd's car broke down, and he almost turned back because he had to work at the post office that afternoon. When he finally arrived at the studio, there were only a few minutes of studio time left. The song was recorded in just one take. The session that day also produced Jean Knight's *Mr. Big Stuff.* [235]

The song was released on the Malaco subsidiary, Chimneyville, as the B side of *What Our Love Needs,* where it languished until New Orleans disc jockey George Vinnett began playing *Groove Me.* WTIX in New Orleans and WLAC in Nashville followed suit. Only then did it attract attention. As the record grew in popularity, Atlantic negotiated the national distribution rights. *Groove Me* climbed to the top of the *Billboard* R&B charts and hit number 6 on the pop charts. It went gold on Christmas Day of 1970. Floyd quit his post office job and went on tour. He returned to the R&B top 10 in 1971 with the follow-up *Got to Have Your Love.* Atlantic next released *Woman, Don't Go Astray,* which earned a gold record three years later.[236]

When Atlantic's agreement with Malaco ended, Floyd split with his label, but the emergence of disco left few outlets for Floyd's brand of soul. He and his wife, Jean Knight's daughter, returned to Los Angeles in 1978 in a futile attempt to revive his career. In 1982 he toured South Africa but afterward drifted in and out of the music scene, until his death from complications of a stroke.[237]

Jean Knight

Jean Knight (January 26, 1943-) didn't have her first hit until 1971. Born Jean Caliste in New Orleans, she got her big break when, at the urging of her first husband, she entered Cosimo Matassa's J&M Studio to record a demo in 1965.[238] One of the songs she recorded was a cover of Jackie Wilson's *Stop Doggin' Me Around.*

Huey Meaux of Winnie, Texas, was also in the studio to record a female singer, Barbara Lynn, whom he'd discovered in nearby Beaumont. He was confident Barbara Lynn's song *You'll Lose a Good Thing* would be a winner—and it was— but Meaux had the presence of mind to take note of Knight. He signed her to a recording contract, and she recorded three singles for Meaux, including a cover of Ernie K-Doe's *Tain't It the Truth*, but nothing really clicked outside New Orleans.

With music now only a hobby, she worked full time baking bread in Loyola University's cafeteria. One day a stranger approached her to inform her that he had written some songs that producer Wardell Quezergue wanted her to sing. She had never heard of Quezergue but was intrigued enough to travel to his Malaco Studio in Jackson, Mississippi. There she listened to a tape of *Mr. Big Stuff* and liked it, but it was a ballad and she decided to liven it up. In the Malaco studios, she nailed the song on her second take.

Knight returned to baking bread while Quezergue tried to find a label interested in picking up not only her record, but

Jean Knight singing My Toot Toot *at her Louisiana Music Hall of Fame induction. (Courtesy of Louisiana Music Hall of Fame)*

also *Groove Me*, which King Floyd had recorded the same day. Quezergue's first choice was Stax Records in Memphis, but they weren't interested. Frustrated, he started his own label, Chimneyville, on which he released *Groove Me*. It became an instant hit in New Orleans. That got the attention of Stax executives, and the company picked up Knight's *Mr. Big Stuff.* The record was an overnight hit in the Washington and New York markets[239] and quickly climbed to number 1 on the R&B charts and to number 2 on the *Billboard* Hot 100, remaining on both charts for sixteen weeks.[240]

As personal appearances piled up for Knight, *Mr. Big Stuff* went on to sell more than three million copies, earning her both gold and platinum records. At the Grammy Awards in New York, the song was runner-up to Aretha Franklin's *Bridge over Troubled Waters* for Song of the Year, and Knight was named Most Promising New Female Artist.[241] At this point Knight was earning five thousand dollars a night. Stax suggested some songs for her to record but Quezergue tossed them, insisting that she record songs from his production company. The dispute between Quezergue and Stax accelerated the end of her association with the record company, but with *Mr. Big Stuff,* her future was secure. The song has brought her a steady income for more than three decades.

In 1981, she charted again at number 57 with *You Think You're Hot Stuff,* which sold 900,000 copies. In 1985, her cover of Rockin' Sidney's *My Toot Toot* sold 850,000 singles. In all, there were three versions of *My Toot Toot* to chart simultaneously, but Knight's was an even bigger hit than the popular Rockin' Sidney release. In 2007, she was inducted into the Louisiana Music Hall of Fame.[242]

Dr. John

Judging from his impressive list of credits, the phrase "Right Place, Wrong Time," taken from his hit song of the same name, doesn't quite do justice to the career of Malcolm John Rebennack, Jr. Rebennack, better known as Dr. John (November 21, 1940-), has moved with grace and style into his role as ex-officio ambassador of goodwill for New Orleans music.

As a child, he spent many hours hanging around Cosimo Matassa's studio, where hit after hit was recorded. His patience paid off when he was called to sit in on sessions and play guitar for Professor Longhair, Frankie Ford, and Joe Tex alongside sidemen Red Tyler, Lee Allen, and Earl Palmer. The session work evolved into one-nighters all over Louisiana, Arkansas, Oklahoma, Texas, and the Gulf Coast. At one of those gigs in Jacksonville, Florida, a fight broke out and Rebennack tried to intervene. A gun was fired and Rebennack was hit in the hand, leaving a mangled left index finger that ended his career on the guitar. With the help of James Booker, however, a new career as a pianist and organist was born.[243]

In the early 1960s, newly elected district attorney Jim Garrison shut down clubs for gambling, prostitution, and anything else he considered morally corrupt. In the process, New Orleans nightlife was threatened with the same fate that had befallen the notorious Bossier City Strip years earlier in north Louisiana.[244] With gigs drying up all over town in the wake of the crackdown, musicians began a mass exodus to more attractive venues, spurred in part by the devastation inflicted on New Orleans by 1965's Hurricane Betsy. Rebennack decided to seek his fortune in Los Angeles. There, he teamed with an old New Orleans friend, Harold Battiste, who was working as a producer for Sonny and Cher. Battiste hired Rebennack for road work with the duo. He also found Rebennack work as a first-call session player for several prominent producers, including Leon Russell and Phil Spector. Battiste encouraged him to develop his Dr. John character and it was Sonny and Cher who gave him free studio time at the end of their own sessions, allowing him to record tracks that eventually became his critically acclaimed *Gris-Gris* album for Atco Records.

Dr. John's persona developed from lackluster in the mid-1950s—in one promotional photo he is wearing a conventional suit and striped tie—to extreme after he recorded his *Gris-Gris*

Dr. John, right, is inducted into the Louisiana Music Hall of Fame by Mike Shepherd, left. (Courtesy of Louisiana Music Hall of Fame)

album. It was only then that his "Dr. John, The Night Tripper" persona emerged, accented by his gravely, raspy voice and garish outfits inspired by the Mardi Gras Indians. His eclectic vocal stylings only served to underscore his image makeover. His outfits, complete with a walking cane that featured a carving of a snake's head, were every bit as outrageous as those of Elton John, whom he pre-dated by at least two decades. The Dr. John name was inspired by a mid-nineteenth-century New Orleans character. Known by several names, including

John Montaigne and Bayou John, he was more commonly known as Dr. John. The original Dr. John was once arrested along with a woman named Pauline Rebennack for running a voodoo operation and for prostitution. Rebennack would later speculate that Pauline Rebennack was one of his ancestors. The temptation was too strong for John Rebennack to resist and the latter-day Dr. John was born.

Word about Dr. John's unique style spread and soon he was being sought out to work with Eric Clapton, Mick Jagger, The Band, and Bob Dylan. The rest of his curriculum vitae includes work varyingly as a keyboardist, vocalist, and multi-instrumentalist from 1968-99 for Canned Heat, B.B. King, Allen Toussaint, the Rolling Stones, the Sir Douglas Quintet, Ringo Starr, Carly Simon, Harry Nilsson, Van Morrison, Joe Cocker, Hoyt Axton, Bob Seger, Emmylou Harris, Leon Redbone, Johnny Winter, the Neville Brothers, and the Edgar Winter Band.[245]

As proof of his versatility, Dr. John won Grammy Awards for Best Jazz Vocal Performance (1989), Best Traditional Blues Album (1992), Best Rock Instrumental Performance—a collaboration with B.B. King, Bonnie Raitt, Eric Clapton, and others (1996)—and Best Pop Collaboration with Vocals with B.B. King for *Is You Is, Or Is You Ain't My Baby* (2000). He also wrote and performed the score for the 1982 Nick Nolte movie *Cannery Row.* Dr. John is best known, however, for his June 1973 hit *Right Place, Wrong Time,* named as one of 500 Songs That Shaped Rock and Roll.[246] The song reached number 9 on the *Billboard* Hot 100 and number 19 on the R&B charts, was backed by the Meters, and produced by New Orleans' Allen Toussaint at his Sea-Saint Studio. It was included, along with Fats Domino's *White Christmas,* in the soundtrack of the 2000 John Travolta movie *Lucky Numbers.* In October of 1973 he reached number 43 with *Such a Night.*

A member of the Louisiana Music Hall of Fame, Dr. John remains active and is considered an icon among New Orleans musicians.

4

The Baton Rouge Connection

When Louisiana music is the subject of conversation, most think of the rich heritage of New Orleans jazz and R&B or the pioneering rockabilly sound that roared out of Shreveport's *Louisiana Hayride*. Other areas of the state, however, contributed to the music of the 1950s and early 1960s. Southwest Louisiana had Goldband Records, producer Eddie Shuler, George Khoury, the Lyric and Khoury Record labels, Huey Meaux, Bobby Charles, Cookie and the Cupcakes, and Barbara Lynn. The Acadiana area of the state contributed the swamp pop of T.K. Hulin, Rod Bernard, G.G. Shinn, Johnnie Allan, Joe Barry, Rusty Kershaw, Doug Kershaw, mail-order record-store owner and recording executive Floyd Soileau, and Crowley recording executive and songwriter J.D. Miller.

Often overlooked is the talent that emerged from Baton Rouge. Besides Slim Harpo, there were Johnny Rivers, Percy Sledge, Joe Tex, John Fred, Dick Holler, Dale and Grace, Joe Simon, recording executive S.J. Montalbano, and several other blues artists.

Jimmy Clanton

Jimmy Clanton (September 2, 1940-) entered his teen years just as white audiences were beginning to discover rhythm-and-blues music. He formed the Dixie Cats in 1956 while a student at Baton Rouge High School and quickly became one of the few whites who could emulate the sounds

Jimmy Clanton sings one of his hits during a 2008 performance in New Orleans. (Courtesy of Louisiana Music Hall of Fame)

of Little Richard, Johnny Ace, and Fats Domino. His early contemporaries included fellow Baton Rouge musicians John Fred and Johnny Ramistella, who would gain fame as Johnny Rivers. Clanton eventually teamed with Dick Holler, the leader and pianist of the Rockets.[1] Clanton and Holler recorded at Cosimo Matassa's studio in New Orleans in 1957 and the following year, Clanton wrote and recorded *Just a Dream* for Johnny Vincent's Ace Records.[2]

Clanton, with his great voice and feel for the New Orleans sound, had the ability to pursue R&B but was artistically restricted to syrupy ballads by Johnny Vincent, owner of Ace Records. Still, it is difficult to argue with success: *Just a Dream* reached number 4 on the Hot 100 chart. Ironically, it did even better on the R&B chart, going all the way to number 1. It remained on the two charts eighteen and seventeen weeks, respectively. *Just a Dream*, *Venus in Blue Jeans* (number 7), and *Go Jimmy Go* (number 5 pop and number 9 R&B), released on Ace Records, each earned Clanton a gold record.[3]

Clanton's ballad gradually gained airplay not only in Louisiana but in other parts of the country as well. Suddenly, the Baton Rouge teenager was one of the hottest acts in the U.S. Bookings outside the South followed, including an appearance on Dick Clark's *American Bandstand* and a performance at the Hollywood Bowl. He was also booked for performances on Alan Freed's package tours and in 1959 appeared in Freed's jukebox movie *Go, Johnny Go!* along with Chuck Berry, Jackie Wilson, the Flamingos, the Cadillacs, Eddie Cochran, and Ritchie Valens.[4]

On February 3, 1959, Buddy Holly, Valens, and J.P. Richardson (the Big Bopper) died in a plane crash in Clear Lake, Iowa, while on their Winter Dance Party tour. Clanton and Frankie Avalon were signed for the remainder of the tour.[5] When Ace Records folded, Clanton continued recording for Phillips, Mala, Laurie, and Imperial Records, but the British Invasion effectively spelled the end of his string of hits. He became a disc jockey in the 1970s and continues to perform, occasionally teaming with onetime Ace label mate Frankie Ford in oldies shows.[6]

Ike Clanton

The obituary in the *Clark County (AL) Democrat* gave no details as to the cause of death, stating only that he was sixty-four, a native of Baton Rouge, and died June 9, 2004, in Villa Feliciana Hospital in Jackson, Louisiana. It noted that he was survived by a brother, Jimmy Clanton. As a teenager, Ike Clanton, along with Fats Domino's band, played behind John Fred when Fred cut his first record at Cosimo Matassa's studio in New Orleans.[7] He also played for a time with Duane Eddy's band in Las Vegas and managed to crack *Billboard's* Hot 100 a couple of times as a solo artist with *Down the Aisle* (number 91) in 1960 and *Sugar Plum* (number 95) in 1962. Each remained on the charts two weeks.[8]

What the obituary notice did not say was that Ike had suffered a nervous breakdown at one point during his troubled life. He had worked for a time as a truck driver following his brief recording career. Graveside services were held on June 15 in Jackson, Louisiana, and a memorial service was held on June 19 in Coffeeville, Alabama.[9]

John Fred

In 1956, John Fred, born John Fred Gourrier (May 8, 1941-April 15, 2005), formed his first band with classmates at Baton Rouge's Catholic High School.[10] S.J Montalbano booked the band at local dances and scheduled its first recording session on September 23, 1958. Only seventeen, Fred found himself in Cosimo Matassa's J&M Studio in New Orleans. Fats Domino had recorded *Whole Lotta Loving* earlier that day, so his band stayed to back Fred for his session. Featured in the session was band member Ike Clanton, Jimmy Clanton's brother.[11]

The success of *Shirley,* cowritten by John Fred and Tommy Bryan, was enough to get Fred an appearance on Alan Freed's radio show in New York. He was asked by Dick Clark to appear on *American Bandstand,* but Fred was a member of the Catholic High basketball team, which would go on that year to win a state championship, so he declined Clark's offer in order to play in a game for the Bears. *Shirley* reached number 82 on *Billboard*'s Hot 100. It might have done better on R&B stations had black disc jockeys not discovered that Fred was white.[12]

Fred was an outstanding athlete and appeared to be on a path to follow in the footsteps of his father, who played professional baseball for the Detroit Tigers organization. After graduation from high school, he excelled in both basketball and baseball at Southeastern Louisiana University in Hammond, about forty miles east of Baton Rouge.[13]

By 1964, the British Invasion had breached America's shores. John Fred knew he had to change his approach and his sound in order to be heard over the trans-Atlantic din. It started with a song called *Boogie Chillen,* a remake of an old John Lee Hooker song, on Stan Lewis's Jewel Record label

John Fred. (Courtesy of Louisiana Music Hall of Fame)

in Shreveport. That was followed by a pair of singles, *Up and Down* and *Agnes English,* which were big regional hits, reaching number 1 in New Orleans for eight weeks each. The two songs were preludes to better things. *Up and Down* was recorded in Tyler, Texas, where Fred teamed with his idol, Dale Hawkins.[14] Even though *Up and Down* was released on Jewel, Stan Lewis's predominantly R&B label, Fred's chances of getting black disc jockeys to play the song was again doomed when Lewis took out a full page ad in *Billboard* magazine, revealing the singer's white identity.[15]

During the summer of 1967, Fred was lolling on a beach in the Florida panhandle, thinking about his next song. The Beatles had just had a hit with *Lucy in the Sky with Diamonds* and the song kept running through his mind. As the lyrics repeated themselves, another song began to take shape. Soon he was in the studio recording *Judy in Disguise (With Glasses)*, a parody of the Beatles' hit. Released on

Paula, a label also owned by Lewis, the success of the song, instantly identifiable by its rapid-fire bass guitar intro, was immediate and dramatic.[16] By January of 1968, it was the number 1 song in the country. It remained number 1 for two weeks and stayed on the charts for sixteen weeks, but it went far beyond those mere statistics. The song has sold more than five million copies, has been featured in as many as twenty movies, and has appeared on nearly forty hit record compilations. It has turned up on a half-dozen TV commercials. It also became a number 1 hit for Elton John when he recorded the song in 1974.[17]

The song led to tours and television appearances on Dick Clark's *American Bandstand* and on Johnny Carson's *Tonight Show,* but the zenith of Fred's career came in August of 1969 when he met Elvis Presley at the International Hotel in Las Vegas.[18] When Fred's buddy Wayne Cochran said, "Elvis, I'd like you to meet John Fred," Elvis spun around, stuck out his hand, and said, "John Fred, *Boogie Chillen!*"

It turned out that Elvis knew all about Fred and had heard him late one night while listening to disc jockey Wolfman Jack. Fred and Elvis talked about Louisiana music for a couple of hours before Elvis's show and the King gave Fred front-row tickets. They met again in late 1973 at Graceland and the two played pool and talked. Elvis wanted to know all about Baton Rouge blues artist Slim Harpo. When Fred met the Beatles, John Lennon was interested in Harpo too.

Following *Judy in Disguise*, Fred left Paula Records for Los Angeles-based Uni Records, but he never repeated the success of *Judy*. In 1979, he turned to producing other artists and one of his first efforts was the critically acclaimed Irma Thomas comeback album, *Safe with Me.* He also wrote, performed, and produced jingles for Greyhound Bus Lines and Ban deodorant and wrote and recorded *Baseball at the Box* for the Louisiana State University baseball team.

With royalties from *Judy* continuing to pour in, Fred was able to indulge his first love. He worked as a volunteer baseball coach at Catholic High. After a stint as vice president of Cyril Vetter's Record Company of the South, he returned to performing in 1983. In 1992, he formed the Louisiana Boys with Joe Stampley and G.G. Shinn.[19] He died in Tulane Hospital in New Orleans following a kidney transplant.[20]

Jay Chevalier

Jay Chevalier (March 4, 1936-) traveled with three-time governor Earl K. Long during Long's 1959 political campaign. Barred constitutionally from succeeding himself as governor, Long ran for lieutenant governor.[21] Chevalier composed and recorded *The Ballad of Earl K. Long* in 1959 and followed that with *Come Back to Louisiana.* The latter, first recorded in 1963, was featured in *Blaze,* the Paul Newman movie about Long. Chevalier served as a consultant for the movie and played the role of Sen. Paul Braden. The song was re-recorded in 2006 to encourage victims of Hurricane Katrina to return home.[22] The Louisiana legislature adopted it as the official state song in 2006, giving Louisiana three state songs. *You Are My Sunshine* and *Give Me Louisiana* are the others.

Chevalier enlisted in the Marine Corps in 1954 and formed his first band, which appeared on Jimmy Dean's national television show in 1957. Today, Chevalier opens his shows with *Billy Cannon,* a rollicking tribute to LSU's only Heisman Trophy winner (1959). Cannon carried the team on his strong legs to the 1958 national championship and on Halloween Night, 1959, electrified a partisan LSU crowd and stunned the Ole Miss Rebels with a fourth-quarter, eighty-nine-yard punt return to give the Tigers a 7-3 victory. Chevalier, not really a football fan, was attending the game with Governor Long. Caught up in the pandemonium of the Tiger Stadium crowd after the touchdown, he wrote the song that night. Chevalier's Pel Records release, backed with *High School Days Are Almost Over,* was out within days, adding to Cannon's already mythical appeal and making Jay Chevalier's name a household word from Shreveport south to Lake Charles and east to New Orleans.

Other songs he recorded and continues to perform include *Castro Rock, Khrushchev and the Devil,* and *Rock and Roll Angel.*[23] Chevalier was inducted into the Louisiana Political Hall of Fame in January of 2003. He is also a member of the Rockabilly Hall of Fame.[24]

Dale and Grace

Dale Houston (April 23, 1940-September 27, 2007) and Grace Broussard (1939-) had known each other barely twenty-four hours when they teamed up as Dale and Grace to record a song that would skyrocket to the number 1 position in America in late 1963.[25]

Dale, born in Seminary, Mississippi, moved with his family to Baton Rouge when he was seven. He recorded a

song entitled *Lonely Man,* which cracked the Hot 100 list briefly, and that was enough to convince him he wanted to make music his life's calling. S.J. Montalbano, owner of Montel Records in Baton Rouge, was impressed enough with Houston to sign the eighteen year old as a songwriter.[26]

Grace, born a year before Dale in Prairieville, just south of Baton Rouge, was nineteen at the time and had been singing in her brother Van Broussard's band since she was sixteen. Montalbano also had Grace under contract.[27]

Versions of how the two came to record together

Dale Houston and Grace Broussard after receiving their gold records for their 1963 number 1 hit I'm Leaving It All Up to You. *(Courtesy of Dale Houston estate)* differ. Montalbano, who operated a demo studio for local musicians inside his father's produce company, says Dale was working a gig in a bar in Ferriday. He and a friend drove from Baton Rouge to Ferriday because Montalbano wanted Dale to sing harmony with a promising female singer. "We picked up Dale that night and drove back to Baton Rouge, then went to Prairieville and picked up Grace."

Montalbano had a piano at his home and the two singers started rehearsing in preparation for a recording session the next day. It was after midnight and the duo had been at it for about four hours doing old songs and some new ones that Montalbano had given them to learn. Dale started playing the old Don and Dewey Squires song from the mid-1950s called *I'm Leaving It All Up to You*. Montalbano came out of a dead sleep when he heard it from his bedroom, ran into the living room still in his underwear, and screamed, "Play it again. . . . That's a hit!" The next day he took Dale and Grace to the recording studio where they cut four songs. Montel Records then released *I'm Leaving It All Up to You* as a single and by October 1963, it was the number 1 record in the nation.[28]

Not so, say both singers. Dale had been touring with singer Jay Chevalier in Colorado, Nevada, and California. During a break in their tour, Dale returned to Baton Rouge in order to record. "I was contracted with Sam [Montalbano] and Montel Records and had three or four tracks I needed to get laid down while we were on the break," Houston says. "I met Grace at a cookout at Sam's home the night before I was to go to Lafayette for the session. She decided to ride to Lafayette with us."[29]

Grace, in a separate interview, agreed with Dale's version. "We had the same manager and we went to La Louisianne Studio in Lafayette the day after the cookout. Dale was supposed to record some songs and I was supposed to record a single for Sam." During a break in the recording session, Dale wrote the first verse to the lyrics of *I'm Leaving It All Up to You*. He had first sung the song for Grace only the night before at the cookout and when he scribbled the lyrics at La Louisianne Studio, he omitted the second verse. "We recorded it anyway," she recalls.[30]

"I finished my songs and I asked her to sing a few with me," Houston says. "We did a couple of numbers, including the Buck Owens song *Foolin' Around*. Then I asked her to sing *I'm Leaving It All Up to You* with me and she said she didn't know the words. I told her I'd write them down for her and I completely forgot to include the second verse. I called Jay Chevalier and told him I was bringing Grace with me to our next show in Wichita Falls, Texas. We started making plans to return to La Louisianne to lay down the second verse.

"By the time we got to the Golden Nugget in Las Vegas, Sam was calling us to say we had to get back to Baton Rouge right away," Houston continues. "I asked him why and he said he had released one of our songs and it was a big hit. I asked what song and he said, *I'm Leaving It All Up to You*. I was shocked because we never even got the chance to do the second verse. Sam took the tapes to Houston and added backup vocals and violins. The violins played in the wrong key but that was the way they released the song and it went to number 1."[31]

The song was initially released on Michelle, a regional label named for one of Montalbano's daughters, and later rereleased on his national label, Montel. "It wasn't S.J. Montalbano's idea to team us together," Grace explains.[32] "It was just a situation of the right place and right time. After we recorded it, I went on the road with Dale and Jay Chevalier and we were in Vegas when S.J. called and said we had to get back to Baton Rouge because the song was a hit. We didn't know what he was talking about because the song wasn't even finished."

The song debuted on the national charts in October of 1963 and the pair joined the Dick Clark Caravan of Stars. On November 17, 1963, Clark joined them onstage in Cincinnati to make an announcement. The duo had no idea what was unfolding. Grace says, "He went on to read the telegram that informed us that *I'm Leaving It All Up to You* had reached number 1 in the country." Both Dale and Grace still had copies of that telegram over forty years later, and Houston, shortly before his death, still had a copy of the *Billboard* Hot 100 chart for the week of November 17, 1963.[33]

The tour took the performers to Dallas the next week. It was in Dallas on November 22 that Dale and Grace, Brian Hyland, Bobby Vee, and Jimmy Clanton waved and shouted to Pres. John F. Kennedy as the motorcade passed. Only three blocks farther, the presidential motorcade met gunshots. It was not until later that the singers learned those shots killed Kennedy.[34]

"We followed *I'm Leaving It All Up to You* with *We've Got to Stop and Think It Over* and it went to number 8," Dale describes. "It would have gone to number 1 too, but the Beatles hit right at that time and they bumped us" in 1964 with *She Loves You.* However, Dale and Grace did receive gold records for each of the songs.

The British Invasion changed America's musical tastes overnight and contributed to the duo's eventual breakup, but their split was hastened by personal problems. "Grace and I stayed together from '63 to '65," Dale says. "I was more interested in country music and she wasn't into country that much. She sings country now with Van, and she does a great job, but she wasn't interested at the time, so I left. I went to Atlanta first, then to Panama City, Knoxville, and to Nashville. I did a couple of songs in Nashville, but nothing ever really hit."

According to Dale, he received only about twelve thousand dollars for each of the two top 10 songs, and only after a protracted legal battle. He also filed suit to stop another duo from falsely billing themselves as Dale and Grace.[35] The real Dale and Grace were inducted into the Delta Music Museum Hall of Fame in Ferriday on April 7, 2007. Dale was scheduled to reunite with Grace Broussard on October 27, 2007, for a special performance at their induction into the

Louisiana Music Hall of Fame but exactly a month earlier, he was hospitalized with stomach pain and died that night. He was sixty-seven.

Van Broussard

Grace Broussard's brother, Van Broussard (1937-) remains a celebrity in and around Baton Rouge for helping to blaze the trail for swamp pop music, and he has been performing steadily for half a century.[36] Originally a Dixieland musician, he abruptly switched to R&B when he heard Elvis Presley and eventually became a fixture in area clubs. Broussard, who first performed with his sister Grace, of Dale and Grace, when she was just sixteen, is again performing with her as part of his Bayou Boogie Band, comprised completely of local musicians. "Some of my players have been with me for forty-five years," he says. One such player is Junior Bergeron, who also performed with Baton Rouge singer-songwriter Dick Holler.

A retired heavy equipment operator and former drag racer, Broussard performed with Joe Stampley, Fats Domino, Al Downing, Jerry Lee Lewis, Tommy McLain, Elvis Presley drummer D.J. Fontana, and John Fred. Self-taught for the most part, he acknowledged that a black man named Pete Franklin taught him much about playing guitar. He recorded two regional hits, *Lord, I Need Somebody Bad Tonight* and *Feed the Flame*, songs that deserved more national attention but because his record labels' distributors were underfunded, it was not to be. "*Feed the Flame* was a song I'd heard on a Clarence Carter album and I liked it, so I recorded it," he recalls.

Broussard admits it sometimes can be amusing to think about what might have been. "Once, I was playing at Bear Creek [a night club in St. Helena Parish, near the Mississippi state line] when this woman drags her underage daughter into the club and tells me I have to listen to her sing because she's great, she has a lot of talent, and all the other things that mamas say about their kids. I'm the kind of guy who will give anyone a chance to sing, so I told her I'd let her. She chose the Patsy Cline song *Crazy.* This poor little kid just butchered it. It was terrible, so I told her mama to keep that little girl in school because she had no future in music. The girl was Britney Spears," he says, shaking his head and chuckling. "But I got no regrets. I love what I do and I love seeing the same people show up to hear us play and to dance wherever we might be performing." As he finished speaking, he leaned over to pick up his guitar, looking around as he did so at the retirees and middle-aged audience members waiting to resume dancing. "That's why I do this," he concludes, nodding in their direction.[37]

Bobby Lovless

Another little-heralded but gifted musician of the era was saxophonist and singer Bobby Lovless (1940-September 18, 2005). Lovless performed in the 1960s with Jimmy Clanton and Johnny Rivers but left Rivers, who relocated to Los Angeles, so that he could remain close to home. He joined swamp pop favorite Van Broussard and later left to form his own band, the Night Owls. He named the band after his regional hit *Night Owl,* released by S.J. Montalbano's Montel label. *Night Owl* was a number 1 hit in several Louisiana parishes and received considerable air play in Houston.

Lovless, besides playing with Clanton and Broussard, also teamed with drummer Junior Bergeron and Dr. John as part of a pickup band of Baton Rouge and New Orleans players who backed Bobby Darin, Jerry Lee Lewis, and Frankie Ford during their performances at the Saenger Theater in New Orleans.

As a teenager in the 1950s, he would sneak up to the back door of Town and Country Night Club in his hometown of Donaldsonville. From his vantage point he would listen to Fats Domino and his band. It was saxophonist Lee Allen, however, who got his attention. Allen's style made an impression on the young Lovless, who learned to emulate his sax hero so well that he was occasionally referred to as "Little Lee Allen." Lovless's high-pitched voice was reminiscent of not only Lee Allen but also Motown singer Jr. Walker.[38]

Johnny Rivers

Johnny Rivers (November 7, 1942-) was born John Henry Ramistella in New York City. When his father lost his job, the family moved to Baton Rouge, where an uncle procured Johnny's father a job painting houses and antiquing furniture. Johnny got his first guitar at age eight, and his career is, for the most part, a story of good timing, beginning with his attraction to south Louisiana rhythm-and-blues.[39] When performers like Fats Domino, Jimmy Reed, and Irma Thomas played at school dances at Baton Rouge Junior High, it only aroused in Johnny an even more intense drive to make his own music.[40]

He entered talent shows at the old Paramount Theater in downtown Baton Rouge, winning seven straight times before he was asked not to return so that others would have a chance. He started his own band, the Spades, while still in junior high and cut his first record at age fourteen.[41] A year later, in 1957, he returned to New York for a visit. He stationed himself outside the WINS studio at Columbus Circle and waited in the freezing rain until Alan Freed returned from lunch with his manager, Jack Hooke. Rivers drew on all the courage a fifteen year old could muster. Introducing himself, he said he would like Freed to hear his music. Incredibly, Freed handed him his business card and suggested that Ramistella come to his office in the Brill Building on Broadway the next day.

During his meeting the following day, he played several songs for Freed and Hooke. Hooke called George Goldner, owner of the Gone and End record labels, to set up a recording session. Songwriter Otis Blackwell, who wrote *Don't Be Cruel* for Elvis and *Great Balls of Fire* for Jerry Lee Lewis, arranged Johnny's debut single, *Baby, Come Back*, backed with *Long, Long Walk*. The record didn't sell,

*Johnny Rivers during a performance in south Louisiana.
(Courtesy of Louisiana Music Hall of Fame)*

but as it was being prepared for release, Freed turned to
the youngster, telling him he needed to come up with a
name a little more musical than Ramistella. The boy said
something about how had grown up in Baton Rouge on the
Mississippi River and somehow "Rivers" emerged.

The new singer with the new name returned to Baton
Rouge and got another career break. He began touring as
a solo act with popular southern comedian Brother Dave
Gardner. At a show in Birmingham in 1959, Rivers met
Audrey Williams, widow of Hank Williams. Audrey brought
Rivers to Nashville and secured a contract for him with Cub
Records, a subsidiary of MGM. He cut two records with the
studio backing of several of Nashville's best session artists,
including Floyd Cramer. Rivers formed a close friendship
with the late Roger Miller, then an upcoming songwriter
who owned his own publishing company, Tree Music.

Rivers' New York and Nashville experiences honed
his instincts for selecting songs and writers for his own
recording career. In New York, writers like Otis Blackwell
would bring him a new tune and ask him to record a demo

with an Elvis Presley sound. At twenty-five dollars per demo, Rivers made a comfortable living and in 1960, he got a spot on the *Louisiana Hayride* through the efforts of KWKH disc jockey Merle Kilgore.

The *Hayride* appearance led to yet another break with an introduction to former *Hayride* house guitarist James Burton, a Shreveport native then playing for Ricky Nelson's band in California but home on vacation at the time. Burton took a tape of Johnny's song *I'll Make Believe* to California, and a few weeks later he called to tell Rivers that Nelson would record it for inclusion on his Imperial LP *More Songs by Ricky.*

Much had happened in a relatively short span, but Rivers still did not have a hit record. All his contacts, all his writing, and all the records he had recorded in Baton Rouge, New York, and Nashville had failed to chart. He moved to California in 1961, met Ricky Nelson, and recorded *Long Black Veil* for Capitol Records, which also was a commercial flop. Nevertheless, he landed on his feet when he obtained work as a writer and producer.

Everything changed two years later. Following late nights at the recording studio as a producer and musician, he would often stop at a little late-night Italian restaurant and bar that featured a jazz trio. One night the band failed to show and the restaurant's owner, Bill Gazzari, asked Rivers to fill in. With only drummer Eddie Rubin and no act, Rivers settled in for what he anticipated would be a three- or four-day gig. Instead, word spread and the house was packed every night with throngs of people who came to hear Rivers and Rubin play rock and R&B at the heretofore jazz venue. When Rivers was ready to leave, Gazzari offered him more money and hired a bassist, Shreveport native Joe Osborne.

Again, Rivers would have the good fortune to meet someone—actually two someones—who would have significant impacts on his career as a performer. The first was Lou Adler, who became his producer. The other was Elmer Valentine, who was preparing to open the Whiskey a

Go-Go Club on the Sunset Strip. Valentine offered Rivers a year's contract to perform at the new club. He opened at the club on January 15, 1964.[42] Three days later the Beatles' *I Want to Hold Your Hand* hit the *Billboard* charts.[43]

Rivers brought his Gazzari's following with him to the Whiskey a Go-Go and the new club was a success from the first night. Rivers and his familiar red Gibson ES-335 guitar were at the club only a short time before Adler conceived the idea for a live album. After recording over two nights, they could not find a record company that wanted any part of the project. Finally, Liberty Records president Al Bennett released it on Imperial, which Bennett had purchased from founder Lew Chudd. Rivers was excited at the prospect of recording for the label that had made stars of Ricky Nelson and Fats Domino. That he and Adler were given complete autonomy in selecting which songs he would record only made the deal sweeter.

The album, *Johnny Rivers Live at the Whiskey a Go-Go*, reached number 12 on the charts. A cover of Chuck Berry's *Memphis,* a cut from the album released as a single, reached number 2 in the midst of Beatlemania, sending a statement that American artists were not ready to concede their turf to the Brits just yet. Other hits included another cover of a Chuck Berry song, *Maybeline* (number 12), and a cover of Harold Dorman's 1960 hit *Mountain of Love* (number 9), both in 1964; *Midnight Special* (number 20), *Seventh Son* (number 7), and *Where Have All the Flowers Gone* (number 26) in 1965; *Under Your Spell Again* (number 35), *Secret Agent Man* (number 3), (*I Washed My Hands*) *In Muddy Water* (number 19), and *Poor Side of Town* (his only number 1 record), all in 1966; *Baby I Need Your Lovin'* (number 3), *Tracks of My Tears* (number 10), and *Summer Rain* (number 14) in 1967; a cover of Huey "Piano" Smith's *Rockin' Pneumonia and the Boogie-Woogie Flu* (number 6) in 1972; *Blue Suede Shoes* (number 38) in 1975; and *Swayin' to the Music (Slow Dancin')*, his last top 10 song (number 10) in 1977.[44]

Rivers played harmonica on *Maybeline* but was unhappy with the results because he played out of tune. Of his cover of Louisiana State University graduate Mose Allison's *Seventh Son*, he acknowledged he had been a fan of the blues singer for years, since hearing Allison sing the song in a Gulfport, Mississippi, jazz club. For *Poor Side of Town*, Imperial tried to discourage him from changing directions in his music but he insisted on cutting the song.

He nearly pulled off another big hit, *Fire and Rain*, but circumstances and corporate decisions have a way of intervening in the music business. Rivers heard the song on an obscure album and though he had not heard of James Taylor, he liked *Fire and Rain* and decided to record it. It did so well that Warner Bros., seeing that Rivers' record was making a move, decided to release Taylor's version as a single. Radio stations suddenly switched and started playing Taylor's release, which climbed to number 3 in the country.

In all, Rivers had nine top 10 hits, seventeen that made *Billboard*'s top 40, and seventeen gold records. He recorded go-go style records, folk, blues, rock oldies, and slow-moving ballads, selling more than thirty million records in the process. In 2000, he teamed with Tom Petty, Paul McCartney, and Eric Clapton to record a tribute album dedicated to Buddy Holly's band, the Crickets.

He also founded his own record company, Soul City Records, and was recognized for giving songwriter Jimmy Webb his first break when the 5th Dimension recorded his composition *Up, Up, and Away*. As producer of the 5th Dimension's 1967 hit, he received two Grammy Awards, for Best Contemporary Single and for Record of the Year. He also produced singer Al Wilson's hit recording, *The Snake*.

In a long and notable career, Rivers was the first rock and roll act ever to play New York's famed Copa Cabana. He broke all existing Las Vegas audience records in 1966 when he appeared at the Riviera. He performed with the E Street Band at Pres. Bill Clinton's 1992 Inaugural Ball. Other honors for Rivers include a Heroes and Legends 1995

Lifetime Achievement Award and a feature in *The History of Rock and Roll* television series. His *Secret Agent Man* was named fourth as TV's Best Theme Song of all time by *TV Guide* in June 1999. The song was hot again in the 1990s with the success of 1960s-themed spy film *Austin Powers* and new James Bond films featuring Pierce Brosnan.[45]

Joe Tex

Joseph Arrington, a.k.a. Joe Tex (August 8, 1933-August 13, 1982), was born in Baytown, Texas. He struggled with three different record labels for nearly a decade before he found success with *Hold What You've Got* in late 1964. By January of 1965, the song, distributed by Atlantic Records, entered both the R&B and pop charts. It remained on the R&B charts for eight weeks, peaking at number 2, and stayed on the pop charts for eleven weeks, reaching the number 5 position.

In 1954, at the age of eighteen, he had entered and won a talent contest in Baton Rouge. First place was a two-week trip to New York, where he showed up on amateur night at the Apollo Theater and again won. His New York stay was extended to four weeks and offers from other nightclubs followed. In 1956, he was discovered at a Long Island club by a scout for King Records. He failed to chart for King and moved to Johnny Vincent's Ace Records the following year. Four years later, following a string of recordings that failed to catch the public's fancy, he signed with Dial Records, based in Nashville and headed by Buddy Killen.[46]

Killen had the idea of recording material delivered in the style of a black preacher. In preparation for recording his songs, Tex would make himself hoarse so as to achieve a raspy delivery that he felt made him sound more authentic. He had written only four lines of *Hold What You've Got* when he showed it to Killen. From that tentative start, the two men created the first of two dozen songs Tex would chart during the 1960s and '70s, eight of which made *Billboard's* top 10.[47] His biggest hit, 1972's *I Gotcha,* climbed to number

2 on *Billboard*'s Hot 100 and number 1 on the R&B charts, remaining on the charts for twenty-two weeks.[48]

While *I Gotcha* and *Hold What You've Got* were his biggest commercial successes, Joe Tex is probably best remembered for a novelty tune called *Skinny Legs and All,* which peaked at number 10 on *Billboard*'s Hot 100 in December 1967 and number 2 on the R&B charts. All three songs sold well over a million copies each and earned Tex three gold records.

Soon after *I Gotcha* climbed to the number 2 spot on the pop charts, Tex abruptly announced his retirement. He converted to Islam and changed his name first to Joseph X and later to Yusuf Hazziez. He moved to a farm outside Houston and became a rabid Houston Oilers fan, emerging briefly from retirement to record a tribute to running back Earl Campbell.

He was unable to stay away from the secular world permanently, however, and in 1977, he reassembled his band to record one final hit, another comedy record called *Ain't Gonna Bump No More (With No Big Fat Woman).* It hit number 7 on the R&B charts and number 12 on the *Billboard* Hot 100. In 1981, he became a member of the Soul Clan, which included Wilson Pickett, Don Covay, Solomon Burke, and Ben E. King.

Tex died of a heart attack on his farm only five days after his forty-ninth birthday. Among his pallbearers were Buddy Killen; Soul Clan's Pickett, King, and Covay; and Louisiana native Percy Mayfield.[49]

Joe Simon

Joe Simon (September 2, 1943-) was born in the town of Simmesport, about seventy miles up the Mississippi River from Baton Rouge, and began his music career after moving to Oakland, California.[50] His first major hit came in 1965 with *Let's Do It Over,* which reached number 13 on the R&B charts. He scored again in mid-1966 with *Teenager's Prayer,* which peaked at number 66 on the pop charts and number

11 on the R&B charts. That was followed by *My Special Prayer* and *Nine Pound Steel* in 1967 and *No Sad Songs* and *(You Keep Me) Hangin' On* in 1968. A 1969 cover of Nat King Cole's *Looking Back* reached number 70 on the pop charts.

In May of 1969, Simon teamed with country songwriting legend Harlan Howard to record *The Chokin' Kind,* which reached number 13 on the pop charts and number 1 on the R&B charts, earning Simon the first of three gold records. His other gold records, both in 1972, were *Power of Love* and *Drowning in the Sea of Love.* Each reached number 11 on the pop charts. In 1980, he returned to Nashville and retired from active performing in favor of devoting his life to the church.[51]

Percy Sledge

A stellar second baseman, he planned to become a professional baseball player, but when he recorded *When a Man Loves a Woman,* everything changed for Percy Sledge (November 25, 1940-). On April 10, 1966, wearing his baseball uniform, he walked into a recording studio in Muscle Shoals, Alabama, to record his signature hit. "Yeah, you heard right," he confirms when asked about the accuracy of the story. "I think I was well on my way to a professional baseball career. I was a pretty good second baseman back then. My dream was to play for the Cincinnati Reds."

Born in Leighton, Alabama, he moved to Baton Rouge in 1966. With his characteristic grin, as much his trademark as his distinctive vocal stylings, he nods toward his wife, seated at the opposite end of the table during an interview. "I met her," he says by way of explanation. "She's from Morgan City and we moved to Baton Rouge. You couldn't drag me away from here now with a team of horses."[52]

Typically, the road to stardom was less than smooth. He worked in the farming fields of Leighton before securing a job as an orderly at Colbert County Hospital in Sheffield, Alabama. All the while he played baseball and performed and toured when he could with the Esquires Combo. One of his hospital patients was a friend of record producer

Percy Sledge performs at the Louisiana Music Hall of Fame induction ceremonies in 2006. (Courtesy of Louisiana Music Hall of Fame)

Quin Ivy and introduced the two. An audition followed and Sledge was signed to a recording contract. *When a Man Loves a Woman* was his very first effort and it was an instant success. Ivy released the single as an independent and licensed it to Atlantic Records. Atlantic lost no time in buying out Sledge's contract and by May 1966, the song had climbed to number 1 on both the pop and R&B charts, remaining on the charts for thirteen and sixteen weeks, respectively. Other hits followed, including *Warm and Tender Love* (number 17) and *It Tears Me Up* (number 20), also in 1966; *Baby, Help Me* (number 87), *What Am I Living For?* (number 91), *Out of Left Field* (number 59 and featured in the Tom Cruise/Paul Newman movie *The Color of Money*), *Love Me Tender* (number 40), and *Cover Me* (number 42) in 1967; *Take Time to Know Her* (number 11) and *Sudden Stop* (number 63) in 1968; and *My Special Prayer* (number 93) and *Any Day Now* (number 86) in

1968. *My Special Prayer* is the song with which he opens each of his concerts.[53]

His first gold record for Atlantic, *When a Man Loves a Woman*, was a song Sledge had only hummed while picking cotton as a youth. He improvised the lyrics while performing at a frat party at the University of Mississippi. Atlantic executive Jerry Wexler called the recording session for what would become the cornerstone of Sledge's career "a transcendent moment." He described the song as a "love hymn."[54]

As if its first time around were not enough, the song was revived when it was featured in television commercials, in the soundtrack of the 1987 Academy Award-winning movie *Platoon*, and in the 1994 Meg Ryan film *When a Man Loves a Woman*.[55] When it hit the charts a second time, reaching number 2 in Britain, it led to personal appearances by Sledge on *Saturday Night Live* and *Entertainment Tonight,* which in turn led to extended concert tours in the U.S., as well as in Africa and Europe, where the song was featured in a Levi's Jeans commercial. Sledge plays about a hundred dates per year in the U.S. and Europe.[56]

Despite, or perhaps because of the resurgence of his career, Sledge, in 1994, fell into a trap familiar to entertainers from Willie Nelson to Redd Foxx. The IRS said Sledge failed to report more than $260,000 in income. He was subsequently ordered to pay more than $95,000 in back taxes, penalties, and interest, sentenced to six months in a Baton Rouge halfway house, and placed on five years' probation.[57]

Besides picking up five gold and two platinum albums while at Atlantic, Sledge also was the first recipient of the Rhythm & Blues Foundation's Career Achievement Award. He is a regular feature at events such as the Gulf Coast Jam, Port Arthur's Mardi Gras celebration, and other southwest Texas productions.[58] A member of the Louisiana Music Hall of Fame, he was inducted into the Rock and Roll Hall of Fame in 2005,[59] and *When a Man Loves a Woman* was chosen by the Rock and Roll Hall Fame as one of 500 Songs That Shaped Rock and Roll.[60]

Louisiana's LeRoux

When it started out in Baton Rouge as the Jeff Pollard Band in 1975, there was little indication that it would lead to an African tour with Gatemouth Brown, a new identity as Louisiana's LeRoux (familiarly known as just LeRoux), and a recording session at Bogalusa's Studio in the Country that would produce the best New Orleans-themed song of the twentieth century.[61]

The 1977 tour with Brown led to the band's big break. Bassist/producer Leon Medica gave a demo tape to a Screen Gems-EMI representative and that encounter led to a recording contract with Capitol Records and a name change to Louisiana's LeRoux.[62] LeRoux takes its name from the Cajun French word for the thick gravy base used to make gumbo, and the band's first album was described as a musical gumbo that blended instruments, vocals, and

Louisiana's LeRoux. (Courtesy of Leon Medica)

Jeff Pollard. (Courtesy of Louisiana Music Hall of Fame)

arrangements into a mixture of blues, funk, R&B, jazz, rock, and swamp pop. Their debut album, *Louisiana's LeRoux*, produced the energetic *Take a Ride on the Riverboat*, written by Jeff Pollard. Also included on the album was *New Orleans Ladies*.[63] Cowritten by Alexandria native Medica, *New Orleans Ladies* climbed to number 59 in July of 1978 and quickly became the band's signature anthem and a must in the repertoire for local cover bands.[64]

Chosen by readers of *Gambit Weekly*, a New Orleans weekly newspaper, as the Best New Orleans Song of the 20th Century, *New Orleans Ladies* was almost never recorded. Medica said that he and Hoyt Garrick composed the song for a French musician named Dick Rivers who was seeking material with a New Orleans theme. Rivers rejected the song so Medica took it to Pollard, who indicated he was disinterested as well. However, audience response to live performances of the song was so overwhelming Pollard had a change of heart and allowed LeRoux to record the number. Besides reaching number 59 on *Billboard*'s Hot 100, the song ascended to number 1 in the Southeast.

Pollard subsequently left the band to establish a

Christian ministry. His exit was followed by trumpeter, percussionist, and vocalist Bobby Campo. Dennis "Fergie" Frederiksen and Jim Odom were brought in to replace the two and LeRoux continued to turn out critically acclaimed albums. It soon became the session band for Bogalusa's Studio in the Country, backing Gatemouth Brown and Clifton Chenier.[65]

Besides Brown and Chenier, LeRoux has also toured with a host of other musicians and musical groups: the Allman Brothers Band, Amazing Rhythm Aces, Beach Boys, Marshall Tucker Band, John Mellencamp, Blood, Sweat and Tears, Blues Brothers, Chicago, Alice Cooper, Charlie Daniels Band, Nitty Gritty Dirt Band, Doobie Brothers, Foreigner, Emmylou Harris, Heart, Journey, Kansas, Kinks, Little River Band, Lost Gonzo Band, Kenny Loggins, Willie Nelson, Randy Newman, the Neville Brothers, Ozzy Osbourne, Pure Prairie League, Bonnie Raitt, REO Speedwagon, Santana, Bob Seger, Stephen Stills, Jerry Jeff Walker, Steve Wariner, Muddy Waters, Edgar Winter, and ZZ Top.

LeRoux television appearances include *Don Kirshner's Rock Concert, Solid Gold, Midnight Special*, and MTV spots, as well as the band's own PBS live video "Rocking the Nottaway," filmed at Louisiana's antebellum Nottaway Plantation in Iberville Parish in 1997. The special *Unplugged* concert for MTV was more than a LeRoux reunion with Randy Knaps sitting in for Pollard. It also featured performances by John Fred, who sang *Judy in Disguise* in the final set, and Luther Kent of Denham Springs, who sang *Hoochie Koochie Man* and Rosco Gordon's 1963 hit, *Just a Little Bit.*[66]

LeRoux was inducted into the Louisiana Music Hall of Fame in 2009.

Leon Medica

It would be impossible to write about LeRoux without discussing the career of Leon Medica because the fortunes of the two are so intertwined. Few Louisiana producers and session players, with the possible exceptions of Dave

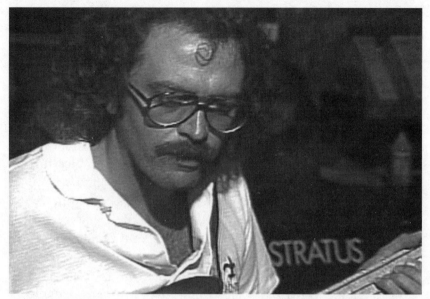

Leon Medica. (Courtesy of Louisiana Music Hall of Fame)

Bartholomew and Allen Toussaint, have achieved so much in their entertainment careers.

Medica, a native of Alexandria, Louisiana, now lives in Hendersonville, Tennessee. His first gigs were playing bass at clubs and LSU fraternity parties in Baton Rouge in the 1960s and he eventually recorded with a succession of Baton Rouge blues artists. By the end of the decade, his bands opened for Strawberry Alarm Clock, The Who, and Creedence Clearwater Revival. Two highlights of his early career were performing at the New Orleans International Pop Festival and playing in Chuck Berry's band at the Festival of Man and Earth.[67]

In 1972, New Orleans disc jockey C. C. Courtney and cousin Ragan Courtney, both Ruston natives, recruited Medica to act and perform music in their Broadway production, *Earl of Ruston*, at the Billy Rose Music Hall. *Earl of Ruston* was about a gangly uncle of the Courtney cousins who was, to put it in polite terms, Ruston's town character.[68]

With Earl's mother sitting in a rocking chair strategically spotlighted on a corner of the stage, cousins Ragan and C. C. portrayed Earl in various aspects of his wonderfully eccentric personality. When he wasn't playing bass, Medica was to walk over to the elderly Mrs. Woods and admonish her for some transgression, real or imagined. Critics loved the play, and Johnny Carson visited backstage on several occasions. Best suited to off-Broadway, the play was unable to compete with glitzier shows like *Chicago*, *A Chorus Line*, and a revival of *No, No, Nannette*.[69]

Medica followed *Earl of Ruston* with the off-Broadway hit *Iphigenia* which starred Tommy Lee Jones. He then returned to Baton Rouge, where he recorded and toured with Potliquor. He also worked in Bogalusa's Studio in the Country and recorded with Clifton Chenier, Gatemouth Brown, Betty Davis (Miles Davis's wife), and French singer Dick Rivers, for whom Medica wrote *New Orleans Ladies*.[70] Following the tour with Gatemouth Brown as a member of the Jeff Pollard Band, he commuted between Nashville recording sessions and Aspen, where he played bass parts for a Nitty Gritty Dirt Band album.

Medica produced and wrote songs for four of the five LeRoux albums and was part of numerous tours and television appearances. It was also during this period that Medica wrote and produced songs for movies and served as tour manager for Randy Travis and Patty Loveless.[71] He recorded and performed with Cajun rocker Zachary Richard from 1987 to 1989 and on one occasion he was onstage with Richard, Jimmy Buffett (on guitar), and former *60 Minutes* reporter Ed Bradley (on percussion). He described the experience as "an absolute blast." He played bass on recordings for artists as diverse as country singer Vern Gosden, R&B singer Maurice Williams, Charlie Daniels, the Nitty Gritty Dirt Band, Uriah Heep, John Fred and the Playboys, Wayne Toups, and Baton Rouge's Floyd Brown.[72]

His crowning achievement, however, was producing Doobie Brothers member Tom Johnson on the multi-platinum *Dirty Dancing* album, one of the all-time biggest-selling soundtracks. Besides *Dirty Dancing*, he has recorded for the soundtracks of *Rent-a-Cop, Steel Magnolias, Private Resort, The New Kids,*

Private School, Fled, Trial & Error, Following Her Heart, Crocodile Shoes, and *At Close Range.*[73] In all, Medica's name appears on more than ninety albums and ten movies.

He is the recipient of an American Music Award, a Grammy, two gold records for domestic sales, thirteen platinum records for domestic sales, twelve platinum records for international sales, the Times Music Best Bassist Award, and *Gambit Weekly's* Best New Orleans Song of the 20th Century award for *New Orleans Ladies.*[74]

Duke Bardwell

Duke Bardwell (August 19, 1943-), like his siblings, was named for a university. A brother, Stanford Bardwell, Jr., once served as U.S. attorney for Louisiana's Middle District in Baton Rouge. Other siblings include Harvard, Princeton, Auburn, Cornell, and Duke's twin sister, Tulane. Even parents Stanford, Sr., and Loyola, were in on the act. Duke's interests were in music, however, and by age thirteen, he had his first garage band, Duke and the Losers. That was 1957 and three years later, he got his first road gig playing guitar, bass, and trumpet for Lenny Capello and the Dots.[75]

He enrolled at LSU in 1961 and began playing in a pickup

LSU fraternity band the Greek Fountains, circa 1970. At left is Duke Bardwell, who went on to tour with Elvis Presley. (Courtesy of Louisiana Music Hall of Fame)

band at frat houses. When the British Invasion hit, Bardwell and friends got together at a local club and did a mix of covers from the Beatles, the Stones, the Animals, and other British bands. People turned out to hear the group calling themselves the Greek Fountains. Several regional hits ensued, and the band worked the college and club circuit for the next five years.[76]

Greek Fountains cofounder Casey Kelly moved to New York and procured Duke Bardwell a job playing bass with folk artist Tom Rush. He performed with James Taylor, Gordon Lightfoot, Jackson Browne, and Jerry Jeff Walker. Bardwell returned to Baton Rouge and formed another band with his cousin, Luther Kent. The two fronted for Cold Gritz and the Black-Eyed Peas. The band signed with Lou Adler's Ode Records in Los Angeles, but the band broke up before its first album was released.[77] Kelly, meanwhile, had his own record deal and was touring with Loggins and Messina, so Bardwell moved to L.A. and joined Kelly as a duo opening for Loggins and Messina for two years.

In 1971, Bardwell signed on as a singer-songwriter for Jose Feliciano and played bass during recording sessions for Feliciano as well as during appearances on *The Tonight Show*, *The Dinah Shore Show,* and *Soundstage* in Chicago. In 1974, he toured and performed in 181 shows with Elvis Presley and played bass on Elvis's album recorded live at the Mid-South Coliseum in Memphis on March 20, 1974.[78]

Casey Kelly

Casey Kelly (April 30, 194?-), who grew up in Baton Rouge as Danny Cohen, played rock, country, Cajun, and New Orleans music. Working with Bardwell as the two toured with Tom Rush, Kelly played guitar, keyboard, and harmonica. After touring with Loggins and Messina, he relocated to Nashville, where he wrote for House of Gold Music and was nominated for a Grammy for the number 1 Kenny Rogers-Dottie West hit, *Anyone Who Isn't Me Tonight*. He also wrote

Casey Kelly. (Courtesy of Louisiana Music Hall of Fame)

songs for America, Helen Reddy, T. G. Sheppard, George Strait, the Remingtons, Tanya Tucker, and Joe Diffie.[79]

5

Blues Artists

Country and rhythm-and-blues merged to form the hybrid that we know as rock and roll. Before country, however, there was Celtic folk music brought over from Europe that would evolve into Appalachian mountain music, or bluegrass. Before rhythm-and-blues, there was simply blues, largely a holdover from American slave music imported from western Africa. Blues music in this country mostly sprang from the Mississippi Delta cotton fields and moved north to Memphis, St. Louis, and Chicago and west to Kansas City. Many of the blues greats like B.B. King, Bo Diddley, Muddy Waters, John Lee Hooker, and Howlin' Wolf were from Mississippi, but Louisiana has more than its share of blues legends. Their contributions, like those of their Mississippi cousins, have survived the onslaughts of Elvis, the Beatles, Motown, hip-hop, and rap. Moreover, the influence of Louisiana and Mississippi blues artists is evident in the recordings of Stevie Ray Vaughn, Janis Joplin, Kenny Wayne Shepherd, the Rolling Stones, Eric Clapton, and George Thorogood, among others.

Slim Harpo

James Moore (January 11, 1924-January 31, 1970), born in the Lobdell community of Port Allen, Louisiana, was the most famous harmonica player in the swamp blues tradition, performing professionally first as Harmonica Slim and later as Slim Harpo.[1] Self-taught on guitar and harmonica, when both his parents died while he was still in his teens he left school to work days as a dockhand while playing club gigs around Baton Rouge at night.

Moore married in 1948 and began appearing and recording with his brother-in-law Otis "Lightnin' Slim" Hicks. His harmonica riffs and arrangements, reminiscent of Jimmy Reed, soon attracted the attention of Crowley, Louisiana, producer J.D. Miller. Miller, after first using him as a backup to Lightnin' Slim, convinced him to sing in a more nasal tone. Miller also convinced him to change his name when it was learned there was another Harmonica Slim performing on the West Coast.[2] Moore's wife, Lovelle, added an o to the end of the word "harp," and he became Slim Harpo.

Harpo's best material was cowritten with his wife. His first recording for the Nashville Excello label, 1957's *I'm a King Bee*, was affiliated with Miller's studio and was later covered by the Rolling Stones on their first album. In 1961, he recorded *Rainin' in My Heart,* which featured Lightnin' Slim on guitar.[3] The song was his best seller, climbing to number 17 on the R&B charts and number 34 on *Billboard's* Hot 100.[4] The Rock and Roll Hall of Fame included it as one of 500 Songs That Shaped Rock & Roll.[5] The Stones also covered his 1966 song *Shake Your Hips.* Others who covered his songs include the Yardbirds, the Kinks, Warren Smith (*Got Love if You Want It*), Van Morrison (*Don't Start Crying Now*), Dave Edmunds (*Shake Your Hips*), and Hank Williams, Jr. (*Rainin' in My Heart*). The Moody Blues took their name from one of Harpo's songs. His 1966 hit *Baby, Scratch My Back* reached number 16 on the pop charts and number 1 R&B and revitalized his career. It led to a 1967 national tour with Lightning Slim on the blues/rock circuit in Chicago, New York, and Los Angeles. That same year, *Tip on In* reached number 37 on the R&B charts.[6]

While he never pursued music full time (he operated a trucking company during the 1960s), Harpo saw that his star was suddenly on the rise and his first European tour and London recording session were put together in early 1970.[7] Shortly after arriving in London, Harpo was felled by a fatal heart attack only twenty days after his forty-sixth birthday.[8] He was buried in the back of weed-and-briar-infested Mulatto Bend Cemetery in Port Allen, across the Mississippi River from Baton Rouge. His grave, situated in an above-ground concrete vault, is adorned with rusty harmonicas and a few foreign coins left there by admirers.

Lightnin' Slim

As the first great star of producer J.D. Miller's blues talent pool, Lightnin' Slim (March 13, 1913-July 27, 1974) developed his style on little more than his primitive guitar work, with the support of a harmonica and a drummer. The formula of combining his gritty vocals with his electric guitar and the backing of home-grown musicians was a perfect blend. He recorded several regional hits in Miller's Crowley studio that were issued on the Nashville-based Excello label for over a decade. His *Rooster Blues* reached number 23 on R&B charts in 1959.

Slim was a brilliant blues storyteller, even when adapting the material of others to his own world-weary style. His worry-laden voice, austere and expressionless, made other blues singers sound almost euphoric by comparison. His familiar "blow your harmonica, son" became one of the great mournful catchphrases of blues numbers.[9]

Born Otis Hicks in St. Louis, Missouri, he moved to St. Francisville, Louisiana, with his family at age thirteen. He learned guitar early. Because he only changed keys on his recordings when using a capo, it is probable that his boyhood teachers knew how to play in only the key of E.[10] After playing local clubs during the late 1930s and early 1940s he moved to Baton Rouge in 1946 and played weekends in local bars. A local disc jockey persuaded Miller to record him. Starting on Miller's Feature label, he spent twelve years as an Excello artist. After a move to Detroit in the late 1960s, he found new life in his career when European blues discovered him and he toured the continent. He also performed for the American festival circuit with protégée Slim Harpo as a double act.[11] When Harpo died unexpectedly in 1970, Lightnin' Slim went on as a solo performer, recording sporadically and performing as part of the American Blues Legends tour until his death.

Silas Hogan

J.D. Miller's tiny studio in Crowley, Louisiana, produced many outstanding blues records by several superb musicians for Excello Records of Nashville. Included among Miller's all-star lineup was Silas Hogan (September 15, 1911-January 9, 1994).

Hogan learned the basics of guitar from two uncles in the late 1920s. He began by playing house parties and picnics, but in the early 1950s he moved to Baton Rouge. Equipped with a Fender electric guitar, he formed his first combo, the Rhythm Ramblers.[12] In 1962, at the age of fifty-one, he was introduced to J.D. Miller and for four years, he released solid swamp blues songs on the Excello label.

His association with Excello ended in 1966 and he disbanded his group and went back to his job at the Exxon refinery in Baton Rouge. He returned to recording in 1970 when he released songs for the Arhoolie and Blue Horizon labels while continuing to perform live. In 2008, he was posthumously named a recipient of the Baton Rouge Blues Foundation's Slim Harpo Award.[13]

Whispering Smith

Whispering Smith (January 25, 1932-April 28, 1984), born Moses Smith, arrived on the music scene just as the Baton Rouge swamp blues movement was ending. Often playing with the likes of Lightnin' Slim and Silas Hogan, he sang and accompanied himself on the harmonica. He was one of several fine blues performers who did some of his best work in the Crowley studio of J.D. Miller. There, he recorded such numbers as *Mean Woman Blues, I Tried So Hard, Don't Leave Me, Baby, Live Jive,* and *Hound Dog Twist.*

Excello Records of Nashville, for whom Miller had produced many of its blues successes, decided to try swamp pop again in 1970, but without the studio expertise of Miller, who had left the recording industry, Smith was unable to recapture the magic.[14]

Henry Gray

Born in Kenner, Louisiana, Henry Gray (January 19, 1925-) moved to Alsen on the outskirts of Baton Rouge while still a young boy. There, he was exposed to the piano through radio, church, records, and an elderly neighbor who gave him lessons. As with many families, blues music was not allowed in his home. At the age of sixteen he finally gained the courage to tell his father he had been invited to perform with a band at a club near his home. The elder Gray allowed him to go—but only if he accompanied his son. Henry played his first paying gig and his dad had a change of heart, opening the door to sixty years of playing the blues.[15]

Gray moved to Chicago in 1946 and ten years later joined blues legend Howlin' Wolf's band where he remained as pianist until 1968. He has played with blues notables Muddy Waters, Johnny Shines, Lazy Lester, Little Walter Jacobs, Jimmy Reed, Otis Rush, Little Milton, Whispering Smith, Raful Neal, Kenny Neal, B.B. King, Tabby Thomas, Buddy Guy, Guitar Kelly, and Guitar Slim.[16] He has performed at almost every New Orleans Jazz Festival, two Chicago Blues Festivals (1987 and 1989), the 1988 Festival International de Jazz de Montréal, virtually every Baton Rouge Blues Festival, several Festival International de Louisianes in Lafayette, the Mississippi Valley Blues Festival, and the King Biscuit Blues Festival in Helena, Arkansas.

He received a Grammy nomination for his 1998 Telarc Records album *A Tribute to Howlin' Wolf.* He was featured on the Kenny Wayne Shepherd release *10 Days Out,* also nominated for a Grammy. In 2006, he was named a National Endowment for the Arts National Heritage Fellow for his contribution to folk art. He is also the recipient of the Baton Rouge Blues Foundation's Slim Harpo Award.[17]

Clarence "Gatemouth" Brown

His first Grammy was for traditional blues; he won a cluster of W.C. Handy Awards, was awarded the Rhythm & Blues Foundation's Pioneer Award, and was inducted into the Blues Foundation Hall of Fame in 1999. Yet Clarence "Gatemouth" Brown (April 18, 1924-September 10, 2005) never considered himself a bluesman. He referred to himself as one who played American music—Cajun, country, bluegrass, and jazz.[18] Born in Vinton, Louisiana, he grew up in Orange, Texas, and died there eighty-one years later, a cancer-stricken evacuee of Hurricane Katrina, the storm that destroyed his home in Slidell, Louisiana. In between, Brown established himself as one of the most versatile musicians in America. A master of the guitar, violin, viola, harmonica, bass, mandolin, and drums, he learned guitar and fiddle from his father.[19]

He kicked off his professional music career as a drummer during World War II and after serving in the army made his debut as a guitarist as a fill-in when an ailing T-Bone Walker had to quit in the middle of his performance at Houston's Peacock Club. Gatemouth, who was in the audience, went onstage, picked up Walker's Gibson electric guitar, launched into his rendition of *Gatemouth Boogie,* and within minutes was showered with six hundred dollars in tips. Walker made a sudden recovery and rushed back onstage. Don Robey, owner of the club, soon had Gatemouth fronting a twenty-three-piece band for a tour throughout the South and Southwest. In order to exploit Gatemouth's sound for a national audience, Robey founded Peacock Records, the first successful postwar black-owned record label.[20]

In 1949 he had a double-sided hit for Peacock, *Mary Is Fine* and *My Time Is Expensive*, which peaked at numbers

8 and 9, respectively, on the R&B charts. Dozens of hits followed, including *Okie Dokie Stomp, Boogie Rambler,* and *Dirty Work at the Crossroads,* before he eventually split with Robey and moved to Nashville, where he added country music to his repertoire. There he recorded with Roy Clark and appeared on the syndicated television show *Hee Haw.*[21]

At the age of seventy-seven, he was still hard at work, producing a CD entitled *Back to Bogalusa.* The CD featured two tracks, *It All Comes Back* and *Why Are People Like That,* composed by Louisiana songwriter Bobby Charles Guidry. The album was recorded at Brown's favorite studio, Bogalusa's Studio in the Country.

Gatemouth called Louisiana one of the few places left in America where people and nature can coexist in harmony. Only thirty-two miles from New Orleans, he loved his Slidell home until Hurricane Katrina ripped through southeast Louisiana on August 29, 2005. The storm destroyed his home and left him a devastated, broken man in his final anguished days.[22]

Mr. Google Eyes

He was born Joseph Augustus (September 13, 1931-) and began by singing in the church choir. With his eyes always on the female patrons of Dooky Chase's restaurant where he worked as a delivery boy, he earned the name "Mr. Google Eyes" from his boss, who also sponsored a local jazz band with whom Augustus occasionally sang.[23]

He made his recording debut in 1946 at age fifteen for black-owned Coleman Records with *Poppa Stoppa's Be-Bop Blues.* The record label promoted him as "the world's youngest blues singer." *No Wine, No Women* was his follow-up release and it earned him an endorsement deal with Monogram Wine. Columbia Records bought out his Coleman contract after his third hit, *Rock My Soul.*[24] Augustus signed with Duke Records when his Columbia contract expired and recorded *Play the Game* in 1953. He wrote Johnny Otis's hit *Please Forgive Me* before relocating to California.

He returned to New Orleans and in 1960 was emceeing for an all-star revue at the Sho-Bar on Bourbon Street. During that time he was dating a white woman and harassed by police for it. His lover shot him in the abdomen when he attempted to break off the relationship. He survived but terminated his Bourbon Street shows—and relationships with white women.

In 1965, Allen Toussaint produced his final record, *Everything Happens at Night*, released under the name Joe August. He then turned to bartending and sporadically emceed and performed with Earl King and Deacon John.[25]

Ernest "Tabby" Thomas

Ernest "Tabby" Thomas (January 5, 1929-), born in Baton Rouge, is King Emeritus of the Swamp Blues, having retired from operating his popular nightclub in Baton Rouge in 2004.[26] As a young man in the military in the mid-1950s, he won a San Francisco talent contest, beating out Etta James and Johnny Mathis, and signed for his first recording session. When *Midnight Is Calling* failed to sell, he moved back home and cast his lot with the blues movement in Baton Rouge. He formed his own band and went through a number of record labels before having a hit on Excello Records in 1962 with *Hoodoo Party*. A versatile musician, he played a New Orleans piano style in the tradition of Professor Longhair and Fats Domino and played lead guitar as well. He often teamed with harmonica players Whispering Smith and Lazy Lester and did several recording sessions for Floyd Soileau's Maison De Soul and various labels owned by J.D. Miller.

Thomas wasn't able to record a hit follow-up to *Hoodoo Party* and by the end of the 1960s, he had retired from performing. In 1970, however, he founded Blue Beat record label. Besides releasing his own recordings, Blue Beat promoted emerging Baton Rouge talent. When the label proved successful, Thomas began his own blues club, Tabby's Blues Box and Heritage Hall.[27]

The idea behind the club is a story unto itself. While

Tabby Thomas makes a rare appearance at the 2006 Baton Rouge Blues Festival. (Courtesy of Louisiana Music Hall of Fame)

having lunch one day at an eatery on North Boulevard, Thomas noticed the building space next door was vacant. He asked about renting it for a blues club. The owner, a white pharmacist, handed Thomas the keys and told him to come back in three months and they would discuss the rent.[28] Thomas went about restoring the ragged old building with the peeling paint and in 1979, Tabby's Blues Box and Heritage Hall opened its doors. It was the first and only blues club in Baton Rouge that featured blues exclusively and it was the only club in Baton Rouge that welcomed all blues lovers, black or white. It was the most popular blues joint in Baton Rouge by the mid-1980s. The misspelled items on the hand-written menus only added to the charm.

Musicians were not allowed to bring their own equipment into the club. Instead, they had to make do with what was there. One of the club's early performers was Tab Benoit. What was there, Benoit said, was a leaky roof and an outdated, 1970s bass amplifier PA system. Despite, or perhaps because of, the antiquated sound system and the less-than-adequate creature comforts of the club, people started pouring into the tiny, crowded, dimly lit edifice. Many of those were students at Louisiana State University who initially came for the draft beer and free hot dogs but who came back for the music.

Local musicians who made their debuts on Tabby's creaky stage include Silas Hogan, Guitar Kelly, Henry Gray, Whispering Smith, Raful Neal, Kenny Neal, and Tabby's son, Chris Thomas King, who signed his first recording contract in the club. Besides the performers who would move on to their own successful careers, visitors to Tabby's Blues Box included Mike Tyson, Shaquille O'Neal, author Harold Robbins, the O'Jays, Bruce Springsteen, and actor Paul Newman. A persistent but unconfirmed rumor has it that Mick Jagger and Keith Richards visited the club incognito during a break from a tour that took them to nearby New Orleans. As the Blues Box grew in stature, so did the Tabby Thomas legend. He became a regular at the New Orleans Jazz and Heritage Festival and he performed throughout the world to enthusiastic audiences.[29]

In 1999, highway construction forced Tabby to move the Blues Box to downtown Baton Rouge. In January 2004, Tabby had a stroke while waiting to perform at the relocated club. Though he eventually recovered, Tabby closed the doors of Tabby's Blues Box and Heritage Hall forever in November 2004. In a rare appearance in April of 2006, he told an appreciative audience it was his first performance since his wife died the previous December. "Listen to me, people," he said in a gravelly baritone voice choked with emotion, "and remember this: it gets lonely in your bedroom all alone at night."

Somewhere in that poignant pronouncement lies a great blues song.[30]

Tab Benoit

Tabby Thomas once told Tab Benoit (November 17, 1967-), "If you play the blues, you'll always have a job." Benoit took the advice to heart and went on to build a reputation as an accomplished musician and vocalist by playing about 250 dates a year across the U.S., Canada, and Europe.[31] A resident of Houma, Louisiana, he is a recipient of the Baton Rouge Blues Foundation's Slim Harpo Award.

His first album was 1992's *Nice and Warm* on Houston-based Justice Records. The album drew praise from critics who said his guitar licks were reminiscent of Albert King, Albert Collins, and Jimi Hendrix, a characterization he refuted though he does admit being influenced by them.[32] Several of his recordings have been heard on prime-time television shows, including *Northern Exposure*, *Melrose Place*, and *Party of Five*. He also appeared on camera in the premiere of the *Baywatch* spin-off, *Baywatch Nights*. His *Brother to the Blues* CD was a 2007 Grammy nominee and on May 11, 2007, *Fever for the Bayou,* released on Telarc Records, was named Best Contemporary Blues Recording for 2006. He was named Contemporary Blues Male Artist of the Year and B.B. King Entertainer of the Year at the Blues Music Awards (previously called the W.C. Handy Awards) that same year.

Night Train to Nashville was recorded live on May 9, two nights before the 2007 Blues Music Awards. Benoit is backed on the album by Louisiana's LeRoux and guest artists Jim Lauderdale, Waylon Thibodeaux, and harmonica players Kim Wilson, Jimmy Hall, and Johnny Sansone. Members of LeRoux featured on the album include Jim Odom (guitar), Nelson Blanchard (keyboards), Tony Haselden (banjo), Leon Medica (bass), David Peters (drums), and Mark Duthu (percussion).

Benoit and members of the Voice of the Wetlands All-Stars performed at both the Democratic and Republican national conventions in Denver and Minneapolis in 2008.[33]

Raful Neal

Raful Neal (June 6, 1936-September 1, 2004) was an important architect of the Baton Rouge blues and rhythm-and-blues scene. Born in Chamberlin, a small town outside

Raful Neal, Sr. (Courtesy of Louisiana Music Hall of Fame)

Baton Rouge, he built a following in south Louisiana while attaining the status of international blues icon. He began harmonica at age fourteen and three years later formed his first band, the Clouds, which originally included Leslie Johnson (Lazy Lester). At age twenty-two, he was signed by Peacock Records of Houston.

In the late 1970s and early '80s, Neal toured with Buddy Guy.[34] He first broke onto the national scene in 1987 when *Man, Watch Your Woman* was released on the Fantastic label. The song was nominated as the Blues Single of the Year. His first album, *Louisiana Legend,* was released on the King Snake label and reissued on Alligator in 1990. In 1998, he recorded *Old Friends* for the Club Louisianne label in Lafayette. He also recorded on Whit, an imprint label of Stan Lewis's Jewel Records in Shreveport.

He was inducted into the Louisiana Blues Hall of Fame in 1995 and was a recipient of the Baton Rouge Blues Foundation's Slim Harpo Award.[35] He continued to play in festivals throughout the world until his death.

Kenny Neal

The eldest of Raful Neal's ten children, Kenny Neal (October 14, 1957-) grew up listening to his father perform with Buddy Guy, Lazy Lester, and Slim Harpo.[36] When Harpo gave three-year-old Kenny a harmonica to stop him from crying, his destiny was sealed. He mastered the instrument he calls a "Mississippi saxophone" in the same manner as Harpo, flipping it over and playing low notes on the right and high notes on the left. He played piano at age six during one of his father's gigs and by thirteen was the regular bass player in the band. When he was seventeen, Buddy Guy hired him as his bass player.

Kenny Neal performs for the Louisiana Music Hall of Fame in 2007. (Courtesy of Louisiana Music Hall of Fame)

Following his tour with Buddy Guy, Neal moved to Toronto and, along with brothers Noel, Larry, Ronnie, and Raful, Jr., formed the Neal Brothers Band. To pursue a solo career, he moved back to Baton Rouge and teamed with producer/arranger Bob Greenlee in 1987 to cut a series of albums that featured his blues background. *Bio on the Bayou* was released on King Snake Records in 1987. That project netted him a recording contract with Alligator Records in 1988. His first release on

Alligator was 1988's *Big News from Baton Rouge. A Tribute to Slim Harpo and Raful Neal* won him a W.C. Handy Award for Best Blues Album of the Year.[37] In 1991, he starred in the Broadway musical *Mule Bone,* a role that won him the prestigious Theatre World Award for Most Outstanding New Talent On and Off Broadway.

Neal's music is a curious blend of Louisiana swamp blues, soul vocals, and funky rhythms. His driving guitar and mournful harmonica made him a leader among the younger generation of bluesmen. Neal has performed with B.B. King, Bonnie Raitt, Muddy Waters, Aaron Neville, and John Lee Hooker. In 1993, he toured seven African countries for the U.S. government.

Kenny Neal has known enough misery to qualify him to sing a bucketful of blues. In April 2004, his brother Ronnie died. Five months later, his father, Raful Neal, Sr., died. In March 2005, his sister, Jackie Neal, an accomplished blues singer in her own right, was murdered. *Fly Away*, a cut from his *Let Life Flow* album, was dedicated to the three. Other performers on that album include Neal's brothers Darnell and Frederick and his son, Kenny Neal, Jr.[38]

Like his father, Kenny Neal is a recipient of the Baton Rouge Blues Foundation's Slim Harpo Award.

Raful "Lil' Ray" Neal, Jr.

The list of those with whom Raful "Lil' Ray" Neal, Jr. (March 16, 1960-) has performed reads like an all-star blues lineup: Bobby Blue Bland, Big Momma Thornton, Little Milton, James Cotton, Bobby Rush, and of course brothers Kenny, Ronnie, Larry, and Noel and father Raful Neal, Sr. Lil' Ray followed his brothers and father into the family business of blues and eventually became the genre's "gentle giant." He takes a back seat to no one while living out his motto of "nothing but the blues."[39]

He was born in Erwinville, just west of Baton Rouge. His uncle owned a club where his father and his band would play. After the shows, Lil' Ray would often sneak into one of the vans and play around with the guitars, invariably breaking strings and then replacing the instruments as though nothing had happened.[40]

When one of his father's band members failed to show for a gig, Lil' Ray stood in and soon he was backing dad on a regular basis. In 1975, he and brothers Ronnie, Larry, and Noel formed their own band and were regulars on Baton Rouge radio station WXOK. In 1980, he traveled to Canada to join older brother Kenny's band and to play with Bobby Blue Bland, Big Mama Thornton, Little Milton, and Bobby Rush. Weary of the road, he returned to Baton Rouge and played off and on with his father until the elder Neal's death in 2004.[41]

In 2008, he was honored by the Baton Rouge Blues Foundation with its Slim Harpo Award.[42]

Larry Garner

Playing blues for a living wasn't Larry Garner's first career choice. Born in 1952, he at first restricted his performing to moonlighting gigs, but one night an auto accident forced

him onto an alternate route that took him past Tabby's Blues Box. He didn't make it home until 2:30 A.M.

Playing nights at Tabby's, he met and performed with Tabby Thomas, Raful and Kenny Neal, Whispering Smith, Silas Hogan, and Arthur Kelly. One night at Tabby's, he was speaking with Kenny Neal, who had just come off tour. When Garner insisted he needed to leave because he had to work the next morning, Neal implored him to quit his job at Dow Chemical and play full time. Garner made a difficult choice and resigned from the plant.[43]

Blues singer Larry Garner performs at the Alive at Five event in Baton Rouge in 2008.

His parents didn't approve of his playing blues, but in the ensuing years Garner has built a devoted following in both the U.S. and Europe. He tours Europe twice a year because, he says, Europeans appreciate authentic blues. He is a recipient of the Baton Rouge Blues Foundation's Slim Harpo Award.[44]

Little Walter

Little Walter (May 1, 1930-February 15, 1968) was born Walter Marion Jacobs in Marksville, Louisiana, just north of Simmesport. An unruly but talented child, he taught himself the harmonica by age eight. He ran away at age twelve and worked the streets and clubs of New Orleans. Heading north, he performed on the *King Biscuit Time* radio broadcast in Helena, Arkansas, from 1943-1946. From there, he found his way to Chicago via Memphis and St. Louis and in 1948 joined Muddy Waters' band.

He played amplified harmonica by holding a small microphone next to the instrument in his cupped hands, producing a saxophone-like sound.[45] One source said his 1952 instrumental hit *Juke* was recorded when Waters had some time left at the end of one of his recording sessions.[46] Actually, *Juke* was the very first song recorded during the session and Jacobs then performed several takes of *Can't Hold on Much Longer*. It was only after he finished those two songs that Muddy Waters recorded his only song of that session, *Please Have Mercy*. *Juke* spent twenty weeks on the *Billboard* charts in 1952, including eight weeks at number 1. From 1952 to 1958, Walter had fourteen top ten R&B hits. With the Chicago blues scene entering a period of dormancy, he managed only one more major hit, 1959's *Everything Gonna Be Alright*.

By the 1960s, Walter was on the path of self-destruction and not even a 1964 tour of Great Britain with the Rolling Stones could salvage his career. He died of head injuries suffered in a street fight at the age of thirty-seven.[47]

Lonnie Brooks

Born Lee Baker, Jr., in the tiny community of Dubuisson, Louisiana, Lonnie Brooks (December 18, 1933-) found that the path to stardom reads like something out of a B movie. His grandfather arose each day at 4 A.M. to play his banjo. Baker, though, didn't purchase his first guitar, a Fender Stratocaster, until he was twenty-two. Early influences included B.B. King, T-Bone Walker, Fats Domino, and Elvis Presley.

His first break came one day when he was practicing on a second-story porch and a Cadillac stopped on the street below. The driver, Clifton Chenier, "the King of Zydeco," was in need of a guitar player. After listening for a few minutes, he invited Baker to join his band. When Chenier signed with Specialty Records and moved to California, Baker stayed in Louisiana to perform with Lonesome Sundown. When Sundown got its own recording contract, Baker was forced from guitarist to singer. He didn't know the words to most of the songs the band played, so he made up his own words.

Before long, Baker began to compose his own songs. *Family Rules* was rejected by his Houston producer, but a disc jockey caught one of his shows and invited him on his radio show the next day. He played several songs and toward the end of the program, he was asked to do another. *Family Rules* was the only piece he had not performed, so he sang it to favorable audience response. Thus reassured, he recorded the song under the name Guitar Junior on Eddie Shuler's Goldband Records of Lake Charles. It became a regional hit, prompting his boss to fire him from his forty-three-dollars-a-week pipefitting job in order to convince Baker to accept an offer to play for five hundred dollars a night in Baton Rouge. He followed *Family Rules* with *The Crawl,* which became the signature song in live performances by an Austin, Texas, group, the Fabulous Thunderbirds.

After a chance meeting with Sam Cooke in a taxi in Georgia, Cooke invited Baker to Chicago. Because Chicago already had a guitar player calling himself Guitar Junior,

Baker dropped the name in favor of Lonnie Brooks. He went on to record for Chess, Mercury, and Alligator Records and worked with Clarence "Gatemouth" Brown and Jimmy Reed. He also appeared in the movie *Blues Brothers 2000*.

Brooks, like so many other musicians of his time, neglected to retain the publishing rights to his earlier songs. He believes he was typical of most young and experienced musicians who didn't know the business and only wanted to cut a record. Like many, he trusted the recording executives without protecting the rights to his music.[48]

Buddy Guy

A protégée of Muddy Waters and Guitar Slim, Buddy Guy (July 30, 1936-) was born in Lettsworth, Louisiana, and grew up in his sharecropper parents' home. He didn't own a real guitar until he was fifteen.[49] Instead, he would strip screen wire from the front door and string four strings to a cigar box to fashion a primitive instrument.[50]

Guy performed with Baton Rouge bands for several years

International blues musician Buddy Guy performing in his hometown of Baton Rouge in 2008. (Courtesy of Louisiana Music Hall of Fame)

before leaving behind local blues clubs for those of Chicago in 1957. In the ensuing years he became known as the bridge between blues and rock and earned the open admiration of guitar virtuosos Eric Clapton, Stevie Ray Vaughan, and Jimi Hendrix. He racked up a handful of Grammy awards and opened one of Chicago's most successful blues clubs.[51]

When he arrived in Chicago on September 25, 1957, he was stranded for three days with no food but vowed he would never sell or pawn his guitar. A stranger gave him a salami sandwich and took him to a blues club called the 708 Club. The stranger who befriended him was blues legend Muddy Waters. Otis Rush was onstage at the 708 Club, and Little Walter was playing harmonica. Guy was able to secure his own performance at the club and soon established himself as a force to be reckoned with when he walked into the audience playing his guitar in much the same manner as he had seen Guitar Slim do back in clubs around New Orleans.[52]

Slim was the first guitar player Guy had seen; he had been thirteen at the time. At that moment, Guy decided he wanted to sound like B.B. King but play guitar like Slim. As homage to Slim, he cut a record entitled *You Sure Can't Do*. Guy has recorded for the Cobra, Chess, Atlantic, Vanguard, and Silvertone labels.[53]

In February 1965 he made his first trip to England, touring with the Yardbirds. Rod Stewart served as his valet during the tour. Eric Clapton once told Guy he had slept in his van in order to get a chance to see the guitarist play. Clapton later said he got his idea for a blues-rock trio while watching Guy's trio perform in England during that tour. Guy has said he performed with more energy back then, playing guitar with his feet and throwing it up in the air.

Despite his success in Britain, he still had no record. He assumed it was because he played too loud and with too much feedback until he saw Clapton and Hendrix selling millions of albums using the same techniques—techniques they had learned from him.[54] When crossover audiences discovered Buddy Guy in the late 1960s, they thought he was ripping off Jimi Hendrix. The truth wasn't forthcoming until a 1968 videotape revealed Hendrix squatting near Guy, taping his concert. Hendrix was so determined to learn from the master that he occasionally canceled his own concerts to attend Guy's club dates.

In 1970, Eric Clapton coproduced an album for Atlantic Records, *Buddy Guy & Junior Wells Play the Blues.* Guy won his first Grammy in 1991 with his Silvertone album *Damn Right, I've Got the Blues* and picked up his second award in 2003 with *Blues Singer,* performed exclusively on acoustic guitar.[55] He played in the Rolling Stones concert movie *Shine a Light* and appeared with Tommy Lee Jones in *In the Electric Mist.*[56]

Guy has received five Grammy awards, twenty-three W.C. Handy Awards (the most of any blues artist), *Billboard's* Century Award for distinguished artistic achievement, the Congressional Medal of Arts, and induction into the Rock and Roll Hall of Fame. While appreciative for all the awards, Guy, generally acknowledged as the greatest living electric blues guitarist, has said he wishes lesser-known blues musicians who influenced him could be recognized and honored. Instead, he notes, some of them, like Guitar Slim, don't even have headstones on their graves.

Passing the torch just before his death, Muddy Waters told Guy, "Don't let them goddamn blues die with me."[57]

Marva Wright

Though she did not begin singing professionally until she was nearly forty, New Orleans-born Marva Wright (March 20, 1948-) is generally recognized as the Blues Queen of New Orleans. Even when she did begin performing in public, it was on a part-time basis and she initially held a second job in order to support her family. As her popularity grew, however, so did her commitment to full-time performing and her singing career has taken her all over the globe.

In 1989, during a performance at Tipitina's in New Orleans, she made her first recording, *Mama, He Treats*

Your Daughter Mean, and made her national TV debut on a Super Bowl special in 1991.[58] She has performed with Allen Toussaint, Glen Campbell, Joe Cocker, Aaron Neville, Fats Domino, Lou Rawls, and Marcia Ball. Her first album, *Heartbreakin' Woman*, was released in 1991 and the *New Orleans Times-Picayune* ranked it among the year's top ten albums in the city.[59]

She suffered a debilitating stroke in 2009 and no longer performs.

Fird "Snooks" Eaglin, Jr.

Fird "Snooks" Eaglin, Jr. (January 21, 1936-February 18, 2009) developed glaucoma shortly after his first birthday so when given a guitar at the age of five, he learned to play by listening to other musicians and the radio. At age eleven, he won a talent contest and three years later, he dropped out of the Louisiana School for the Visually Impaired to become a professional musician.[60]

In 1952, he joined the Flamingos, a seven-piece band started by Allen Toussaint. While with the band, the blind Eaglin claims, he once drove a car home from a gig when the rest of the band members were too drunk to drive.[61] With vocal stylings reminiscent of Ray Charles, he billed himself in the early 1950s as "Little Ray Charles." He also was known as "Blind Snooks Eaglin." He finally settled on just "Snooks Eaglin."

Eaglin claimed to have as many as two thousand songs in his repertoire and was sometimes called the "human jukebox." With no set list during his shows, he preferred playing audience requests and whatever came to mind.[62] Dr. John has said Eaglin played guitar, piano, horn, and bass parts of Dr. John's *Drown in My Own Tears*.[63] Discovered by folklorist Harry Oster, he recorded briefly for Imperial and later signed with Black Top Records. Besides the five albums he recorded for Black Top, he backed several other artists for the label, including Earl King and Tommy Ridgley.[64]

Once, Cowboy Mouth drummer Fred LeBlanc was allowed

to sit in with Eaglin at Mid-City Lanes Rock 'n' Bowl in New Orleans. Of all the songs Eaglin could have chosen to play with LeBlanc, he picked *Back That Ass Up*. LeBlanc said only in New Orleans can a white guy in a punk rock band perform a rap song with a black, blind blues guitar legend and make it seem natural.[65]

Eaglin resides with his wife in the New Orleans suburb of St. Rose and continues to perform at the annual New Orleans Jazz Fest, though his conversion to the Seventh Day Adventists means he does not perform between sundown Friday and sundown Saturday. Eaglin died at age seventy-two on February 18, 2009.[66]

Etta James

Etta James (January 25, 1938-) was born in Los Angeles. She had no direct ties to New Orleans but did come to the Crescent City for recording sessions with saxophonist Lee Allen and producer Allen Toussaint.[67] In 1956, she teamed with Jimmy Beasley for her first New Orleans recording session and later recorded both in that city and in Los Angeles. Lee Allen produced her album *Hickory Dickory Dock* during the late 1950s. Her third sojourn into New Orleans and Toussaint's Sea-Saint Recording Studios resulted in the 1992 album *The Right Time*. In 2002, she issued *Burning Down the House*, a live album recorded at the New Orleans House of Blues.[68]

Well into her late seventies, she has kept busy recording and performing. She was inducted into the Rock and Roll Hall of Fame in 1993 and her record *Tell Mama* was named one of 500 Songs That Shaped Rock and Roll. She was also inducted into the Blues Hall of Fame.[69]

Memphis Minnie

She spit tobacco juice while singing in a chiffon ball gown, worked as a twelve-dollar prostitute, and was married to three different guitar players. Under the name Memphis Minnie, she also played her own guitar with the best of the period's blues singers. Born Lizzie Douglas (June 3, 1897-August 6, 1973) in Algiers, Louisiana, across the Mississippi River from New Orleans, she moved with her family to Wall, Mississippi, when she was seven. In 1910, she ran away to Memphis and lived on Beale Street where she sang for change and worked as a prostitute, commanding twelve dollars for her services, a premium price for the times. Out of necessity, she became proficient at self-defense, whether using a knife, pistol, or her guitar.[70]

In the 1920s, she met and married Will Weldon, who performed under the name Casey Bill. By 1929, the marriage was over and she married Kansas Joe McCoy. She changed her name to Memphis Minnie and together she and her husband released *When the Levee Breaks*. In 1930, she released one of her favorite songs, *Bumble Bee*. Minnie and Joe recorded songs on a frequent basis in New York and Memphis for Columbia, Vocalion, Decca, Okeh, and Bluebird records.[71] In 1933, after moving to Chicago, Minnie participated in a showdown with blues guitar king Big Bill Broonzy. The judges, fellow musicians, awarded Minnie the prize of a bottle of whiskey and a bottle of gin for her performance of *Chauffeur Blues* and *Looking the World Over*.[72]

In 1939, she married Ernest "Little Son Joe" Lawlars, a Memphis guitarist. In 1952, she recorded a session for the fledgling Chess label but soon her health began to fail. She retired from music and returned to Memphis.[73] In 1960, she was wheelchair-bound after experiencing a stroke. Little Son Joe died the following year and Minnie suffered a second stroke. She died in a nursing home in 1973.[74] In 1980, she was among the first twenty artists to be inducted into the Blues Hall of Fame.[75]

Barbara Lynn

She had a pronounced limp because one leg was shorter than the other but Barbara Lynn Ozen (January 16, 1942-) never took her eyes off her goal. When she was sixteen she wrote a poem after a breakup with her boyfriend.

You'll Lose a Good Thing was written in 1958, recorded two years later, and two years after that, it bumped Ray Charles' *I Can't Stop Loving You* from the number 1 spot on the R&B charts. It reached number 8 on the pop charts.[76]

Ozen taught herself to play left-handed guitar but after hearing Guitar Slim, Bobby "Blue" Bland, and others, she set her sights on a singing career. Risking expulsion from high school, she played clubs throughout the Golden Triangle of Beaumont, Orange, and Port Arthur, Texas, as well as roadhouses like the Big Oaks, Lou Ann's, and the Palomino just over the state line in Louisiana. By the time she graduated from Beaumont's Hebert High School in 1960, she had written enough songs to complete an album.[77]

Singer Joe Barry caught her act at Lou Ann's and approached Huey Meaux, a music producer in Winnie, Texas, to tell him about the girl. Meaux heard a tape of her singing and playing and scheduled a recording date for her at Cosimo Matassa's J&M Studio in New Orleans. Matassa provided the session musicians, one of whom was Dr. John. The superb guitar instrumental that emerged from the song came not from any of the studio musicians, but from Lynn herself. She established herself in a single session not only as a talented vocalist, but also as an accomplished instrumentalist.

She was in the kitchen of her Beaumont home when her song came on the radio. "I couldn't believe it was really me on the radio," she has said. She toured with Otis Redding, Sam Cooke, James Brown, Al Green, Carla Thomas, Marvin Gaye, Ike and Tina Turner, and the Temptations. She followed *You'll Lose a Good Thing* with several more songs that made *Billboard*'s Hot 100, and the Rolling Stones covered *Oh Baby (We Got a Good Thing Goin')* on their 1964 album *Rolling Stones Now!* She bought a house near where she grew up and continues to reside there.[78]

Janis Joplin

Rock and roll's first female superstar, the best white blues singer of her era, was not from Louisiana nor did

Janis Joplin (January 19, 1943-October 4, 1970) record in Louisiana. But the state left an indelible imprint on her meteoric and turbulent musical career.[79]

Joplin, born in Port Arthur, Texas, was a hard-living, hard-drinking, insecure artist who burst onto the scene with her memorable performance at the Monterey International Pop Festival in June of 1967. It was just a year after she first arrived in San Francisco as part of the great hippie migration to that city. Before that, however, she was part of a smaller, unnoticed migration that helped define her tumultuous career.[80]

In Houston, ninety miles west of Port Arthur, the sounds of Bobby "Blue" Bland and Lightnin' Hopkins came in over the static of AM radios. To the east, the Louisiana swamp pop sounds of Dale and Grace, Rod Bernard, Tommy McLain, Slim Harpo, Phil Phillips, and Clifton Chenier held sway on jukeboxes.[81] Enhancing the lure of the juke joint music that flowed like a siren's song from the roadhouses and dancehalls along U.S. 190 across the Sabine River was the convenient fact that Louisiana's legal drinking age was eighteen as opposed to twenty-one in Texas. It was a natural attraction that pulled kids from Beaumont, Port Arthur, and Orange into Louisiana's promised land of booze, blues, and good times. The road trips, known as "going on the line," were considered a rite of passage for Joplin and the high-school boys with whom she made the weekend forays. Bands like the Boogie Kings and singers like T.K. Hulin, Jay Chevalier, and G.G. Shinn played the hits of the era and worked dirty dancing and grinding moves into their musical selections that blasted their brassy sounds into the night.[82]

The rowdy swamp pop of Lake Charles and the rhythm-and-blues of New Orleans exposed her to the state's rich ethnic musical culture and inspired Joplin to an appreciation of blues. Unable to read music, she was encouraged to learn guitar and take up singing. By the time she graduated from Thomas Jefferson High School in 1960, her knowledge of music, particularly blues, stimulated her desire to push her proficiency to its limits. She began playing the folk circuit and coffee houses in Austin. In 1966, she left for San Francisco where she indulged in an orgy of music, booze, heroin, and bisexual liaisons.[83]

Signing on with an obscure band Big Brother and the Holding Company, Janis brought the 1967 Monterey International Pop Festival to a standstill with her electrifying version of Big Mama Thornton's *Ball and Chain*. Columbia Records purchased the band's recording contract and in 1968 released the album *Cheap Thrills*. The album included *Piece of My Heart*, *Ball and Chain*, and *Turtle Blues* and quickly went to number one on the *Billboard* charts, remaining in that position for eight weeks. The album went gold within a month of its release. By 1969, she left Big Brother and formed the Kozmic Blues. *I Got Dem Ol' Kozmic Blues Again Mama* went to number five on the *Billboard* charts just as the Kozmic Blues broke up. That same year she formed the Full Tilt Boogieband and entered the studio to begin work on a new album, *Pearl*. Featuring *Me and Bobby McGee* and *Mercedes Benz*, *Pearl* again topped the charts in 1971 but Joplin would not live to see it.

Unfortunately, her life ended tragically—and early. On October 4, 1970, only four years after her escape from the authoritative and constrictive confines of Port Arthur and just two weeks after the death of Jimi Hendrix, the rebellious Joplin died of a heroin overdose in her room at the Landmark Hotel in Los Angeles. She was twenty-seven at the time of her death, and alone.[84] She was inducted into the Rock and Roll Hall of Fame in 1995.

Marcia Ball

Texas's Golden Triangle, along with Lake Charles, Louisiana, has produced many great blues artists. Examples of what can happen when East Texas blues meshes with southwest Louisiana swamp pop include Janis Joplin, Johnny Winter and Edgar Winter, George Jones, Kenny

Neal, Barbara Lynn, Clifton Chenier, Zachary Richard, Stevie Ray Vaughan, the Fabulous Thunderbirds, Clarence "Gatemouth" Brown, and Marcia Ball (March 20, 1949-).

Ball grew up in Vinton, Louisiana. She began playing piano at age five and was influenced early on by performers like Shirley and Lee, Irma Thomas, Fats Domino, James Booker, Professor Longhair, and Etta James.[85]

She enrolled at Louisiana State University and while pursuing an English degree, she played in the psychedelic rock band Gum. In 1970, she and her first husband were stranded in Austin when their car broke down and they decided to remain in the Texas capital. There she performed for awhile with Freda and the Firedogs. Upon leaving the band, she signed with Capitol Records as a solo artist and released her first album, *Circuit Queen*, an artistic triumph but a commercial failure.[86]

In the 1980s, she began concentrating on Gulf Coast rhythm-and-blues and signed with Rounder Records.[87] In 1997, after five critically acclaimed albums, she collaborated with Irma Thomas and Tracy Nelson to record *Sing It!*[88] The album, released in January 1998, was nominated for both a Grammy and a W.C. Handy Blues Award as Best Contemporary Blues Album.[89] She received the W.C. Handy Award for Female Vocalist of the Year for her work on the album and was nominated again in 2000. She also joined Cajun music legends the Hackberry Ramblers on their album *Deep Water,* on which she sings in Cajun French (*Les Blues de Bosco*). In 1999, Marcia and her band, along with B.B. King and Della Reese, performed at the White House in a concert aired nationally on public television.[90]

In 2001, she again changed record labels, moving to the Chicago blues Alligator label. Her first album, *Presumed Innocent,* spent seven months on the *Billboard* blues chart and won the 2002 W.C. Handy Blues Award for Blues Album of the Year. Her 2005 album *Live! Down the Road* was nominated for two Grammy awards and four W.C. Handy Awards. A virtuoso on the piano, Ball stays on the go, performing in the U.S., Europe, and Canada. No matter where she travels, however, her loyalties are divided between Austin, where she lives, and New Orleans, where she plays each year at the New Orleans Jazz & Heritage Festival.[91]

Luther Kent

Luther Kent (June 23, 1948-), born in New Orleans, began singing professionally at age fourteen and later signed with Baton Rouge-based Montel Records. His first record, released under the name of Duke Royal, was *I Wanna Know.*[92] Kent and Duke Bardwell sang for Cold Gritz and the Black-Eyed Peas in 1970. Kent was lead singer for the group, which previously played the rhythm section for Atlantic Records at its Miami Criteria Studios. The group left Atlantic when it was signed to Lou Adler's Ode Records in Los Angeles. After the breakup of Cold Gritz, Kent became

Luther Kent sans Trick Bag as he fronts for the Fabulous Boogie Kings during a 2008 performance in Baton Rouge.

lead singer for Blood, Sweat and Tears. Though he toured with the group in the mid-1970s, he was never allowed to record with it because Ode Records refused to grant a release.[93]

In 1978, Kent and Charlie Brent formed a New Orleans horn band, Luther Kent & Trick Bag. This became the after-hours band for artists to sit in with when visiting New Orleans.[94] Guest artists included B.B. King, Bobby "Blue" Bland, Greg Allman, Etta James, Joe Cocker, Bo Diddley, Rita Coolidge, the Righteous

Brothers, Ike and Tina Turner, Wilson Pickett, and ZZ Top, as well as many New Orleans performers. During its ten-year existence, Trick Bag released three CDs and won a Cleo Award for a collaboration with John Fred.

In 1987, Kent signed with FM Records and released the album *Past Due.* He was also cast in a singing role for the show *Cop Rock.* He lives in Denham Springs, near Baton Rouge.[95]

Kenny Acosta

Kenny Acosta, (November 9, 1949-), a native of Baton Rouge, spent most of the 1970s in Austin, Texas, performing with W.C. Clark, Stevie Ray Vaughan and Jimmy Vaughn, and Marcia Ball. In 1978, he returned to Baton Rouge and formed his own band, Kenny Acosta and the House Reckers. He traveled throughout the Gulf Coast and the southern states during the 1980s and '90s and in 1984 he released his first solo album, *Hot Dog. Justice Blues*, from the album, was named the best original song at the 1989 Baton Rouge Blues Festival. From 1986 through 1994, he

Kenny Acosta performs during the 2008 Baton Rouge Blues Festival. (Courtesy of Louisiana Music Hall of Fame)

was a regular performer at the New Orleans Jazz Fest.

Acosta produced the Fall Full Moon Festival of Blues, originally staged at Hemingbough Plantation near St. Francisville, and in the festival's second year, it was featured on Louisiana Public Broadcasting's award-winning documentary *Raining in My Heart*.[96] Acosta ultimately discontinued the festival in order to spend more time with his family.

Chris Thomas King

Grammy-winning New Orleans musician and actor Chris Thomas King (October 14, 1964-) lost his uptown New Orleans home and studio to Hurricane Katrina in August of 2005. Reacting as any blues artist would, he wrote a song about it.[97] Initially known for his daring blending of blues and hip-hop, King reached a whole new audience with the Coen Brothers film *O Brother, Where Art Thou?* Not only did he appear on the award-winning soundtrack, but he also established himself as a serious actor.[98]

Chris Thomas King has emerged from the shadow of his father, Tabby Thomas, to become one of the premier blues musicians in the country.

The son of Louisiana bluesman and club owner Tabby Thomas, he was surrounded by music from a young age, soaking up as much as he could while hanging out at his father's club. Even so, the young Thomas didn't turn to blues until his late teens when he accompanied his father on a European tour. There he found the audiences larger and more enthusiastic than back home. Upon his return to the States, Thomas landed a deal with Arhoolie Records, playing all the instruments on his 1986 debut album, *The Beginning*.

Blending music and acting, he costarred as bandleader Lowell Fulson in the Oscar-winning movie *Ray*. The soundtrack *O Brother, Where Art Thou?* was a *Billboard* number 1 album, sold over eight million records in the U.S., and won a Grammy for Album of the Year. King also co-headlined the *Down from the Mountain* tour that grossed twenty million dollars and was certified gold with U.S. sales of one million records. He was voted one of the Entertainers of the Year by *Entertainment Weekly* in 2001.[99]

Kenny Wayne Shepherd

Kenny Wayne Shepherd (June 12, 1977-) is not the prototypical blues singer. Shepherd is a blues-rock musician more in the tradition of Duane Allman and Stevie Ray Vaughan than B.B. King or Muddy Waters. He doesn't have the proper name for a blues singer, eats pasta in a Manhattan restaurant, vacations in Cancun, and married the eldest daughter of popular movie star Mel Gibson.[100]

Born in Shreveport, he displayed his musical potential at an early age by learning Muddy Waters guitar licks off his father's records. With his first guitar, he taught himself most of Stevie Ray Vaughan's catalogue but considered abandoning music when Vaughan died in a helicopter crash.[101] His ambition was refueled when he saw Buddy Guy perform.

Before the age of eighteen and still in high school, he landed a major-label record deal and released his debut album, *Ledbetter Heights*.[102] His next project was to pack a portable recording studio and a documentary film crew and hit the road in search of veteran blues players on their home turf. The result was the exemplary album and film *10 Days Out (Blues from the Backroads)*, which was nominated for a Grammy.[103]

Henry Butler

He is not only an eight-time nominee for the W.C. Handy Best Blues Instrumentalist Award, but Henry Butler (September 21, 1949-), blinded since birth by glaucoma, also is a world-class photographer whose works have been exhibited throughout the U.S. No less an authority than Dr. John compares him to Professor Longhair, James Booker, Tuts Washington, and Jelly Roll Morton.[104]

A New Orleans native displaced by Hurricane Katrina in 2005, Butler moved to Colorado where he still resides. A master of all genres, he has recorded for the Impulse, Windham Hill, and Basin Street record labels. Besides piano, Butler learned the baritone horn, valve trombone, and drums while attending the Louisiana School for the Visually Impaired in Baton Rouge and continued his education under the tutelage of Southern University clarinetist Alvin Batiste.

Though his early recordings were jazz trio albums, he naturally gravitated toward New Orleans music and the blues. In 2002, he released the all-electric blues-rock album *The Game Has Just Begun* on Basin Street Records, a New Orleans-based independent label. The album represented a turning point for him in that it was the first time he brought a blues and R&B band into the studio with him. He has said that work made him feel closer to his roots.[105]

Spencer Bohren

Born in Casper, Wyoming, Spencer Bohren (1950-) is more closely associated with New Orleans than his birthplace, but it took a meandering course for him to decide which city he wanted to call home. Drawn first to the Kingston Trio then, beginning with the British Invasion, to the Beatles, the Stones, and Bob Dylan, and finally to the stylings of Jimmie Rodgers and Hank Williams, he has finally settled into his musical niche: blues.

In 1975, he and wife Marilyn found their way to New Orleans where he fell under the musical influence of Dr. John, James Booker, Clifton Chenier, Earl King, Professor Longhair, the Neville Brothers, and BeauSoleil. His 2000 album *Carry the Word* was chosen Best CD of the Year by a Louisiana Artist by the *New Orleans Times-Picayune*.

Other releases include a Delta blues album, *Down in Mississippi* (1986), and *Down the Dirt Road Blues* (2005). Following Hurricane Katrina, he recorded the critically acclaimed *The Long Black Line*.[106]

6

Cajun and Zydeco

Zydeco originated among the Creoles of southwest Louisiana during the early nineteenth century. Influenced by the music of the area's French-speaking Cajuns and the African-American-rooted genres of jazz, blues, and R&B, it is heavily syncopated, fast-tempoed, and dominated by the button, or piano, accordion and a form of washboard known as a *frottoir*. Zydeco's rural origins and the difficult social conditions experienced by people of color at the time of its inception are evident in the song titles, lyrics, and soulful vocals. The first recordings of what was originally known as *zodico* were made by Amédé Ardoin in 1928.[1]

Boozoo Chavis and Clifton Chenier introduced zydeco to the American mainstream in the mid-1950s.[2] Chavis recorded what is thought to be the first modern zydeco recording, *Paper in My Shoe,* in 1954. After Chavis left the music business, Clifton Chenier became the first major zydeco superstar and introduced the word "zydeco" to the musical lexicon in 1965. He has said that zydeco is a corruption of *les haricots,* or "the beans," from the title of one of his early hits *Les Haricots Sont Pas Salés.*[3] In the mid-1980s, Rockin' Sidney rekindled interest in zydeco music nationwide with the hit remake of the classic *My Toot Toot.*[4]

Although Zydeco, like Cajun music, draws heavily on Acadian French influence and they share similar origins and lyrics, the two followed different evolutionary paths. Cajun music originated from ballads but gradually morphed

211

into dance music—with or without words—to accompany
any of the several Cajun dances. Whereas zydeco features
a syncopated beat like that of a jitterbug, Cajun music
provides the beat for the Cajun one step, two step, or
waltz. The music was essential for the popular all-night
house dance, the *bal de maison*, as well as the *fais do-do*,
held at a public dance hall. By the middle of the twentieth
century, Cajuns began gravitating toward country music
and Nashville with the fiddle out front.

Some of the earliest recordings of Cajun music were of
farmhands in the late 1920s by historian Alan Lomax. The
first commercial recording of a Cajun song was *Allons à
Lafayette,* by Joe Falcon and Cleoma Breaux in 1928. The
first songs were mixtures of folk influences from black,
white, and Native American traditions with early song lyrics
entirely in Cajun French. Today some younger singers like
Damon Troy and Jamie Bergeron sing in English.

In the ever-evolving world of Louisiana music, the
various genres, including Cajun and zydeco, borrowed
from and contributed to each other to develop a unique
cross-section of musical styles that makes Louisiana stand
alone as a bastion of popular music. Ample evidence of this
is found in the fact that multiple songs from each of the
musical disciplines have appeared on the *Billboard* Hot 100
and R&B charts since the 1940s.

Terrance and Cynthia Simien
In June of 2007, the Recording Academy announced the
creation of a Best Zydeco or Cajun Music Album category
with the first winner to be chosen at the 50th Grammy
Awards in February 2008. The announcement was a victory
for zydeco music veteran Terrance Simien (September 3,
1965-) and his wife Cynthia Simien (August 4, 1961-) not
only because they had been lobbying the Academy for
six years for creation of the category, but also because
Terrance won the first Grammy in the new category for
his album *Live! Worldwide* on Aim International Records

of Australia. Zydeco and Cajun musicians previously had been nominated in the Grammy's Folk category. Rockin' Sidney won a Grammy for Best Ethnic Recording for *My Toot Toot* in 1985 and Lafayette Cajun band BeauSoleil won for Best Traditional Folk Album in 1987.[5]

Terrance, born in Eunice, Louisiana, first heard zydeco at local dances as a boy but did not show any interest in the music until the early 1980s. After learning the accordion and writing a few songs, he formed a band with his brother Greg, playing local clubs at night and working as a bricklayer during the day. Paul Simon heard him play at the New Orleans World's Fair and enlisted him to collaborate with him on a cover of Clifton Chenier's *You Used to Call Me*. He also appeared in the Dennis Quaid movie *The Big Easy*.

Cynthia, a member of the National Academy of Recording Arts and Sciences, called the approval of the new category a major step toward wider exposure of zydeco music. "Now every Louisiana musician has a chance to win a Grammy," she said.[6]

The Hackberry Ramblers

The oldest existing Cajun band, the Hackberry Ramblers, may well be the oldest band in America. Blending Cajun with western swing, the band dates back to 1933 when it was founded by fiddler Luderin Darbone (January 1913-November 21, 2008). Born in the Acadia Parish town of Evangeline, Darbone was living in Hackberry in Cameron Parish during the Great Depression. It was there that he played music with neighbor Edwin Duhon (June 11, 1910-February 26, 2006).[7] Other early members of the band include guitarists Floyd and Lonnie Rainwater and Lennis Sonnier. The Ramblers' membership has undergone several changes over the years.[8] At one time, the band included Eddie Shuler, owner of Lake Charles' Goldband Records.[9]

The band first played amplified music by hooking its sound system to the battery of Darbone's idling Model-T. Its first recording was in 1935. The Ramblers recorded

Edwin Duhon, Glen Croker, Luderin Darbone, Ben Sandmel, Johnny Farque, and Johnny Faulk of the Hackberry Ramblers. (Photo used by permission of Philip Gould, copyright 1992)

for the Goldband, Bluebird, Deluxe, Arhoolie, and Hot Biscuits labels. During the 1930s and '40s, the band hosted a radio program broadcast throughout southwest Louisiana and east Texas. In 1998, the Hackberry Ramblers were nominated for a Grammy for their 1997 album *Deep Water.* The band was featured on *MTV Live* in 1998, appeared in a Memorial Day performance at the Kennedy Center in Washington, and was featured in the *Oxford American*'s annual Southern Music Issue.

On December 4, 1999, the Hackberry Ramblers made its Grand Ole Opry debut. The band has also been featured on *Entertainment Tonight, Music City Tonight,* NPR's *Weekend Edition*, and in the *New York Times, Rolling Stone,* and *Musician.* "The Hackberry Ramblers has to be one of the coolest bands in the world," said *Cashbox* and the *Dallas Morning News* described the band members as "party animals."[10]

Today the Ramblers are absent their longtime leaders. Edwin Duhon died on February 26, 2006, at the age of ninety-five. His last performance was at the Shaw Center for the Arts in Baton Rouge three months earlier.[11] Darbone last performed at the New Orleans Jazz Fest in May of 2008, only six months prior to his death on November 21. For his funeral Mass and burial, he was dressed in the suit he wore while performing. His fiddle was placed beside him in his coffin for the service but retrieved and kept by his son, Edward. The Lost Bayou Ramblers, the band that accompanied him at his final Jazz Fest performance, played *Jolie Blonde* as his casket entered Our Lady of Prompt Succor Catholic Church in Sulphur and played his favorite song, *Beaumont Rag*, as it left the church for the cemetery. The Hackberry Ramblers, said Edward Darbone, died with his father.[12]

Leo Soileau

Taught the fiddle by Dennis McGee and Sady Courville, Leo Soileau (January 19, 1904-August 2, 1980) became one of the most important Cajun musicians of the 1930s and '40s. He made his debut recording in 1928 when he hooked up with Mayeus Lafleur to record *He Mon*. He went on to cut more than one hundred more records, including *Hackberry Hop, La Gran Mamou, La Valse De Gueydan,* and *Jolie Blonde*.

In the early 1930s, he formed the Three Aces, later renamed the Rhythm Boys. They drove to Chicago to record the first of their many recordings in 1941. Dropped by Decca Records at the beginning of World War II, the Rhythm Boys played the Silver Star Club in Lake Charles for eight years and the Showboat Club in Orange, Texas, for another two years. Soileau eventually left music to work with his brothers in a general contracting firm in Ville Platte.[13]

Nathan Abshire

Nathan Abshire (June 27, 1913-May 13, 1981) was unable to earn a living with his music, so he was forced to take a job at the Basile, Louisiana, town dump. Influenced by Amédé Ardoin, he was one of the first musicians to take Cajun music beyond the borders of the state.

Born in Gueydan, he took up the accordion at age six

and soon was in demand throughout southwest Louisiana. He began his professional career in the 1920s and first recorded with Happy Fats and His Rayne-Bo Ramblers in the early '30s on the RCA subsidiary Bluebird Records. Following World War II, he cut *Pine Grove Blues* for D.T. Records. He also recorded for Swallow, Khoury/Lyric, La Louisianne, and Kajun records and during the 1950s and '60s played on sessions with the Balfa Brothers.

A revival in interest in Cajun music during the 1970s put Abshire in demand for festivals and colleges. He was featured in Les Blank's 1971 documentary *Spend It All* and in the 1975 PBS-TV Cajun documentary *Good Times Are Killing Me*.[14]

Amédé Ardoin

Known for his high-pitched voice and his skill on the ten-button (diatonic) accordion, singer Amédé Ardoin (March 11, 1898-November 4, 1941) is credited with opening the door for Cajun music in the early part of the twentieth century.

Born in l'Anse des Rougeaux, an unincorporated community between Eunice and Mamou, he was popular among both whites and blacks and often played white dances with Creoles Alphonse LaFleur and Douglas Bellard and with white Cajuns Sady Courville, Shelby Vidrine, and Dennis McGee. In December of 1929, he and Dennis McGee teamed to record six songs for Columbia Records.[15]

The black-white combo did not come without a cost. Ardoin was severely beaten while walking home from a house party he'd played in Eunice. His social faux pas was in accepting a handkerchief from a white woman with which to wipe sweat from his face. The attack left him with a crushed skull and throat, resulting in damaged vocal chords. He was found the next day lying in a ditch more dead than alive.[16]

Cajun performers Canray Fontenot and Wade Fruge, interviewed on *American Patchwork* on PBS, said Ardoin was struck by a car before he was beaten. Dennis McGee theorized he was poisoned by a jealous fiddler. Others said Ardoin suffered impaired mental and musical abilities, probably because of the attack. He spent his final years in Pineville State Hospital (now Central Louisiana Hospital), at the time a facility for the insane. He died there, a victim of venereal disease, according to recent studies.

His unique accordion stylings and his high, wailing vocals remain a prominent factor in today's Cajun music. He was a major influence on Nathan Abshire, Austin Pitre, and Iry LeJeune and many of his songs are still found in the Cajun repertoire.[17]

Dennis McGee

Dennis McGee (January 26, 1893-Octoctober 3, 1989) was named Honorary Dean of Cajun Music by the University of Louisiana-Lafayette shortly before his death in 1989 at the age of ninety-six. Composer, vocalist, and fiddler, McGee, born in the l'Anse des Rougeaux community, was one of the earliest recorded Cajun musicians.[18] In the 1920s and '30s, he played and recorded alongside black Creole accordionist Amédé Ardoin as well as fellow fiddler and brother-in-law Sady Courville. He received his first fiddle from a cousin and within six months was playing for house parties throughout southwest Louisiana. He also played the squeezebox but preferred the fiddle.[19]

Signed at various times with Vocalion, Brunswick, Melotone, and Swallow labels, he recorded the classic *Madame Young Donnez Moi Votre Plus Jolie Blonde* in 1929. The song borrowed the tune of another popular Cajun song, *Allons Danser Colinda*.

McGee's recordings with Courville and fiddler Ernest Frugé are among the few surviving examples of Cajun music as it existed before introduction of the accordion. McGee continued to perform at festivals and concerts and recorded for various American and French record labels until shortly before his death.[20]

John Delafose

As a child, John Delafose (April 16, 1939-September 17, 1994) constructed homemade fiddles from window screen wire and wooden cigar boxes. He took up harmonica and at age eighteen, he learned the button (diatonic) accordion. Unable to make a living from music, he relied on farming and did not pursue music seriously until the early 1970s when he played accordion and harmonica for several local zydeco bands. By the mid-1970s, he had formed his own band, the Eunice Playboys, with Charles Prudhomme on guitar and his brother Slim Delafose on bass. Eventually, the band was joined by sons John "T.T." on frottoir, Tony on drums, and Geno on frottoir, accordion, and vocal leads.

The Eunice Playboys' recording debut in 1980 was *Joe Pete Got Two Women* from the album *Zydeco Man.* As interest in traditional Creole culture grew, the group became one of the hottest attractions on the Gulf Coast circuit. John Delafose's final album with his beloved Eunice Playboys was *Blues Stay Away from Me* in 1993. Geno succeeded his father as bandleader upon the elder Delafose's death.[21]

Geno Delafose

At age seven, Geno Delafose (February 6, 1972-) was already playing *frottoir* (washboard) in his father John Delafose's band, the Eunice Playboys. He went on to perform on seven of the band's albums and collaborated with his father on 1992's *Pere et Garcon Zydeco.*[22] When his father's health began to fail, Geno switched to accordion and continued on the squeezebox following the elder Delafose's 1994 death.

Born in Eunice, Delafose is influenced by Cajun and country and western music. The title of his debut album on Rounder, *French Rockin' Boogie,* also became the name of his band. He released two more albums on Rounder before switching to the Time Square label for the release of *Everybody's Dancin'* in 2003.[23]

Geno Delafose during an Alive at Five performance in Baton Rouge.

His 2007 album, *Le Cowboy Creole,* was nominated for a Grammy. It was recorded at the Master Trak Enterprises Studio in Crowley, the same studio used by John Delafose for his Eunice Playboys debut album *Zydeco Man* twenty-seven years earlier. Studio owner Mark Miller engineered and mastered both albums.[24]

Geno raises horses on his Double D Ranch in a rural section of Duralde, a few miles north of Eunice. Each fall he hosts a fan appreciation day that he calls a "Creole zydeco hootenanny," complete with free barbeque. He invites fans to "bring a chair, your best dancin' shoes, and a beverage. Geno, his family, and band, will provide the rest."[25]

Wilson Anthony "Boozoo" Chavis

Although he went thirty years between recording sessions, Wilson Anthony "Boozoo" Chavis (October 23, 1930-May 5, 2001) was a pioneer of zydeco music. Born in Lake Charles to tenant farmers, he was given the nickname Boozoo as a child.[26] He was raised by his mother who cleaned houses and sold barbecue at horse races. His father gave him his first accordion and once he learned the instrument, he played area barn dances. When his mother opened a dance club, he began to play with Morris Chenier and his sons, Clifton and Cleveland.[27]

In 1954, he recorded *Paper in My Shoe,* acknowledged as the first zydeco hit, under Eddie Shuler's Goldband label. He then withdrew from recording or performing in public.[28] His distrust of the music industry in general and Eddie Shuler in particular was fed by his conviction that Shuler and Goldband Records cheated him out of royalties. He also denied Shuler's claim that he once got so drunk he fell off his stool while recording *Paper in My Shoe.*[29] Shuler has said he gave Chavis a pint of Seagram's 7 in order to get the sound he wanted and when Boozoo fell off the stool, he somehow managed to continue playing his accordion.[30]

For the next three decades he raised champion racehorses in Texas and Shreveport and Lafayette, Louisiana. In 1984, he returned to music when he signed a five-year contract with Maison de Soul and recorded four albums for the label: *Louisiana Zydeco Music, Boozoo Zydeco, Zydeco Homebrew,* and *Zydeco Trail Ride.*[31]

Chavis performed with his band, the Majic Sounds, at the Newport Folk Festival and the New Orleans Jazz & Heritage Festival.[32] Scott Billington, A&R vice president for Rounder Records, credited Chavis with reviving the moribund zydeco music scene in South Louisiana.[33] He also was featured in the 1994 Robert Mugge video documentary *The Kingdom of Zydeco* and was inducted into the Zydeco Hall of Fame in 1998. He died in Austin, Texas, of complications from a heart attack.[34]

Canray Fontenot

Canray Fontenot (October 23, 1922-July 29, 1995), one of the last players of pre-zydeco Creole music, punctuated his primitive fiddle style with barefoot stomping. Unable to subsist off music alone, he worked as a sharecropper and in a hardware store to make ends meet. Still, he managed to put four of his six children through college and a daughter through law school.

In 1937, Fontenot was asked to join Amédé Ardoin for his

recording of *Les Portes de la Prison,* but Fontenot's mother refused to grant him permission to make the trip to New York on the grounds that he was too young. A few years later he joined accordion player Alphonse "Bois-Sec" Ardoin to form a duo, and the two continued to play together for more than forty years, traveling outside Louisiana for the first time in 1966 to perform at the Newport Folk Festival. Five songs from that performance were included on the 1976 album *Louisiana Cajun French Music from the Southwest Prairies, Vol. 2.*

Fontenot released his last album for Arhoolie Records, *Louisiana Hot Sauce Creole Style,* in 1993. He was featured in the film *J'ai Ete au Bal.* He died in 1995 following a lengthy battle with cancer.[35]

Doug Kershaw

Born in Tiel Ridge in Cameron Parish, Doug Kershaw (January 24, 1936-) is Cajun music's ambassador to the world, thanks to his 1969 national television debut on the *Johnny Cash Show.*[36] Two months later, *Louisiana Man,* recorded in 1961, was the first song broadcast back to earth from the lunar surface by

the Apollo 12 astronauts. The song, recorded with brother Rusty Kershaw, was eventually covered by more than eight hundred artists. Doug signed a contract with Warner Bros. Records in 1969 and he topped off the year with a week-long gig at the Fillmore East in New York as the opening act for Eric Clapton's Derek and the Dominos.[37]

With his appearance on the *Johnny Cash Show,* Doug's popularity skyrocketed, though in reality, he and Rusty had already sold more than eighteen

Doug Kershaw (Courtesy of Louisiana Music Hall of Fame.)

million records. *Louisiana Man* was a top 10 country hit on the Hickory label and *Diggy Liggy Lo* had done nearly as well.[38]

The son of an alligator hunter, Doug is the seventh of nine children. He was raised in a home where Cajun French was spoken and did not learn English until he was eight—the same year his father committed suicide. Starting with the fiddle at age five, he eventually taught himself to play twenty-eight instruments. His first paying job was at a Cajun bar, the Bucket of Blood, where he was accompanied by his mother. He and brothers Rusty and Peewee formed their first band, the Continental Playboys, in 1948.[39]

Peewee Kershaw soon left the band but Rusty and Doug continued recording in French for J.D. Miller's Feature Records. Miller convinced them to switch to English and in 1955 they recorded *So Lovely Baby,* which Miller leased to the Hickory label. The song was a top 5 country hit and the brothers soon became members of the *Louisiana Hayride* in Shreveport.[40]

A sketch still hangs on the wall of Miller's recording studio that depicts Rusty and Doug Kershaw and members of their band during a recording session. Each member is clad only in underwear. Studio owner Mark Miller explained that the studio had no air conditioning and it was so hot and humid during the session that band members stripped down to their skivvies.[41]

Doug earned a degree in mathematics from McNeese State University in Lake Charles and in 1958 both brothers enlisted in the army. Reunited following their discharges in 1961, the two collaborated on *Louisiana Man* but by the time their first album, *Rusty and Doug,* was released in mid-1964, they had decided to split up.

On June 21, 1975, Doug married wife Pam in the Houston Astrodome before an Astros game. Following the game, he performed a concert for the Astrodome crowd. He has five sons. One son, Tyler, is a drummer in his band. In 1988 he recorded *Cajun Baby,* a duet with Hank Williams, Jr. He currently runs Doug Kershaw's Bayou House, a restaurant in Lucerne, Colorado, where he continues to play regularly.[42]

Clifton Chenier

Born in Port Barre in St. Landry Parish, Clifton Chenier (June 25, 1925-December 12, 1987) put zydeco music on the international map with his frenetic accordion playing and boundless energy. Along with his brother Cleveland, Clifton moved to Port Arthur, Texas, in 1947 to work in the oil refineries. There they formed the Hot Sizzling Band, which played the Gulf Coast areas of Texas and Louisiana.[43]

Elko Records signed Chenier to his first recording contract, though he also recorded for the Imperial, Specialty, Chess, Argo, Checker, and Zynn labels.[44] On May 11, 1965, the Chenier brothers entered Gold Star Studio in Houston, spoke a few words to each other in Creole French while the tapes rolled, and then, backed by drummer Madison Guidry, launched into *Zydeco Sont Pas Sale,* the song that would become Chenier's signature piece about, of all things, two mischievous dogs named Hip and Taiaut.

Often wearing a crown signifying his title as King of Zydeco, Chenier took his mixture of rock and French all over the world and even toured with bluesman Lowell Fulson. Sometimes called the Jimi Hendrix of accordion, he was a long way from being confined to the nameless black clubs in and around Lafayette, New Iberia, Cankton, and Grand Coteau—clubs no white person ever entered.[45]

While recording Chenier was loath to spend much time on any one number. He believed that an artist's work diminished in quality with each take. Chenier won a Grammy for his album *I'm Here.* It was also the first Grammy for the little-known Alligator Records.

Chenier died of kidney disease but he bequeathed his accordion and his Red Hot Louisiana Band to his son, C.J. Chenier, who continues to carry the torch of zydeco music to the world.[56]

Paul "Lil' Buck" Sinegal

Allen Toussaint called him "the Gentle Giant" of the guitar, guitarist Raymond Monet called him "the Hawk," and Clifton Chenier gave him the handle "Buckaroo," but it was while he was performing with the Jive Five that Paul Alton Sinegal (January 14, 1944-) got his permanent nickname, "Lil' Buck."[47]

The fourth of six children, he was born in Lafayette to Creole parents. He received his first guitar around 1955, and a year later spent three days with Creole guitarist Raymond "Swank" Monet of Lafayette. Monet showed Sinegal chord progressions and riffs. The first song he learned was *Honky Tonk*. After those sessions, Sinegal was able to figure out nearly any tune he heard and maintains that Monet was one of the "baddest" guitarists he ever knew.[48]

Sinegal's first band was the Jive Five. From that group, he graduated in 1958 to the Top Cats, a fifteen-piece band. The band, which included Buckwheat Zydeco on keyboard, was influenced by James Brown, Jackie Wilson, and Joe Simon and backed Barbara Lynn, Otis Redding, Percy Sledge, Millie Jackson, and Joe Tex.

In 1969, Sinegal accompanied his cousin to the Blue Angel Club in Lafayette. When they entered, a big, tall man in a Mexican hat and yellow shirt standing at the bar asked if he was the guitarist Lil' Buck. The stranger was Clifton Chenier and as fate would have it, Chenier's guitarist was a no-show for that night's performance. Chenier asked Sinegal to stand in. He did and that was the start of a musical relationship between the two that lasted fourteen years. Sinegal left Chenier's Red Hot Louisiana Band only when Chenier cut back on appearances because of failing health. Sinegal then went on to work with Rockin' Dopsie, Sr., Rockin' Dopsie, Jr., and Buckwheat Zydeco.[49]

Sinegal is credited as a sideman on over three hundred recordings, including Paul Simon's 1987 Grammy-winning *Graceland* album. It wasn't until 1998, however, that his album *The Buck Starts Here* was produced and released on the NYNO label by Allen Toussaint. Sinegal's CD charted in *Living Blues* magazine's top 20 for several months during 1998 and introduced Sinegal to a new generation of blues fans.[50]

Buckwheat Zydeco

Stanley Joseph Dural, Jr. (November 14, 1947-) was the natural successor to the title vacated with the death of Clifton Chenier. By blending his synthesizer- and trumpet-dominated music with strains of rock and R&B, he fused traditional and contemporary zydeco, reaching a more mainstream audience than any artist before him.[51]

Born in Lafayette, he was exposed to traditional zydeco as a child. He preferred R&B, however, and by the mid-1950s was playing professionally. One morning in 1957, he made his way to the Truman Court Motel, a Lafayette motel for blacks. He waited patiently for the arrival of a pink Cadillac. Opening the door of the vehicle, he stammered hello to his hero, Fats Domino. That night, he managed to sneak into the back entrance of the Jazz Room and watched the Fat Man's show.

Dural's reputation as a keyboardist garnered him jobs backing Joe Tex and Clarence "Gatemouth" Brown.[52] In 1971, Dural founded Buckwheat and the Hitchhikers, a sixteen-piece funk band. In 1976, he fell under zydeco's influence when recruited to back Chenier on tour. Originally signed as an organist, Dural picked up the accordion within two years and learned from the master himself, rechristening himself "Buckwheat Zydeco" in homage to the *Our Gang* Little Rascals character.[53]

By 1979, he had formed his own combo, Ils Sont Partis (translated, "They're off!" in honor of the starting shout for each horse race at the Lafayette track). After signing with the Blues Unlimited label, the group debuted in 1979 with *One for the Road*, followed in 1980 by *Take It Easy, Baby*. After 1983's *100 Percent Fortified Zydeco*, the group moved to the Rounder label and released the Grammy-nominated *Turning Point*. Its 1985 follow-up, *Waitin' for My Ya Ya*, was similarly honored.[54]

In 1986, Buckwheat Zydeco landed a deal with Island Records, becoming the first zydeco act ever signed to a major label. The band made its Island debut in 1987 with the Grammy nominee *On a Night Like This.* That same year they appeared in the movie *The Big Easy.*[55] Buckwheat and his band performed at both of Bill Clinton's presidential inaugurations, and in 2006, he performed at the Atlanta Summer Olympics closing ceremonies before a worldwide television audience of three billion. He also appeared on *CBS Morning News, The Today Show,* and *Late Show with David Letterman.*

Zachary Richard

Singer-songwriter Zachary Richard (September 8, 1950-) was born in southwest Louisiana and was influenced by Cajun, zydeco, and New Orleans R&B. While remaining true to his musical traditions with *Coeur Fidèle* and *Cap Enragé,* he cites the Rolling Stones' *Out of Their Heads,* the Byrds' *Turn! Turn! Turn!,* and Simon & Garfunkel's *The Sound of Silence* as early rock and roll influences.[56]

At about thirteen, he decided he wanted to get a guitar and become the next Mick Jagger. His family, however, expected

Cajun singer Zachary Richard is an advocate of the preservation of the French culture and of saving Louisiana's wetlands. (Courtesy of Louisiana Music Hall of Fame)

him to become a lawyer or a doctor. They associated musicians with debauchery because they stay out late and drink while making little money. Accordingly, he enrolled at Tulane University in pre-law. But then, he said, he smoked a "big joint, and it was over." He graduated summa cum laude in history in 1971, but his heart belonged to music.[57]

Zachary resided in Montreal from 1976 to 1981 where he recorded seven French-language albums, two of which were certified gold. Returning to Louisiana he started recording in English for the Rounder and A&M record labels. In 1995, he returned to recording in French.[58]

Sonny Landreth

Although Sonny Landreth (February 1, 1951-), "the King of Slydeco," slide guitar played with a strong zydeco influence, is an extremely skilled guitarist in the conventional form—Eric Clapton described him as perhaps

Sonny Landreth. (Courtesy of Louisiana Music Hall of Fame)

the most underestimated musician on earth and probably one of the most advanced—he is best known for his slide playing.[59] He is tagged as a blues artist, but the Cajun/zydeco influence is easily apparent in most of his recordings. Born in Canton, Mississippi, he was moved by his family to nearby Jackson before they settled in Lafayette, in the heart of Cajun country. When not touring and performing, he resides in Breaux Bridge, Louisiana.[60]

Following his first professional job with Clifton Chenier in the 1970s (where for a time, he was the only white person with the Red Beans and Rice Revue), Landreth recorded two albums for the Blues Unlimited label in Crowley, *Blues Attack* in 1981 and *Way Down in Louisiana* in 1985. The second album got him noticed in Nashville, which led to work with John Mayall, who recorded Landreth's *Congo Square*. He has worked with New Orleans bandleader and pianist Allen Toussaint, who, along with Dire Straits guitarist Mark Knopfler, guests on several tracks on Landreth's 1996 album *South of I-10.*[61]

Rockin' Dopsie

Clifton Chenier may have been the King of Zydeco, but Rockin' Dopsie (February 10, 1932-August 26, 1993), with stage antics that overshadowed his proficiency on the button accordion, was its crown prince. Dopsie was devoted to preserving the old French songs that form the basis of zydeco.

Born Alton Rubin in Carencro, near Lafayette, he spent much of his childhood picking cotton and working in the cane fields. His father played accordion and performed at local house parties on weekends, often bringing young Alton along with him. His father gave him a small accordion when Rubin was fourteen, telling him he would have to teach himself to play.[62] Learning songs from the radio, Rubin, a "southpaw," developed the unorthodox style of holding the accordion upside down.

He eventually moved to Lafayette and began performing

Rockin' Dopsie, Jr., performs at the inauguration of Louisiana governor Bobby Jindal in 2008. (Courtesy of Louisiana Music Hall of Fame)

in blues clubs in the 1950s, working days in construction as a hod carrier. Taking his stage name "Dopsie" from a Chicago dancer, he was given the additional name of "Rockin'" to describe his lively accordion playing. Rockin' Dopsie performed zydeco in clubs and against Clifton Chenier's advice continued working in construction, eventually becoming an electrical contractor. Through the 1950s and '60s, Dopsie occasionally recorded with independent record companies, including six albums for Sweden's Sonet label and soon became a popular performer across the Atlantic.[63]

In 1979, he launched a series of European tours, but his U.S. career got a huge boost in 1985 when he recorded *That Was Your Mother* with Paul Simon on Simon's Grammy-winning *Graceland* album.[64] Simon hired him after seeing him perform at the Lone Star Café in New York City. The song was recorded in J.D. Miller's studio in Crowley. Later Dopsie was nominated for a Grammy for his 1991 album *Louisiana Music*. He also appeared in the film *Delta Heat*.

He continued performing and recording until his death of a heart attack in Opelousas. His son David Rubin is the only metal washboard player known to front a zydeco band and son Alton Rubin, Jr., is a drummer. David has taken over leadership of the band as well as the name Rockin' Dopsie, Jr.[65]

Rockin' Sidney Simien

Sidney Simien, better known as Rockin' Sidney (April 9, 1938-February 25, 1998), became an international sensation with his recording of *My Toot Toot*.[66] Born in St. Landry Parish, he wrote the song and in October 1984, included it on his third album, *My Zydeco Shoes Got the Zydeco Blues*. Sidney played all the instruments on the album, recorded in Eddie Shuler's Goldband Records studio in Lake Charles, Sidney's home studio.[67]

A veteran Cajun-zydeco musician who played almost every style of music, Sidney took up the guitar at an early age and by his late teens was leading his own band as Sidney Simien and His All Stars. Although his success is based upon his reputation as a zydeco musician, Sidney did not start out as either a zydeco artist or an accordion player, morphing to the genre only after first trying swamp pop and blues. Heavily influenced by Slim Harpo and Cookie and the Cupcakes, he cut his first R&B recording in 1957 on the Fame label of Muscle Shoals, Alabama.[68]

After a brief stint with Fame, Sidney switched labels and began releasing records for Floyd Soileau's Jin Records of Ville Platte, Louisiana. For nearly six years, Sidney pumped out material for the label and in 1963, his single *No Good Woman* clicked with the record-buying public in south Louisiana and east Texas. Soileau released nine Rockin' Sidney singles between 1957 and 1964. He suggested that Sidney learn the accordion and start playing zydeco, which was then making a comeback.[69]

Sidney signed with Goldband Records of Lake Charles in 1965 and started wearing a turban, referring to himself as

"Count Rockin' Sidney." Between the mid-1960s and the late '70s, Sidney cut over fifty contemporary blues, soul, and R&B singles for Goldband.[70] By the late '70s he was playing solo organ gigs at Lake Charles hotels and lounges when he signed with Bally Hoo Records and started Sid Sim Publishing. He also signed an agreement with Soileau for the distribution of his records on Soileau's Maison de Soul Records. In return, Soileau's Flat Town Music Company would share the profits.[71]

One of only a few zydeco artists to gain commercial success outside south Louisiana, Rockin' Sidney scored big time in 1984 when his single *My Toot Toot* was certified a platinum record and won a Grammy. It was the first zydeco song to get major airplay on pop, rock, and country radio stations. Many listeners mistook the phrase "don't mess with my toot-toot" as holding either sexual or drug connotations; however, its actual meaning is steeped in the Cajun French language as a term of endearment.[72]

The song has been covered by Fats Domino, Rosie Ledet, Jean Knight, Terrance Simien, Doug Kershaw, Denise LaSalle, Jimmy C. Newman, and John Fogerty. Fogerty's version, in fact, was recorded in J.D. Miller's studio in Crowley in 1985. Rockin' Sidney's version was released on the Maison de Soul label in Ville Platte but became so popular as a novelty dance number that Soileau found it impossible to keep up with the sales demand. He entered into an agreement with Huey Meaux who leased the song to Epic Records, a division of Columbia, for national release.

Rockin' Sidney surged into the country top 40 with the song and it remained there for eighteen weeks. It spent one week at number 98 on the pop charts. He was featured in *People* magazine, *Rolling Stone, Billboard,* and *Music City News* and appeared on TNN (now Spike TV), *Hee Haw, You Can Be a Star,* and John Fogerty's Showtime special *New Country.* He has performed at the Charlie Daniels Jam and Austin City Limits Music Festival. *My Toot Toot* was included in the soundtracks of the movies *Hard Luck, One Good Cop,* and *The Big Easy.*[73]

Decades after *My Toot Toot* debuted, it is still drawing royalties from commercial use in Europe and cover versions done in several languages by dozens of musicians. Sidney used royalties from the song to purchase radio station KAOK-AM in Lake Charles and also bought Festival City, a six-acre entertainment complex there. Additionally, he started a new record label, ZBC Records. *Hot Steppin'*, a song from his first ZBC effort, was nominated for a Grammy in 1986.

Rockin' Sidney Simien died in 1998 following a lengthy battle with cancer.[74]

Wayne Toups

Accordionist and vocalist Wayne Toups (October 2, 1958-) was born in Lafayette and grew up in neighboring Crowley. A progressive Cajun musician, he combines Cajun and zydeco elements with mainstream rock and English lyrics. Toups has recorded for Polygram Records and toured in over twenty-six countries while promoting a musical style he calls "zydecajun."[75]

Wayne Toups, one of the more popular zydeco singers in Louisiana, performs in Baton Rouge.

He began his recording career in J.D. Miller's recording studio in Crowley when he was only about ten years of age. Miller's son Mark, who now runs the studio, has produced several of his albums.[76] His constant touring and festival and television appearances make him one of the most visible musicians of his genre, and his work can be heard on soundtracks for television (*Broken Badges*) and the movies (*Steel Magnolias*).

Toups lists as his musical influences R&B stars Otis Redding and Aretha Franklin and rockers the Allman Brothers and the Doobie Brothers, adding their styles to his own unique musical gumbo that has won him a huge following of zydeco converts. Bursting full throttle onto the stage with his accordion, his electrifying—and energizing—presence is fed by his persona.[77] Often clad in a Hawaiian shirt, he is in perpetual motion onstage as he melds the bluesy sounds of zydeco, traditional Cajun, and gyrating rock and roll.[78] In 1992, he was named Accordionist of the Year by the Cajun French Music Association, which also named his *Late in Life* Song of the Year.

Jo-El Sonnier

For Jo-El Sonnier (October 2, 1946-), the road to fame wasn't always a smooth one. Born in Rayne, Louisiana, to French-speaking sharecroppers, he worked in the cotton fields while learning to play his brother's battered accordion. His radio debut was at age six, and at age eleven he had his first recording session. A south Louisiana club favorite, he chased his dreams to California. There, he built a reputation as an accomplished session player but he never connected as a solo artist. His next stop was Nashville, where he signed with Mercury Records, but he returned to Louisiana discouraged and ready to abandon the accordion. Fate, however, intervened.[79]

Merle Haggard hired him as his opening act and Sonnier hit the road with the country icon, eventually making his way back to Los Angeles. This time he formed friendships with Albert Lee and Garth Hudson of The Band, who assisted him in obtaining solo shows. Top 10 country hits *Tear Stained Letter* and *No More One More Time,* both on the *Come on Joe* album, thrust him into prominence and allowed him more creativity with his Cajun-based roots.[80] He has also played accordion on albums by Alan Jackson, Neil Diamond, Johnny Cash, Elvis Costello, Emmylou Harris, Hank Williams, Jr., Bob Dylan, and George Jones.[81] Sonnier has written songs for Cash, George Strait, Mel McDaniel, John Anderson, and Jerry Lee Lewis and appeared in the movies *Mask, A Thing Called Love,* and *They All Laughed.*[82]

He was named New Country Artist of the Year by *Performance* magazine in 1987.[83] In 1995, Sonnier was honored as Male Vocalist of the Year by the Cajun French Music Association, and he won Song of the Year for his recording of *La Valse de Chere Bebe.* His 1997 release, *Cajun Pride,* was nominated for a Grammy. In 1999, he was awarded the Male Vocalist of the Year and also had the 1999 Song of the Year for *Here to Stay* at the Golden Music Awards. That same year, he performed on the Grand Ole Opry.[84]

He continues to tour when his schedule permits.

Joe Hall

Born and raised in Eunice, Joe Hall learned accordion from the late Bois Sec Ardoin and drew inspiration from Creole musician Nolton Simien, whom he met in 2005 when Simien was playing at Lafayette's Blue Moon Saloon. With his newly formed band, the Louisiana Cane Cutters, he recorded the 2006 CD *La Danse Finit Pas: Classic Louisiana Creole Music.* The release includes songs that Hall learned by visiting the Archives of Cajun and Creole Folklore at the University of Louisiana-Lafayette. He dedicated the CD to the memory of Freeman Fontenot (1900-1986), a Creole musician from Basile who worked to preserve Creole culture.

Hall and the Louisiana Cane Cutters released their CD *Good Times, Good Music* on May 5, 2007. The CD features on fiddle Blake Miller, who played both fiddle and accordion with the New Pine Grove Boys. Other members of the Louisiana Cane Cutters include Kevin Murphy on guitar, Jay Miller on drums, and Dexter Ardoin on bass.[85]

The Pine Leaf Boys

The Pine Leaf Boys, all youngsters by comparison to many of their industry counterparts, play traditional music from southwest Louisiana, drawing inspiration from Amédé Ardoin to the contemporary Mamou Playboys.[86] Choosing the unaffected name of their group in an effort to focus less on a band name than the music, they sing exclusively in French even though each band member had to learn the language later in life. They often perform with Geno Delafose and the Red Stick Ramblers and were twice nominated for a Grammy in the Best Zydeco or Cajun Music Album category.[87]

BeauSoleil avec Michael Doucet

Garrison Keillor of the radio variety show *A Prairie Home Companion* has called BeauSoleil avec Michael Doucet "the world's greatest Cajun band." While Keillor's qualifications to evaluate Cajun music might be questionable, the band, still pumping out CDs in its fourth decade of existence, does have a Grammy to show for its efforts.[88]

Since its inception in 1975, BeauSoleil avec Michael Doucet has taken the rich traditions of Cajun music and blended it with zydeco, New Orleans jazz, Tex-Mex, country, and blues. Taking its name from Joseph Broussard dit Beausoleil, who organized Acadian resistance to British deportation efforts in Nova Scotia in 1755 then led 193 French exiles to Louisiana, the band includes brothers Michael (fiddle, vocals) and David Doucet (guitar, vocals), Jimmy Breaux (accordion), Billy Ware (percussion), Tommy Alesi (percussion), and Mitchell Reed (bass, fiddle).[89]

BeauSoleil has contributed to the movie soundtracks of *The Big Easy, Passion Fish,* and *Belizaire the Cajun.* The band plays at jazz and folk festivals including the Newport Folk Festival, New Orleans Jazz Fest, and Austin City Limits Music Festival and has appeared on *Late Night with Conan O'Brien, Emeril Live,* and the Grand Ole Opry stage. They regularly visit Keillor's *A Prairie Home Companion* radio show. BeauSoleil has also performed with Mary Chapin Carpenter and the Grateful Dead.

In 2008, BeauSoleil was among several groups and individual artists who performed in a mini-Jazz Fest in England. The event was held in conjunction with the NFL game between the New Orleans Saints and San Diego Chargers.[90]

7

Swamp Pop

Swamp pop is indigenous to south Louisiana and southeast Texas. Drawing from a combination of New Orleans rhythm-and-blues, the rockabilly sounds of northwest Louisiana, and traditional French Louisiana music, swamp pop evolved in the late 1950s and '60s, trading fiddles, accordions, and washboards for keyboards, guitars, and horns—lots of horns. Exemplified by soulful lyrics, piano triplets, pulsating bass lines, brash horn sections, and a dominant R&B backbeat, swamp pop is personified by Cookie and the Cupcakes, Bobby Charles, Warren Storm, Phil Phillips, Rod Bernard, Joe Barry, Johnnie Allan, T.K. Hulin, and Clint West, among others.[1]

Having developed their own sound, swamp pop musicians began showing up in dance halls all over south Louisiana and recording on Floyd Soileau's Jin Records, Eddie Shuler's Goldband, George Khoury's Khoury label, Carol Rachou's La Louisianne, Huey Meaux's Crazy Cajun label, and J.D. Miller's Feature and Excello labels. To disguise their Cajun and black Creole surnames, swamp pop artists often adopted stage names. John Allen Guillot became Johnnie Allan; Robert Charles Guidry dropped his last name in favor of Bobby Charles; Joe Barrios switched to Joe Barry; Warren Schexneider changed to Warren Storm; and Terry Gene DeRouen became Gene Terry. Motivated by the free market, they wanted to sell records to consumers, producers, and disc jockeys who found their ethnic surnames difficult, if not impossible, to pronounce.[2]

237

More than twenty swamp pop songs appeared on the *Billboard* Hot 100. Five songs broke into the top 10 and three reached number 1. Swamp pop's impact can be heard in the Rolling Stones' cover of Barbara Lynn's *You'll Lose a Good Thing* and *Oh Baby (We Got a Good Thing Goin'),* the Honeydrippers' rendition of Phil Phillips' *Sea of Love,* Elvis Presley's remake of Johnny Ace's *Pledging My Love,* Bruce Channel's *Hey, Baby,* and Creedence Clearwater Revival's songs. Paul McCartney wrote *Oh! Darling* to emulate the swamp pop sound. Louisiana audiences elevated Freddy Fender to the status of honorary swamp pop musician because of the genre's influence evident in his hits *Before the Next Teardrop Falls* and *Wasted Days and Wasted Nights.*[3]

Rod Bernard

At age ten, Rod Bernard (August 12, 1940-) talked an automobile dealership into sponsoring a weekly fifteen-

minute show on his Opelousas hometown radio station KSLO. It was an auspicious start for a man who would help establish the swamp pop genre.[4] Within two years, he was a disc jockey at the station but left in 1954 when he and his family moved to Winnie, Texas. There he struck up a friendship with Huey Meaux, the full-time barber, part-time talent agent-recording executive and formed his own band, the Twisters.[5]

In 1958, Bernard and his band recorded *This Should Go on Forever* for

Rod Bernard. (Courtesy of Shane Bernard)

Jin Records in Ville Platte. Meaux took time off from his barbershop duties to take the records around to several Winnie-area radio stations. Some disc jockeys refused to play the record, claiming it was bad song, while others declined because it contained a perceived risqué line: "If it's a sin to really love you/Then a sinner I will be." Meaux pushed the record on his own show on Port Arthur's KPAC and also gave a copy of the record to a Beaumont disc jockey named J.P. Richardson, who later gained fame as the Big Bopper. Richardson not only played the song, but made it his pick of the week.[6]

It took seven months, but by April 1959, Soileau leased the song to Argo Records and *This Should Go on Forever* climbed to the number 20 *Billboard* position. It remained on the charts for twelve weeks. An appearance on *Dick Clark's American Bandstand* followed after Bernard scrubbed the objectionable lyrics.[7]

In 1962, he signed with Hall-Way Records where many of his recordings were backed by Johnny and Edgar Winter. From those sessions came *Colinda* and *Fais Do Do,* two Cajun rock songs performed in a combination of English and Cajun French. Both songs did well in south Louisiana and along the Gulf Coast.[8]

Bernard eventually settled into a sales job at a television station in Lafayette and lives there today. His son, Shane, authored a history of swamp pop music.[9]

Johnnie Allan

John Allen Guillot, a.k.a. Johnnie Allan (March 10, 1938-), has led an interesting odyssey during his decades as a swamp pop pioneer, educator, and historian.[10] Allan earned enough money to purchase his first guitar at the age of eleven and formed the Krazy Kats while still a teenager. In 1958 he teamed with Ville Platte recording executive Floyd Soileau to record *Lonely Days, Lonely Nights.* He followed that with *Letter of Love.*

During that time, he was attending the University of

Johnnie Allan. (Courtesy of Louisiana Music Hall of Fame)

Southwestern Louisiana in Lafayette (now the University of Louisiana-Lafayette). In 1961 he began his teaching career only to be called into active duty in the National Guard for the Berlin Crisis six weeks later. Upon his return, he learned that another song he and the Krazy Kats had recorded, *Your Picture,* was playing well on local radio stations and that *Lonely Days, Lonely Nights* almost cracked the national charts.[11]

A two-year hiatus from music between 1967 and 1969 allowed Allan to obtain his master's degree in education and he returned to teaching.[12] In 1970, he reunited with the Krazy Kats and in 1974, they recorded an old Chuck Berry hit, *Promised Land,* with Soileau. A huge hit in the U.K., it was overshadowed by Elvis Presley's release of the song six weeks later. He took early retirement from teaching and launched his third career—that of compiling photographs to document the history of south Louisiana music. Volume I of *Memories, a Pictorial History of South Louisiana Music, 1920s-1980s* was published in 1988 and Volumes I and II were published in combined form in 1995 by Omnibus Press.[13]

Warren Storm

Born Warren Schexneider in Abbeville, Warren Storm (February 18, 1937-) started his professional career when he filled in at age twelve for his father, a drummer in the Rayne-Bo Ramblers, a Cajun band that drew its name from its home town of Rayne, Louisiana.[14] He was one of the most sought-after session drummers in south Louisiana even before he recorded *Prisoner's Song* as his first single in 1958. The record sold a quarter-million copies and soon became the prototype swamp pop song.[15]

In 1962, Storm teamed with fellow swamp poppers Rod Bernard and Skip Stewart to form the Shondells (not to be confused with Tommy James and the Shondells or singer Troy Shondell) while continuing to record as a solo artist. He recorded *Lord, I Need Somebody Bad Tonight* and *My House of Memories.* He formed the Cypress Band in 1980 with saxophonist Willie Tee Trahan.[16]

Willie Tee Trahan

Collaboration with Warren Storm is just one of the career highlights for Willie Tee Trahan (March 1, 1944-) who, after more than thirty-five years of performing, is still considered one of south Louisiana's most respected musicians. Born in Lafayette to sharecropper parents, he played his first professional gig in 1958 at St. Anthony's Hall in Lafayette at age fourteen. That same year his father cosigned a loan for a Sears and Roebuck saxophone and in 1959, with Kenny Tibbs on vocals, he cut his first record, *I Promise,* at J.D. Miller's studio in Crowley under the name Willie and the Jokers. The record sold more than eleven thousand copies locally. The band followed up with *They Played Our Song Last Night,* written by Abbeville native Bobby Charles Guidry.

From 1965 to 1969, he played with the Fabulous Boogie Kings, which he has described as the best R&B band he ever played with. He played baritone saxophone on the band's album *Live at the Purple Peacock,* Tommy McLain's *Sweet*

Dreams, Clint West's *Big Blue Diamonds,* and Charles Mann's *Red Red Wine.*

He joined Tommy McLain's band, the National Soul Revue, in 1969 for two years and rejoined McLain and his Mule Train Band in 1974. The band happened to be playing at a hotel lounge in Lafayette at the same time Warner Bros. was filming the Paul Newman movie *The Drowning Pool.* Movie executives caught his act and signed him to sing Fats Domino's *Margie* in the movie.

In 1976, he recorded his first solo single, a cover of Chris Kenner's *Sick and Tired,* on Huey Meaux's Crazy Cajun label. That same year the Mule Train Band joined Freddy Fender on a two-week tour of Canada. Willie Tee joined Warren Storm to form the Cypress band in 1980, and they had their own weekly half-hour TV show from 1981-1983. His second single, an instrumental cover of Freddy Fender's *Before the Next Teardrop Falls,* was recorded in 1982. In 1985, he teamed up with Rockin' Sidney and Creedence Clearwater Revival lead singer John Fogerty for a remake of *My Toot Toot,* which was featured on Fogerty's hour-long Showtime special.

Trahan reunited with the Fabulous Boogie Kings in 1994, and in 1995 the band recorded *Swamp Boogie Blues.* Guest vocalists on the album include Rod Bernard, Johnnie Allan, Tommy McLain, Warren Storm, Wayne Toups, Cookie and the Cupcakes, and Dale and Grace. In 1998, he joined T.K. Hulin and Smoke. Willie Tee is also featured on *Louisiana Legends,* a CD produced by Paul Marx, owner of KBON radio station, which plays Louisiana swamp pop music almost exclusively. He also performs with Warren Storm and Cypress.[17]

Jivin' Gene Bourgeois

Huey Meaux attributed the first hit he produced to his idea of placing Jivin' Gene Bourgeois (February 9, 1940-) in the bathroom "surrounded by porcelain" to create a reverb effect. Born Gene Bourgeois in Port Arthur, Texas, the singer was given the name Jivin' Gene by Meaux. Bourgeois wrote and recorded *Breaking Up Is Hard to Do,* a classic swamp pop song, not to be confused with Neil Sedaka's 1962 pop song of the same name.[18]

A Port Arthur refinery worker, he walked into Meaux's barbershop/office in jeans, bare feet, and horn-rimmed glasses and announced he wanted Meaux to record his band. The ensuing session—recorded in mono on an old Magnecord—was held in the KPAC radio station studios in Port Arthur where Meaux worked part-time. Bourgeois had to sing in the corner of the studio over a toilet to achieve the sound Meaux wanted. The recording executive said he thought he would have to place the drums in the street because they were so loud. He sent the demo tape to Floyd Soileau in Ville Platte, who suggested recording under better conditions. A second session was booked at J.D. Miller's studio in Crowley and the song was leased to Mercury Records.[19]

The song climbed to number 69 and though Bourgeois never had another national hit, *Breaking Up* secured his place in swamp pop lore as certainly as *Mathilda* did for Cookie and the Cupcakes. Every swamp pop band is required to include those two songs in its repertoire if it expects to be taken seriously.[20]

Cookie and the Cupcakes

There are several songs that would qualify as the official anthem of swamp pop music, but none is more qualified than *Mathilda* by Cookie and the Cupcakes. Fronted by Hugh "Cookie" Thierry (August 16, 1936-September 23, 1997), the band was one of the first racially integrated rock and roll bands in Louisiana.

Mathilda rode the charts for fifteen weeks in early 1959, cresting at number 47 and quickly becoming the requisite song for every club band in Louisiana and east Texas.[21] Beginning at the Moulin Rouge Club in Lake Charles in 1953, the band succeeded in blending Cajun music with traditional rock and roll to create the hybrid that became swamp pop.

The song's success led the band to tour as the opening act for Jerry Lee Lewis and Fats Domino, but the group generally limited its work to the Louisiana-Texas area.

Cookie and the Cupcakes approached several record labels with *Mathilda* as early as 1957. George Khoury finally released the song on his Khoury label, selling thousands of copies before leasing it to Judd Phillips, brother of Sun Records owner Sam Phillips, for national distribution. *Mathilda* was followed by *Belinda,* indistinguishable from *Mathilda* except for the lyrics.[22] The band founds its way into the top 100 again with *Got You on My Mind,* which spent four weeks on the charts, reaching number 94 in May of 1963.[23]

Not everything came easy to the band or to Thierry, a black Creole of mixed-race ancestry. He sang Creole music as a child but never performed the genre in public. His early idols were Fats Domino and Hank Williams, Sr., a bridge that effectively defined swamp pop. He began his musical career in 1952 when, at the age of sixteen, he escorted his two sisters to a dance at the all-black Horseshoe Club in Lake Charles. The Boogie Ramblers, with Ernest Jacobs on trumpet and piano, Shelton Dunaway on tenor saxophone, and Marshall LeDee on electric guitar, were performing Fats Domino's *The Fat Man.* The vocalist, who was not a regular band member, was singing in the wrong key. Thierry insisted he could sing the song better and finally the drummer invited him onstage. The crowd—and the band—loved his singing and Thierry was hooked.

Bandleader Jacobs would not promote Cookie to lead singer, however, relegating him to the lowly status of stagehand. As he learned more songs, he was eventually given more opportunities to perform. By 1956, he had worked his way up to lead singer, and the band eventually changed its name to Cookie and the Cupcakes.

About the same time that the new name was adopted, Thierry discovered the song that would become the swamp pop national anthem. Thierry claimed the original lyrics to *Mathilda* were "But still I cried and cried for you," but saxophonist Dunaway said it sounded like Cookie was singing "Mathilda" instead of "But still I." They took the song to Goldband Records owner Eddie Shuler, who turned it down. Thierry continued taking the song to different producers, but everyone turned them down until George Khoury of Lake Charles arranged for them to get an acceptable version of the song on tape at the KAOK radio studios in Lake Charles.[24]

The station had a single-track recorder and a single microphone and the musicians were required to stand directly in front of it for *Mathilda.* When the group later recorded *Got You on My Mind,* everyone was in a separate room wearing earphones so that each member of the band could hear the other players and singers.[25]

Despite the band's popularity around south Louisiana, there was the constant threat of trouble because Thierry had a voracious appetite for white Cajun ladies, who in turn were attracted to him in an era when race mixing was taboo. There were times when the band needed sheriffs' escorts as they traveled into and out of several south Louisiana parishes for performances. The racial tensions continued and finally contributed to Cookie's sudden disappearance in August 1965. Rumors abounded of Thierry's death; some reports had him crippled in an auto accident. Finally, in 1992, Cupcakes pianist Ernest Jacobs traveled to California and found him working in a car wash in South Central Los Angeles. Twenty-seven years after his unexplained disappearance, Cookie returned with Jacobs to Louisiana and the Cupcakes were reunited. Joining him were original saxophonist Dunaway and guitarist LeDee. The band continues to play in southwest Louisiana and southeast Texas but without Thierry, who died in Lake Charles in 1997.[26]

Lil' Alfred Babineaux

Alfred Babineaux (January 5, 1944-), known professionally as "Lil' Alfred," was only sixteen and had to obtain his parents' permission before he could record *Walking Down the Aisle* for George Khoury's Lake Charles label. The song was a regional hit and prompted Shreveport's Stan Lewis to pick it up for national distribution.

As a teenager, Lil' Alfred was often accompanied by his parents to venues because they disapproved of his performing in clubs without adult supervision. After his first hit, he began using Cookie and the Cupcakes as his studio band. Then, in 1964, after Cookie (Hugh Thierry) mysteriously disappeared, he replaced the missing singer as lead vocalist for the Cupcakes. He also performed with the Fabulous Boogie Kings.

Cookie and the Cupcakes and the Fabulous Boogie Kings were among the first racially mixed bands in Louisiana. According to Lil' Alfred, there was less commotion about the issue than people might think. "If you entertain long enough in south Louisiana, you play with everybody sooner or later," he has been quoted as saying.[27]

Phil Phillips

Born John Phillip Baptiste in Lake Charles, Louisiana, Phil Phillips (March 14, 1926-) had only one hit. *Sea of Love* crested at number 1 on the R&B charts and number 2 on the *Billboard* Hot 100, remaining on the charts for eighteen weeks in 1959.[28] Contractual disputes stymied his career, but the song lived on, selling two million copies and earning Phillips a gold record. Moreover, the song has appeared in the soundtracks of half a dozen movies, including the Al Pacino Universal Pictures film *Sea of Love*.[29]

Phillips, who still resides in Jennings, Louisiana, began his musical career as a vocalist for the Gateway Quartet while working as a bellhop in Lake Charles.[30] He composed *Sea of Love* for a girlfriend during this period. Confounded by how to prove his affection, he was sitting on her porch with his guitar thinking, "If I could just take her out on a sea of love I could convince her—just her and me with all that water."

The song was arranged and produced by Goldband

Phil Phillips received a standing ovation from an appreciative crowd at the Louisiana Music Hall of Fame induction ceremonies in 2007 when he sang his popular hit Sea of Love. *(Courtesy of Louisiana Music Hall of Fame)*

Records owner Eddie Shuler for friend George Khoury's label. Shuler knew the song was a hit the first time he heard it. Khoury brought Phillips into his studio on February 23, 1959, for an audition but Shuler rejected Khoury's offer of a fifty-fifty deal, with Shuler doing the production and paying for a recording session and the subsequent release. Shuler said later he wished he had taken Khoury up on the offer. They finally agreed that Shuler would arrange and produce the song in exchange for publishing rights.[31]

They took their time with the arrangement, building up the vocal group and trying out different musicians. After three months they felt they were ready.[32] Cookie and the

Cupcakes, fresh off their own hit *Mathilda,* were called in to provide the swirling backup for the session. Finally, the record was released on Khoury Records, but it wasn't an immediate hit.[33]

When it was first released, many disc jockeys tossed the record into the trash. A disc jockey in Baton Rouge, however, played *Sea of Love* and listeners began to request it over and over.[34] Suddenly, the public was demanding the song and disc jockeys were Dumpster diving to retrieve the record even as Khoury negotiated a distribution deal with Mercury Records. Mercury leased the song and signed Phillips to a contract, but after a year or so, Mercury and Khoury got into a legal dispute, catching Phillips in the middle, unable to get out of his five-year contract. The dispute effectively killed his recording career.

The song was covered by Del Shannon in 1982. His version climbed to number 33 on the pop charts. In 1984, the Honeydrippers recorded *Sea of Love,* and it reached number 3, spending fourteen weeks in the top 40.[35] Because Phillips wrote the song, he receives royalties not only from his own version, but also from movie soundtracks and cover versions.

Phillips eventually became a disc jockey at KJEF in Jennings. In the late 1960s, he attempted a recording comeback in Muscle Shoals. The Fame Studio magic didn't work for Phillips, however, so *Sea of Love* remains his musical legacy. He rarely performs in public, though he did perform at the 2003 and 2005 Ponderosa Stomps in New Orleans. In October of 2007, at the age of eighty-one, he brought an appreciative crowd to its feet when he reprised the song at his induction into the Louisiana Music Hall of Fame in Baton Rouge.[36]

Joe Barry

His professional recording career spanned only eleven years and two appearances on the *Billboard* Hot 100. But swamp rocker Joe Barry (July 13, 1939-August 31, 2004), born Joseph Barrios in the Lafourche Parish town of Cutoff, was a major contributor to swamp pop music.[37]

Rolling Stone described him as a "Cajun Fats Domino."[38] Growing up deep in Cajun country, he listened to both black gospel and Cajun music, thinking there must be a way to combine the two. When he heard Ray Charles sing *Come Back Baby,* he knew the two distinctly different genres were indeed compatible. Barry released his first recording in 1956, *Greatest Moment of My Life,* which created a few regional sales.[39] In 1961, he broke out with *I'm a Fool to Care,* a slow, melancholy ballad recorded for Jin Records. Most listeners unfamiliar with the song took the voice, piano, and orchestra for those of Fats Domino. That may be because the song was recorded in Cosimo Matassa's J&M Studio where Fats recorded many of his hits.[40]

Barry recorded in New Orleans because it was closer to Cutoff than Floyd Soileau's Jin Records studio in Ville Platte. *I'm a Fool to Care* was intended as the "B" side for *I Got a Feeling.*[41] When Soileau, who was eager to record Barry because he thought he sounded like Ray Charles, heard *I Got a Feeling,* he was disappointed. But once he heard *I'm a Fool to Care,* he realized he had lost Ray Charles but gained something just as good—a Fats Domino clone.[42]

Once it was released, disc jockey Bobby Van of WSMN in New Orleans pushed the song on his show until other stations picked it up and it soon was the number 1 song in the city.[43] As the song gained popularity, Soileau, lacking the financial resources for national distribution, turned to Huey Meaux, who leased the song to Smash Records, a subsidiary of Mercury.[44] It remained on the Top 40 charts for twelve weeks, peaking at number 24 and selling over a million copies. It also debuted on the U.K. chart, reaching number 49. Barry followed that success with *Teardrops in My Heart* just two months later, and it reached number 63.

Barry left Smash Records for the Princess label and played frequently at Papa Joe's strip club in New Orleans and the Esquire Ballroom in Houston. According to Barry, crowds would boo the strippers because they wanted to hear the music. In 1965, Freddy Fender, just released from Angola State Penitentiary, joined Barry's band.[45]

In 1960, Barry discovered a young female vocalist and brought her to the attention of Meaux, who arranged a recording session for Barbara Lynn Ozen. She dropped her last name on the recording *You'll Lose a Good Thing*.

Barry, convinced he was defrauded of royalties, left the music business in 1967. Despite serious health problems, he made a comeback over three decades later when he completed the *Been Down That Muddy Road* album in 2003. He died of multiple medical problems the following year.[46]

Fabulous Boogie Kings

The Boogie Kings, a.k.a. the Fabulous Boogie Kings, began as a trio of white kids who played only black music in the mid-1950s in Eunice, Louisiana. No one knew then that the band would endure despite changes in members, evolving musical tastes, internal turmoil, and lawsuits. But as the new millennium dawned they were still rocking, bigger than ever. From the beginning the band built a loyal following throughout southwest Louisiana and the Texas Golden Triangle area.[47]

Band members comprised an honor roll of Louisiana swamp pop, some of whom had major hits as solo artists: Bert Miller, Tommy McLain, Clint West, G.G. Shinn, Ned Theall, Dwayne Yates, Jerry LaCroix, Linda Clark, Norris Badeaux, Mike Pollard, Murphy Buford, Dan Silas, Jon R. Smith, and Doug Ardoin. Originally comprised of Bert and Harris Miller and Douglas Ardoin, the Boogie Kings' ranks swelled at one point to twelve members.[48]

Although the band had never played outside Acadiana, at the group's inception each original member purchased seven different tuxedos—one for each day of the week—and began seeking bookings in Houston and New Orleans. While they were packing the houses in those two markets, they

The Fabulous Boogie Kings, led by Ned Theall, far right. Theall discovered Edgar Winter during a Boogie Kings performance in Beaumont, Texas.

were booked into Reno, Lake Tahoe, Las Vegas, Hollywood, and San Francisco.[49]

Once, the band was booked into Ball's Auditorium in Houston before an all-black audience. B.B. King played the first show and stayed around as part of a packed house to hear the Boogie Kings. After the band had played a few songs, auditorium owner Reginald Ball came onstage to inform the band that King wanted to join them for a few songs. When King returned to the stage, pandemonium reigned. The more enthusiastic the crowd got, the better the band played, and the better the band played, the more enthusiastic the crowd became. Afterwards, King told them they were the blackest band he had ever heard.[50]

Drugs, pills, booze, and women took their toll on the band, which had Clint West as its ex-officio leader after the release of its initial album, *Clint West and the Boogie Kings.* However, West, experiencing marital problems, was missing occasional gigs much to the growing consternation of other band members.[51] One night the band was booked into the Continental Club in Beaumont and West did not show. Ned Theall was sitting on the organ bench at nine o'clock cursing the fact that there was no drummer and, consequently, no show, when an albino kid walked up and asked, "What's wrong?" Theall tried to brush the boy away, but the youth was persistent, so Theall explained the band's predicament. "I can cut the gig," the kid said.

"I told him he was too young to understand the band's music," Theall explains. "But he just repeated, 'I can cut the gig.'" When he asked the boy how long he had been playing drums, the boy responded that he was a trumpet player. Theall, intrigued at confidence bordering on cockiness, asked him his name. "Edgar Winter."

Theall told him he had one shot and if he proved good enough, he could play the show. He sensed that Winter was capable; the difficulty lay in convincing skeptical band members. The young man aced the test on the first song and stayed on, never missing a beat all night.[52]

Band members grew increasingly disenchanted with West's leadership. In 1964, the Moulin Rouge Club offered Clint a partnership with the club. At the time, the band was the house band for the Bamboo Club so a vote was taken. West had to reject the Moulin Rouge offer and return to the Bamboo or leave the band. Theall gave him the news right after a New Year's Eve show, and West left. A protracted legal fight over the Boogie Kings' name ensued with Theall eventually winning. West signed with Swallow Records in Ville Platte while the remainder of the band went with Montel Records in Baton Rouge. And a half-century later, the band plays on.[53]

Tommy McLain

Tommy McLain (March 15, 1940-) had a bigger hit with *Sweet Dreams* than did Patsy Cline. Her version climbed to number 44 in June 1963 while McLain's went to number 15 in August 1966, selling more than three million copies (McLain claims it was ten million) and earning him a gold record. He also racked up scores of state, national, and international awards. His version was featured in the Paul Newman-Joanne

Tommy McLain sings Sweet Dreams *just prior to his induction into the Louisiana Music Hall of Fame during ceremonies in Baton Rouge in 2007. (Courtesy of Louisiana Music Hall of Fame)*

Woodward movie *The Drowning Pool,* filmed in Lafayette.[54]

McLain, born in Jonesville, Louisiana, formed his own band while still in high school and later worked as a disc jockey at Oakdale radio station KREH. Despite its success, McLain's song almost never made it beyond a self-promoted hometown hit.[55]

Floyd Soileau ran Floyd's Record Shop in Ville Platte, Louisiana, and also owned a recording studio as well as the Swallow record label. He sold records wholesale to a shop in Alexandria, about fifty miles north of Ville Platte. The record shop owner told Soileau about a young man who had recorded a song on his own that was selling briskly in central Louisiana. After hearing the poorly done record, he attempted to reach McLain, but the phone numbers given to him were incorrect and he was unable to locate the singer.[56]

Swamp pop had been in a state of steady decline since the arrival of the Beatles, the Stones, and the Animals, but Soileau stayed the course in trying to promote south

Louisiana musical talent. One of those groups was the remnants of the Boogie Kings, led by Clint West. When West came in for a scheduled recording, Soileau learned that the band's new bass player was McLain. Soileau immediately told McLain he had been looking for him to redo the song. With West and his band, McLain recorded *Sweet Dreams,* backed with *I Need You So.*

Despite his initial enthusiasm over the song, Soileau did not like the new recording and delayed releasing it for several months. "It was something with the sound or the multiple voices, but I just didn't like it," he has said. Soon after the song's release, the proprietor of a local bordello purchased the record. A few weeks after including *Sweet Dreams* on his establishment's jukebox, he told Soileau, "The women play it over and over and they know what's going to sell in a record." Thus did *Sweet Dreams,* like Joe Barry's *I'm a Fool to Care,* become a certified whorehouse hit.[57]

As the song gained momentum, Soileau called old friend Huey Meaux, by now relocated to Houston, for assistance. As sales continued to climb for *Sweet Dreams,* publishers Acuff-Rose rushed Roy Orbison into the studio to do the song. That was enough to encourage more aggressive promotion of McLain's record, which was released on MSL, for Meaux, Soileau, and Lipsius. MSL retained southern regional rights, while Jamie Records obtained U.S. and world rights.[58]

McLain toured with Dick Clark's Caravan of Stars and appeared on Clark's variety show *Where the Action Is,* performing with Tommy James and the Shondells, the Yardbirds, Paul Revere and the Raiders, and Jimmy Page. He was inducted into the Swedish Rock and Roll Hall of Fame and into the Louisiana Music Hall of Fame.[59]

McLain later recorded Abbeville native Bobby Charles' composition *Before I Grow Too Old* and teamed with Clint West to record *Try to Find Another Man,* but he never was able to equal the success of *Sweet Dreams.*

G.G. Shinn

G.G. Shinn (August 25, 1939-) has been an integral part of the swamp pop scene for many years. Although he has cut back on public appearances, he still performs around Baton Rouge. He operates his own club, GG's in Alexandria, Louisiana.

G.G. performed with the Fabulous Boogie Kings from 1963 to 1966. In 1966 he formed his own band, the Rollercoasters, with whom he recorded two R&B albums. In Los Angeles, he recorded the album *Chase* with Bill Chase and his band. The album was nominated for a Grammy in 1971. He also toured with Chase and performed with the Fabulous Chicken Hawks before teaming up with Joe Stampley and the late John Fred in 1997 to form the Louisiana Boys.[60]

Swamp pop veteran performer G.G. Shinn. (Courtesy of Louisiana Music Hall of Fame)

T.K. Hulin

It is rare that an original version of a swamp pop song cannot be found at Floyd's Record Shop in Ville Platte, but in the case of the 1963 recording of *I'm Not a Fool Anymore* by T.K. Hulin (August 16, 1943-) a search of Floyd's shop came up empty. The song, nevertheless, still stands as a classic swamp ballad.

Hulin, known as "the voice with a tear," began his singing career at age fourteen when he recorded *Many Lonely Nights* in St. Martinville. When he was seventeen, he put together a twelve-piece band, the Lonely Knights.[61] One of the band members was Edgar Winter of Beaumont, Texas. Winter, who drove to St. Martinville on weekends and stayed in Hulin's home, once described Hulin as a "soulful entertainer, much like Otis Redding, with a whole lot of drive and funk."[62]

In August of 1963, *I'm Not a Fool Anymore* was released on LK Records, a label owned by Hulin's father and local songwriter Robert Thibodeaux. The song cracked the Hot 100 at number 92. Though it remained on the charts only two weeks, it sold five hundred thousand copies, thanks to the promotional efforts of Huey Meaux, who negotiated a distribution deal with Smash Records. Sales were sufficient to secure Hulin a spot on a tour with Bobby "Blue" Bland, Jerry Lee Lewis, B.J. Thomas, and the Everly Brothers. He followed *I'm Not a Fool Anymore* with *As You Pass Me By on Graduation Night, I'm Ashamed Enough to Die,* and a cover of Eddy Raven's *Alligator Bayou.*[63]

Asked if he still keeps in touch with Winter, Hulin shakes his head. "You know, we used to stay in touch but awhile back, I called him to see if he would like to perform in a reunion concert," he says. "I got a call back from his manager who told me the price would be ten thousand dollars. Well, first of all, I called Edgar, not his manager, so I just told him to forget it."[64]

Roy Head

Huey Meaux had a direct hand in guiding the careers of four rock and roll stars, beginning with Barbara Lynn in 1962 and capping off his career with Freddy Fender in 1975. Sandwiched between those two were the Sir Douglas Quintet with *She's about a Mover* and Roy Head and his *Treat Her Right.* Head (September 1, 1941-), like the other three Meaux artists, was a native of south Texas.[65] The driving horns and pulsating beat make *Treat Her Right* unmistakable from its first notes. It remained on the *Billboard* Hot 100 for eleven weeks, eight of those at number 2, and also made the R&B charts for fourteen weeks. Subsequent to its tenure on the charts, *Treat Her Right* took on a life of its own in TV commercials and in the Leonardo DiCaprio movie *Catch Me if You Can.*[66]

Head wrote the song in high school with Gene Kurtz, a bass player for the Traits, a band Head started in the late 1950s when he was sixteen. The Traits' first single, *One More Time*, received airplay on Gordon McClendon's chain of radio stations strewn across the Texas landscape: KILT in Houston, KTSA in San Antonio, and KLIF in Dallas. Head and his band were booked on tours with Roy Orbison, Eddie Cochran, Jerry Lee Lewis, Bobby "Blue" Bland, and B.B. King. In 1963, Head and the Traits made an appearance in Houston where they were brought to the attention of Meaux. Before long, Head and the Traits were ushered into the Gold Star Studio in Houston to record *Treat Her Right*.[67]

The only white artist on Don Robey's Peacock label, Head played for a convention of black disc jockeys in Houston. Soon *Treat Her Right* was being played on every black radio station in the U.S. The song battled the Beatles' *Help!* for the number 1 spot on the charts. *Help!* won out in the end, but that did little to diminish the impact of *Treat Her Right*, which sold over a million copies and earned Head a gold record.[68] It was as much his dance moves as his music, however, that drew crowds wherever he went. Copied from Joe Tex and Jackie Wilson, his steps were so good that James Brown booted Head off the Godfather of Soul's tour.[69]

When Meaux went to prison after his conviction for transporting a teenage girl across state lines, ostensibly for a record showcase, Head found himself without a band, producer, or record label. He made a brief comeback in 1977 as a country artist and had a major hit with a cover of Rod Stewart's *Tonight's the Night* on ABC Records. Other hits followed, but out of principle, he rejected a four-million-dollar recording contract and a twenty-five-thousand-dollar signing bonus when he saw what he perceived to be the initial signs of the creeping corporate takeover of music.[70]

Freddy Fender
It might seem curious to include a Tex-Mex singer in a work about Louisiana stars, but after Freddy Fender (June

4, 1937-October 14, 2006) spent three years in Angola State Penitentiary, scored a *Billboard* number 1 hit, and then decided to become a permanent resident of Louisiana, it would be difficult—and unfair—to exclude him.

Born Baldemar Huerta in the Texas Rio Grande town of San Benito, he grew up in a barrio that he described as differing from a ghetto only in that it was a poor Hispanic neighborhood.[71] His blues background stems from when he worked alongside blacks as a migrant farm worker during picking season. He was convinced that many of those black workers were good enough to have sung professionally. After a three-year stint with the Marines, he returned to San Benito, where he started his recording career. In 1957, he released *No Seas Cruel* (*Don't Be Cruel*) on Falcon Records. The record was distributed by Peerless Records of McAllen, Texas. It climbed to number 1 in Mexico and South America, giving birth to Hispanic rock and roll.[72]

In an attempt to broaden his appeal with the gringo audience, he adopted the name Freddy Fender in 1959, but in 1960 he was arrested in Baton Rouge for possession of two marijuana joints. Fender was sentenced to five years at Angola. While imprisoned, he cut three records for the Goldband label of Lake Charles. In 1963, he was released by Gov. Jimmie Davis. A provision of his parole stipulated that he not involve himself in the music business for a period, so he again returned to San Benito, where he worked as an auto mechanic. During this time, he also went back to school and majored in sociology at Del Mar College.

After his parole and while living in Corpus Christi, he met recording executive Huey P. Meaux. Meaux owned the Houston-based Sugar Hill Recording Studio and the Crazy Cajun record label. Impressed with Fender's music, Meaux insisted that he record *Before the Next Teardrop Falls*. Released in 1975, it soared to the number 1 position on both the pop and country charts, making it the first time in history that an artist's initial single reached number 1 on both charts. It remained on the pop chart for twenty-one weeks, reaping Fender a gold record in the process.[73]

His next release, *Wasted Days and Wasted Nights,* was originally recorded for Imperial Records but released on Dot. Again, it topped the country charts. It reached number 8 on the pop charts in September 1975, earning him his second consecutive gold record. That was followed by *Since I Met You Baby* in November of that same year. Fender's personal favorite, it reached number 45 on the pop charts. *Secret Love,* released in December of 1975, climbed to number 20.[74] In April 1976, Fender did a remake of *You'll Lose a Good Thing,* which climbed to number 32 on the pop charts. Between 1975 and 1977, nine of his songs placed in the top 10 on the country charts. His spate of hits was enough to gain him recognition as Most Promising Male Vocalist by the Academy of Country Music, and the Country Music Association named *Before the Next Teardrop Falls* its Single of the Year.[75]

Thanks to chart successes, Fender, in his own words, had "enough money to get into the heavy stuff, like cocaine," though drinking remained his vice of choice. Making matters worse, he got into a running battle with Meaux over money. The dispute, he said, left him owing the IRS sixty thousand dollars.

Music industry honchos approached Fender in 1989 to team him up with three other Texans, Doug Sahm, Flaco Jimenez, and Augie Meyers, to form the Texas Tornados. The trio released three albums between 1990 and 1992. The releases met with such critical acclaim that the group embarked on sold-out tours in South America, Europe, and the U.S.[76]

Fender settled on the northshore of Lake Pontchartrain in Slidell, Louisiana. He received a kidney from his daughter in 2002 and a liver transplant in 2004. He also suffered from diabetes and hepatitis C. In late August 2005, he was forced to flee the onslaught of Hurricane Katrina and relocated with his family to Corpus Christi, Texas.[77]

Fender, who won his third Grammy in 2002, was diagnosed with terminal cancer in late 2005. He was scheduled for surgery in January of 2006 to remove the upper left lobe of his lung, but when surgeons found two large tumors, it was decided to leave the lobe intact. Chemotherapy treatment was then stopped because of side effects. A subsequent scan found two more tumors and he resumed chemotherapy treatments of lower dosages. Fender died in October in his Corpus Christi home with his family at his bedside.[78]

Lucinda Williams

Born in Lake Charles, Lucinda Williams (January 26, 1953-) found time to crank out some folk songs during a brief stay in New Orleans before beginning an odyssey at age twenty-one that took her to Austin, Texas, New York, and Jackson, Mississippi, where she recorded her first album at Malaco studios. Released in 1979, *Ramblin'* featured traditional blues, country, folk, and Cajun selections.[79]

In 1998, her album *Car Wheels on a Gravel Road* featured a rock sound with strong country and blues influences. It won a Grammy for Best Contemporary Folk Album and won *The Village Voice* "Pazz & Jop survey."[80]

8

The Louisiana Hayride

Shreveport's *Louisiana Hayride* was instrumental in transforming traditional country music into rockabilly. Several factors conspired to help the *Hayride* succeed. From 1948-1952, cities were restricted to a single television station by federal law, thus limiting entertainment options. The *Hayride's* flagship station, 50,000-watt, clear-channel KWKH, beamed broadcasts into twenty-eight states. CBS Radio aired delayed broadcasts on Saturday nights. The *Hayride* got another boost when KWKH sister station KTHS of Little Rock, Arkansas, also a 50,000-watt, clear-channel station, broadcast the *Hayride* live, giving the show an even larger audience. In 1954, the Armed Forces Network started airing thirty-minute segments of *Hayride,* bringing the radio series to overseas listeners.

Gaggles of singers and pickers responded to the siren song that was the *Louisiana Hayride.* Collectively, they transformed the venue into a rockabilly mecca. Two singers in particular—a frail, nasal balladeer from Alabama and a self-conscious teenager from Memphis who billed himself as the "Hillbilly Cat"—did more to validate the show as a major player in the live entertainment field than any other artists. But while the impact of Hank Williams and Elvis Presley remains indisputable, there were other contributors.

As the 1950s moved into the 1960s and television began to assert itself as the center of family activity, stars like Jack Benny and Bob Hope moved from radio to television.

The popular radio show *Gunsmoke* followed suit. The trend forced radio to move away from live programming in favor of pre-recorded music, and the *Louisiana Hayride* was no longer as important to aspiring stars as it once was. Television was now the vehicle that gave them their national exposure, as evidenced by the appearances of Elvis and the Beatles on the *Ed Sullivan Show* and Jerry Lee Lewis on the *Steve Allen Show. American Bandstand* and *Shindig!* also accelerated the exodus to the new medium. By the mid-1960s, the *Hayride* was surviving on past momentum and reputation. By the '70s, it had virtually ceased to exist, its glory relegated to a bygone era.[1]

In 1975, Dave Kent, who had had no previous role in the music industry, approached KWKH to purchase the *Hayride* name. He was informed that the name was never registered and since the station had no intention of using the name again, he was welcome to it.[2] Even more unbelievable than the fact that the station had never trademarked its star program's name were the slipshod methods employed in preserving the history of this important show. About the same time that Kent was reviving the original *Louisiana Hayride,* KWKH was preparing to move from its longtime Texas Street home in downtown Shreveport to a new location on I-20. Movers boxed up some things and threw away others. Station management asked Kent if he wanted an old box of reel-to-reel tapes of shows. Son Joey Kent was sent to pick up the tapes and while he was there, he was asked to help move a desk. When the desk was moved, a tape reel wedged between it and the wall fell and started unwinding across the floor. Joey Kent stopped it with his foot and noticed it had Elvis Presley's name on it. When he and his father listened to it, it turned out to be a recording of Elvis's *Hayride* debut.

Station engineers occasionally recorded segments to document that sponsors were getting the promotions they paid for. Elvis made only one product endorsement his entire career, a live *Hayride* ad for Southern Maid Doughnuts on November 6, 1954:

> You can get 'em piping hot after 4 P.M.,
> You can get 'em piping hot.
> Southern Maid Doughnuts hit the spot;
> You can get 'em piping hot after 4 P.M.

Typically, the engineer on duty picked a tape at random and placed it on the recorder. After turning it on, the engineer would go about his business and allow the tape to run through that segment of the program in order to catch the commercial. That's how the majority of about six hundred song recordings owned by Kent were captured. The Presley tape began recording about ten minutes before Elvis came out on stage and runs out about twenty minutes after he finished. Kent also has a tape of Johnny Cash doing a live Southern Maid Doughnut commercial from the *Hayride* stage.[3]

The *Hayride* studio was important not only for its broadcasts of musical performances, it also provided a location for many musicians of the day to cut tapes of new songs. Dale Hawkins recorded *Suzy-Q* in the KWKH studios after the station went off the air. In fact, many of the *Hayride* stars recorded some of their biggest hits that same way. The Saturday broadcast ended around 11:30 or midnight, and the station would sign off at 1:00 A.M., with programming not resuming until 5:00 on Sunday morning. That left four hours that the studio was not in use. Hank Williams, Slim Whitman, Jim Reeves, and others would adjourn to the station's studios. Inexplicably discarded during the station's move was documentation of recording sessions held by Jim Reeves in the studio.[4] Many Hank Williams recordings survive only because the singer had a regular morning show on KWKH and often recorded shows in advance so that he could go on the road to perform. When Williams died on New Year's Day, 1953, a station disc jockey named Ray Bartlett retrieved the tapes and sold them to Leonard Chess of Chess Records. Chess in turn, sold them to Hank's record label, MGM. Bartlett, for his part, was fired.

Shreveport's Municipal Auditorium, longtime home of the Louisiana Hayride.

Hayride recordings of Elvis Presley and Johnny Cash have been compiled by Kent, and CDs of those performances are readily available today, a half-century after they were performed live in the stately old Municipal Auditorium. The CDs, while not the best in terms of audio quality, nonetheless provide a refreshing bridge between the *Hayride's* glory days and today. In a sense, though, the *Hayride* never really went away. Statues of Elvis and James Burton stand silent watch in front of the auditorium. Inside, posters and publicity photos of Hank Williams, Elvis, Johnny Cash, Johnny Horton, Merle Kilgore, Webb Pierce, Kitty Wells, Jim Reeves, George Jones, Doug Kershaw, Gene Autry, and scores of others can still be viewed by the touring public in the spacious foyer and along the hallowed halls along both sides of the auditorium. If you listen carefully, you just might hear the faint echo of Hank crooning *Lovesick Blues*. And if you close your eyes, you almost certainly will hear the deafening roar of thirty-eight hundred appreciative fans as they give Hank one standing ovation after another, screaming for yet another encore.

Horace Logan and Tillman Franks

Two men crucial to the success of the *Hayride* were Horace Logan (August 3, 1916-October 13, 2002) and Tillman Franks (September 29, 1920-October 26, 2006).[5] Logan was ten years old when he and his mother moved to Shreveport. At sixteen, he accompanied a friend to an announcer contest at KWKH. When one of the other contestants dropped out, Logan was asked to audition. He won the prize of a job as a 5:00 A.M. radio announcer.

After World War II, he was offered the job of program director at KWKH. Station management wanted to revamp an old program called *Saturday Night Roundup.* He was given the assignment to put together the *Louisiana Hayride* and placed in charge of booking the show's talent. He produced the *Hayride* from 1948 to 1958.[6]

The first breakthrough for the *Louisiana Hayride* came when Hank Williams became a regular on the show in August of 1948. His participation placed it on an even footing with the older and more established Grand Ole Opry. Six years later, Logan and talent manager Tillman Franks became aware of a young singer from Memphis. They decided to give him a chance to perform on the broadcast. On October 9 or 16, 1954 (there are conflicting dates given by those who were there), Elvis Presley was introduced to his first national radio audience. He was quickly signed to a contract to appear weekly on the *Hayride* and tour with other regular *Hayride* performers.[7]

When Logan retired in 1958, Tillman Franks became the *Hayride* producer, a position he would hold for the next two years. Franks also taught guitar to Jerry Kennedy, Tommy Sands, and Merle Kilgore. It was in his capacity as manager of singers, however, that he built his reputation, working with Slim Whitman, Webb Pierce, Johnny Horton, Claude King, Jimmy C. Newman, David Houston, and even Terry Bradshaw. Franks claims it was he who secured a recording contract for Bradshaw with Mercury Records. He also wrote several of Horton's songs.[8]

Franks was also responsible for the trademark suit Hank Williams wore during performances. When Williams first appeared in Shreveport, he didn't have a suit so Franks gave him the white suit that would become so familiar to his audiences. It was the same suit Williams was wearing in a picture that was later used on a commemorative U.S. postage stamp.

Logan died in Victoria, Texas in 2002.[9] Franks died in Shreveport four years later. Their deaths marked the end of an era during which some of the hottest talent in rockabilly music blazed a trail across the stage of the *Louisiana Hayride*, an era of artistic achievement that most surely will never be duplicated.[10]

Hank Williams

Hank Williams (September 17, 1923-January 1, 1953) was neither blues nor rockabilly. Still, because his voice carried so much feeling, he could mesmerize female audience members simply by making eye contact. He joined the *Louisiana Hayride* in the show's inaugural year, 1948, and in 1949—the same year Fats Domino debuted with *The Fat Man*—he released *Lovesick Blues,* which besides being a huge country hit, crossed over to mainstream audiences. The song was a radical break from traditional country and was emblematic of things to come. It was not close to rock or even rockabilly, but it burst open the doors that allowed Dale Hawkins, Elvis Presley, Carl Perkins, Gene Vincent, and Johnny Cash, among others, to walk through virtually uncontested. Williams, in his brief career that barely spanned seven years, was so recognized for his contributions to the genre that he was inducted into the Rock and Roll Hall of Fame in 1987.[11] Before he was through, he would write and record such classics as *Your Cheatin' Heart, Cold, Cold Heart, Hey Good Looking, Take These Chains from My Heart, I'm So Lonesome I Could Cry,* and *Jambalaya,* all of which shot to number 1 on *Billboard*'s country music chart. Other hits by Williams included *You*

Win Again, Wedding Bells, Honky Tonk Blues, Kaw-Liga, Half as Much, and *(I Heard That) Lonesome Whistle.* Not only would his versions of the songs sell millions of records, but they also would be recorded by scores of other artists, including Fats Domino, Tony Bennett, and Ray Charles.[12]

The *Louisiana Hayride* had its first performance on April 3, 1948, but Hank was not on the bill. He was placed on a six-month probation to ensure he could remain sober. When he finally did perform, he was an instant hit and was quickly signed to a one-year contract. He moved his family to an apartment in nearby Bossier City.

Soon after he began his *Hayride* career, Hank and wife Audrey traveled to Cincinnati for his first recording session in over a year. Among the four songs recorded during that session held shortly before Christmas in 1948 was *Lovesick Blues.* It was released six weeks after the session, but Williams performed the song at the *Hayride,* prompting the *Shreveport Times* to write on January 9, 1949, that capacity crowds clamored for encores of the song.

His final *Hayride* performance was on June 3, 1949, and it was a memorable event. A standing-room-only crowd of thirty-eight hundred called him out for seven encore performances of *Lovesick Blues*—something no *Hayride* performer, not even Elvis, ever duplicated—and then gave him a final, deafening standing ovation. Later, when he stepped up to the microphone at the Opry, he launched once again into *Lovesick Blues* and got the same results. This time he was called out for six encores, an event unprecedented in the history of the Opry.

His career hit its peak in 1951 when his composition *Cold, Cold Heart* became the most popular song in America, even though it was not Hank's version, but Tony Bennett's, that recorded the most sales. Although it was unheard of for a country song to cross over into the pop field, it quickly became commonplace for Hank's. Of all his hit songs, only *Lovesick Blues* was not one of his compositions.[13]

Beset by excruciating back pain brought on by spina bifida

and aggravated by several accidents, including a fall from a stage when he tried to perform drunk, Williams was addicted to pain killers. That and his fondness for alcohol created a lethal combination. A man known as Dr. Toby Marshall kept Hank supplied with pills that all but guaranteed his meteoric career would burn out much too quickly.[14]

Nevertheless, for most of the time that he lived in Bossier City, he managed to stay sober. He even lived in Bossier City long enough for Audrey to give birth to their son, Hank, Jr., giving Louisiana a claim to "Bocephus" as a native son. Inevitably for one bent on self-destruction, as Hank seemed to be, he fell back into his deadly cycle of drugs and alcohol. Following his divorce from Audrey, Hank married Billie Jean Jones Eshliman on October 18, 1952. Less than three months later, on New Year's Day, he died while en route to a show in Canton, Ohio. His last song, fittingly, was *I'll Never Get out of This World Alive.*

Even though his star was extinguished in what seems the blink of an eye, his tenure in Shreveport sent the metaphorical flare into the southern skies. His career, brief though it was, encouraged, even commanded, others to journey to the mecca that was the *Louisiana Hayride* to launch their careers via live broadcasts of the fledgling show over powerful KWKH radio. Collectively, they not only succeeded, but in doing so, they transformed the *Hayride* into a rockabilly promised land, validating the show's self-proclaimed designation as the "Cradle of the Stars."[15]

Elvis Presley

It was the *Hayride,* not Sun Records, that gave Elvis Presley (January 8, 1935-August 16, 1977) his first national exposure, launching the career of the single greatest phenomenon in popular music history. Likewise, it was Elvis Aaron Presley who catapulted the *Louisiana Hayride* from respectability to fame. Before his death, six Louisiana musicians would either record or tour with Elvis. They were drummer D.J. Fontana, pianist Floyd Cramer, and guitarists Gerry McGee, Duke

Statue of Elvis Presley outside the Municipal Auditorium in Shreveport. Presley received his first national exposure over the Louisiana Hayride.

Bardwell, James Burton, and Fred Carter, Jr.[16]

To say Elvis exploded into the national music consciousness during his *Hayride* debut would be an embellishment of the facts. The truth is, he got only a lukewarm reception exactly one week—or two weeks—after hitting a low point in his fledgling career; the exact date of his first appearance on the radio show remains in question. Producer Horace Logan said it was October 9, 1954; others say the date was October 16. Either way, on October 2, he bombed at the Grand Ole Opry in Nashville and was told by Jim Denny, who ran the Opry's talent office, to stick to truck driving. Then and there he swore an oath to never again have anything to do with "them sumb——" at the Opry. On stage for the *Hayride's* early show, he found the audience's demographic makeup similar to that of the Opry. The middle-aged country music traditionalists were neither ready nor willing to connect with this wild man from Memphis, Tennessee, who had the brass to call himself the Hillbilly Cat.

KWKH had been playing both sides of his first Sun record (*That's All Right* and *Blue Moon of Kentucky*) for a couple of weeks, and younger fans had been listening and liked what they heard. His was a different sound than what they were accustomed to. Even those in the audience who still weren't sure if they liked his sound were curious enough to hang around for the second part of the show.

Elvis and his backups Scotty Moore and Bill Black wanted and needed exposure so they had driven all the way from Memphis to Shreveport, a round trip of nearly seven hundred miles, for what even in those days was a pittance. Elvis got eighteen dollars per show, and Scotty and Bill got twelve dollars each. The *Hayride* didn't pay expenses for travel, lodging, or meals so the three would usually stay at the Al-Ida motel and subsist on hamburgers. They would have breakfast with Stan Lewis, who picked up the checks. Just a few doors down Texas Street from the KWKH studios, Lewis operated Stan's Record Shop, where Elvis held regular autograph sessions.[17]

Elvis, who had a girlfriend back in Memphis, began keeping company with fellow *Hayride* performer Carolyn Bradshaw whenever he was in town, which became more and more frequent. He would hang out at Murrell Stansell's Bantam Grill and Harry's Barbecue and regularly attended movies at the Strand or Don Theaters.

Hayride producer Horace Logan said that Elvis called him at home early on the afternoon of his historic performance and asked if Logan would allow him, Scotty Moore, and Bill Black to enter the Municipal Auditorium early so that they might get a feel for the place. Logan acquiesced and met the three there. He said Elvis, the youngest, was wearing white pants and a pink shirt and sported bushy sideburns. He also noticed that Elvis's guitar was undersized, a child's instrument.[18]

That night the CBS segment was broadcast live over KWKH and taped for delayed broadcast the following Saturday night over some two hundred CBS affiliates across the U.S. With time for six numbers during the fast-paced CBS portion, Logan placed Elvis near the middle of the lineup. When it was his turn to sing, Elvis was plainly nervous. Still wearing the white pants, pink shirt, and slicked-back hair, he had added a bow tie and a sport coat that Logan said looked second-hand. Logan leaned into his microphone and introduced Elvis to America with these thirty prophetic words: "Ladies and gentlemen, you've never heard of this young man before, but one day you'll be able to tell your children and grandchildren that you heard musical history made tonight."

Elvis communicated as much unease as talent to the audience during that performance. The second segment of the show, however, was quite different. After the older fans had filtered out of the auditorium, leaving in their stead the younger college kids, and secure in the knowledge that CBS was not carrying his second set, he seemed to grow more confident. Merle Kilgore said Elvis thought the crowd was afraid of him during his first appearance, but when he came back out, the audience was more prepared.[19]

Country-Cajun singer Jimmy C. Newman described the new kid as an amateur and said he had rings of dirt on his neck. Shreveport disc jockey T. Tommy Cutrer's first impression of Elvis was his long, greasy hair and dirty appearance. Even Cutrer's wife observed that Presley needed to wash his neck. Elvis still didn't get an encore, but the change that came over the audience from the first to the second set, especially among the female members, convinced Logan to give Elvis two more appearances on the *Hayride*.[20]

It never occurred to *Hayride* officials to have Elvis close the show. But as younger and younger crowds poured into the Municipal Auditorium and as he gained more confidence, Elvis Presley soon became the act no one could follow. None of the other performers wanted to close the shows, especially those who disliked his music and resented him—and there were several.

After the October 23 performance, Logan approached Elvis with a one-year contract offer that called for the same pay scale of eighteen dollars per show for Elvis and twelve dollars each for Scotty and Bill. The three leaped at the opportunity, though Elvis, because he was only nineteen, needed his parents' signatures on the contract. When Gladys and Vernon Presley arrived in Shreveport on

November 6 (Elvis skipped the October 30 show because of a prior commitment), they stayed at the city's best hotel, the Captain Shreve. Knowing they could not afford such accommodations, Logan assumed that Sun Records owner Sam Phillips provided them money for the trip. That night, playing the first of more than fifty contract performances for the *Hayride,* Elvis got his first encore as his parents sat in the audience.[21]

It was also around this time that Elvis added Shreveport's D.J. Fontana as the band's drummer, though their first show together was a disaster. Elvis and his musicians had been asked to fill in for a local band at the Lake Cliff Club just outside Shreveport, but the substitution was not announced to the crowd. The audience, expecting the regular band, was not thrilled at the greasy kid gyrating on stage in front of them and by the time they had finished their show, they were singing only to the bartender and waitresses.

By September of 1955, nearly a year later, Elvis had signed Tom Parker as his manager and his contract with the *Hayride* was nearing an end. Logan knew he had to act fast to secure Presley's services for another year. He offered the singer two hundred dollars per week to sign early and over Parker's loud objections, both his parents signed the new contract.

As Elvis's popularity grew, so did the lines of girls outside the Al-Ida motel. Logan claimed to have seen as many as three hundred girls outside Elvis's room one night. He said Elvis did his best to accommodate as many of them as possible.[22]

On January 7, 1956, Elvis played before a packed house at the Municipal Auditorium and then celebrated his twenty-first birthday the following day. On January 10, it was off to Nashville with Scotty, Bill, D.J., and *Hayride* pianist Floyd Cramer for an RCA recording session. Accompanied by guitarist Chet Atkins and backup singers Gordon Stoker, Ben Speer, and Brock Speer, he cut *I'm Counting on You* and *I Was the One.* Then it was back to the *Hayride* for another Saturday show.

Another song Elvis recorded in that session would eclipse everything he had done before and in the process kill any chance the *Hayride* had of holding him to the terms of his contract. May Axton had written a song that was based loosely on the words in the final note left by an anonymous suicide victim. The song was considered a "morbid mess" by Sam Phillips, who had sold Elvis's contract to RCA for thirty-five thousand dollars. By the spring of 1956, the song was number 1 on both the country and pop charts and number 3 on the R&B charts. Virtually everyone in America under the age of twenty-five was singing *Heartbreak Hotel.*

In April, Elvis approached Logan to say he was going to have to buy out the rest of his contract. While Logan was convinced that the *Hayride*'s contract was enforceable, he had no intention of holding his star back by forcing him to work for two hundred dollars per night while he could be making forty times that amount. The *Hayride* penalized Elvis four hundred dollars for every missed show over and above the five absences per year allowed under his contract. With seven months to go, Elvis calculated he owed twelve thousand dollars. Logan made Elvis a counteroffer of ten thousand dollars with the provision that he would return for one final *Hayride* appearance before the end of the year, with all proceeds over and above expenses being donated to a charity. Two days later, Logan had a ten-thousand-dollar check from Elvis and Presley's final *Hayride* show was scheduled for December 15, 1956.[23]

The only place in Shreveport large enough to accommodate the crowd was the Youth Center (now Hirsch Memorial Coliseum) at the state fairgrounds. Tickets were $2 in advance and $2.50 at the door. Proceeds went toward building a new swimming pool for the YMCA camp south of the city. More than thirteen thousand people jammed into the center, making it the largest crowd ever to witness a *Louisiana Hayride* show.

Shreveport police, charged with keeping Elvis safe from female fans, created the first Elvis impersonator. A Shreveport patrolman named Robert Catts had the same build and sleepy eyes as Elvis, so he was outfitted as the singer and ushered into a rented pink Cadillac. The Caddy, with police escort, headed for the front entrance of the youth center and thousands of hysterical teenagers. Catts was predictably mobbed while Elvis slipped unnoticed through the center's rear doors.[24]

During that show Logan coined a phrase that would be repeated hundreds more times at the conclusion of Elvis concerts. Once Elvis had completed his forty-five-minute set and he had sung his encore, the crowd headed for the exits even though there were other acts waiting to go on. In the ensuing pandemonium, Logan sought to restore order before announcing in desperation, "Please, young people . . . Elvis has left the building. He has gotten into his car and driven away. Please take your seats."[25]

Once, when he was performing in the middle of a field in Jacksonville, Florida, a couple of thousand teenage girls rushed the stage. D.J. Fontana watched in horror as the girls tore at Elvis's clothes. Even as Fontana feared they very well might not escape with their lives, he was hit with a revelation that rock and roll music was catching on.[26]

Webb Pierce

Webb Pierce (August 8, 1921-February 24, 1991) was the consummate honky-tonk singer. Between 1952 and 1982, he had nearly one hundred songs make the charts, several of which became crossover hits. Not always popular among his peers, he nevertheless developed a loyal fan base.

Born near West Monroe, Louisiana, he was three months old when his father died. After his mother remarried, he was raised on a farm seven miles outside of Monroe. He hosted his own weekly radio show, *Songs by Webb Pierce,* on Monroe's KMLB, when he was just fifteen years old.[27] After getting married, he and his wife moved to Shreveport, where he got a job working in the men's department of the Sears and Roebuck store. In 1947, the couple appeared on the KTBS morning show. He moved to KWKH and was made a member of the *Louisiana Hayride* during its first year of operation in 1948. In 1950, Webb and his wife divorced and he started his solo career. He signed with Decca and made his first recordings there in 1951. His initial effort, *Wondering,* spent four weeks at number 1 on the country charts. The next year, 1952, he left the *Hayride* and joined the Grand Ole Opry.

Among his most famous songs are *There Stands the Glass* (1953), *In the Jailhouse Now* (1955), and *Fallen Angel* (1960). His recording of *Slowly* was one of the first recordings to feature the pedal steel guitar. By 1960, rock and roll had taken some of the steam out of his career, much as it did for most other hardcore country singers.[28] By this time, however, Pierce was extremely wealthy and was known as one of the most flamboyant country singers of his day. He built a thirty-five-thousand-dollar guitar-shaped swimming pool at his house and wore gaudy outfits designed by Nudie, the Hollywood western tailor.[29]

He appeared in several movies, including *Buffalo Guns, Music City USA, Second Fiddle to a Steel Guitar,* and *Road to Nashville.* In the late 1960s, he opened his home to tourists, sparking a feud with neighbor Ray Stevens, who sued Pierce over the increased traffic. He had one last hit, charting in 1982 with a remake of *In the Jailhouse Now* with Willie Nelson. For the most part, however, like so many of the older singers, he was forgotten. He waged a long battle with cancer that he finally lost in 1991.[30]

Faron Young

Faron Young (February 25, 1932-December 10, 1996) grew up on his father's dairy farm. A Hank Williams soundalike, he formed his own band while still in Fair Park High School and later dropped out of college to pursue a career in music. Swept up in the wake of the Williams honky-tonk sound, he toured with Webb Pierce and in 1951 became a regular on the *Louisiana Hayride.*[31]

In the summer of 1952 he was dating a woman named

Billie Jean Jones Eshliman and double-dated with Hank Williams, recently estranged from wife Audrey. Williams, taken with Billie Jean, claimed her for himself, convincing Young to break off his relationship with the woman by threatening him with a gun.[32]

From 1954 to 1969, Young recorded sixty-three country hits, forty-six of those making the top 20. In doing so, he gave precious exposure to a number of struggling band members, including Roger Miller, Don Gibson, Roy Drusky, Kris Kristofferson, and Willie Nelson.[33] It was the Willie Nelson classic *Hello Walls* that catapulted both men to musical immortality. Nelson pitched the song to Young in Tootsie's Orchid Lounge in Nashville for five hundred dollars, but Young, seeing the potential profitability in songwriter royalties, refused, telling Nelson to keep the rights to the song and he would record it. Young, true to his word, recorded *Hello Walls,* and it reached number 12 on the pop charts in June 1961 and number 1 on the country charts. Nelson recalled that Young loaned him the five hundred dollars anyway.[34]

Young also was involved in stock-car racing, a booking agency, a recording studio, and co-ownership of the country music publication *Music City News.*[35] In the early 1990s, Young was diagnosed with emphysema. As his health deteriorated, he became convinced that the country music industry had turned its back on him and other older country singers. As the two factors combined to feed his depression, he put a gun to his head and pulled the trigger. Gravely wounded, he died in Nashville the following day. He was posthumously inducted into the Country Music Hall of Fame and Museum in 2000.[36]

Johnny Cash

The *Hayride* crowd of December 10, 1955, was more receptive to Johnny Cash (February 26, 1932-September 12, 2003) than it had been fourteen months earlier for Elvis Presley's debut on the show. Cash had released his first record on Sun Records only six months before. Both sides, *Hey Porter* and *Cry, Cry, Cry,* were doing well in the Memphis area but nowhere else. He sang both songs on the *Hayride,* then encored with *Folsom Prison Blues,* a song he had cut a few months earlier but which was not yet released. When Cash exited the stage upon completion of his set, Logan asked him to join the *Hayride* as a regular and he signed the contract in January 1956. His and Elvis Presley's bands formed a weekly carpool from Memphis to their Saturday night *Hayride* shows.[37]

In April of 1959, three years after signing with the *Hayride,* he recorded *I Walk the Line.* It took off immediately, climbing to number 17 on the *Billboard* Hot 100 and number 2 on the country charts. Seven months after its release, it was still number 3 on the country charts and remained on the pop charts for twenty-two weeks, becoming his first million seller. Both *Folsom Prison Blues* and *I Walk the Line* were chosen by the Rock and Roll Hall of Fame for inclusion among the 500 Songs That Shaped Rock and Roll.[38]

Cash's popularity grew so fast Horace Logan knew that the *Hayride* couldn't hold him long. Still, the Man in Black remained to fulfill his contractual obligations, and when he did leave in July 1956, he took out a full-page ad in *Billboard* thanking the *Hayride* and Logan.[39]

One of seven children, Cash grew up dirt poor in Kingsland, Arkansas, working with his parents by day and listening to his mother sing at night. By age twelve, he was writing poems and songs. When the Korean War started, he enlisted in the air force. While stationed in Germany, he bought his first guitar and formed a band that played at clubs around the air base.[40]

By 1958, Cash had published fifty songs and by the time he left Sun Records to sign with Columbia, he had sold over six million records. His 1960 theme album *Ride This Train,* his 1963 album *Ring of Fire* (the title song written by *Hayride* performer Merle Kilgore and June Carter, Cash's future wife), and 1968's *Johnny Cash at Folsom Prison* all won gold records. His bestselling record didn't come until fourteen years after he had signed his first recording contract and it was on Columbia, not Sun. *A Boy Named Sue,* recorded live at his San Quentin concert, climbed all the way to number 2.[41] Cash was certified multiplatinum for three of his albums: *Greatest Hits, Folsom Prison,* and *San Quentin,* each of which topped two million in sales. The latter two were recordings of live performances at the prisons for which the albums were named.

Although it is easy to tag Johnny Cash as country, such a label would be overly simplistic. He could belt out a good rockabilly song (*I Will Rock and Roll with You*) or folk (*Understand Your Man* and *It Ain't Me, Babe*). He teamed with former Sun artists Roy Orbison, Carl Perkins, and Jerry Lee Lewis in 1986 to record a rockabilly reunion album, *Class of '55,* netting him a Grammy nomination.[42]

Those first few modest shows at the *Louisiana Hayride* in Shreveport played a significant role in launching his career. He would go on to record almost 1,500 songs on more than 470 albums. He placed 130 songs on the country charts and 48 on the *Billboard* Hot 100 pop charts—more than the Rolling Stones. Between 1955 and 1972, he had 26 albums on the pop charts, the same number as the Beatles during that same time span. In all, he sold more than fifty million records.[43] In 1992, he was inducted into the Rock and Roll Hall of Fame, making him the only artist ever inducted into the Rock and Roll Hall of Fame, the Country Music Hall of Fame (1980), and Nashville Songwriters Hall of Fame (1989).

The Man Comes Around album was released in early March of 2003 and featured his cover of the Nine Inch Nails song *Hurt.* The video of that song contains footage of June Carter Cash and highlights of Cash's career and is a poignant music video, coming as it did only months before both their deaths. On May 15, 2003, June, his wife of thirty-five years, died from complications following heart surgery. Just four months later, Johnny Cash died of respiratory failure.[44]

Merle Kilgore

Merle Kilgore (August 9, 1934-February 6, 2005) was a disc jockey at KRUS radio station in Ruston before graduating to the *Louisiana Hayride* in Shreveport. He then went on to a career as a songwriter and Hank Williams, Jr.'s personal manager, general manager of Williams' publishing companies, and executive vice president and head of management of Hank Williams Jr. Enterprises. Along the way he appeared in several movies.

Born in Chickasha, Oklahoma, Kilgore moved to Shreveport where he attended Creswell Elementary School and Byrd High School. He began his musical career at age fourteen by carrying Hank Williams, Sr.'s guitar and became a performer on the *Hayride* at sixteen. Two years later and while a student at Louisiana Tech, he got a job at KRUS, where he hosted the morning show on the predominantly country station. The following year, while hosting the *Tall Texan* television show on KNOE-TV in Monroe, he wrote his first number 1 hit, *More and More,* which became a million-seller for West Monroe native Webb Pierce.[45]

There followed a succession of radio and television jobs from 1955 to 1960, including stints at KBSF in Springhill, KCU and KENT in Shreveport, a return to KBSF as disc jockey and manager, and host of the *Big Ten Jamboree* on KTVE-TV in El Dorado, Arkansas. During his second tour at KBSF in 1959, he wrote and recorded his first top 10 record, *Dear Mama,* on Starday Records. The same year, he wrote *Johnny Reb,* a million-seller for *Hayride* performer Johnny Horton. On May 23, 1960, he made his first appearance on the Grand Ole Opry and received the WSM Mr. DJ Award.[46]

Kilgore's watermark year was 1962. It was then that he began performing as a regular on the Grand Ole Opry and wrote the blockbuster number 1 crossover hit *Wolverton Mountain* for *Hayride* regular Claude King of Shreveport. He joined the Johnny Cash road show and performed at Carnegie Hall in New York and in the Hollywood Bowl. The momentum carried over into 1963 when he was

named one of *Billboard* magazine's Top Ten Songwriters
and then cowrote *Ring of Fire* with June Carter, a song
that sold sixteen million copies. The song is credited with
saving Cash's career, as Columbia Records was considering
dropping Cash because his last two albums had sold poorly.
In all, Kilgore wrote more than three hundred songs, most
of which were recorded by other artists.

He came full circle from carrying Hank Williams, Sr.'s guitar
in 1948 when in 1964 he joined Hank Williams, Jr.'s road show
as the opening act. In 1986, his two-decade-long association
with Williams paid huge dividends when he negotiated the
deal with ABC for Williams' opening promo for *Monday Night
Football.* Each fall from 1986 through 2006, football fans
heard him ask, "Are you ready for some football?"[47]

In March of 2004, the estate of June Carter Cash squelched a
potential million-dollar deal for Kilgore when it refused to allow
Ring of Fire to be used in a television commercial for hemorrhoid
cream.[48] That same year, at age seventy, he underwent heart
surgery and two back surgeries and was diagnosed with
cancer. Following a trying day of tests at Vanderbilt University
Medical Center, he arrived with his wife at an International
Entertainment Buyers Association dinner to present a Lifetime
Achievement Award to Hank Jr. Only after he arrived did he
learn that he was to be the recipient instead.

He regaled the audience at the event, relating an account
of the time he booked Little Richard into Shreveport's
Municipal Auditorium. The auditorium was sold out and
the crowd was rocking. A young black performer was
screaming, "Tutti frutti" when three or four people came
up to Kilgore and said the singer was an imposter. "Well,
we didn't have TV in Louisiana back then . . ." he said, his
voice drowned out by the crowd's laughter. He said he only
had to refund four tickets.[49]

Kilgore died of congestive heart failure in Mexico, where
he was undergoing treatment for cancer.[50] Hank Williams,
Jr., who called Kilgore a father figure and his best friend,
said he was numbed at the news of his death.[51]

Chet Atkins watches as Tommy Blake, accompanied by Ed Dettenheim, practices in RCA's Studio B in Nashville. Blake was the first to use that studio, later used by Elvis Presley exclusively for his Nashville sessions. (Rockabilly Hall of Fame)

Tommy Blake

Harry Chapin could have been singing about Tommy Blake (September 14, 1931-December 24, 1985) when he recorded *WOLD* in 1973. Blake, an unwanted, illegitimate child, was born Thomas Van Givens in Dallas, Texas. He epitomized the small-town disc jockey, roaming from town to town, station to station in a worn-out car, supplementing a meager income with concerts and dances in stuffy high-school gymnasiums. One of those stops was in Ruston, Louisiana, in 1956, where he worked at 250-watt KRUS, the same station where Merle Kilgore broke into radio.

Blake joined the KRUS house band, the Rhythm Rebels as lead vocalist. The Rhythm Rebels had Carl Adams on lead guitar, Tom Ruple on drums, Ed Dettenheim on rhythm guitar, and Eddie Hall on bass. The band got regular gigs on KTBS Radio in Shreveport and other stations around north Louisiana in the mid-1950s. In 1956, Blake cut his first record with the band, *Koolit,* on Buddy Records of Marshall, Texas.[52]

Blake signed a recording contract with RCA, but he was soon dropped by the label. A bit of trivia emerged from his RCA recording session, however. Blake and his band were the first group to record in RCA Studio B on McGavock Street in Nashville. Studio B later was used for Elvis Presley's Nashville recording sessions and is now the RCA Museum on Music Row.

Guitarist Ed Dettenheim says Blake would write a song and if he couldn't sell it immediately, he would give it away. "That's what happened with *Story of a Broken Heart* that Johnny Cash recorded," he said. "Same thing with *Lonely Street* [a number 5 hit for Andy Williams] and *Tender Years* [a number 11 song for George Jones]." Dettenheim explains that Blake also wrote two Jim Reeves songs, *Am I That Easy to Forget?* and *What's He Doing in My World?*[53]

By the 1970s, Blake had exited music altogether. On Christmas Eve, 1985, his second wife, Samantha, shot him to death in their Bossier City home. Details of the shooting vary but the most credible version of the shooting was given by John Andrew Prime, an entertainment editor for *The Shreveport Times* who knew both Samantha and Blake.[54]

"I'd run into Van [Blake] and Sam and Dean Mathis [keyboard player for the Newbeats] at clubs around town," Prime relates. "Dean and Van were good friends. Occasionally, I'd see Van after he'd started drinking and it was ugly. You just wouldn't want to be around him like that.

"As to the shooting," Prime continues, "Sam was never prosecuted. Sam was defending herself." He said he saw Samantha several times after the shooting. "You know how some people can do something bad or wrong and never feel bad or remorseful about it, never feel a pang of conscience?" he asked. "That wasn't Sam. Whenever I ran into her after the shooting, I saw a stricken woman. It devastated her."[55]

Dale Hawkins

Dale Hawkins (August 22, 1938-) was born Delmar Allen Hawkins in Goldmine, Louisiana, near Ferriday. He was

Dale Hawkins is still rocking more than a half-century after his hit Suzy-Q. He closes the show during the 2007 induction ceremonies of the Louisiana Music Hall of Fame in Baton Rouge. (Courtesy of Louisiana Music Hall of Fame)

an early innovator of American rock and roll as a singer, songwriter, and rhythm guitar player. It was while working in the cotton fields around Mangham that he first became exposed to blues as he toiled alongside black field hands. And it was while attending elementary school that he met Carl Adams, one of a succession of skilled guitarists who worked with Hawkins during a career that has spanned nearly half a century. Others include Joe Osborne, Roy Buchanan, and James Burton of Shreveport, and West Monroe's Kenny Bill Stinson.[56]

After spending time in the navy, Hawkins took a job as a counter clerk in Stan's Record Shop in Shreveport. The jukeboxes of the time were loaded with the records of Howlin' Wolf, Lonnie Johnson, and Guitar Slim. Hawkins became an authority on the R&B hits, selling them by day and singing them by night in various dives along the Bossier

Strip that catered to Barksdale Air Force Base personnel seeking easy access to prostitutes and liquor.[57]

Hawkins found himself at the right place at the right time with the right sound in 1957. America was emerging from the postwar doldrums. Teenagers were weary of the endless offering of stodgy melodies by middle-aged balladeers. The time was perfect for white acceptance of rhythm-and-blues and for "hillbilly" music to make the transition to rockabilly. Complicit in this cultural upheaval were scores of independent recording companies popping up across the nation's landscape. Radio, losing programming to television, was looking for alternative entertainment. This trifecta of good fortune was perfectly poised to take full advantage of the blasé attitudes permeating the boardrooms of the four major recording companies.

Into the breach stepped Dale Hawkins, James Burton, and Joe Osborne. While playing area clubs in 1956, Hawkins began experimenting with a song he had written. The song, influenced by what Scotty Moore was doing on guitar for Elvis, retained its own Louisiana sound and featured a heavy blues influence.[58] "It took five months for me to get *Suzy-Q* right," Hawkins says, "and in 1957 we paid KWKH engineer Bob Sullivan twenty-five dollars for studio time when the station went off the air at midnight for equipment changes. Sullivan was the engineer on the song and I was the producer. It took us seven takes to get it down right." Besides Hawkins, the band included Osborne (bass), Ronnie Lewis (drums), and fifteen-year-old future Rock and Roll Hall of Fame member Burton (lead guitar). *Suzy-Q* kicked off with the rhythmic beat of a cowbell as Burton fell in on guitar before Hawkins came in on the vocal. "It was a one-track recording because we didn't have multitrack tapes back then," Hawkins recalls. "Our band had the riffs for *Suzy-Q* for some time, and we kept putting them together until one day I finally said, 'That's it.' We went into KWKH to cut the song. I know that sounds unusual today, but they used to do a lot of recording there."[59]

The tape was sent to Chess Records in Chicago because Hawkins' boss, Stan Lewis, had worked with Leonard Chess before moving back to Shreveport. Chess told Hawkins he wanted the song, but after several weeks passed with no further word from Chicago, Hawkins sent a copy of the tape to Jerry Wexler at Atlantic Records. Wexler said if Chess wasn't interested, he was. Two weeks later, Chess released the record, and it broke in different parts of the country at different times. "We knew it was a hit after only a week and a half," Hawkins says.

Independent labels like Chess were coming into their own about this time because major labels like Capitol, Columbia, Decca, and RCA were not interested in the new sound, which they considered a passing fad. It was Stan Lewis, taking advantage of his friendship with Leonard Chess (Lewis was the largest distributor of Chess and Checker Records in Louisiana), that resulted in the management deal with the Chicago record label. "The special sound of the guitar was a reverb technique they added in Chicago," Hawkins explains. "The basic sound was ours, though, heavy on Louisiana influence, with some blues."

Payola can take many forms, from cash to gifts to vacations. Sometimes, it can adversely affect an artist. In the case of *Suzy-Q*, Hawkins and Burton collaborated to compose the song, but when Chess issued the record, Burton was not credited. Writers named on the record were Hawkins, Stan Lewis, and Eleanor Broadwater. Broadwater was the maiden name of the wife of WLAC disc jockey Gene Nobles. The one-third of royalties was Chess's way of expressing its appreciation to Nobles for promoting the label's records on the Nashville station.[60]

Suzy-Q climbed all the way to number 27 on the *Billboard* Hot 100 in July of 1957 and number 7 on the R&B chart. It remained on the pop chart for nineteen weeks. Author Jeff Hannusch called the song "two minutes and sixteen seconds of flawless music." *Rock & Blues News* said it was a record "that helped define just exactly what was (and what was not) rock 'n' roll."[61] *Suzy-Q* was chosen as one of the Rock and Roll Hall of Fame's 500 Songs That Shaped Rock and Roll and *OffBeat* magazine, a New Orleans publication, included the song on its list of the 100 Most Essential Louisiana CDs. Creedence Clearwater Revival covered the song to launch the career of John Fogerty in 1968.[62]

Hawkins followed *Suzy-Q* with *La-Do-Dada* (number 32) in October 1958, *A House, a Car and a Wedding Ring* (number 88) in December of 1958, and *Class Cutter* (number 52) in April 1959.[63] He capitalized on his early experience in production in the KWKH studios by moving into a successful career in producing hits for Joe Stampley and the Uniques (*Not Too Long Ago*), the Five Americans (*Western Union*), and Bruce Channel (*Mr. Bus Driver*), as well as songs by The In Crowd, Michael Nesmith, John Fred, Ronnie Self, and Harry Nilsson. He worked for a time as A&R representative for RCA Records, scouting for rock and roll groups all over the country, but mainly in the Texas-Arkansas-Louisiana area. He also hosted *The Big Beat*, a.k.a. *The Dale Hawkins Show,* on WCAU-TV in Philadelphia.

In 1998, Ace Records released a compilation CD, *Dale Hawkins, Rock 'n' Roll Tornado.* In 1999, he released his first new CD in thirty years, *Wildcat Tamer,* which received favorable reviews in *Rolling Stone.* A member of the Rockabilly Hall of Fame and the Louisiana Music Hall of Fame now living in Arkansas, he continues to play events throughout the U.S., including the New Orleans Jazz and Heritage Festival and the Ponderosa Stomp. *Rock and Roll News* called Hawkins "a master of swamp rock, lowdown boogie, and straight ahead rock 'n' roll." *High Times* said he had "the type of wild genius it takes to create truly inspired rock & roll."[64]

Jim Reeves

Jim Reeves (August 20, 1923-July 31, 1964) was born in Galloway, Texas, where he grew up listening to Jimmie Rodgers. By age twelve, he was playing guitar and singing with a band on Shreveport radio station KRMD. He also was a first-team pitcher for the University of Texas baseball team. While playing in the St. Louis Cardinals' minor league system in 1947, he suffered a career-ending leg injury. He turned to radio where he found announcing jobs at several east Texas stations that allowed him to promote his personal appearances, and by 1953, he had moved to the *Louisiana Hayride* where he had hits with *Mexican Joe* and *Bimbo* on Abbott Records.[65]

He signed with RCA in 1955 and quickly turned out five top 10 country hits, including *Am I Losing You.* But his breakthrough was with *Four Walls,* which remained at the top of the country charts for two months and peaked at number 11 on the pop charts in May of 1957, remaining for twenty-two weeks. RCA producer Chet Atkins was reluctant at first to record the song. Because the lyrics were about a person waiting at home for a wayward spouse, it was assumed to be a woman's song.[66]

Four Walls represented a melding of country lyrics and pop arrangements. Fiddles and steel guitars were dropped in favor of rhythm sections, strings, and background vocals for a richer, fuller sound that suited the velvety smooth voice of Reeves perfectly. The song's crossover appeal earned Reeves appearances on *Dick Clark's American Bandstand,* the *Ed Sullivan Show,* and the *Steve Allen Show.* He ditched his cowboy outfits in favor of sports coats and slacks and even the occasional tuxedo.

On December 7, 1959, Reeves recorded *He'll Have to Go* and by March of 1960, it was the number 1 country song and had reached number 2 on the *Billboard* Hot 100. Intended as a B-side, it remained on the pop charts for twenty-three weeks, earning Reeves his second gold record. In 1966, he had a number 1 record in the United Kingdom with *Distant Drums.* In Norway alone, his record sales earned him sixteen silver, gold, and platinum albums in the '60s.[67]

On July 31, 1964, Reeves and manager Dean Manuel were in a small airplane piloted by Reeves when it crashed near Nashville in a thunderstorm. Both men died. Reeves was inducted posthumously into the Country Music Hall of Fame in 1967 and in 1998, he became a member of the Texas Country Music Hall of Fame.[68] Though he died in 1964, his hit songs kept coming. *I Guess I'm Crazy* cracked the top 100 at number 82 in September, less than two months after he was killed. Two months later, *I Won't Forget You* reached number 93. In September 1965, *Is It Really Over?* climbed to number 79 and *Distant Drums* topped out at number 45 in May of 1966. *Am I That Easy to Forget?*, released in 1973, nine years after Reeves was killed, was his last major hit.[69]

Johnny Horton

It was a circuitous route that carried Johnny Horton (April 30, 1925-November 5, 1960) from Los Angeles to the fishing waters of Alaska to Shreveport and eventually to the number 1 song for six weeks in 1959. Then, at the peak of his career, his life was snuffed out.

Born John Gale Horton in Los Angeles, he bounced between California and east Texas with his sharecropping parents, eventually calling Tyler, Texas, home. After graduating from high school in 1944, he attended Methodist seminary. He soon left, moving to Alaska in 1949 to work as a fisherman, writing songs in his spare time. He returned to east Texas in 1950, where he won a talent contest hosted by Jim Reeves. In 1951, he performed on several Los Angeles television and radio programs. By the end of the year, he had relocated to Shreveport and become a regular on the *Louisiana Hayride* but encountered two major setbacks when his wife left him and his manager severed ties to take over management of Jim Reeves.[70]

Hank Williams took Horton under his wing. After Williams died on New Year's Day of 1953, Horton began a relationship with Williams' widow, Billie Jean, and they were married on September 26 of that year. Billie Jean received a settlement from Williams' estate, but she and Horton quickly spent the money and Horton found himself broke and unemployed. Talent manager and future *Hayride* producer Tillman Franks also was unemployed at the time, and the Hortons approached him to manage Johnny. Billie Jean convinced Franks that Horton could go to the top if he took him on.

Under Franks' guidance, Horton changed his vocal stylings from country to honky-tonk and left Mercury Records to sign with Columbia. His first hit in 1956, *Honky-Tonk Man,* was covered by Dwight Yoakam half a century later. He followed *Honky-Tonk Man* with *One Woman Man* and his first number 1 song, *When It's Springtime in Alaska.*[71] In June 1959, his recording of Jimmy Driftwood's *Battle of New Orleans* soared to number 1 on both the country and pop charts in June, remaining atop the charts for six weeks. Altogether, it stayed on the charts for twenty-one weeks and sold nearly three million copies. Those successes led to an invitation to perform on the *Ed Sullivan Show.* The appearance was painful. Stiff and ill at ease, he lip-synced the song while wearing a silly coonskin cap.

He also had problems when it came to the powers that be in Nashville. One of the few country stars to reject overtures from the Grand Ole Opry, he became a pariah to the country music elite. His marriage to Hank Williams' widow just nine months after Hank's death did nothing to soothe their feelings. Even the *Encyclopedia of Folk, Country & Western Music* contains no mention of Horton.

In December 1960, *North to Alaska* reached number 4 on the *Billboard* charts, earning him his third gold record. Sadly, he never lived to see it. Nor did he ever see the John Wayne movie of the same name that featured the song in the opening credits. A month earlier, on November 5, Horton, Franks, and guitarist Tommy Tomlinson were en route to Shreveport from a performance in Austin, Texas. It was 1:30 A.M. and as Horton approached the crest of a railroad overpass near Milano, Texas, an oncoming car crossed over the center line, crashing into his vehicle.

Franks and Tomlinson were seriously injured but survived. Franks was knocked unconscious by the crash, and when he awoke, he was lying against Horton. Horton was pronounced dead at St. Francis Hospital in Cameron, Texas, at 1:45 A.M. In a twist worthy of a Hollywood B movie, Horton, married to Hank Williams' widow, was returning from a performance at Austin's Skyline Club when he died. Williams' final performance also was at the Skyline Club.[72]

Claude King

Johnny Horton was racing to get back from Austin to meet Claude King (February 5, 1923-) for opening day of duck season when he was killed in a head-on collision. King duplicated Horton's success with his own theme song from a John Wayne movie a year after Horton's *North to Alaska. The Comancheros* reached number 71 on the pop charts and cracked the top 10 on the country charts in December 1961.[73]

Born in Keithville near Shreveport, King shares one other characteristic with Horton: he insisted on remaining in Shreveport even as other *Hayride* artists gravitated to the greener pastures of Nashville and beyond. And like Jim Reeves and Bob Luman, King's first love was baseball. He played for the University of Idaho Vandals in Moscow, Idaho, but returned to Shreveport where he worked during the late 1940s and '50s as a construction engineer while performing music in local clubs and on radio and TV.[74]

Tillman Franks got him on the *Hayride.* He signed with Columbia and hit with *Big River, Big Man,* which cracked the top 10 in the country charts and reached number 82 on the pop charts in September 1961, three months before *The Comancheros.*

The following July, he struck gold with a song he cowrote with Merle Kilgore. *Wolverton Mountain* was initially turned down by several singers, including George Jones, so King decided to record it himself. It went to number 6, remaining on the pop charts for sixteen weeks, selling ten million copies and earning King a gold record. It also occupied the number 1 spot for nine of its twenty-six weeks on the country charts. In October of 1962, he cracked the *Billboard* Hot 100 again with the Civil War-themed song *The Burning of Atlanta,* which made it as high as number 53.[75]

King also dabbled in cinema, appearing in the 1982

television miniseries *The Blue and the Gray* and two feature films, 1971's *Swamp Girl* and *Year of the Wahoo*.[76]

Bob Luman

Bob Luman (April 15, 1937-December 27, 1977) was born near Nacogdoches, Texas. He formed his own country music band while a student at Kilgore High School and promptly won a talent contest judged by Johnny Horton.[77] In May 1955, he saw Elvis Presley in concert. Presley came out clad in red pants, green coat, and pink shirt and socks, Luman remembered years later. For the next several days, Elvis played one-nighters around Kilgore and every day after school, Luman and his girlfriend went to see Presley play. That was the last time he tried to sing like Webb Pierce or Lefty Frizzell, he said.[78] That same year, Luman recorded the original version of *Red Cadillac and a Black Moustache* and *Red Hot* for Imperial Records.

He became a member of the *Hayride* when he was called on as a replacement in a 1956 talent contest. Carl Perkins was a no-show, so Horton asked Luman if he knew *Blue Suede Shoes*, Perkins' hit song. He sang the song, did several encores, and was booked for a guest spot on the *Hayride*. Following Luman's *Hayride* debut, Logan asked if he wanted to come back. That marked the beginning of the end of a budding baseball career, even though he continued to play semi-professional ball for three more years.[79]

In 1959, after almost accepting an offer from the Pittsburgh Pirates, he was convinced by the Everly Brothers to record *Let's Think About Living*. By October 1960, the song had climbed to number 9 on the country chart and to number 7 on *Billboard*'s Hot 100, remaining on the charts for fourteen weeks.

His follow-up, *The Great Snowman*, was a minor hit, but then he was drafted and spent the next two years in the army. In 1973, *Still Loving You* climbed to number 7 and remained on the country charts for 11 weeks. More interesting than its chart success was Luman's vocal styling.

Even to the trained ear, his voice, whether unintentional or by design, bore an indisputable likeness to Presley's.[80]

On December 15, 1977, he returned home from a Grand Ole Opry performance feeling ill. On December 19, he was admitted to the hospital suffering from pneumonia and on December 27, he died at age forty.[81]

David Houston

David Houston (December 9, 1938-November 30, 1993) was born in Bossier City and made his *Louisiana Hayride* debut at the age of twelve. Finding trouble securing work as a singer, he first worked as an insurance underwriter. Later, he signed with Epic Records and his first release, a cover of Harold Dorman's *Mountain of Love,* reached number 2 on the *Billboard* Hot Country charts in 1963 and was the fledgling record label's first big hit.[82]

In 1966, he topped the country charts and reached number 24 on the Billboard Hot 100 with *Almost Persuaded.*[83] The song spent nine weeks atop the charts. It also earned Houston two Grammy awards in 1967, for Best Country & Western Recording and for Best Country & Western Performance, Male Artist.

Almost Persuaded was the first of a string of top 5 country songs for Houston through 1973. He joined the Grand Ole Opry in 1972 and made his last Opry appearance on November 6, 1993. Nineteen days later, he suffered a brain aneurism and remained in a coma for five days until his death.[84]

9

The Others

In the history of Louisiana's music scene, there are those who defy genre or attempts at labeling. Jerry Lee Lewis, for example, is neither blues, R&B, Cajun, nor zydeco. He never performed on the *Louisiana Hayride*. Nor can he be assigned to the Baton Rouge, New Orleans, or Shreveport geographic regions of the state. Likewise, it would be difficult to pigeonhole Ivory Joe Hunter, Susan and Barry Cowsill, Jimmy Elledge, and Tony Joe White. Randy Jackson was born in Baton Rouge but made little or no impact locally. That each musician listed here made an undeniable contribution to Louisiana's rock and roll legacy, however, is evident and without question.

Ivory Joe Hunter

Ivory Joe Hunter (October 10, 1914-November 8, 1974) had his own radio show on KFDM in Beaumont.[1] Though he was born in Kirbyville, Texas, and spent most of his professional career on the West Coast, he lived for a time in Monroe, Louisiana. Three decades after his death, a former neighbor, Brittany Edwards, could still remember visits to his home by famous performers. She also recalls his TV appearances on the *Ed Sullivan Show*. "I grew up playing in his house," Edwards says. "I saw so many celebrities there, like Johnny Mathis. It didn't mean anything to me then because I was just a little girl." Edwards, who is white, remembers the African-American Hunter often referred to her as his niece.[2]

After moderate success in California in the late 1940s, Hunter signed with MGM Records in 1950 and recorded *I Almost Lost My Mind.* It topped the R&B charts that same year and was his biggest of several hits. Six years later, Pat Boone had a number 1 pop hit with the song.[3] In 1956, after moving to Atlantic Records, Hunter recorded *A Tear Fell,* which also went to number 1 on the R&B charts. Teresa Brewer covered *A Tear Fell* that same year, and it reached number 5 on the pop charts. Ray Charles also had a number 50 hit with his 1964 cover. Altogether, the five versions of the two songs generated substantial songwriting royalties for Hunter. In December of 1956, *Since I Met You Baby* reached number 1 on the R&B charts, remaining on the charts for eighteen weeks. It also became his only Top 40 pop hit and stayed on the charts for twenty-two weeks, peaking at number 12.[4]

Ivory Joe Hunter wrote as many as seven thousand songs by some estimates, including two hits that were recorded by Elvis Presley: *My Wish Came True* in 1959 (number 12) and *Ain't That Loving You Baby* in 1964 (number 16).[5] When he developed lung cancer and medical expenses drained his financial resources, a benefit was held for him at the Grand Ole Opry on October 1, 1974. The event was attended by George Jones, Tammy Wynette, and Isaac Hayes, among others. He died broke a month later.[6]

Jerry Lee Lewis

He had only three *Billboard* top 10 hits (Elvis had thirty-eight). He already had two failed marriages when at twenty-two he married his thirteen-year-old cousin, a union that came before his second divorce was final. That seemed to follow a trend: he wed for the second time before he was legally divorced from his first wife. By mid-1958, his career seemed to be over. Yet in 1986, Jerry Lee Lewis (September 29, 1935-), whose name is synonymous with "rock and roll," was unanimously voted as the first artist inducted into the newly opened Rock and Roll Hall of Fame. Others in

Rock icon Jerry Lee Lewis in his home in Nesbit, Mississippi, during his induction into the Louisiana Music Hall of Fame in 2008. (Courtesy of Louisiana Music Hall of Fame)

that historic first class include Elvis Presley, Chuck Berry, James Brown, Ray Charles, Sam Cooke, Fats Domino, the Everly Brothers, Buddy Holly, and Little Richard.[7]

Born in Ferriday, Louisiana, across the Mississippi River from Natchez, he grew up listening to the *Louisiana Hayride* and Grand Ole Opry broadcasts and gospel singing at the Assembly of God Church. To round out his musical education, he regularly snuck into Haney's Big House, a local juke joint that catered exclusively to blacks. It was there that he first heard and saw Roy Milton, Bobby "Blue" Bland, a young Ray Charles, and an eighteen-year-old B.B. King. Joining him in those prepubescent, furtive eavesdropping sessions were cousins Mickey Gilley and Jimmy Swaggart, who would go on to lucrative careers as a country singer and TV evangelist, respectively.[8]

Egocentric and self-absorbed Jerry Lee, the self-proclaimed "Killer," was not the first of the '50s wild men (that distinction would have to go to Little Richard or

Esquerita), but he certainly was one of the most extreme. Of the early stable of talent at Sun Records—Charlie Rich, Roy Orbison, Carl Perkins, Johnny Cash, Warren Smith, and Elvis Presley—it is improbable that Lewis would be the last one standing. Not only did he survive all of his Sun peers and the scandal of marrying his teenage cousin, but over the years he stared down a laundry list of woes that would have destroyed lesser men: expulsion from seminary, the deaths of two wives and two sons, four divorces, the accidental shooting of his bass player, a gun-waving arrest outside Graceland, a heart attack, a losing battle with the IRS, drug addiction, and a near-fatal bout with a perforated stomach brought on by bleeding ulcers. In the end, the Killer weathered each of those withering blows with the characteristic defiance that was his trademark.[9]

His parents, dirt poor, mortgaged their farm to buy him a used upright Stark piano, and he practiced almost nonstop, eventually becoming master of the glissando (sliding his fingers down the white keys of the piano). He never took a formal lesson, and he told Johnny Carson on the *Tonight Show* decades later that he could not read music.[10] In 1949, Jerry Lee, in his mid-teens, made his first public appearance, playing piano and singing *Drinking Wine, Spo-Dee-O-Dee* at the grand opening of a Ferriday Ford dealership. His father passed the hat and collected thirteen dollars. He also landed his own twenty-minute show on a Natchez radio station. A steady gig at the Hilltop Club in Natchez followed and by age fifteen, he was playing professionally for a traveling revival. In the summer of 1951, he cut his first demo record at Cosimo Matassa's J&M Studio on North Rampart Street in New Orleans.[11]

That same year, his mother enrolled him in the Assembly of God's Southwestern Bible Institute in Waxahachie, Texas. Less than three months later, at a church talent show, he ripped into a barrelhouse rendition of *My God Is Real.* Those who heard it liked it, but the dean did not and Lewis was expelled.[12] Years later, he was asked if he was still playing the "devil's music" and Lewis said he was but pointed out that the same music that got him kicked out of school was the same kind then being played in churches.[13]

On February 21, 1952, he married Dorothy Barton, a revival preacher's daughter. He soon abandoned her, however, and a year and a half later, on September 15, 1953, he married Jane Mitcham, twenty-three days before his divorce from Barton was final. On November 2, 1954, Jane gave birth to a son, Jerry Lee Lewis, Jr. During this time Lewis took a job playing at the Wagon Wheel in Natchez and failed as a door-to-door sewing machine salesman.[14]

His music career fared little better. He was turned down by Nashville studio executives, some of whom suggested he learn guitar, and by the *Louisiana Hayride*.[15] Told by producer Horace Logan that the *Hayride* already had a piano player in Floyd Cramer, Lewis returned to Ferriday after cutting a demo record at the KWKH studios. Years later, after he became a star, he met Logan again. "You're the sonofab— who wouldn't hire me for the *Hayride*," Lewis said. "You're the sonofab— who didn't tell me you sang," Logan replied.[16]

In 1956, he was twenty-one and still without any prospect of a recording contract. He heard about a small company in Memphis that had recorded an unknown singer named Elvis Presley. With a glimmer of hope that his opportunity lay 260 miles to the north, he and his father sold thirty-three dozen eggs to finance the trip up U.S. 61. Arriving in Memphis, they were told Sun Records owner Sam Phillips was vacationing in Florida. Undaunted, Jerry Lee prevailed upon producer Jack Clement to allow him to record demo tapes for Phillips to hear on his return.[17] Clement called in studio guitarist Roland Janes and drummer J.M. Van Eaton to help with the session. Lewis, with his fluid left hand, made the bass all but redundant. The date was November 14, 1956. Though there was no way of knowing at the time, the combination of Lewis, Janes, and Van Eaton was a godsend for Phillips, giving him yet another million-dollar sound. It was less than a year after he had sold Elvis Presley's contract to RCA for thirty-five thousand dollars.

During the session, Janes took a restroom break and Lewis launched into *Crazy Arms.* Clement was in the studio at the time, not in the control room, but he had left the tape machine running. Sun recording artist and session musician Billy Riley walked in and picked up Janes' guitar and started playing. Janes exited the bathroom about halfway through the song and picked up an upright bass and joined in. He wasn't near a microphone so the drums and piano are the only instruments audible on the recording.[18]

Jerry Lee was back in the studio within the month to re-record *Crazy Arms* and *End of the Road.* Ray Price had done well with *Crazy Arms* but Phillips nevertheless decided to test Jerry Lee's version. It sold three hundred thousand copies. Thus encouraged, Phillips brought his new prodigy back into the studio, first to back Carl Perkins on his recording of *Your True Love* and *Matchbox,* and then to play on Billy Riley's recordings of *Red Hot* and *Flying Saucer Rock 'n' Roll.*

It was just after Jerry Lee finished playing on Perkins' recordings that Presley dropped by to visit Phillips. The three joined in on an impromptu jam session. Phillips turned on the tape recorder and called in Johnny Cash, who stayed only long enough to sing a couple of songs and stand in for a photo-op with the group. Presley, Perkins, and Lewis remained and sang several songs together.[19]

Phillips sent Lewis on tour to support Cash and Perkins. Hearing Lewis complain that he was too restricted sitting at the piano, Perkins asked him if he could play standing up. Lewis responded that he could play lying down. With the encouragement to do whatever came naturally, Lewis would kick the piano stool backward at some point in his set and play while standing.[20] Lewis was paid one hundred dollars a night for the thirty-day tour. Thinking he had struck it rich, he purchased a new Buick. When he returned from the tour, he had a high-mileage, used Buick and seventy-five dollars.

Finally, it was time to turn Jerry Lee loose to see what he could do with rock and roll, still considered to be in its formative stages. Backed by his uncle J.W. Brown on bass, Janes on guitar, and Van Eaton on drums, Lewis cut a song he had learned earlier in Nashville.[21] The group needed only one take to record *Whole Lotta Shakin' Goin' On,* though Jerry Lee had to cover for forgetting the lyrics only a minute into the song. When he couldn't remember the original version, he simply backed the band down and talked over the music in a routine he had developed on club dates. He then stormed back for the blistering finish to the song. To this day, Jerry Lee insists he didn't even know the tape machine was running when he recorded the song.[22]

Phillips was hesitant to release the song because he felt it was too suggestive. If the buying public agreed with him, they still liked it well enough for it to ascend to the number 1 position on both the country and R&B charts and the number 3 position on the *Billboard* Hot 100 in September 1957. The song received a major boost on July 28 when Lewis was featured on the *Steve Allen Show*. A repeat performance on Allen's show the following week eclipsed the *Ed Sullivan Show* in the ratings for the first time ever. Taking advantage of his three minutes of precious national exposure, Lewis put on a performance described by author Colin Escott as "demonic." At the top of the last chorus to *Shakin',* Lewis, totally mesmerized, abruptly stood up and kicked the piano stool back across the stage in a maneuver that he had learned on the road. Television viewers at home immediately saw the stool come flying back from the opposite direction as Allen, standing off-camera, grabbed it and sent it sailing past an oblivious Lewis.[23]

Whole Lotta Shakin' Goin' On was originally banned for broadcast by Broadcast Music, Inc., but Judd Phillips successfully petitioned BMI to lift the ban. From that point, the only one who could stop Jerry Lee Lewis was Jerry Lee. He shattered Frank Sinatra's attendance records during a twelve-day engagement at New York City's Paramount Theater.[24] He outsold Elvis in 1957 with three more rock and roll classics: *Great Balls of Fire, Breathless,* and *High School Confidential.*[25]

Great Balls of Fire was basically a duet between Lewis and Van Eaton with Phillips' slapback echoes serving as a third instrument.[26] The song was recorded with thumbtacks stuck into the piano hammers to produce the clicking sound heard on the record. Lewis opened the song's piano solo with four glissandi and then banged away at the same note for six hectic bars as Janes and Van Eaton kept the beat. *Great Balls of Fire* climbed to numbers 2 and 3 on the pop and R&B charts, respectively, and was Lewis's all-time bestselling record. He was viewed as a legitimate threat to Elvis as the main rock and roll heartthrob. He followed *Great Balls of Fire* with *Breathless,* which continued his incredible momentum by climbing to number 7 on the *Billboard* Hot 100 and number 3 on the R&B charts.[27]

To everyone, with the possible exception of Warren Smith, Lewis could do no wrong. Smith, who reached number 72 with *So Long I'm Gone* for Sun in 1957 and who also recorded *Rock and Roll Ruby,* seemed always to be on the cusp of a breakthrough. His fate was sealed, however, when Sam Phillips threw the entirety of his limited financial resources behind the promotion of Lewis, creating tensions between the two singers. Resentment intensified when Lewis, who started out on the road with the others at the bottom of the bill, started moving up in the pecking order. Smith felt a monstrous ego had been unleashed in the person of the cocky and brash Lewis. Jerry Lee did not help matters when, at every eatery on the tour, he played his own songs on the jukeboxes. Smith retaliated by going into record stores in every town they played, buying up all of Lewis's records, and ceremoniously smashing them to bits in front of incredulous customers and store employees.[28]

When forced into a subordinate role, Lewis could make the winner pay. Once, when disc jockey Alan Freed decided to close a show with Chuck Berry instead of Lewis, legend has it that the Ferriday Flash poured lighter fluid over his piano at the end of his set, ignited it, and snarled to Berry as he came offstage, "Follow *that.*" Lewis refused to deny or confirm the story, which over the years has grown to mythical proportions.[29]

But even as *Breathless* was making its way toward the top of the charts, trouble was on the horizon and within months Lewis's career would be in tatters. His performance fee plummeted from $10,000 per night to $250—when he could even find a booking at that price. He started down his personal road to rock and roll purgatory via Hernando, Mississippi, on December 12, 1957. There he took Myra Gale Brown, the daughter of his bass-playing uncle, J.W. Brown, and Lewis's second cousin twice removed, to be married. She was thirteen and he was twenty-two as he embarked on his third marriage.[30] What's more, Lewis repeated his earlier sin by marrying before the divorce from his previous wife was final. He defended that technicality by claiming that since he had married Jane Mitcham before the final divorce from wife number one, Dorothy Barton, he had never really been legally married to Mitcham, thereby making the marriage to cousin Myra Gale legal. And it mattered little that she claimed on her marriage license application to be twenty. Nor did it matter that it was not uncommon in the South to marry distant kin at a young age.

The scandal broke just as Lewis was embarking on a tour of Europe. The first leg of the tour was England, and it never progressed beyond that. The British press, upon learning Myra's true age, pounced on the singer, who appeared baffled at all the hoopla. Lewis fibbed, telling reporters she was a mature fifteen, as if that would assuage the tabloids' outrage. An enraged press demanded Lewis's deportation, and promoters had no choice but to cancel the tour. The newlyweds returned to the U.S. only to find that the scandal had beaten them home. Adding to the embarrassment was the fact that his newest song, which charted at number 21, was—perhaps appropriately—titled *High School Confidential.* Lewis, unsophisticated and clearly ill-prepared to deal with hostile reporters, lamented, "I plumb married the girl, didn't I?"

Four years later, in 1961, a twenty-six-year-old Elvis Presley moved sixteen-year-old Priscilla Ann Beaulieu into Graceland without even the pretense of marriage. He met the fourteen-year-old girl when he was twenty-four and stationed in Germany in 1959, but he didn't "plumb marry the girl" until 1967. America chose to give Elvis a pass on the issue of underage relationships. At least Elvis wasn't hypocritical, telling reporters that if Lewis and his young wife were in love with each other, it was fine by him.[31] One of Jerry Lee's sisters, Linda Gail Lewis, married the first of her eight husbands at age fourteen and another, Frankie Jean Lewis, first married at age twelve. On February 27, 1959, Myra Gale gave birth to Steve Allen Lewis, named for the television host who gave Jerry Lee his first national exposure.[32]

With radio station disc jockeys refusing to play his records, it took him a dozen years, a change in music, a new record label, and a sympathetic producer to get him back on top, though he did reach number 30 with a cover of Ray Charles' *What'd I Say* for Sun in 1961. In 1963, Lewis signed with Smash Records and switched to country music. Producer Jerry Kennedy, a fellow Louisianian, negotiated an uneasy truce with country disc jockeys and slowly the Killer made his way back.

His first big hit as a country artist was *Another Place, Another Time,* which climbed to number 2. In December 1963, he reached number 1 with *To Make Love Sweeter for You.* Then in 1971 and 1972, he did something that even Hank Williams never did. Back to back records saw both sides go to number 1—two records, four number 1 hits. The first was *Would You Take Another Chance on Me,* backed with a remake of Kris Kristofferson's *Me and Bobby McGee,* in 1971. He followed that in 1972 with a cover of the Big Bopper's *Chantilly Lace* backed with *Think about It Darlin'.*[33]

In 1973, he and producer Huey Meaux entered a Memphis studio with a plan to reverse the recent trend of overproducing Lewis songs. Backed by Steve Cropper, Carl Perkins, fellow Louisianian Tony Joe White, and the Memphis Horns, Lewis's voice and personality were allowed to dominate on *Southern Roots*. The twelve-song compilation included *When a Man Loves a Woman, Blueberry Hill, Big Blue Diamonds, Hold on I'm Coming,* and *Cry.*[34]

Two years later, Lewis was in Nashville with producer Jerry Kennedy. Backed by Pete Drake, Charlie McCoy, Tommy Allsup, the Jordanaires, and others, Lewis's piano is more subdued on songs like *Jesus Is on the Mainline*, *I Can Still Hear the Music in the Restroom*, and *Red Hot Memories (Ice Cold Beer),* but not, of course, on the album's title cut, *Boogie Woogie Country Man.* The *Southern Roots* album reached the top 10, while *Boogie Woogie Country Man* made the top 20 and earned Lewis a Country Music Association award for Instrumentalist of the Year.[35]

Once he established himself as a country singer, the hits started coming in regular succession. If his career was revived, however, his personal life was falling apart. In 1962, his three-year-old son Steve Allen Lewis drowned in the family swimming pool, and in 1973, Jerry Lee Lewis, Jr., nineteen, was killed in an automobile accident. Lewis's mother died in 1970 and that same year, Myra Gale divorced him after thirteen years of marriage. The following year, his father died. Wife number four, Jaren Pate, also drowned in the family pool, after she and Jerry Lee had separated. Wife five, Shawn Michelle Stevens, died of an accidental methadone overdose only weeks after she married Jerry Lee, and he later was divorced from wife number six.[36]

On April 1, 1976, he appeared for an engagement at the Old South Jamboree in Walker, Louisiana, about ten miles east of Baton Rouge. He showed but didn't play. Instead, he verbally abused the audience, telling them he would play when he was good and ready and if they didn't like it, "Them doors swing both ways." Then he passed out. James

Hodges, the show's promoter, promptly filed suit against Lewis in federal court, and on February 21, 1980, the singer was ordered to pay $8,220 in damages.

Later in 1976, while celebrating his forty-first birthday, he pointed what he thought was an unloaded pistol at his bass player, Butch Owens, and pulled the trigger, shooting Owens in the chest. Miraculously, Owens survived. A few weeks later, on November 23, 1976, he was invited to Graceland by Elvis, who neglected to inform his security detail. When Lewis showed up, he was barred from entering, and when questioned why he was there, he pulled out a pistol and joked that he was there "to kill Elvis."

In 1979, the IRS claimed Lewis owed four million dollars in back taxes. All his assets were seized, including his cars, motorcycles, guns, jewelry, electronic equipment, rare coins, and the Stark upright piano his parents had bought him when he was six years old. Even with that, the IRS continued to harass him, so he moved to Ireland during the 1990s until the tax dispute was finally resolved.[37]

In 1981, he was hospitalized with less than a 50 percent chance of surviving a two-inch perforation in his stomach brought on by a bleeding ulcer. The Killer recovered and, admitting that he was addicted to drugs, checked himself into the Betty Ford Clinic.[38]

Among all the lows, however, there were occasional highs. In 1986, he reunited with former Sun recording artists Carl Perkins, Johnny Cash, and Roy Orbison in the old Sun studios in Memphis to record *Class of '55 (Memphis Rock & Roll Homecoming)*. Though it received less than complimentary reviews, several wonderful tracks were laid down for the recording, which quickly climbed to number 15 on the album charts and won a Grammy. Lewis said the session was like a family reunion and in a rare moment of humility and generosity, said he enjoyed every second of being in the historic studio. He called Orbison one of the nicest and most talented people he had ever met. Lewis is the only surviving member of that memorable session.[39]

If Lewis could be charitable in reminiscing about old friends, he also could be cantankerous whenever he found that he was being cheated out of royalties. He once discovered a rack of eight-track tapes in a convenience store. Calling attention to a row of tapes of his songs, he told the clerk they were counterfeits. The clerk, unaware of who Lewis was, said he knew nothing about the tapes. Lewis persisted in his assertion that the tapes were bootlegs, urging the clerk to examine the plain white labels with black lettering. He even pointed out that the picture of him on the label was of poor quality and unprofessional.

The clerk replied that all he knew was that a man came around every week and stocked the rack. Without another word, Lewis grabbed the rack, walked outside, and placed it in the parking lot. He doused the tapes, rack, and all with gasoline and struck a match. The astonished clerk, who had followed him outside, screamed and asked what he was going to tell the man when he came to check his rack. Lewis turned slowly to the clerk. "Tell him the Killer was here," he said.[40] In 1989, his life was chronicled in the movie *Great Balls of Fire,* starring Dennis Quaid. In 1990 he wrote *It Was the Whiskey Talking, Not Me,* and the song was included in the soundtrack of the movie *Dick Tracy.*[41] In 2005, the National Academy of Recording Arts and Sciences bestowed its Lifetime Achievement Award on Lewis at the 47th Grammy Awards. The academy described him as rock's first wild man who "created his own unique brand of music" by ignoring boundaries and by merging blues, gospel, country, and rock. That award, along with his 1986 induction into the Rock and Roll Hall of Fame was confirmation that he had returned from oblivion.[42]

In March of 2002, Lewis was scheduled to be inducted into the Delta Music Museum in his hometown of Ferriday, but he stood up Louisiana secretary of state Fox McKeithen at the awards presentation. McKeithen had promised to pick Lewis up in a Cessna jet for his flight from Memphis. The pilot, however, had already placed his Cessna in storage so he took a different jet. Lewis refused to board the substitute airplane.[43]

Kris Kristofferson, who called Lewis a self-destructive natural resource, said he loved what Lewis did with his composition of *Me and Bobby McGee*. Lewis was late for the recording session and all the musicians were waiting. As Jerry Lee strode into the studio, producer Jerry Kennedy asked him how he was going to do the session. "Like this," he said as he sat down at the piano and attacked the song. It was a brilliant version. Lewis hated Janis Joplin's version and told Kris he cut his cover to show her how it should be done.[44]

The Killer has racked up a dozen gold records in both rock and country, won several Grammy awards, was the first unanimous inductee into the Rock and Roll Hall of Fame in the hall's inaugural year, was nominated for induction into the Country Music Hall of Fame, and had two of his songs elected to the Grammy Hall of Fame. *Great Balls of Fire* was chosen in 1998 and *Whole Lotta Shakin' Goin' On* in 1999. Both songs are among the 500 Songs That Shaped Rock and Roll. Lewis said he wanted to be remembered not for all his wives, his mansions, or money he made and spent. "I want 'em to remember me simply for my music," he has said.[45] He was inducted into the Louisiana Music Hall of Fame in 2009.

Tommy Sands

Tommy Sands (August 27, 1937-) was born in Chicago but moved with his parents to Shreveport when he was a small child. He appeared on the cover of more teen magazines than any other rock and roll idol in the mid- to late 1950s, including Elvis. He learned to play guitar by age seven and by age eight, he had a regular gig, a twice-weekly show on Shreveport radio station KWKH at $2.50 per show. At age fifteen, he came to the attention of Col. Tom Parker, who signed him to a contract with RCA, and the hype hailed him as the next Elvis Presley, but it was five years before he scored his first hit.[46]

Sands started his career as a juvenile actor on television,

guest starring on numerous network variety shows. In 1957, he landed the lead role in *The Singing Idol,* a play about the life of a popular rock and roll singer, presumably Elvis Presley, since the part was first offered to him. Presley, because of prior commitments, was unable to do the play and recommended Sands for the part. In March 1957, Sands' *Teen-Age Crush* hit number 2 and remained on the charts for seventeen weeks, earning him a gold record. He followed that success in June 1957 with *Goin' Steady,* which peaked at number 16. He made his movie debut in a feature called *Sing, Boy, Sing* in 1958. With longtime friend Rod McKuen, he wrote the title song for the movie, and it hit number 24 in March of that same year.

He had roles in seven other major motion pictures: *Mardi Gras,* 1958; *Babes in Toyland,* 1961; *Love in a Goldfish Bowl,* 1961; *The Longest Day,* 1961; *Ensign Pulver,* 1964; *None but the Brave,* 1965; and *The Violent Ones,* 1967. In all, he appeared in over 150 television movies.[47]

On September 11, 1960, Sands married Frank Sinatra's daughter Nancy. Sands and Nancy Sinatra were divorced in 1965. After the acrimonious divorce, Nancy, with help from her father, reportedly saw to it that Sands' once promising recording career tanked.[48]

Conway Twitty

Before Harold Lloyd Jenkins was a top rock and roll star and then a top country singer, he changed his name to Conway Twitty (September 1, 1933-June 5, 1993).[49] He chose his name in 1957 by looking at a map, picking Conway, Arkansas, and Twitty, Texas, and then went on to score fifty-five number 1 songs on various charts, more than any other artist, including Elvis or the Beatles.[50] The character Conway Birdie in the musical *Bye Bye Birdie* is purported to have been based on a composite of both Twitty and Elvis Presley.[51]

Born in Friars Point, Mississippi, and named for silent screen actor Harold Lloyd, he moved with his family at the age of ten to Helena, Arkansas. While there he formed his first band and hosted a local radio show each Saturday.[52] Details of his youth are somewhat sketchy, but he attended high school in Tallulah in northeast Louisiana. He played baseball well enough to get an offer from the Philadelphia Phillies but instead was drafted to serve in Korea.[53]

Following his discharge, he made his pilgrimage to Memphis and Sun Records.[54] He wrote *Rock House* for Roy Orbison, but it was not until he hooked up with MGM Records that his fortunes changed for the better.[55] He recorded a song called *I'll Try* that languished for most of 1958. Discouraged and ready to abandon his fledgling career, he learned from a disc jockey that the B side of the record was catching on across the country. Considered an afterthought, *It's Only Make Believe* was recorded in just a few takes. With many convinced that the singer was actually Elvis under a pseudonym, it took nearly a year to reach the top of the charts.[56] It hit number 1 in November of 1958 and remained on the charts for twenty-one weeks.[57] It was the number 1 record in twenty-one different nations, eventually selling more than eight million copies and becoming his signature song as a rock and roll artist.[58] He followed with *Danny Boy* (number 10) in 1959 and *Lonely Blue Boy* (number 6) in 1960.

Despite his success in rock and roll, his real desire was to sing country.[59] Against the advice of those around him, and at a time when other country singers were turning to rock and roll, he made the leap to country in 1965 after walking off the stage in the middle of a rock and roll concert in New Jersey.[60]

Country disc jockeys at first refused to play his new songs. Eventually, though, he made the breakthrough with his first number 1 country song, *Next in Line,* in 1968. In 1970, *Hello Darlin'* became his second signature song. For the remainder of his career, said former band member Al Harris of Lake Charles, he would open his concerts with the first verse of *It's Only Make Believe* from a backstage microphone. He would sing *Hello Darlin'* mid-concert and close with *It's Only Make Believe.*

Younger talent eventually pushed him from the charts and record sales declined. On June 5, 1993, he became ill while performing in Branson, Missouri, and died from an abdominal aneurysm.[61]

Jimmy Elledge

In December 1961, Jimmy Elledge (January 8, 1943-), a resident of Pineville, took Willie Nelson's *Funny How Time Slips Away* to number 22. The song remained on the charts for fourteen weeks, sold over a million copies, and earned Elledge a gold record. It also gave Nelson two gigantic songwriting hits in the same year. Six months earlier, Faron Young took his composition of *Hello Walls* to number 12 on the pop charts.

Elledge, a disciple of the Floyd Cramer slip-note piano-playing style, also had a rollicking version of *Swanee River Rocket.*[62] Still another minor hit for him was *A Golden Tear,* a Roger Miller composition. He also recorded *Reconsider Me,* written by Margaret Lewis of Shreveport.

Elledge eventually left Nashville, where he had recorded his hits, and returned to Louisiana, moving to Gretna, across the Mississippi River from New Orleans. There he settled into playing local venues and was a favorite along Bourbon Street. He was inducted into the Louisiana Music Hall of Fame in 1999 and received the Living Legends Award from the Hall in 2003. He received the One Millionth Air Play Award for *Funny How Time Slips Away* from the Louisiana Music Hall of Fame in 2004. That same year, he was inducted into the West Bank of New Orleans Musicians Hall of Fame.[63]

The year 2005 was not kind to Elledge. First, he suffered a serious stroke during the summer and then had to be evacuated to Texas when Hurricane Katrina hit New Orleans. By mid-November, he was walking with help from a physical therapist. He regained limited speech and could still sing.[64]

A benefit concert for Elledge was held on November 20, 2005, in Lloyd Auditorium in Hendersonville, Tennessee.

Appearing at the benefit were many of those with whom he has performed: Billy Joe Royal, Ace Cannon, Bruce Channel, Carl Mann, Dickie Lee, Gene Simmons, Larry Henley, Merrilee Rush, Robin McNamara, Ronnie Dove, Roy Head, Ronnie and the Daytonas, and disc jockey Dick Bartley.[65]

Randall Hank Williams

Randall Hank Williams (May 26, 1949-) was born in Shreveport a month before his father's first appearance on the Grand Ole Opry. His parents, father Hank, Sr., and mother Audrey, were living in Bossier City at the time, and his father was a regular on the *Louisiana Hayride.* Given the nickname "Bocephus," after Grand Ole Opry comic Rod Brasfield's ventriloquist dummy, he was three when the elder Williams died on New Year's Day, 1953, and just eight when he took the stage for the first time to sing some of his father's songs.[66] He made his Opry debut at age eleven, and at fourteen, he had his first hit record, a cover of Hank, Sr.'s *Long Gone Lonesome Blues.* A year later, he sang all the songs on the soundtrack of *Your Cheatin' Heart,* his father's film biography, a movie that was soon tied up in legal action brought by Hank, Sr.'s second wife, Billie Jean Horton.

The younger Williams learned piano from Jerry Lee Lewis, and in 1969, he and Johnny Cash teamed up at Detroit's Cobo Center for what, at the time, was the largest-grossing country show ever. In 1970, Williams signed the biggest recording contract in the history of MGM Records.

It seemed apparent that his mother Audrey's desire was to groom her son to become a Hank Williams, Sr., impersonator. She even had clothes designed for him that were identical to his father's stage clothes, and she created vocal stylings similar to those of the elder Williams. As much as he loved his father's legacy, he soon grew weary of trying to be a clone at the sacrifice of his own musical identity.[67]

While mountain climbing in Montana on August 8, 1975, he took a fall that shattered every bone in his face and left his brain exposed. Nine major surgeries and two years were needed for reconstruction. The scarring was such that it prompted him to grow a thick, full beard and wear a cowboy hat and dark glasses to conceal the disfigurement. With the help of his manager, Merle Kilgore, Williams reentered the recording studio with a new style that allowed him to turn his back on his father's music and dress code in favor of a new, antiestablishment image. He poked fun at Nashville's expectations of him with his 1979 top 10 signature classic *Family Tradition* and followed it that same year with *Whiskey Bent and Hell Bound.*

The songs reflected his embracing of the southern rock style, but he remained popular with country disc jockeys with hits like *Dixie on My Mind, All My Rowdy Friends (Have Settled Down), A Country Boy Can Survive,* and *Born to Boogie.*[68] He won the Country Music Assocation's Entertainer of the Year award in both 1987 and 1988. He won his first Grammy in 1989 with *There's a Tear in My Beer,* an electronic duet with his late father.[69]

When the radio hits slowed, Williams rebounded by singing the opening theme for ABC's *Monday Night Football,* beginning in 1986. He is probably most recognizable today for his opening line, "Are you ready for some football?" The intro won him four straight Emmy awards from 1991 to 1994. He opened for his last *Monday Night Football* regular season telecast in 2006, though he did open for two playoff games in January 2007 and for the Super Bowl XL on February 5, 2007.[70]

The Newbeats

From 1964 through 1970, the Newbeats were as hot as any American rock and roll group going. Four decades later, the typical response to any mention of the band is met with a blank stare until the lyrics "I like bread and butter" produce instant recognition. The Newbeats were comprised of falsetto Larry Henley and brothers Dean and Marc Mathis, both of Shreveport. The Mathises recorded *Tell Him No* in 1959 after touring first with Bob Wills and the Texas Playboys and then with Dale Hawkins. *Tell Him No* met with only minor success.[71]

In 1964, the Mathis brothers and Henley were signed by Wesley Rose to a recording contract. On June 28, 1964, they entered the recording studio to record *Bye Bye Love, Break Away (From That Boy)*, and *Tough Little Buggy*. *Bread and Butter* was released as the B side of *Tough Little Buggy,* but disc jockeys at WKNR Radio in Detroit flipped the record over. The response was immediate. *Bread and Butter* debuted on WKNR's survey less than three weeks after it was recorded. It soon peaked at number 1 on the station's survey and it had climbed to number 2 in the nation by September, remaining on *Billboard*'s Hot 100 for twelve weeks.

On September 30, 1964, with their song dominating the airwaves, they made their national television debut on ABC-TV's *Shindig!* Next was an appearance on *Dick Clark's American Bandstand* and a sold-out European tour with the Rolling Stones. *Bread and Butter* continues to enjoy widespread popularity and has been featured in several movie soundtracks.

The Newbeats followed *Bread and Butter* with *Everything's Alright,* which reached number 16 on *Billboard*'s Hot 100 in December 1964. *Break Away (From That Boy)* peaked at number 40 in February 1965. Three months later, they had another hit with *(The Bees Are for the Birds) The Birds Are for the Bees,* which climbed to number 40 in February 1965. *Run, Baby, Run (Back into My Arms),* which reached number 12 in November 1965, was the band's last big hit.[72]

The Newbeats dissolved in 1974 and after several solo releases Henley turned his attention to songwriting.[73] With Jeff Silbar, he penned one of the most memorable songs ever written. Recorded by Bette Midler, *Wind beneath My Wings* was the theme song of the movie *Beaches*, was a number 1 song in 1988, went platinum that same year, and earned Midler a Grammy in 1989.[74] It was erroneously assumed by many that the song was written for Midler, but Gladys Knight first recorded the song, and Sheena Easton scored a minor hit with it in 1982.[75]

Joe Stampley. (Courtesy of Louisiana Music Hall of Fame)

Joe Stampley and the Uniques

There was a time before he went country that Joe Stampley (June 6, 1943-) rocked. That was when he fronted a band called the Uniques. The band's name stemmed from critics' difficulty in pigeonholing its singing and playing style. From its bluesy cover of Art Neville's *All These Things* to the upbeat tempo of *Not Too Long Ago,* the Uniques endeavored to play to whatever intensity audiences demanded.[76]

Born in Springhill, Louisiana, Stampley grew up listening to Hank Williams and before he was ten, he was playing piano. Following his family's move to Baytown, Texas, he had an opportunity to sing for Williams on a radio program. Williams encouraged him and after high school, the family moved back to Springhill. By then, Stampley had discovered the Everly Brothers and Jerry Lee Lewis. He was writing songs and cutting demo records at age fifteen with local disc jockey Merle Kilgore. The early efforts by Stampley did nothing, nor did a 1961 session for Chess Records. "We played colleges and dances all around the Ark-La-Tex [southwest Arkansas, northwest Louisiana, and east Texas region]," Stampley says.[77]

He attended Southern Arkansas University in Magnolia, Arkansas. "I majored in pool," he says, half joking. It was while attending Southern Arkansas that he formed the Uniques.

With a band behind him, Stampley set out with renewed vigor to achieve success. "I kept bugging Stan Lewis to hear me play and he kept telling me he didn't have the time," Stampley recalls. Still, he credits Lewis for getting his singing career off the ground. Lewis, owner of Stan's Record Shop in Shreveport, was not content to sell others' records, so he launched his own record labels, Paula, named for his wife, Pauline, and Jewel, intended for black performers, the so-called race records.

"Stan finally got tired of listening to me pester him so he told me to go see this guy Dale Hawkins," Stampley explains. Hawkins started out selling records for Stan, recorded *Suzy-Q,* and was doing production work for Paula Records. "I went to Dale and he asked me if we had anything we'd written and I said 'yes.' He told me to sing him something a cappella and I sang *Not Too Long Ago* for him and he signed us on the spot.

"We recorded *Not Too Long Ago* at the Robin Hood Brian Studio in Tyler, Texas. Dale Hawkins produced the record and Stan released it as Paula No. 219, the very first Paula Record ever released," Stampley relates. The B side was *Fast Way of Living. Not Too Long Ago* reached number 66 on *Billboard's* Hot 100 in April 1965 and remained on the charts for six weeks. Hawkins remembered the recording session for *Not Too Long Ago* in Tyler. "Joe wrote a hot check for $187 to pay for that recording session," he says, laughing.[78]

The Uniques' biggest hit was *All These Things,* a song first done by Art Neville of New Orleans. "I didn't even know the words to *All These Things* when we recorded it, and I just winged the second verse," Stampley remembers. "Art Neville's original version said, 'When you were ten minutes late/I started to cry.' Instead of that line, I sang, 'When you started to go/I started to cry.'

"I'm very proud of *All These Things*. It went to number 1 on KLIF in Dallas, the biggest rock and roll station in that market," he says. Nationally, the numbers were considerably more modest. It barely cracked the Hot 100 at number 97 in July of 1966 and remained on the charts just two weeks. It did, however, secure them a spot on *American Bandstand.*[79]

Stampley turned to country with *Soul Song, Roll on Big Mama, If You've Got Ten Minutes, Do You Ever Fool Around,* and *Hey Joe, Hey Moe* (the latter with Moe Bandy). In 1976, he had eight country singles that charted with *Billboard* and he received *Billboard's* Single Artist of the Year award.[80] In 1980, he and Moe Bandy received the Country Music Association's award for Vocal Duo of the Year. In 1992, he teamed with John Fred and G.G. Shinn to form the Louisiana Boys.[81]

On October 1, 2005, the Uniques reunited for a special show at the Piney Woods Palace in Stampley's hometown of Springhill. The occasion was to commemorate the fortieth anniversary of the band's recording session for *Not Too Long Ago.*[82]

O.C. "Ocie Lee" Smith

O.C. "Ocie Lee" Smith (June 21, 1936-November 23, 2001) made a lasting impact on popular music and then walked away. Smith spent the last sixteen years of his life as minister of the City of Angels Church of Religious Science in Los Angeles. Born in Mansfield, Louisiana, Smith moved with his mother to L.A. at an early age. Upon graduation from Jefferson High School, he joined the air force and spent much of his tour of duty singing in a Special Services vocal group. In 1961, he was chosen as a replacement for Joe Williams in Count Basie's band.[83]

He returned to Los Angeles, where he signed with Columbia Records and worked with songwriters Jerry Leiber and Mike Stoller. He dropped his middle name "Lee" and in April 1968, as O.C. Smith, he scored his first hit with *Son of Hickory Holler's Tramp.*[84] The song, recorded at Fame Studios in Muscle Shoals, Alabama, stayed on the charts for fourteen weeks, peaking at number 40. He followed that in October of that same year with his biggest hit, *Little Green Apples.* It reached number 2 on *Billboard's* Hot 100, remained on the charts for seventeen weeks, and won a

Grammy for Song of the Year for 1968. He had another hit a year later with *Daddy's Little Man,* which reached number 9 on the R&B charts.[85]

In 1980 he began studying for the ministry and graduated in January 1985. In October 1985, he presided at the opening of the City of Angels Church of Religious Science.[86] On November 22, 2001, Smith officiated at a Thanksgiving Day service at his church but died suddenly the next day at his Ladera Heights home.

Tony Joe White

Born in Oak Grove, Louisiana, and raised on a cotton farm, Tony Joe White (July 23, 1943-) achieved fame with one song. *Polk Salad Annie,* unmistakable from its first driving bass note, peaked at number 8 in August 1969 and remained on the charts for twelve weeks. The song was covered by Elvis Presley and more than one hundred other singers, and it catapulted White to stardom in both songwriting and singing.[87]

He followed that with *Roosevelt and Ira Lee* in November

Tony Joe White. (Photo by Bill Ellison, Granada Theater, 2008)

of the same year, a song that climbed to number 44. Several other singers charted with songs written by White. They include Elvis (*For Old Times' Sake* and *I've Got a Thing about You Baby*), Brook Benton and Hank Williams, Jr. (*Rainy Night in Georgia*), and Dusty Springfield (*Willie and Laura Mae Jones*).[88]

White moved to Warner Bros. Records in 1971, but his singing career languished until the late 1980s, when he wrote four songs and played guitar and harmonica for Tina Turner on her *Foreign Affair* album. In 1990, he toured with Eric Clapton and Joe Cocker.[89] His first North American release since 1999's *One Hot July* was 2004's *Heroines*, which features guest vocals by Jessi Colter, Emmylou Harris, Shelby Lynne, and Lucinda Williams.[90]

Kenny Bill Stinson

Superb musical talent has come out of northeast Louisiana: Jerry Lee Lewis, Dale Hawkins, Carl Adams,

At the New Orleans stop of the Lennon Piano's "Imagine Peace Tour," Kenny Bill Stinson of West Monroe plays Imagine *on the instrument on which John Lennon composed the song. (Courtesy Caroline True)*

Fred Carter, Jr., Mickey Gilley, Ivory Joe Hunter, Webb Pierce, Tim McGraw, and Tony Joe White. Kenny Bill Stinson (November 10, 1953-) complements that list. Stinson lives in the Union Parish community of Downsville, about halfway between West Monroe and Farmerville. "I grew up in West Monroe, but we found some good property in Downsville and it's really quiet out here," he says.

"Where I'm from is kind of like a train wreck of country music and blues," he describes. "They kind of crashed together and blew up there. So I play a blend of country, blues, rock 'n' roll—whatever I can throw together to make a living. I call my music 'country' and 'eastern' because it's a lot of country and it's in northeast Louisiana." He named his band the Arklamysteries for two reasons. "First of all, we're from the part of Louisiana that everyone calls the Ark-La-Miss for Arkansas, Louisiana, and Mississippi. Second, it's always a mystery as to who will show up to play on any given night."[91] His band plays all over north Louisiana and as far south as Natchez, Mississippi. It was there, at a club in Natchez-Under-the-Hill in 1999, that he was filmed by *The Mississippi: River of Song,* an ambitious PBS production that explores the musical culture of Middle America as it exists along the 2,350 miles of the Mississippi River. His part of the documentary was shown in the segment entitled *Louisiana: Where Music Is King.*

But Stinson is more than just a barroom picker. He is one of an honor roll of outstanding musicians, including Roy Buchanan, James Burton, and Carl Adams, who have served a stint as guitarist for legendary rocker Dale Hawkins. Besides Hawkins, he has performed with Tony Joe White, Jerry Lee Lewis, Charlie Rich, Rodney Crowell, and James Burton. Stinson also plays piano, bass, and harmonica.

On May 31, 2007, Stinson performed at the Ogden Museum of Southern Art in New Orleans. "I was told that Caroline True of England was touring the country with John Lennon's Steinway piano and that they wanted to set it up at the Ogden Museum," he says.[92] (British singer George Michael purchased the upright Steinway, which Lennon used to compose *Imagine* for $2.1 million, and collectors have placed its value as high as $12 million.) New Orleans was one of several U.S. stops for the Imagine Peace Tour documentary being filmed by British producer True. Stops on the U.S. tour included scenes of major national tragedies such as the site of the World Trade Center, Dealey Plaza in Dallas, Ford's Theatre in Washington, D.C., Waco, Oklahoma City, and Blacksburg, Virginia, among others. *Imagine* is performed at each stop on the tour.[93] "They asked me if I would mind playing the piano and singing *Imagine* for the documentary they were shooting," Stinson explains. "Well, I've always been a Beatles fan and of course, I jumped at the chance."[94]

Although performing on the Lennon piano may have been a unique opportunity, Stinson has found others to be more satisfying. During the early 1990s, he was asked to host a blues show on a Monroe radio station on Sunday afternoons. With no experience in live radio, he plunged in. When the station was sold, he assumed his radio career was over but KEDM, an NPR affiliate housed on the campus of the University of Louisiana-Monroe, was looking for someone to host a live blues show. Stinson got the gig and has been doing his *Blue Monday* show every Monday since, though he occasionally strays from the format to include selections from other genres. Today, the program has evolved into what he describes as "free-form radio," and he considers the show one of the most rewarding things he has ever done.[95]

Kris Kristofferson

Janitor, soldier, Rhodes Scholar, Phi Beta Kappa member, songwriter, singer, actor, political activist, bartender, Golden Gloves boxer, firefighter, or helicopter pilot—pick one. Kris Kristofferson (June 22, 1936-) at some point in his long and colorful career has had experience as each.[96]

Kristofferson was born in Brownsville, Texas. His father was an air force general who wanted a military career for his son. Kris attended Pomona College in California and earned a Rhodes Scholarship to study literature at Oxford University.[97] After Oxford, he joined the army, rose to the rank of captain while completing Ranger school, parachute-jump school, and pilot training. He served as a helicopter pilot in Vietnam.[98] In 1965, he resigned his commission and turned down an appointment to West Point to teach English literature in order to pursue his first love: songwriting.

Taking a job as a janitor at Columbia studios in Nashville, he pushed a broom and emptied ashtrays. He also pushed his songs to anyone who walked through the doors. A stint as a bartender at Nashville's Tally-Ho Tavern followed, and then it was off to Morgan City, Louisiana, where he flew oil workers to rigs located seventy miles offshore for Petroleum Helicopters, Inc. (PHI).[99]

While flying for PHI he wrote the lines "Freedom is just another word/for nothing left to lose," which would become *Me and Bobby McGee.* The song, he felt, had a liberating effect on him because he no longer found it necessary to live up to others' expectations. At PHI, Kristofferson wrote every spare minute, working a week in Morgan City and then heading for Nashville to hawk his songs for a week. Inevitably, it caught up with him and PHI said he had to choose between careers. "I left that job April 15, 1969, and I never have had to work for anybody else since," he has said.[100]

The reason for his newfound independence was his success at peddling his work. In quick succession, he was able to get several big-name country artists to record his songs, several of which crossed over onto the pop charts. In 1969, Kristofferson had not even finished writing *Me and Bobby McGee* when Roger Miller started recording it. Miller also recorded a beautifully moving version of *Loving Her Was Easier Than Anything I'll Ever Do Again,* another Kristofferson composition. Ray Price recorded *For the Good Times* and it climbed to number 11 on *Billboard's* Hot 100 in December of 1970, winning Song of the Year at the 1970 Academy of Country Music Awards. Sammi Smith did even better with *Help Me Make It through the*

Night, a song Kristofferson wrote while sitting atop an oil platform in the Gulf of Mexico. Her version of the song cracked the top 10 at number 8 in March of 1971. Also in March of 1971, Port Arthur, Texas, rocker Janis Joplin took her frenetic version of *Me and Bobby McGee* all the way to number 1 on *Billboard*'s Hot 100, earning her a gold record and establishing Kristofferson as a major songwriter. Kristofferson's music publisher told him he needed to get back to the Louisiana oil patch because his years in Louisiana were his most productive.[101]

His biggest coup came in 1970, and the story behind it has taken on near mythical proportions. Johnny Cash had accepted some of Kristofferson's songs but had done nothing with them. Taking matters upon himself, Kris rented a helicopter and flew from Nashville to Cash's home in nearby Hendersonville. Kristofferson professes to being somewhat hazy about the details but does remember almost landing on Cash's roof. The house was built around a cliff and the lawn almost went over the top of the house, so Kristofferson nearly landed right on the house. He said he was lucky Cash didn't shoot him out of the sky like a giant dove.

Some versions of the story have Cash emerging from his home with a shotgun while other accounts say it was the star's wife, June Carter, who came out armed. The more popular version has Cash demanding why the stranger landed on his property. Kristofferson, exiting the chopper even as the rotors were still turning, said, "Mr. Cash, I have some songs I'd like you to hear."

Cash hesitated for a moment and lowered his gun, muttering something about being obligated to listen to someone that crazy or that bold, whichever description was appropriate. A few nights later, Cash introduced *Sunday Morning Coming Down* to his network television show, and the song peaked at number 46 on *Billboard*'s Hot 100 in September of 1970. CBS tried to prevail on Cash to change the line "Wishing Lord that I was stoned" to "Wishing Lord that I was home," but Cash sensed that the song wouldn't be the same if he changed the lyrics. When Cash performed the song on his show, Kristofferson was seated in the balcony and when Cash came to the line, he looked up at Kristofferson as he sang it the way it was written.[102] More importantly, the brazen act by Kristofferson, coupled with the song's success, solidified a friendship between the two that would culminate with their teaming with Willie Nelson and Waylon Jennings to form the Highwaymen in 1985.

Kristofferson starred in several movies, including *Cisco Pike, Alice Doesn't Live Here Anymore, The Sailor Who Fell from Grace with the Sea, Semi-Tough, A Star Is Born* (for which he won a Golden Globe Award), and *Heaven's Gate.* His marriage to singer Rita Coolidge dissolved around his heavy drinking, and he gave up the bottle in 1976.

He received the Johnny Mercy Award at the 2006 Songwriters Hall of Fame induction ceremony on June 15, 2006. Less than a month later, on July 6, 2006, Kristofferson was inducted into Hollywood's RockWalk on Sunset Boulevard. Other artists with Louisiana ties to be so honored include Cash, Elvis Presley, and Jerry Lee Lewis.[103]

Jimmy Buffett

Despite having only two top 10 songs, Jimmy Buffett (December 25, 1946-), with his bestselling books, personal clothing line, album sales, restaurants, and string of sold-out concerts, manages to earn as much as seventy million dollars per year. Not bad for a guy who spent his formative years in music as a busker, or street performer, in New Orleans, singing for donations and tips. Encouraged by Jerry Jeff Walker, Buffett moved his busking operations to Key West, Florida, where he sang ballads about beaches, bars, and boats, establishing his persona as a laid-back, lovable beach bum.

Born James William Buffett in Pascagoula, Mississippi, he grew up on the eastern shore of Mobile Bay and attended Auburn University and later the University of Southern Mississippi in Hattiesburg, where he received a degree in history and journalism. Though never a dominant figure on the music charts, he has one of the most devoted fan bases this side of the Grateful Dead's fanatically loyal Deadheads. Indeed, as a send-up of their name, Buffett chose a label for his own devotees, who consider it a privilege to be counted among the slightly insane Parrotheads.[104]

A sojourn to Nashville was largely unproductive until he recorded the album *A White Sport Coat and a Pink Crustacean* in 1973—after his move to Key West. That was followed by 1974's *Living and Dying in 3/4 Time,* which produced his first singles chart entry *Come Monday* (number 30). In 1975, he formed the Coral Reefer Band and in 1977 released the album *Changes in Latitudes, Changes in Attitudes*, featuring his first top 10 song. *Margaritaville* peaked at number 8.[105] The song was number 234 on the list of 365 Songs of the Century as compiled in 2001 by the Recording Industry Association of America and the National Endowment for the Arts.

By the time the 1980s rolled around, the Mardi Gras atmosphere of Buffet's live concerts more than made up for the sagging new album sales. He opened his first Margaritaville club in Key West and launched a line of clothing by the same name. While his new album sales were languishing, a compilation of his hits sold millions, earning him a gold record. In 1990, he recorded the live album *Feeding Frenzy*, which also went gold, and in 1992, *Boats, Beaches, Bars, and Ballads* became one of the hottest-selling box sets ever.[106]

Hot Water, released in 1988, featured guest performances by Rita Coolidge, James Taylor, Steve Winwood, and New Orleans musical icons the Neville Brothers. In 2003, he and Alan Jackson recorded the duet *It's Five O'Clock Somewhere*. That song became Buffett's only number 1 hit and won Vocal Event of the Year honors at the 2003 Country Music Association Awards.[107]

Buffett is also one of only a handful of authors to have the *New York Times* number 1 bestseller in fiction and

nonfiction. That distinction puts him in company with
Ernest Hemingway and John Steinbeck. In all, he has written
three number 1 bestsellers. *Tales from Margaritaville* and
Where Is Joe Merchant?, both published in 2003, spent
more than seven months on the *New York Times* Bestseller
fiction list. *A Pirate Looks at Fifty* (2000) shot straight to
the top of the nonfiction list. Among other titles, he also
wrote *Far Side of the World* (2002) and *A Salty Piece of
Land* (2004) and coauthored two children's books, *Jolly
Mon* and *Trouble Dolls,* with daughter Savannah Jane.[108]

In February 1993, Buffett opened his second Margaritaville Café in New Orleans. It is located at the site of the
former Storyville Club in the heart of the French Quarter.
A sign on the wall of the café pays tribute to Buffett's
New Orleans roots by relating how he often came to New
Orleans as a child to meet his grandfather's steamship
(the song *The Captain and the Kid* is his tribute to
his steamship captain grandfather). He thought of New
Orleans as the northern edge of the Caribbean because
his grandfather's ship was always departing New Orleans
for such exotic ports as Buenos Aires and Rio de Janeiro.
Considering the city to be his gateway to the world, he
started his musical career in New Orleans, a place he
always comes back to.

True to his word, Buffett performed at the first post-
Katrina Jazz Fest in 2006. The usually affable Buffett was
almost overcome with emotion when he launched into *City
of New Orleans.* "I got choked up in the first verse," he said
of the poignant return to his beloved Gulf Coast.[109]

The Cowsills

Before the Partridge Family, there were the Cowsills.
Siblings Bill, Bob, Barry, John, Susan, and Paul grew up in
Newport, Rhode Island, although Susan and Barry would
eventually settle in New Orleans. Along with mom Barbara,
they comprised one of the biggest pop acts of the late
1960s. Bill and Bob began their singing careers covering

Everly Brothers hits. They recruited younger brothers Barry and John to play bass and drums. When their mother, Barbara, joined the band, they recorded *The Rain, the Park and Other Things* in 1967. The song climbed to number 2, selling over a million copies. After the band added two more siblings, sister Susan and brother Paul in 1968, *Indian Lake* reached the top 10, and in 1969 the group scored its biggest chart entry with the title song from the rock musical *Hair*.[110]

Susan (May 20, 1959-) and Barry Cowsill (September 14, 1954-September 2005) were both living in New Orleans on August 29, 2005. Susan evacuated ahead of Hurricane Katrina, but her brother did not. She received a phone call from Barry on September 1, two days after the storm, but he was soon reported as missing. His body was found on December 28 but remained unidentified until January 4, 2005. He was fifty-one.[111]

William Alexander "Alex" Chilton

William Alexander "Alex" Chilton (December 28, 1950-) reached the pinnacle of success at age sixteen. Since then, he has gone through a number of transformations. His odyssey included a move to New Orleans, where he worked as a dishwasher and a tree trimmer before making a comeback with a new band.

Born in Memphis, he formed his own band, the Devilles. The band was renamed the Box Tops and in 1967, the group, with sixteen-year-old Chilton as lead singer, recorded *The Letter,* a song that shot to the number 1 position on the *Billboard* Hot 100. *Cry Like a Baby* followed in 1968 and went to number 2.[112]

By early 1970, the band had broken up and in the early 1980s, Chilton moved to New Orleans, where he eventually linked up with jazz musician Panther Burns. In 1984, he split with Burns, but Chilton and the group's bassist, Rene Coman, convinced Memphis drummer Doug Garrison to join them down south. The three began touring and recording at Ardent Studios in Memphis. Their first release was an EP, *Feudalist Tarts,* which featured versions of songs by Carla Thomas, Slim Harpo, and Willie Tee Turbinton. He has since reunited with the Box Tops for concert dates.[113]

Stephen Stills

He is the only artist ever to be inducted into the Rock and Roll Hall of Fame twice on the same night. In 1997, Stephen Stills (January 3, 1945-) was inducted for his work with Buffalo Springfield and with Crosby, Stills and Nash.

Stills moved around as a youngster but claims New Orleans as home. Born in Dallas, he grew up in Texas, Illinois, Louisiana, Panama, Costa Rica, and Florida. He moved back to New Orleans in 1963 at the height of the hootenanny craze to pursue a career as a folk singer but soon realized that Greenwich Village was more suited to folk music than New Orleans.[114]

In New York, he joined a ten-member folk group similar in makeup to the New Christy Minstrels, for whom he wrote and sang in 1964 and '65. With the advent of the British Invasion and the Beatles, Stills headed west to Los Angeles, where he failed auditions for the Monkees and the Lovin'

Stephen Stills. (Courtesy of Louisiana Music Hall of Fame)

Spoonful. He sent for Richie Furay, a former member of Stills' New York group, and the two teamed with Canadians Neil Young and Bruce Palmer to form Buffalo Springfield. In 1967, they scored a number 7 hit with *For What It's Worth*, but the group broke up in May of 1968.[115]

The timing was convenient for forming a powerful new group. The Byrds had recently fired David Crosby, and Graham Nash was becoming increasingly disenchanted with the creative direction of his band, the Hollies. The three combined to create Crosby, Stills and Nash and their first album, helped along by the Judy Collins-inspired *Suite: Judy Blue Eyes* track, sold over two million copies. In 1969, joined by Neil Young, the new group was called Crosby, Stills, Nash and Young. They performed before forty thousand people at the Woodstock Music Festival in upstate New York in August 1969.

After dissolution of the band, Stills remained a solid act. His first solo album, 1971's, *Love the One You're With*, featured Eric Clapton, Jimi Hendrix, and Ringo Starr and went platinum. The title song went to number 14.[116]

In 1979, the Cuban government invited him to perform in the first Cuban American music festival since Fidel Castro took power in the island-nation two decades earlier. Bill Clinton apparently was also a big fan. In 1993, Stills performed at four separate Democratic events during the Clinton inauguration, including the Inaugural Opening Ceremony at the Lincoln Memorial, the official "Blue Jean Bash." The following year, Crosby, Stills and Nash celebrated its twenty-fifth anniversary by performing sixty dates during a summer tour, including headlining at the Second Woodstock Music Festival. The band performed at the White House for President Clinton's birthday and again performed for Clinton and his staff on the White House lawn.[117]

Bobby Kimball

Born in Orange, Texas, Bobby Kimball (March 29, 1947-) was reared in Vinton, Louisiana. He grew up singing and

Bobby Kimball. (Courtesy of Louisiana Music Hall of Fame)

playing piano and performed with a progression of bands, including Baton Rouge's Levee Band, LeRoux, and S.S. Fools. In 1977, he joined with several Los Angeles session musicians to form Toto, a band that would catapult him to new career highs.[118]

Named not for Dorothy's *Wizard of Oz* dog, as many believe, but for spelling simplicity, Toto's self-named first album *Toto* received a Grammy nomination for 1978's Best New Group. In 1983, the band's *Toto IV* album was nominated for eight Grammy awards, winning six. Drug use led to Kimball's being released from the band in 1984, but by 1998, he had made amends and rejoined Toto as lead vocalist.[119]

Randy Jackson

Randy Jackson (June 23, 1956-) was the buffer between benevolent Paula Abdul and caustic Simon Cowell on *American Idol,* for seven years, from 2002 until Abdul's departure at the end of the 2008 season. Jackson's CV, however, is considerably more impressive than just serving as a mediator between his fellow judges.[120]

Born in Baton Rouge, Jackson toured and recorded with the rock band Journey from 1983 to 1986, playing on the group's albums *Frontiers* and *Raised on Radio.* He also has performed with Mariah Carey, Tracy Chapman, Destiny's Child, Bob Dylan, Aretha Franklin, Clarence "Gatemouth" Brown, The Cars, Billy Joel, Bon Jovi, Carlos Santana, Jerry Garcia, Celine Dion, Bruce Springsteen, George Michael, Elton John, Patti LaBelle, Madonna, 'NSYNC, and Charlie Daniels.

Advised to learn the music business from the inside, Jackson moved to production, spending eight years as vice president of A&R for Columbia Records and four more years heading up A&R for MCA. Besides his experience as bassist for Journey, Jackson plays drums, saxophone, guitar, and keyboards. He has worked on over one thousand gold and multiplatinum albums and remains one of the most highly sought-after music industry experts.[121]

Will "Dub" Jones

W.A. "Dub" Jones, the former Cleveland Browns All-Pro receiver and father of NFL quarterback Bert Jones, was born in Ruston. Will "Dub" Jones (May 14, 1928-January 16, 2000) was born and reared seventy miles away in Shreveport.

Though not as well known as the football player, the musician and his deep bass lines are quite familiar. "Meanwhile, back in the jungle" and "Meanwhile, back in the states" originated from the Cadets' 1956 number 11 hit *Stranded in the Jungle.* "Don't talk back," "Slow-walkin' Jones, slow-talkin' Jones," "Why's everybody always pickin' on me?" and "You better leave my daughter alone" were all Jones lines in the Coasters' biggest hits, *Yakety Yak* (number 1 in 1958), *Along Came Jones* (number 9 in 1959), *Charlie Brown* (number 2 in 1959), and *Young Blood* (number 8 in 1957), respectively. The Coasters recorded for Atlantic subsidiary Atco Records. Besides those songs, Jones was rumored to have sung with the Trammps on *Zing! Went the Strings of My Heart* (number 64 in 1972).

He remained with the Coasters until 1965 and in 1988

appeared with other members of the group in New York at the fortieth anniversary celebration for Atlantic Records. He died in 2000 in Long Beach, California, after a lengthy battle with diabetes.[122]

Zebra

Born in February 1975 from the remnants of the band Maelstrom, Zebra is comprised of New Orleans natives Randy Jackson (not to be confused with *American Idol*'s Randy Jackson) and Felix Hanneman and Californian Guy Gelso. In February of 1975, the three were drinking beer and trying to come up with a name for a new band. After a few pitchers of beer, they noticed on the wall a picture of a lady riding a zebra. The photo was a reproduction of a 1922 *Vogue* magazine cover. They liked the photo and chose the subject as the name of the band.

Zebra moved to New York and for several years split gigs between Long Island and New Orleans. The band made two demo tapes during this time and began shopping the tapes to record labels. *Who's Behind the Door?* became a frequent listener request. In late 1982, Zebra was signed by Atlantic and its first album, the self-titled *Zebra,* was released on March 25, 1983. It became the fastest-selling debut record in Atlantic Records history, selling seventy-five thousand copies in its first week. The album remained on the *Billboard* charts for eight months, peaking at number 29.[123]

10

Session Artists

Session musicians labor anonymously and for low pay (the rate was difficult to verify for this work and varies from account to account), playing drums, keyboard, saxophone, bass, guitar; augmenting the lead singer with background vocals; or providing technical advice. It falls to these nameless individuals to turn an ordinary song into a chart buster. Occasionally, an established artist may perform a secondary role. Ernie K-Doe won a gold record with his number 1 hit, *Mother-in-Law*, but it is Benny Spellman's rich baritone that provides the familiar hook. Huey "Piano" Smith played the rolling piano intro for Smiley Lewis's classic *I Hear You Knocking*. Cookie and the Cupcakes provided the instrumental backup on Phil Phillips' *Sea of Love*. "We all knew each other's material and each other's style because we all backed each other up on our recordings," explains Irma Thomas.[1] To their peers, session artists are highly respected professionals. Many have been recognized and honored as such by the industry.

Dave Bartholomew

Dave Bartholomew (December 24, 1920-) was a catalyst in molding and shaping the New Orleans sound during rock and roll's formative years. His contributions were officially acknowledged in 1991 when he was inducted into the Rock and Roll Hall of Fame. Through his association with Cosimo Matassa, he helped develop Smiley Lewis,

Lloyd Price, Huey "Piano" Smith, Chris Kenner, Robert Parker, Frankie Ford, James Booker, James "Sugar Boy"

Crawford, Roy Brown, and Earl King. The biggest name with whom Bartholomew will be eternally linked, however, is Fats Domino. The two collaborated to cowrite more than forty of Domino's hit songs.[2] They produced hundred of millions of dollars in record sales, earning them a spot in the *Guinness Book of World Records.*[3]

Born in Edgard, Louisiana, in St. John the Baptist Parish, Bartholomew moved to New Orleans with his family

Dave Bartholomew. (Courtesy of Louisiana Music Hall of Fame)

when he was a teenager. He was fortunate enough to learn the trumpet from Louis Armstrong's teacher, Peter Davis. Following service in World War II, Bartholomew returned home and put together his own band, which soon became one of the most popular groups in the city. The band was comprised of Bartholomew, saxophonists Lee Allen and Red Tyler, and drummer Earl Palmer.[4]

In 1949, Bartholomew and his band were performing in Houston when he met Imperial Records owner Lew Chudd. Chudd at the time was selling Mexican music and was in Houston to scout for talent. But he was also interested in marketing rhythm-and-blues and hired Bartholomew's band to play sessions at Matassa's J&M Studio. Chudd came to New Orleans to help set up the first session. On a Friday night, he and Bartholomew went to the Hideaway Club and Chudd heard Fats Domino for the first time. He brought Fats into J&M, and the Bartholomew-Domino partnership with Imperial Records and Lew Chudd was born. Their first recording session produced eight songs. One of those was *The Fat Man*.

Fats was Imperial's biggest seller throughout the 1950s (second overall only to Elvis), thanks in large part to Bartholomew's arrangement and production genius.[5] The years 1956 and 1957 were the most productive for Fats and Bartholomew with the pair placing seventeen songs on *Billboard*'s Hot 100. Three of those, *I'm Walkin'*, *Blue Monday*, and *Blueberry Hill*, cracked the top 10.

Blueberry Hill initially created some problems for the two. Bartholomew was not happy with the song, which took the better part of a day to put on tape. Fats had been unable to remember the words and the musicians had performed without sheet music. Several takes were finally spliced together to get a usable copy, a real innovation in those early days of post-production, but Bartholomew was still dissatisfied with the song. He felt it didn't sound right and even tried to convince Chudd not to release the song. Chudd released it anyway for lack of any other recordings from Fats. Bartholomew protested, but two weeks after its release, Chudd called and told him *Blueberry Hill* had just surpassed three million copies sold.

Bartholomew's songs were also popularized by Gale Storm (*I Hear You Knocking*), Elvis Presley (*One Night* and *Witchcraft*), Pat Boone (*Ain't That a Shame*), and Ricky Nelson (*I'm Walkin'*).[6] As his career moved into the 1970s, he worked with Elton John, the Rolling Stones, Paul McCartney, Hank Williams, Jr., Bob Seger, Cheap Trick, Elvis Costello, and Joe Cocker. His songs have also popped up in movies like *The Blues Brothers, American Graffiti,* and *The Girl Can't Help It*.

It became difficult for Bartholomew to turn on the radio and not hear several songs that he had produced. The success of Fats and Bartholomew continued through the decade of the 1950s, Fats scoring his last top 10 hit in 1960 with *Walkin' to New Orleans*. Even after the gravy days finally ran their course, Bartholomew still received offers from New York and the West Coast. He chose to remain in New Orleans.[7]

Roy Montrell

Roy Montrell (February 27, 1928-March 16, 1979) spent more than two decades playing guitar behind some of New Orleans' greatest singers. He is best known, however, as a longtime fixture in Fats Domino's band.

Despite demand as a guitarist in others' recording sessions, he took the opportunity to teach guitar to John Rebennack (Dr. John). So much time did he spend backing other musicians that he cut only two singles of his own— *(Everytime I Hear) That Mellow Saxophone* for Specialty and *Mudd* for Minit Records of New Orleans.

In all, he played on hundreds of recordings for some of the most famous artists of the golden era of New Orleans music. He was equally in demand as a live musician, generally as a member of an artist's tour band. He died suddenly in Amsterdam while on one such tour.[8]

Tommy Ridgley

Tommy Ridgley (October 30, 1920-August 11, 1999) lived and played in the Crescent City. Born Thomas Herman Ridgley, Jr., he grew up outside New Orleans in the Shrewsbury neighborhood of Jefferson Parish. Influenced by Roy Brown, he developed his love of blues while in the navy. He continued his pursuit of music upon his discharge, winning the five-dollar first prize in a talent contest at the Dew Drop Inn.[9]

Signed by Lew Chudd of Imperial Records, he played in Dave Bartholomew's band alongside Red Tyler, Lee Allen, and Herb Hardesty on saxophones; Earl Palmer on drums; Salvador Doucette on piano; Ernest McLean on guitar; and Frank Fields on bass. He was signed by Atlantic Records in 1953 after leaving Imperial. In August of that year, he recorded *Cross That River,* backed with *Ooh Lawdy My Baby*. Piano was provided by Ray Charles.

During the late 1950s, Ridgley and his band, the Untouchables, were the house band at the Dew Drop Inn. They backed Sam Cooke, Clyde McPhatter, Ivory Joe

Hunter, Little Richard, Solomon Burke, Irma Thomas, Ernie K-Doe, Frankie Ford, Eddie Bo, and Little Willie John in appearances at Shreveport's Municipal Auditorium or Lincoln Beach amusement park.[10]

By 1960, Ridgley had signed with Joe Ruffino's Ric label. His affiliation with Ric ushered in one of the most productive and enjoyable times of his career, during which he was billed as the "New King of the Stroll." Chuck Willis, who was the original "King of the Stroll," had just died, and Ruffino thought Ridgley might be his successor.[11]

The turning point of his career came with the introduction of the Beatles to America. Music tastes changed overnight when guitars supplanted horns. Rhythm-and-blues quickly fell into disfavor, and college concerts dried up. Ridgley found himself playing at festivals. In 1995, he developed kidney failure and in May 1998, he received a kidney transplant but died just over a year later.[12]

Earl Palmer

Earl Palmer (October 25, 1924-September 19, 2008) prevailed as a first-call drummer for recording sessions in New Orleans and Los Angeles for more than a half-century.[13] Born in New Orleans, he was first hired by Dave Bartholomew in 1947 for sessions in Cosimo Matassa's studio. Palmer was the session drummer for Fats Domino's historic recording of *The Fat Man,* Lloyd Price's *Lawdy Miss Clawdy,* Little Richard's *Tutti Frutti* and Smiley Lewis's *I Hear You Knocking.* Little Richard said that Palmer was probably the greatest session drummer of all time.[14]

Following a 1957 recording session with Shirley and Lee, he accepted an A&R offer from Aladdin Records and moved to Los Angeles, where he played on thousands of rock, jazz, R&B, and soundtrack sessions.[15] He was a session drummer for Phil Spector's and Berry Gordy's record labels and for dozens of top artists from Ray Charles to Frank Sinatra to Count Basie. He was the drummer on the *Batman, Mission: Impossible, M*A*S*H, The Odd Couple,* and the *Green*

3333333333333

Acres television themes as well as soundtracks for movies *Cool Hand Luke, It's a Mad, Mad, Mad, Mad World, What's Up, Doc?, Top Gun, Predator, The Longest Yard,* and *In the Heat of the Night,* among others.

On March 6, 2000, at the fifteenth annual induction dinner, Palmer was ushered into the Rock and Roll Hall of Fame. Songwriters Mike Leiber and Jerry Stoller served as his presenters at the induction ceremonies.[16] Palmer died in Los Angeles at the age of eighty-three of respiratory illness.[17]

Herb Hardesty

Herb Hardesty (March 3, 1925-) is the architect of the wonderful sax solos on Fats Domino's records *I'm Walking, Blue Monday, Ain't That a Shame,* and *Let the Four Winds Blow.* Hardesty was there from the very beginning of Domino's recording career and played nearly all the saxophone solos until Fats gradually retired from performing.[18]

Born in New Orleans, he started with private lessons, studied at Dillard University, and soon was working with Dave Bartholomew's band. Drafted into Cosimo's studio crew, he began recording with Gatemouth Brown, Big Joe Turner, Tommy Ridgley, Smiley Lewis, and the Spiders. He also toured with Roy Brown and recorded his own songs for the Mercury and Federal labels with tracks like *69 Mother's Place, Perdido Street,* and *Just a Little Bit of Everything.* His Federal sides represent some of the best R&B tracks New Orleans has to offer. Those highlights notwithstanding, Herb Hardesty is remembered for his long association with Domino.

Performing on Fats' debut, 1949's *The Fat Man,* Hardesty laid down great solos for Domino's records for more than half a century. He joined Domino's band full-time in the mid-1950s and has been touring ever since. With his personal and musical sophistication alone, Hardesty stood out from Domino's other musicians, but his wild showmanship—running and sliding across the stage, playing on his back, and even sliding down banisters—added a whole new dimension. After extended periods with Domino in Las

Vegas and Reno, Herb relocated to Vegas in 1970, where he still lives. Under contract to the Las Vegas Hilton, he has backed B.B. King, the Coasters, and Tony Bennett, among others. He also toured with Count Basie, Tom Waits, and Dr. John and continued to perform with Domino off and on throughout the 1970s.[19]

Lee Allen

Listen to songs by Little Richard, Fats Domino, Lloyd Price, Smiley Lewis, Guitar Slim, Charles Brown, Clarence "Frogman" Henry, Dr. John, or the Stray Cats and you are likely to hear the wailing tenor sax of Lee Allen (July 2, 1926-October 18, 1994). Born in Pittsburgh, Kansas, he was offered a music and athletic scholarship to Xavier University in New Orleans in 1943. Once in New Orleans, he began playing weekends at the Dew Drop Inn and the Robin Hood and Tijuana clubs. He never graduated from Xavier because by late 1947, he had joined the Annie Laurie-Paul Gayten band at the Robin Hood. Eventually, Dave Bartholomew invited him to join the J&M Studio Band, which played behind a *Who's Who* of New Orleans rock and roll. His frenetic sax is clear on Little Richard's J&M-recorded *Tutti Frutti*.

Side musicians earned less than fifty dollars a session in those days; a typical four-song session would usually run twelve to eighteen hours. But once the hits started, particularly those of Fats Domino, J&M Studio began attracting recording executives from New York and Los Angeles who used the studio and its musicians. Though Allen would occasionally go on the road with Professor Longhair and Fats Domino, he generally eschewed travel to remain in the New Orleans area so that he could be with his family and take advantage of readily available studio session work.

In 1957, Allen was signed by Al Silver's Herald/Ember label and he produced hit singles for Joe Jones, Ernie K-Doe, and Tommy Ridgley. Despite taking part in the creation of so many hit records for other artists, it was not until 1958 that he came up with a hit of his own, *Walkin' with Mr. Lee,* initially used as a show closer while touring with Fats. Silver suggested that he record the instrumental for Ember Records. It reached number 54 during its eleven-week appearance on *Billboard's* Hot 100. Dick Clark used the song frequently on *American Bandstand,* where it was a number 1 hit for six weeks. With that impetus, Allen formed his own band and played the Apollo in New York and the Howard in Washington and toured Florida, the Carolinas, and Canada. After failing to hit big with anything else, he returned to work for Fats in 1961.

In 1965, with the music scene shifting away from New Orleans, Allen moved to Los Angeles, where he worked at an aircraft manufacturing plant while continuing to participate in recording sessions and play gigs. He returned to New Orleans in the mid-1970s to again work with Fats Domino, a relationship that lasted until 1980. With the rockabilly revival of the late '70s, he was sought out to record with the Stray Cats and was a member of the Blasters for their last two albums. In 1981 he played three shows for the Rolling Stones.[20]

Alvin "Red" Tyler

New Orleans artists who recorded so many hits in Cosimo Matassa's J&M Studio owe much of their success to a group of musicians called the Studio Band. No member of that band was more central to that success than Alvin "Red" Tyler (December 5, 1925-April 3, 1998). Tyler and Lee Allen were officially the co-leaders of the Studio Band, but Tyler was the real leader, though Matassa said he never got the full credit he deserved. It was Tyler, Matassa said, who arranged nearly every song performed in his tiny studio.[21]

Because of finances and his military obligation, Tyler delayed getting into music. The G.I. Bill, however, gave him the opportunity to study at the Grunewald School.[22] He considered himself to be a jazz saxophonist, but rock and roll and blues were more lucrative, paying forty dollars per recording session.

One of the principals of the short-lived A.F.O. record label, he helped form Par-Lo Records when A.F.O. went under. Par-Lo turned out the Aaron Neville classic *Tell It Like It Is*, but distributors made off with the money and neither Tyler nor Neville received a cent for their efforts. Par-Lo soon followed A.F.O. into record label oblivion. Tyler subsequently settled into a job as a liquor salesman and performed occasional gigs.[23]

Peter "Chuck" Badie

Bassist Peter "Chuck" Badie (May 17, 1925 -) collaborated with Allen Toussaint on session work, but he was best known for his unique style on Jessie Hill's *Ooh Poo Pah Doo,* Ernie K-Doe's *Mother-in-Law*, Barbara George's *I Know (You Don't Love Me No More),* and Chris Kenner's *Something You Got.* Following a stint at the Dew Drop Inn, he toured with Roy Brown from 1950 to 1952 and later with Sam Cooke before returning to New Orleans. There he performed with Paul Gayten's band, which led to a tour of duty with Lionel Hampton. In 1961 he teamed with Alvin "Red" Tyler and others to form A.F.O. Records.[24]

Cornelius Jessie Coleman

Some people, it seems, are born to labor in obscurity. Such was the career of Cornelius Jessie Coleman (July 5, 1929-February 20, 1973). An excellent drummer, he was always second banana to Earl Palmer. Never a member of the J&M Studio Band that backed so many great musicians (that distinction was Palmer's alone), Coleman, a native of New Orleans, was Fats Domino's studio and road drummer.[25]

Though Palmer played on Domino's 1949-1950 recordings, Coleman was session drummer on all Fats' recordings from 1951 to 1956. The lone exception was the May 25, 1956, session that produced *When My Dreamboat Comes Home.* He also played on virtually all of Domino's Imperial sessions from 1957 to 1962 but was not on any of his post-Imperial recordings. Even though he did not continue as the studio drummer after Domino moved to ABC-Paramount, Coleman toured with Fats and reappeared on his live Mercury LP recorded in Las Vegas on June 10, 1965.[26]

Eddie Bo

Edwin Joseph Bocage, a.k.a. Eddie Bo (September 30, 1930-March 18, 2009), grew up in New Orleans' Algiers and Ninth Ward neighborhoods. Following a stint in the army he enrolled in the Grunewald School of Music. While there, he developed his unique style of playing the piano, one that drew on the influences of Art Tatum and Oscar Peterson. Throughout his fifty-year career, he made more singles than any other New Orleans artist except Fats Domino. A prolific songwriter, he wrote and recorded *Baby I'm Wise* (recorded by Little Richard as *Slippin' and Slidin'*), *It Must Be Love, Check Mr. Popeye*, and *Hook and Sling*. He also wrote hit songs for Etta James (*My Dearest*

Eddie Bo performs at the New Orleans Jazz Fest. (Courtesy of Louisiana Music Hall of Fame)

Darling) and Tommy Ridgley (*In the Same Old Way*).[27]

Besides writing and recording his own vocals under several names and on a wide assortment of record labels, he also worked as a sideman, arranger, and producer. His piano skills enhanced many records originating in New Orleans. In the early 1950s, Eddie Bo took a group of leading New Orleans sidemen on a tour to back Roy Brown, Big Joe Turner, Smiley Lewis, Lloyd Price, Johnny Adams, and the Platters.[28]

In 1996, he was nominated for a Big Easy Award as Best R&B Artist and was nominated in 1997 as Best Male Artist and Best R&B/Funk Artist. He received the Lifetime Achievement Award from the South Louisiana Music Association, the Big Easy Award for best R&B Player of 2000, the WDSU-TV Making a Difference Award, the Congressional Lifetime Achievement Award in Jazz and Blues, and the Lifetime Achievement Award in Music from New Orleans' *OffBeat* magazine. He was recognized for unwavering loyalty to classic piano playing and R&B traditions by the New Orleans Jazz & Heritage Foundation and for outstanding contributions and dedication to the arts by the New Orleans Museum of Art.[29]

He died of a heart attack at the age of seventy-eight.

James Johnson

Slim Harpo's *Baby, Scratch My Back* was recorded in a single take in J.D. Miller's studio in Crowley. The song features one of music's classic guitar licks by James Johnson (April 8, 1940-), the son of sharecroppers in Pointe Coupee Parish, northwest of Baton Rouge. Miller said Johnson's now-famous "chicken scratch" could have been better if he had put more into it, but Johnson remains satisfied. Johnson also is heard on Slim Harpo's *Rainin' in My Heart*, today considered a classic among south Louisiana blues songs. When *Rainin' in My Heart* was recorded at Miller's studio, it was just another song for the session. Only when it started up the national charts

did Miller, Harpo, and the band members realize they had
something special.

Harpo, Johnson, and the rest once landed a gig in New York
opening for James Brown in Madison Square Garden. The
hardest part of the tour for Johnson was the ordeal of lugging
his guitar and amp all over the city. Despite having become
a famous singer, Slim eschewed hiring a valet, choosing
instead to goad Johnson into hauling his heavy equipment
while Slim was burdened with only a harmonica case.[30]

Lazy Lester

Lazy Lester (June 20, 1933-) was born Leslie Johnson
in Baton Rouge. Now living in northern California, he was
house percussionist, harmonica player, arranger, recording
artist, and session player for J.D. Miller's recording studio.
He can be heard on *Baby, Scratch My Back* tapping the
woodblocks and bongos. Lester said he could hear empty
spaces "and I filled them up with something." He was adept
at improvising with such instruments as newspapers, the
studio's acoustic tile wall, and cardboard boxes stuffed with

Lazy Lester performs at the Baton Rouge Blues Festival in 2006.

an assortment of paper. Members of Elvis Presley's band once told Lester that the percussion in Presley's hit *All Shook Up* was inspired by his cardboard box innovation.

Lester got into recording by accident when he met Lightnin' Slim on a bus. Slim was on his way to a recording session in Miller's Crowley studio, and Lester decided to accompany him. When the session's harmonica player failed to show, Lester boasted that he could play better than the absent musician—a man he had never seen or heard. Miller gave him a chance. Impressed, he hired him as a session musician and gave him the name "Lazy Lester."

Lester recorded several songs that he either wrote by himself or with Miller, but like so many black recording artists of the era, he never saw any royalties. Miller, he claimed, using the pseudonym J. West, gave himself full credit for the songs composed by Lester and reaped the rewards, leaving Lester a bitter man.[31]

John Boudreaux

John Boudreaux began playing drums in elementary school under the guidance of Harold Battiste. He began his professional career with the Hawkettes, who later achieved fame because of Art Neville's tenure with the band. Boudreaux, a native of New Roads, later played behind Clarence "Frogman" Henry before moving on to join Melvin Lastie's band. From Lastie, Boudreaux went on to work with Allen Toussaint, Benny Spellman, Ernie K-Doe, and Dr. John. Boudreaux's energetic drum work is unmistakable on K-Doe's *Mother-in-Law,* Chris Kenner's *Land of 1,000 Dances,* Lee Dorsey's *Sittin' on My Ya-Ya,* and Jessie Hill's *Ooh Poo Pah Doo.*

He also did session work with Lastie's A.F.O Records during its brief existence.[32]

Melvin Lastie

Melvin Lastie (November 18, 1930-December 4, 1972) was introduced to the trumpet at age fifteen and organized his

first professional jazz band during his senior year at Booker
T. Washington High School in New Orleans. The piano player
for that band was Fats Domino. Lastie went on the road at
sixteen and in 1954 he joined Big Joe Turner as the singer's
bandleader. Returning to New Orleans, he performed as a
regular at the Sho-Bar on Bourbon Street before running his
own nightclub, the High Hat, from 1957 to 1959. The club
took up an entire city block and featured three bars.[33]

In the early 1960s, he joined Harold Battiste in forming
A.F.O. Records. During this time, Lastie also served as a
representative for the American Federation of Musicians
Local 496 and he handled all recording transactions for the
musicians' union.[34]

In 1963, Lastie and Battiste moved to Los Angeles, where
they produced Sam Cooke's label. They were instrumental
in producing one of Cooke's greatest songs, *A Change Is
Gonna Come.* Back in New Orleans, they also produced the
Dixie Cups' first hit, *Chapel of Love.*[35]

Wardell Quezergue

Wardell Quezergue (March 12, 1930-) was one of the most
requested arrangers for Crescent City recording sessions.
Quezergue worked behind the scenes to create some of the
best-known material for many New Orleans performers as
well as Rufus Thomas, the Pointer Sisters, and Paul Simon.
Examples of Quezergue's work include *Iko-Iko* and *Chapel
of Love* (Dixie Cups), *Barefootin'* (Robert Parker), *Trick Bag*
(Earl King), *Big Chief* (Professor Longhair), *Mr. Big Stuff*
(Jean Knight), *Groove Me* (King Floyd), Dr. John's Grammy
award-winning album *Going Back to New Orleans,* and
Paul Simon's 1973 album *There Goes Rhymin' Simon*.

Once, he found it necessary to borrow a school bus to
transport participants to the recording sessions for *Groove
Me* and *Mr. Big Stuff*, produced under his struggling Malaco
Record label. Stax and Atlantic Records turned down both
records and only after King Floyd's *Groove Me* began taking
off did Atlantic relent. He also was instrumental in the

production of two outstanding big-band albums by Clarence "Gatemouth" Brown, and he did studio work with Willie Nelson, the Supremes, B.B. King, and the Staple Singers.[36]

Allen Toussaint

Allen Toussaint (January 14, 1938-) created a monster of sorts when he wrote *Mother-in-Law* for Ernie K-Doe. When K-Doe recorded his signature song, Benny Spellman was asked to sing backup. Thus, the rich baritone intoning "Mother-in-law" as the song's introduction is identified with the number 1 song as much as K-Doe's singing. After *Mother-in-Law* became a hit, Spellman approached Toussaint with a request that he write him a hit song. Toussaint wrote *Lipstick Traces (On a Cigarette),* which went to number 28 on the R&B charts and to number 80 on the Hot 100 in

Allen Toussaint. (Courtesy of Louisiana Music Hall of Fame)

June of 1962. He also wrote *Fortune Teller* for Spellman, a song later covered by the Rolling Stones.[37]

Toussaint, born in New Orleans, has been a key part of the city's music scene since the late 1950s. He was hired by Dave Bartholomew to play piano parts for a Fats Domino recording session while Fats was on the road and unavailable to lay down the instrumental track. He also played in recording sessions behind Lee Allen and Smiley Lewis.[38] He became a producer with New Orleans-based Minit Records in 1960.[39]

He was drafted into the army for two years in 1963 and ran head-on into racial stereotyping. On a weekend pass from his Houston base, he and a friend traveled to Dallas where Toussaint decided to purchase a new car. When Toussaint said he was paying cash for the vehicle, the salesman began stalling. It turned out the salesman thought a black man with enough money to pay cash must have stolen it, so he had coworkers call the police.[40]

Toussaint also wrote *Working in the Coal Mine, I Like It Like That, Java* (a number 4 hit for Al Hirt), *Whipped Cream* for Herb Alpert (the theme for the TV show *The Dating Game*), *All These Things* for Aaron Neville, and *Southern Nights* for Glen Campbell. *Southern Nights* was recognized by Broadcast Music, Inc. as the most performed song of the year and was nominated for Song of the Year by the Grammy Awards and the Country Music Association. In 1976, the editors of *Billboard* named Toussaint "One of the Top 200 Executives of Tomorrow."[41]

In 1973, Toussaint and Marshall Sehorn opened Sea-Saint Studio. There, Toussaint produced, arranged, or played with Paul McCartney, Dr. John, Patti LaBelle, Paul Simon, Joe Cocker, Etta James, Ramsey Lewis, and Elvis Costello, among others. He earned gold records for his production and arrangements for Dr. John (*Right Place, Wrong Time*), Patti LaBelle (*Lady Marmalade*), and Paul Simon (*Kodachrome*). In 1998, Toussaint was inducted into the Rock and Roll Hall of Fame[42] and in

2009 he was named a Grammy Trustees Award Winner.

When Hurricane Katrina blew into New Orleans on August 29, 2005, not only was Toussaint's home completely flooded, but his beloved Sea-Saint Studio was also lost to the floodwaters as well. "It was almost surreal," he told *Billboard* magazine. "I've seen all the hurricanes that have come through, and I saw the biggest." Toussaint made his way by bus to Baton Rouge Metropolitan Airport and from there took a flight to New York, where he settled in until he, like others, could start the painful process of recovery in his hometown.[43] Typically, he said Katrina wasn't a drowning, but a baptism.[44]

Gerald James McGee

Gerald James McGee (November 17, 1937-) was born in Eunice to pioneer Cajun fiddler Dennis McGee. He began his own musical career at age fourteen and went on to play with some of the elites of country and rock in California, Nashville, and New York before returning to Louisiana. Besides his father, he drew inspiration from Hank Snow, Jimmie Rodgers, Chet Atkins, Lefty Frizzell, and Guitar Slim. He plays lead guitar, bass, accordion, banjo, and harmonica.[45]

Guitarist Gerald James McGee, left, with Mike Shepherd of the Louisiana Music Hall of Fame. (Courtesy of Louisiana Music Hall of Fame)

One of McGee's first professional gigs was with Bill Mack and Buddy White after they left Gene Vincent's Blue Caps. Billing themselves as Buddy White and the Knights, they embarked from Shreveport on a 1959 tour that lasted four months. McGee returned to Shreveport and contacted James Burton, who at the time was Ricky Nelson's guitarist. McGee took Burton's advice to relocate to California and found work as a session musician. He played guitar on the Jerry Lee Lewis hit *Great Balls of Fire* and has recorded with Sandy Nelson, Elvis Presley, John Mayall, the Monkees, Rita Coolidge, Booker T and the MGs, Nancy Sinatra, Kris Kristofferson, Patti Page, Emmy Lou Harris, Ray Stevens, Jerry Reed, the Everly Brothers, Linda Ronstadt, Dwight Yoakam, and Joe South.[46]

He has extensive movie and television credits, including three Kris Kristofferson movies: *A Star Is Born*, *Heaven's Gate*, and *Convoy*. He also appeared in the ABC miniseries *North and South* and the NBC series *L.A. Law*.[47] In 1968, he joined the Ventures. The most successful instrumental rock band ever, the Ventures continue to tour Europe and Japan. McGee has recorded more than twenty studio CDs with the Ventures as well as several live albums and DVDs.[48] The band was inducted into the Rock and Roll Hall of Fame in 2008.

Deacon John Moore

Deacon John Moore (June 23, 1941-) participated in hundreds of the recording sessions at Cosimo Matassa's studio that produced so many R&B hits of the 1950s and early '60s. Moore was one of thirteen children reared in a musical family on New Orleans' Elysian Fields Avenue. After purchasing a pawn shop guitar, he fell under the influence of Roy Montrell, Justin Adams, and George Davis. Davis and Deacon John traded guitar licks on Robert Parker's *Barefootin'*. He also played sessions for dozens of other New Orleans artists. "I played nearly everything recorded for Minit Records," he said.[49]

John Moore knew he needed something to set him apart from the crowd and for that something, he looked no

Deacon John Moore performs at the inauguration of Louisiana governor Bobby Jindal in 2008. (Courtesy of Louisiana Music Hall of Fame)

farther than Roy Brown's 1947 hit *Good Rockin' Tonight*. A line (absent from cover versions) goes, "Well Deacon Jones and Nelda Brown/Two of the sleekest cats in town/ They'll be there, just wait and see/Stomping an' jumpin' at the jamboree." Moore took the name "Deacon" from that song.[50]

Besides their regular gig at New Orleans' Dew Drop Inn, Deacon John and the Ivories played behind a different artist every Sunday as the house band at the College Inn in Thibodaux, backing Huey Smith and His Clowns and national acts Chubby Checker, the Midnighters, Marvin Gaye, Wilson Pickett, and Little Esther.[51] "I remember when [James] Booker went on the road with the Clowns and impersonated Huey 'Piano' Smith," Moore has related. No one knew any better because there was no television and without that medium to familiarize audiences with musicians' appearances, it was easy to sell a phony.[52]

Before the popularization of television, such substitution of artists was common. Deacon John said the first time he met Earl King, King was posing as Chuck Berry. He came out with his hair and nails done, wearing a long coat down to his knees, Moore described. But King was a charismatic performer in his own right. In the style of the times, Earl King was a master at "walkin' the bar." He would walk up and down the bar, playing his saxophone. People would stuff money in the horn, and if Earl knocked over a drink, he would go behind the bar and replace it, all the time playing with one hand. Moore said he could never forget that scene even though he was only sixteen or seventeen at the time.[53]

At an after-party show for the 1999 Big Easy Awards, Deacon John reunited with Cyril Vetter, whom he had known at the beginning of his career. Vetter earned a living as a Baton Rouge attorney, television executive, musician, and songwriter. He was a member of the 1960's LSU fraternity band the Greek Fountains and wrote *Double Shot of My Baby's Love*, a number 17 hit for the Swingin' Medallions in 1966. Their chance reunion in New Orleans spawned the idea for the *Deacon John's Jump Blues* CD, produced by Vetter and his daughter Gabrielle, and recorded at Ultrasonic Studios in New Orleans. The session included songs of Dave Bartholomew, Ray Charles, Smiley Lewis, Professor Longhair, and Shirley and Lee. That project was followed by a concert video of the same name, recorded in the historic Orpheum Theater in New Orleans.[54]

One of the reasons Moore agreed to the project was because the documentary portion of the video, "Going Back to New Orleans," did not include a second line or other overused traditions such as flambeaux dancers that he feels have become a cliché under the guise of preserving New Orleans heritage. Moore said he likes the brass bands and the Mardi Gras Indians but the sight of grown men picking up pennies that people have tossed onto the street during Mardi Gras parades is demeaning. Keeping these traditions alive just perpetuates a negative stereotype, he said in an interview.[55]

Moore was inducted into the Louisiana Blues Hall of Fame in 2000,[56] and in 2006 he became president of New Orleans Local 174-496 of the American Federation of Musicians.[57]

D.J. Fontana

In early October 1954, Shreveport drummer Dominic Joseph Fontana (March 15, 1931-) was asked to come by the *Louisiana Hayride* offices to listen to some records by a new singer. He had never heard of the kid who called himself the "Hillbilly Cat," but his first *Hayride* show with Elvis Presley would forge a friendship between the two that would last until Presley's death.

Because drums were generally frowned upon by country music fans in those pre-rockabilly days, Fontana always remained behind the curtain when accompanying *Hayride* guests, including Elvis in his debut. Reflecting their movement away from the country sound, Elvis and his band members Scotty Moore and Bill Black were happy for the chance to perform with a drummer for the first time. Prior to the show, D.J. decided to complement the three rather than crowd them with his drums, so he eschewed cymbals and played the back beat. After that first performance with Presley, D.J. emerged from behind the curtain to play up front with the rest of the band.

Agreeing to share the cost of his one-hundred-dollar-per-week salary between them, Scotty and Bill persuaded Elvis to add D.J. as a permanent member of the band. When Sam Phillips sold Presley's contract to RCA in late 1955, Elvis, Scotty, Bill, and D.J. entered the RCA studios for Elvis's first session, which included *I Got a Woman* and *Heartbreak Hotel*. It was his first recording session with Elvis. On July 2, 1956, they had a follow-up session in New York that produced *Hound Dog, Don't Be Cruel,* and *Any Way You Want Me.* Three appearances on the *Ed Sullivan Show* between September 1956 and January 1957 netted Elvis $50,000 while D.J., Scotty, and Bill each were paid $78.23 per show. From that first RCA session to the time

D.J. left Elvis's employ in 1969, he played on about four hundred RCA songs with Elvis, participating in nearly fifty recording sessions.[58]

Floyd Cramer

Floyd Cramer (October 27, 1933-December 31, 1997) was everything Jerry Lee Lewis was not—and vice versa. Lewis sang; Cramer did not. Lewis pounded the piano in such an aggressive boogie-woogie style that kids jitterbugged in the aisles. They slow danced when Cramer caressed the keys. Lewis, with his ego, could settle for nothing less than star billing. Cramer, even with three top 10 hits as a solo artist, was content in his role as a session pianist, backing up some of the hottest names in country and popular music.

Born in Campti, Louisiana, Cramer grew up in the tiny (population 1,500) sawmill town of Huttig, Arkansas. By age five, he was teaching himself to play the piano, eschewing formal lessons. Upon graduation from high school in 1951, he left Huttig for Shreveport and a job as pianist for the *Louisiana Hayride.* There he backed up Jim Reeves, Webb Pierce, Hank Williams, Lefty Frizzell, and Elvis Presley, among others. He also backed Reeves on his 1951 RCA recording of *Mexican Joe.* The friendship he made with Elvis at the *Hayride* developed into a close relationship as the two toured high-school auditoriums together throughout Texas in 1952 and '53.[59]

After a year or two alternating between working with Elvis and commuting to Nashville, he approached Chet Atkins about becoming a session pianist. Encouraged, he made the permanent move from Shreveport to Tennessee in 1955 and within a year, he was busy day and night playing sessions for various artists. One of the few times he did not play piano in a session was for Jimmy Dean's 1961 number 1 smash hit *Big Bad John.* For that session, he created the pickaxe sound effect by suspending an iron doorstop from a coat hanger and striking it with a hammer. By one estimate, Cramer played on a quarter of all releases during the heyday of the Nashville sound. "I've worked with about everybody," he once said.[60] He participated in Elvis Presley's first recording sessions for RCA in 1956. Among the songs that came from those sessions were *Heartbreak Hotel, Too Much, Hound Dog, Any Way You Want Me, Don't Be Cruel, I Was the One, Money Honey,* and *I Want You, I Need You, I Love You.* Others with whom he recorded include Roy Orbison, the Everly Brothers, Patsy Cline, Charley Pride, Connie Smith, Boots Randolph, Chet Atkins, Eddie Arnold, Brenda Lee, and Ray Price.[61]

Then, in 1960, Cramer recorded a slow, melodic instrumental ballad entitled *Last Date.* It was the first of three consecutive top 10 songs that would earn him gold records. The song featured a style of playing called the "slip note" or "bent note," wherein two notes are struck almost simultaneously so that one leads effortlessly into another with a slurred sound. *Last Date* was a pop hit, reaching number 2 for four weeks, beginning in December, and remaining on the charts for twenty weeks altogether. The record that kept it from reaching number 1 was Presley's *Are You Lonesome Tonight,* on which Cramer also played.[62]

He followed *Last Date* with *On the Rebound,* which reached number 4 in April 1961, and *San Antonio Rose,* which climbed to number 8 in July 1961. He also had a number 49 hit with *Java,* a song written by Allen Toussaint. Following a spate of other moderate hits, Cramer stopped releasing singles, concentrating on albums, though in 1979, *My Blue Eyes* won a Grammy for Best Country Instrumental.[63] His thirty-ninth album, *In Concert,* was recorded in the cafeteria of his ninth-grade daughter's junior high school in Nashville. She was on the school's entertainment committee and prevailed on her father to perform. Cramer, in turn, convinced RCA Nashville operations chief Chet Atkins that the album would be a good project. His instincts were correct as the album turned out to be one of his best efforts.[64]

In 1997, Cramer was diagnosed with cancer. He died at his home at the age of sixty-four.[65]

Carl Bailey Adams

Carl Bailey Adams (November 7, 1935-February 24, 1965) was uniquely gifted as a musician despite having only two fingers on his left hand. Events in his early childhood that led to his disfigurement left him even more scarred emotionally and psychologically than physically.[66]

Born in Rayville, Louisiana, Carl was the last of ten children born to Monroe and Lura Adams. Four of his siblings died at birth.[67] On October 11, 1941, less than a month before his sixth birthday, his grandfather placed a double-barreled shotgun on the dining room table in preparation for a hunting trip. Carl inserted the two middle fingers of his left hand into one of the gun barrels. The gun's safety was off and there was one shell in the chamber. Startled at his sister's scream of alarm, he jerked his hand, causing the loaded shotgun to roll and discharge. The scene that ensued was both horrific and unimaginable. The two fingers Carl had jammed into the gun barrel were blown off. Even worse, his infant cousin Charles Alvis was in the line of fire and was decapitated.[68] Devastated, a guilt-ridden Carl spent the remainder of his life believing he was responsible for his cousin's death.

With surgery, Carl's hand was partially repaired and his remaining fingers were shaped into a semblance of a claw so that he could grasp objects. To encourage the use of his damaged hand, Carl's mother bought him a guitar when he was twelve and he taught himself to play left-handed with picks taped to his thumb and little finger while holding the guitar upside down and backwards.[69] Instead of reversing the order of the strings to allow him to pick the instrument in the manner of most left-handed players, he left the strings as they were and learned to play by pulling on the strings instead of pushing on them, according to Ed Dettenheim, who, with Adams on lead, played rhythm guitar for the Rhythm Rebels band. The unique method of playing allowed Adams to develop a sound that baffled other players, a sound Dettenheim described a half-century later as "a screaming, wailing guitar sound." According to Dettenheim, Chet Atkins called Carl's playing "the most commercial guitar sound he'd ever heard."[70]

Carl met Dale Hawkins while attending elementary school in Mangham, Louisiana. Sharing a common love for music, the two struck a lasting relationship that would see them perform together professionally. Playing lead guitar for Hawkins in 1957, he collaborated on several recordings, including *Number Nine Train* on Norton Records and the Checker label's *Don't Treat Me This Way*, *Little Pig*, and *Baby, Baby*. "I was the first person Carl worked for," Hawkins says. "I went to his house to get him. My second release, *Baby, Baby,* which was recorded in Chicago, was the first session Carl ever played on." That session was held in the Sheldon Studio on August 29, 1957. Margaret Lewis of Shreveport sang backup vocals. "I took him [Adams] to Chicago with me several times," Hawkins continues.[71]

Around that time Adams and Ed Detteneheim were serving as the session band for KRUS radio station in Ruston. When Tommy Blake came to work as a disc jockey in 1955 or '56, he convinced the two to join him for live performances on KTBS in Shreveport and they began to tour north Louisiana.[72]

Long hours and too many gigs eventually took their toll on Carl's health and ultimately, his life, according to the Rockabilly Hall of Fame. He struggled with over-the-counter drugs for several years, and in late February of 1965, he made a desperate call to his mother from El Paso, Texas. At his mother's insistence, he purchased a bus ticket to California, where his mother and his sister Vaudie lived. Vaudie, an operating room nurse, met him in Long Beach. Recognizing the symptoms of kidney failure, she took him directly to the hospital where he was rushed into surgery. He never made it out of surgery. At the age of twenty-nine and at the apex of his career, he died.[73]

Fred Carter, Jr.

Fred Carter, Jr. (December 28, 1933-), a native of Winnsboro, wears three hats—musician, singer, and composer—but it was as a prolific guitarist that he earned his reputation. Carter, who also plays fiddle, bass, mandolin, and piano, did not take up guitar until he was in his early twenties. In his stellar career, he has backed Dale and Ronnie Hawkins, Elvis Presley, Webb Pierce, Kitty Wells, Faron Young, Johnny Horton, Chet Atkins, Les Paul, Roy Orbison, Johnny Cash, Jerry Lee Lewis, Willie Nelson, Waylon Jennings, Bobbie Gentry, Floyd Cramer, Muddy Waters, Simon & Garfunkel, The Band, Bob Dylan, Joan Baez, Neil Young, and Dean Martin.

Although he played on several of Simon & Garfunkel's recordings, his presence is most evident on *The Boxer,* a number 7 *Billboard* hit in 1969. In all, he played four different guitars for the recording, including the superb introduction and conclusion. He also played on their number 1 hit *Bridge over Troubled Waters* in 1970, Bobby Goldsboro's number 1 *Honey* in 1968, Kenny Rogers' number 1 *Lucille* in 1977, and bass on Bob Dylan's *Lay, Lady, Lay,* which climbed to number 11 in 1969.[74]

The first vocalist for whom he played guitar on a recording was Slim Whitman. "Our recording session was held in the KWKH studios after the station went off the air," he remembers. Two songs that came from that session were *Among My Souvenirs* and a gospel song, *Lord Take My Hand and Show Me How,* written by Kathleen Quarles of Ruston.

Carter retired at age fifty-five in 1990. "I got tired of playing others' music and wanted to play some of my own," he explains. "I went back to my family home in Winnsboro for most of the '90s. I built my own studio, not for others to record in, but for me to play around in and experiment." He later sold the Winnsboro property and moved back to Nashville. "Music is music whenever, wherever, whether you're playing a lute or a synthesizer," he says. "Music is multilingual; it knows no color and recognizes no boundaries or time limitations. You see, music is like water—it fits in anything and will go anywhere."[75]

Already a dialysis patient and a diabetic, he suffered a

stroke in 2009 that left him almost totally blind. "I'm not in too good a shape," he says.

Maylon Humphries

Maylon Humphries (March 18, 1935-) never seemed to be able to grab the brass ring for himself. Born in the Jackson Parish village of Kelly, Louisiana, he attended high school in Pineville and Alexandria. He was in the KWKH radio studio in 1957 helping with the hand clapping on Dale Hawkins' recording of *Suzy-Q*. It was also in 1957 that Humphries cut a demo of *Worried about You, Baby* which, like *Suzy-Q*, had James Burton on lead guitar and Ronnie Lewis on drums.

Ronnie Lewis's brother, Stan Lewis, sent *Worried about You, Baby* to Chess Records in Chicago. Leonard Chess, however, decided against releasing the song because his style too closely resembled Hawkins'. It remained in the Chess vaults until 1976 when it was inadvertently included in the All Platinum Record Group release of a Dale Hawkins album.

Humphries followed James Burton and Bob Luman to California in 1958 but returned to Shreveport following the death of his brother. In 1960, he married Betty Jo Abbott, whose sister, Louise, was married to Burton.[76]

Charles "Keep-a-Knockin'" Connor

Because Little Richard played and sang with such flamboyance, he easily overshadowed other members of his band. Still, drummer Charles "Keep-a-Knockin'" Connor (January 14, 1935-), born in the heart of the New Orleans French Quarter, was one of music's few successful left-handed drummers. Inspired by Gene Krupa and Buddy Rich, he started playing at local parties. In 1950, when he was fifteen, Professor Longhair hired him as a last-minute fill-in for a Mardi Gras gig, marking the beginning of his professional career.[77]

In 1953 he was in Nashville playing with Smiley Lewis. Little Richard was playing a few doors away. Without a band of his own, Richard asked Connor and saxophonist

Lee Diamond to join him.[78] Only seventeen, Connor had to call home and get permission from his mother. "What's a 'little Richard'?" she asked. "Is that the boy with the long hair who looks like a woman?" She consented and Connor became an original member of the Upsetters.

One of the first things Little Richard did was take Connor to the train station in Macon, Georgia. "I don't know the name of the beat and I'm not familiar with notes or anything, but I want you to play like a choo-choo train pulling out from the station," the singer said. "That's the kind of beat I want you to play behind me. No other drummer is playing the beat and we've got to sound different and look different." Connor replied, "Yeah, nobody's doing it because it's hard to do." Despite the difficulty, the drummer mastered the sound. Connor explains, "Now, to understand what I was doing, I was playing four-four time on my bass drum. On my sock cymbal, I'm playing eighth notes and I'm playing those same notes on my snare drum. That's how Little Richard's style was created. I created that choo-choo beat way before any *Tutti Frutti* or *Long Tall Sally* or any of Little Richard's Specialty hits."[79]

In order to project a nonthreatening image to white music patrons and hostile black boyfriends alike, Little Richard required that band members wear pancake makeup and act effeminate. "All the band members had to wear makeup and earrings and act gay," Connor says. "White men relaxed, thinking the colored boys were gay. Likewise, black men weren't jealous of 'gay' band members, but the only one who was actually gay was Richard. Back then, we all had to be actors." He continues, "We looked like a bunch of Negro sissies but that's how we got to play rock and roll in the white honky-tonks. Remember, this was in 1954. We played a lot of places where other bands wouldn't. It was all about attitude."[80]

During breaks from touring with Little Richard, he worked with Kenner native Lloyd Price. He also took advantage of the fact that Little Richard and James Brown shared the same booking agent and played with the Godfather of Soul when Little Richard was not working. Two years after he joined Little

Richard, the band toured the U.S., playing Turner's Arena and Howard Theatre in Washington, D.C., Royal Theatre in Baltimore, Apollo Theater in Harlem, and Paramount Theater in Brooklyn as part of an Alan Freed promotion. It was in New York that he first witnessed white teenagers dancing in the aisles with black teens. "The Civil Rights Act may have been passed in 1964, but rock and roll music brought young people together a decade earlier. Our popularity cut across racial lines." It was also in New York that Little Richard, with Connor on drums, recorded *Lucille,* which was a number 1 R&B hit and number 21 on the pop charts.

"A lot of Little Richard's tunes were recorded with a studio band at Cosimo Matassa's studio in New Orleans because the musicians had a little syndicate thing," Connor says. "We were in all the movies with Little Richard and we played all his concerts but they wouldn't let him or Guitar Slim or Fats Domino or Joe Turner or Ernie K-Doe or Jessie Hill use their traveling bands. They had that studio thing so controlled. That's how those musicians made a living, by recording behind about ten or twelve acts."[81]

Occasionally, though, Little Richard would record away from New Orleans. In 1957, *Keep-a-Knockin'* was recorded by the road band in Washington, D.C. "We were playing at the Howard Theatre and had a two-hour break between shows. We rushed over to a radio station to record the old Louis Jordan song *Keep-a-Knockin'*. Richard wanted a four-bar intro but when he tried it on the piano, it didn't sound powerful enough for him. I suggested that I try it on the drums. I came up with that little choo-choo train thing with all kinds of New Orleans gumbo tossed in. Little Richard liked it so much he gave me a five-hundred-dollar bonus on the spot. My drum intro became the signature for *Keep-a-Knockin'*."[82] Connor's first four-bar drum intro helped propel *Keep-a-Knockin'* to number 8 on *Billboard*'s Hot 100 and number 2 on the R&B chart, making it the singer's second-biggest hit behind *Long Tall Sally*.

Some sources give credit for the introduction to *Keep-a-*

Knockin' to Earl Palmer, who was Richard's regular studio drummer, but Connor insists it was he, not Palmer, on the song and that it was recorded in Washington, not New Orleans. Connor also takes credit for giving Little Richard the phrase "A-wop-bop-a-loo-bop-a-lop-bam-boom," the opening line to *Tutti Frutti.*[83]

His distinctive four-bar drum intro is duplicated on Led Zeppelin's *Rock and Roll* from the *Led Zeppelin IV* album. "That was John Bonham," he says of the Led Zeppelin drummer who died in 1980. "That was my eight-note choo-choo train intro and he took it right off *Keep-a-Knockin'.* But he didn't have the soul to pull it off the way I did. He didn't have any red beans and rice."

When Little Richard retired from music in favor of the ministry in 1957, Conner and the Upsetters joined Sam Cooke. During breaks from performing with Cooke, Conner also worked with Big Joe Turner, the Coasters, and Jackie Wilson. He recorded with Jack Dupree, Larry Williams, Larry Birdsong, and Dee Clark. His drumming is prominent in Clark's recording *Hey Little Girl.*

Connor and his wife live in Los Angeles, where he is still active as a musician and songwriter. He also devotes much of his time to motivational speaking appearances. His drumsticks are on display at the Rock and Roll Hall of Fame.[84]

Joe Osborne

The bass lines of Joe Osborne (August 28, 1937-) are heard on half the hit songs recorded in Los Angeles. He played on more than four hundred Top 40 country hits and over two hundred Top 40 pop hits, twenty of which were number 1 songs. He played bass for Dale Hawkins on his recording of *Suzy-Q* in 1957 and was the first to record Karen and Richard Carpenter, doing so in his four-track recording studio in his home.[85]

Osborne was born in the Madison Parish town of Mound, Louisiana, across the Mississippi River from Vicksburg. He grew up in Shreveport and at age twelve learned to play guitar by listening to the radio. He started out working area clubs before teaming with Hawkins. He headed to Los Angeles and, finding himself without work, contacted Shreveport native Bob Luman, who hired him for a year-long gig at the Las Vegas Showboat Hotel in 1959. He returned to Shreveport briefly in 1960 but soon returned to L.A. For the next four years he played bass on Rick Nelson's recordings and was a regular guest, along with James Burton, on the *Adventures of Ozzie and Harriet.*

Osborne soon was in demand as a recording session sideman. Among those soliciting his services were producers Bones Howe and Lou Adler; songwriters Jimmy Webb, Steve Barry, and P.F. Sloane; and singers Tommy Boyce and Bobby Hart. While making a demo for Adler's Dunhill Records in 1963, he played with drummer Hal Blaine and keyboardist Larry Knechtel. It was the first time to play together for the three, who later became known as the Wrecking Crew, which for the next decade was the top rhythm section on the West Coast. The trio played on recordings by Glen Campbell, the Beach Boys, Monkees, Fifth Dimension, Partridge Family, the Mamas and the Papas, the Carpenters, the Association, Gary Lewis and the Playboys, America, Spanky and Our Gang, and the Grass Roots. Baton Rouge native Johnny Rivers, by then living in Los Angeles, recruited Osborne to play bass on his albums and to help open the Whiskey a Go-Go in 1964. Osborne traveled to New York to play on recordings by Simon & Garfunkel, Bobby Sherman, Richard Harris, and Barry McGuire. He also performed on many movie soundtracks and television commercials.[86]

Attempting to cut back on his workload, he demanded double and triple scale. The tactic backfired when demand for his services increased to as many as twenty sessions per week. To force a cutback in his schedule, he moved to a Nashville farm. There he experienced a slower pace of occasional jingles and sessions with Chet Atkins, Eddie Rabbitt, Merle Haggard, Reba McEntire, Kenny Rogers, and Jimmy Buffett. In 1990, he moved to a Shreveport suburb where he continues to record original songs on his four-track recorder. He still flies to Dallas, Los Angeles, and Nashville for occasional recording dates. But after four decades of nonstop picking, he has finally succeeded in reducing his work schedule.[87]

James Burton

He got his first guitar at age thirteen and within a year, James Burton (August 21, 1939-) was a member of the *Louisiana Hayride* staff band. At fifteen, he joined Dale Hawkins in the KWKH studio in Shreveport to record *Suzy-Q*. Besides Hawkins, he would record with Elvis Presley, Elvis Costello, Rick Nelson, Jerry Lee Lewis, John Denver, Merle Haggard, Emmylou Harris, Randy Newman, and Roy Orbison.[88]

Burton was born in Minden and his family moved to nearby Shreveport when he was ten. He and Hawkins cowrote *Suzy-Q* in 1956, Burton writing the music and Hawkins penning the lyrics. Burton remains philosophical about not receiving writer's credits, saying he was only fifteen

Statue of James Burton outside Shreveport's Municipal Auditorium. Burton played for many years with Elvis Presley.

and knew nothing about the music business. He said he was only doing something he really loved and enjoyed.[89]

At the *Hayride,* he backed George Jones, Johnny Horton, and Bob Luman. Ricky Nelson overhead him as he played behind Luman at the Imperial Records studio and recruited him for his band. The two remained together from 1958 to 1965. Millions of viewers watching the *Adventures of Ozzie and Harriet* each week saw Burton playing behind Nelson in the closing musical performance of each show.[90]

In 1965, the TV show *Shindig!* debuted, featuring Burton as guitarist for the show's house band, the Shindogs.[91] During this time, Bob Dylan tried to lure him to work in his touring band, but the contract with *Shindig!* prevented him from accepting the offer. In 1966, he released *Corn Pickin' and Slick Slidin'* with Buck Owens' pedal steel guitar player Ralph Mooney.[92]

In 1968, Burton was asked to participate in NBC's 1968 Elvis Presley "Comeback Special," but he was doing studio work on an album with Frank Sinatra and was unable to accept yet another exciting opportunity. He had seen Elvis perform at the *Hayride* but the two never met until Elvis decided to resume touring in 1969. Burton was the first person he called, asking him to play guitar and be his band leader. This time Burton accepted the offer to replace Scotty Moore. The two remained together until Presley's death on August 16, 1977.[93]

Burton remembered that on the day of Presley's death, he was on board a plane en route to Portland, Maine, for Presley's scheduled August 17 show. During the flight, they were asked to return to Las Vegas. The plane landed in Pueblo, Colorado, to refuel and trombonist Marty Harrell called Vegas for answers. Harrell came up to Burton and put his arm around him. He said that Elvis had died, Burton remembered, adding that cold chills went through him. He and the others attempted to come to grips with the finality of the news during the long flight back to Vegas. "It was an incredibly sad time," he said in an interview.[94]

During downtimes with Elvis, Burton also performed with Gram Parsons and Emmylou Harris as part of their Hot Band. He toured for several years with John Denver and was a member of Jerry Lee Lewis's road band in the early 1980s. In 1971, with Presley's producer Felton Jarvis, he recorded his only solo album, *The Guitar Sounds of James Burton.* Other stars with whom he has performed include Hoyt Axton, Judy Collins, Buffalo Springfield, the Everly Brothers, the Beach Boys, Sonny and Cher, Buck Owens, the Fifth Dimension, and Phil Spector's roster of singers. In 1988, he performed in the Cinemax special "Roy Orbison and Friends: A Black and White Night," playing a guitar duel with Bruce Springsteen.[95]

Accolades for James Burton have come from a wide range of artists and critics. John Fogerty said Burton was one of his earliest influences. Emmylou Harris called him a poet, saying there is no one comparable to him. John Denver echoed Harris, saying Burton is the best guitar player there is. Chet Atkins called him "the greatest," and Carl Perkins said one would be hard pressed to meet a finer gentleman or a better guitar player. George Harrison called Beatles material "feeble by comparison." On March 19, 2001, Burton was inducted into the Rock and Roll Hall of Fame. Burton fan Keith Richards of the Rolling Stones presented his induction speech.[96]

Al Harris

Al Harris (June 9, 1936-) is another Louisiana instrumentalist who played in Rick Nelson's band. Besides

Nelson, Harris, a pianist, also worked for ten years for Conway Twitty and found time to play for Nat Stuckey, Johnny Horton, and Dale Hawkins. "I played behind Conway at Gilley's in Pasadena [Texas] and afterwards, Gilley waited until we were alone and asked me to teach him the Albert Ammons piano lick," Harris says.

Raised in a musical family in a hamlet called Jigger, Louisiana, Harris replaced Floyd Cramer on the *Louisiana Hayride* when Cramer left for Nashville. Harris later recorded for Capitol Records where Glen Campbell backed him on guitar.[97]

Al Harris of Lake Charles, like James Burton, played for Rickey Nelson for several years. He also played with Conway Twitty. (Courtesy of Al Harris)

Jon R. Smith

A self-taught musician, saxophonist Jon R. Smith (June 8, 1945-) is a veteran musician who has crammed several lifetimes of recording experience into his fifty-year career as a sideman for some of the best acts in the annals of rock and roll. Will Lee, a member of the CBS Orchestra, noting that he had followed Smith since he left the Edgar Winter White Trash Band. "I couldn't leave Antone's [in Austin, Texas] until I knew he'd played his last note of the night." The *Dallas Observer* said Smith has been "a helluva sideman in some big-a— bands," and the path of rock and roll is littered with acts he had a hand in forming.[98]

Born in Lake Charles, Smith lives with his wife in the rural area of Lafayette, Louisiana. With an admitted obsessive compulsive disorder (he requested two post-lunch toothpicks wrapped in a napkin during this interview), he said everything in his home must be arranged so that he can find them in the dark. That idiosyncrasy aside, he was a charter member of Edgar Winter's White Trash Band in 1969. He also has toured and/or recorded with Percy Sledge, Boz Skaggs, Toto, Dr. John, Ike and Tina Turner, Johnny Winter, Delbert McClinton, the Isley Brothers, Dale Hawkins, Larry Henley, Bobby Charles, Johnny Lee, Clarence "Gatemouth" Brown, Randy Newman, the Doobie Brothers, the Rascals, Jerry LaCroix,

Jon R. Smith of Lafayette has played saxophone behind dozens of popular singers during his career. He also plays for the Fabulous Boogie Kings.

Albert Collins, Larry Garner, Sonny Landreth, the Forever
Fabulous Chickenhawks, C.J. Chenier and the Red Hot
Louisiana Band, Luther Kent, the Fabulous Boogie Kings,
and Wolfman Jack (including Wolfman Jack's first recording,
Live at the Peppermint Lounge in Bossier City in 1963).[99]

He continues to tour with the Fabulous Boogie Kings.[100]

11

Songwriters

Some historians believe that prehistoric man may have made up and sung his own songs. In fact, many adults, at the dawn of rock and roll, were convinced that's where the strange, new music originated. African slaves, many coming to New Orleans via the West Indies, did in fact bring their unwritten music with them to America. As the written language evolved, more and more tunes were composed. It was inevitable that lyrics would be affixed to paper. With the availability of musical instruments, humankind became even more prolific in picking out melodies to accompany lyrics on the piano and guitar. From the chants of the Mardi Gras Indians to New Orleans rhythm-and-blues, soul, and funk, music is ingrained in our heritage. The professional songwriter has played a crucial role in this development and like its singers and musicians, writers have had a profound influence on America's popular music.

Songwriters can ply their trade in several different ways. They may serve as their own music publishers, have outside publishers, or simply work as staff writers for musicians. For example, Percy Mayfield was a staff writer for Ray Charles, and many country songwriters work as staff writers. Some songwriters, like Dave Bartholomew and Allen Toussaint, also work as record producers, and others, like Kris Kristofferson and Hank Williams, are singer-songwriters who record their own songs.

There have been some outstanding songwriting teams,

namely Motown's Brian Holland, Lamont Dozier, and Eddie Holland; Jerry Leiber and Mike Stoller; John Lennon and Paul McCartney; George and Ira Gershwin; and Mick Jagger and Keith Richards.

Some songwriters, like Hank Williams and Huddie Ledbetter (Lead Belly), were unable to read music, choosing to write the lyrics and simply work the music out in their heads. Both Williams and Lead Belly played instruments but some, like Bobby Charles Guidry and J.D. Miller, did not.

No matter which route the songwriter takes, songwriting often can be more lucrative than recording. Dick Holler's *Abraham, Martin and John* is probably the only song to make *Billboard's* Top 40 five times by five different artists.[1] Roy Hayes, who wrote *I'm Gonna Be a Wheel Someday,* has made a comfortable living from that one song. It was a big hit for Fats Domino (number 17) and was included in the soundtracks of five movies.[2]

Eight singer-songwriters who wrote or recorded in Louisiana on a regular basis or who lived for a time in the state are members of the Songwriters Hall of Fame. They are Dave Bartholomew, Sam Cooke, Fats Domino, Kris Kristofferson, Huddie Ledbetter, Little Richard, Randy Newman, and Hank Williams. John Fogerty and Paul Simon, both of whom recorded in Louisiana studios, also are members.[3]

In addition, eight singer-songwriters who lived, wrote, recorded, or began their careers in Louisiana are in the Nashville Songwriters Hall of Fame: Jimmy Buffett, Johnny Cash, Jimmie Davis, Merle Kilgore, Kris Kristofferson, Lead Belly, Conway Twitty, and Hank Williams. Lead Belly, Kristofferson, and Williams are members of both shrines.[4]

Dorothy Labostrie

Dorothy Labostrie (May 18, 1938-) is remembered for penning several hit songs. Born in Rayland, Kentucky, and reared in Mobile, Alabama, until the age of thirteen when her family moved to New Orleans, she worked as a domestic servant and waitress. She wrote poetry between work and visits to the blues joints along Rampart Street.

Accounts differ as to the manner in which it was done, but the consensus is that she wrote *Tutti Frutti* in about fifteen minutes. She claims to have written the song outright after responding to a radio advertisement for songwriters. Others say she simply cleaned up Little Richard's lyrics after the singer launched into an impromptu performance of his more risqué version of the song during lunch at the Dew Drop Inn. Regardless of which version is accurate, producer Robert "Bumps" Blackwell offered her an exclusive songwriting contract with Specialty, but she refused.

One day while she was writing *I Won't Cry,* she heard roofer Johnny Adams singing a gospel tune in his apartment down the hall. She asked him to sing a few lines from her song and decided he was the perfect match. She convinced Joe Ruffino to sign him to a contract with his Ric record label, and Adams had a number 41 R&B hit with *I Won't Cry.*

She also wrote *You Can Have My Husband (But Don't Mess with My Man)* for an up-and-coming eighteen-year-old Irma Thomas. The song became a number 22 R&B hit for Ruffino's other label, Ron Records. Claiming she was never paid the songwriting royalties owed her, Labostrie eventually split with Ruffino and joined Cosimo Matassa's White Cliffs Publishing. She wrote hundreds of songs over the ensuing years but never duplicated her early successes.

She was seriously injured in an automobile accident in 1970 and after her mother died, she quit the commercial music business and moved to New York City.[5]

Bobby Charles Guidry

Bobby Charles Guidry (February 21, 1938-) lost everything he owned in the fall of 2005 to Hurricane Rita. The storm struck southwest Louisiana on September 24, leveling practically every building in Guidry's Cameron Parish.

Born in Abbeville, Guidry grew up listening to Cajun music but discovered rock and roll as a teenager. Soon he

Bobby Charles wrote See You Later Alligator, Before I Grow Too Old, *and the Fats Domino hit* Walkin' to New Orleans. *(Courtesy of Louisiana Music Hall of Fame)*

was singing at local dances with a band called the Cardinals. During this time he penned a song called *See You Later Alligator*, which stemmed from a long-running routine of saying, "See you later, alligator" to friends. One night when he was leaving a dance, his piano player was seated in a booth, and Charles gave him his familiar farewell. There were a couple of people in the booth with him, and one of them responded with, "After awhile, crocodile." Charles went straight home and wrote the song in twenty minutes, with some interruption by his father, who repeatedly called to him to turn out the light and go to bed.[6]

Guidry maintains he has never sat down for the explicit purpose of writing a song. He describes his lyrics as coming to him fully composed, and he only puts them to paper. Once, he said his wife was yelling at him while he was taking a bath. He asked her to bring him paper and a pencil and then leave him alone. The result: *The Jealous Kind*. His wife served as similar inspiration for the song *Before I*

Grow Too Old. She asked him if he was going to lie around and write music for the rest of his life. He responded that he was going to do as much as he could before he grew too old.[7]

A record store owner in Crowley heard *See You Later Alligator,* liked the fourteen-year-old's song, and secured Guidry a telephone audition with Chess Records founder Leonard Chess. Chess was sufficiently impressed to arrange a recording session at Cosimo Matassa's studio in New Orleans. Upon entering the studio, Charles found that Fats Domino's band had been booked to back his recording session. He balked at the arrangement, insisting instead on using the Cardinals.

Upon hearing the recording and never having met the songwriter, Chess signed Guidry to a contract, learning only later that he was not black, but a white Cajun. Phil Chess, Leonard's brother, met him at the Chicago airport and his first reaction was to say that he could not be Bobby Guidry. Once assured of the boy's identity, Chess said, "Leonard's going to s—t but there's nothing we can do about it now; the record's already out and it's a hit."

Guidry changed his name to Bobby Charles after signing with Chess. His Chess release of *See You Later Alligator* reached number 14 on the R&B charts early in 1956. Five months later, he charted again with the R&B hit *Only Time Will Tell,* which went to number 11. Bill Haley and the Comets released *See You Later Alligator* almost simultaneously to Charles' release. That version climbed to number 6 on *Billboard*'s Hot 100 in early 1956.[8]

The only white artist on a black label, he fronted an all-black band while on tour with Chuck Berry and Frankie Lymon and the Teenagers. One tour stop was the University of Mississippi. Taking a restroom break, he was followed by several Ole Miss football players who were unhappy that he was riding with Chuck Berry. Berry saw the players enter the restroom after Charles and suspected they were not seeking autographs. He and several other band members went in after the players. Charles credits Berry and the others with saving his life.[9]

Charles moved to Imperial Records in 1958 but was unable to duplicate his Chess achievements as a vocalist. His triumphs as a songwriter continued, however, when he wrote *Walkin' to New Orleans* for Fats Domino. The song climbed to number 6 on the pop charts in August 1960 and to number 2 on the R&B charts. In 1961, another Bobby Charles composition, Clarence "Frogman" Henry's *(I Don't Know Why) But I Do* reached the number 4 position on *Billboard*'s Hot 100 and number 9 on the R&B charts. The song was given new life when it was included in the soundtrack of the 1994 Academy Award-winning movie *Forrest Gump.*

When he wanted to start his own publishing company, Leonard Chess told him he was making a mistake.[10] Nevertheless, Charles, determined to take control of his own songwriting career, left Chess and entered into a partnership with Stan Lewis. Charles recorded *The Jealous Kind* for Lewis's Paula/Jewel label, but a dispute over royalties to the song led to his departure.[11]

Charles never played an instrument, nor did he read or write music. Whenever he had an idea, he jotted down the lyrics and sang it into a recorder or to a musician. It only took him twenty to thirty minutes to write a song, he has claimed. He also wrote *On Bended Knee, Bye Bye Baby,* and *One Eyed Jacks.* His songs have been recorded by Delbert McClinton, Joe Cocker, Lou Rawls, Ray Charles, Tom Jones, Kris Kristofferson, Etta James, David Allen Coe, Gatemouth Brown, Bo Diddley, Rita Coolidge, and Junior Wells.[12]

Roy Hayes

Roy Hayes (January 25, 1935-) would never stand out in a crowd, but Fats Domino fans know his composition *I'm Gonna Be a Wheel Someday.* Born in Henderson, Louisiana, he worked for a pharmaceutical wholesaler. "Some of the guys and I were sitting around one day talking about our bosses," he says, speaking of the song's origins during an interview. "One of the men said what everyone has said at one time, in one way or another: 'That's okay, I'm gonna be a wheel someday.' Something clicked when he said that, so I wrote the phrase on a packing slip and stuck it in my wallet. About six months later, sometime in 1956, I came across the note while cleaning out my wallet and I sat down and wrote the song in less than five minutes."

He says the song's hook was obvious. "Everybody has the sentiment that someday he's going to be a big wheel and he'll be the one giving the orders. It clicked just like *Mother-in-Law* did for Ernie K-Doe and for the same reason: everyone has a mother-in-law and they identified with his song just like they did with *Wheel*."

At the time he wrote the song, Hayes subscribed to a music magazine that featured stories about singers and published the lyrics to popular songs. "I noticed that many of the songs were written by Dave Bartholomew. I saw where he was playing at Carl's Club in Prairieville. I wrote him a letter and left it with the club's bartender and he gave it to Bartholemew." A few days later Hayes received a letter from Bartholomew. "He wanted to record me," Hayes explains, "so I recorded four songs with Dave Bartholomew's band over about six hours, and he signed me to a five-year recording contract with Imperial and at the same time signed a publishing contract for four songs. He paid my bus expenses back to Baton Rouge."

In 1957, New Orleans singer Bobby Mitchell was the first to record *I'm Gonna Be a Wheel Someday*. The song did well in the New Orleans area but did not chart nationally. About that time Imperial wrote Hayes to inform him that record executives had decided not to release any songs he had done in his New Orleans session for Bartholomew. "But they told me they were going to use other singers for the songs," he says. "Actually, I wasn't disappointed; I was relieved."[13]

Then, in 1959, Fats Domino recorded *Wheel* for Imperial and by September, it had peaked at number 17, staying on the charts for thirteen weeks. That was far from the end of the story for Hayes and his song, however. *Wheel* was also covered by Clyde McPhatter, Mitch Ryder, Paul McCartney, and Sheryl Crow. Crow was nominated for a Grammy for her version of the song.[14] In all, an Amazon.com search for *I'm Gonna Be a Wheel Someday* turned up more than one hundred different CDs.[15] Additionally, *Wheel* has been part of the soundtrack of five movies: *A Fine Mess, Confessions of a Sorority Girl* (Sheryl Crow's version), *Hot Rods, Return to Macon County,* and *Holes.* The Disney film *Holes* has provided him with his single largest source of songwriter royalties.

"Every time someone records that song or every time it appears in a movie, I get royalties on it," he says of *Wheel.* Unlike many other singers and writers of the era, Hayes has no complaints about the financial remuneration he has received from his writing. "I know many artists never got their fair share from a lot of their music. I've heard all the stories and they're all sad and heart wrenching. But personally, I have nothing but good feelings about the way I've been treated. Dave Bartholomew took 50 percent of songwriting royalties on virtually all of Fats Domino's songs. But even though I wrote the lyrics, it was Bartholomew who did the arrangements on those songs. Besides, if he is getting 50 percent, he's going to be more enthusiastic about pushing the song," he relates.

His songs have also been recorded by Baton Rouge's Slim Harpo (*The Music's Hot* and *You Can't Make It on Your Own*), New Orleans duo Shirley and Lee (*Somebody Put a Jukebox in the Study Hall*), and New Orleans R&B singer Joe Jones (*Oh Gee, How I Cried*). "I've probably written a couple hundred songs," Hayes says. "I write for the fun of it; it's my hobby."[16]

Hayes, who today lives with his wife in a comfortable garden home in Baton Rouge, was inducted into the Louisiana Music Hall of Fame on April 16, 2000.

Percy Mayfield

Percy Mayfield (August 12, 1920-August 11, 1984) was one of the few R&B artists with no ties to New Orleans. He first saw the light of day more than three hundred miles to the north, in the Webster Parish town of Minden. Tucked away in the northwest corner of Louisiana, Minden is about thirty miles east of Shreveport and a comparable distance south of the Arkansas border. Instead of gravitating to New Orleans, he headed west to Los Angeles.[17]

He called on Supreme Records in 1947, hoping to coax singer Jimmy Witherspoon into performing a song he had written. But when the Supreme executives heard his rendition of *Two Years of Torture,* they insisted he record the song instead. The record was a good seller on the West Coast, and Art Rupe signed Mayfield to a contract with Specialty Records. His first record for Specialty in 1950 was *Please Send Me Someone to Love,* which quickly became a top seller, making Mayfield a popular act in the Los Angeles area. When sales topped 250,000, Rupe signed Mayfield to a five-year contract and doubled his royalties. By the end of the year, he had returned to north Louisiana to perform at a sold-out show in Shreveport. The show was part of a national tour that consisted of sixty one-nighters across the U.S., including the Apollo Theater in New York. In 1951, he was part of the L.A. Cavalcade of Jazz, performing with Lionel Hampton, Billy Eckstine, Joe Liggins, Roy Brown, Jimmy Witherspoon, and Wynonie Harris. More than twenty-five thousand people turned out for a cavalcade performance at Chicago's Wrigley Field.

A string of hits kept his career on the fast track well into the following year, but in September 1952, while returning to Los Angeles from a Las Vegas performance, Mayfield was seriously injured in an automobile accident, putting his career on indefinite hold. His recuperation was lengthy and left his face terribly disfigured. He returned to his hometown of Minden, where he soon grew depressed, but not before writing a poignant song entitled *Stranger in My Own Home Town.* The reasons for his discontent at returning home were driven by the cultural and social customs of the day. Minden in the early 1950s was radically different for a black man than Los Angeles. Dining and restroom facilities, waiting rooms, and even water fountains were strictly segregated in north Louisiana, making it necessary for him to readjust to an old way of living he thought he had left behind. Disillusioned, he returned to the Los Angeles area to continue his rehabilitation.

Mayfield returned to the Specialty studio in January 1953 and recorded several songs over the next two years that did brisk regional sales. In April 1955, he signed with Leonard Chess and Chess Records of Chicago. Two years later, the Moonglows recorded *Please Send Me Someone to Love* on Chess. It was an even bigger hit than Mayfield's version of seven years earlier, and it sparked a renewed interest in Mayfield as a writer. He signed on as a writer-singer with Atco, a division of Atlantic Records. As the 1950s reached an end, however, he had faded into relative obscurity, sharing a common fate with many other R&B performers who reached their creative peaks in the years before their music became the sound of mainstream America.[18]

Then, in 1961, he got the biggest break of his career when he wrote *Hit the Road Jack.* The song was a megahit for Ray Charles, surpassed on the charts only by *I Can't Stop Loving You* the following year. *Hit the Road Jack* soared to the number 1 spot on *Billboard*'s Hot 100 on October 9 and remained on the charts for thirteen weeks, earning Charles a gold record.[19]

Charles was starting his own Tangerine record label at the time. Charles liked the song so much that he signed Mayfield to a singer-songwriter contract for his fledgling record label, which had a distribution contract with ABC-Paramount. Mayfield quickly became Charles' favorite songwriter with such hits as *Hide nor Hair, At the Club, Danger Zone,* and *On the Other Hand, Baby.* The two maintained a productive relationship for two decades, until Mayfield's death on the day before his sixty-fourth birthday.[20]

Dick Holler

What do Whitney Houston, Ray Charles, Dion DiMucci, Marvin Gaye, Smokey Robinson, Kenny Rogers, Harry

Belafonte, Bob Dylan, Lobo, Garth Brooks, Cher, the Bellamy Brothers, and the Royal Guardsmen have in common? All have recorded or performed songs written by Baton Rouge native Dick Holler (October 16, 1934-).

Born Richard Louis Holler in Indianapolis, Indiana, he moved with his family to Baton Rouge in 1951. He graduated from University High School the following year and attended Louisiana State University for five years. It was while attending LSU that he began to play piano and organize bands with his college friends. Holler performed for two years on the local WBRZ-TV teen show *Hit or Miss*. Others who performed on the show were future actresses Donna Douglas and Elizabeth Ashley and movie critic Rex Reed. Holler also appeared occasionally on disc jockey Dave Davidson's Saturday morning radio show *Teen Town Rally*. It was during a January 1956 *Teen Town Rally* that he met Baton Rouge High student Jimmy Clanton and brothers Ike and Tommy.

"They were quite precocious," Holler remembers. "I tried to sign Jimmy, but his mother informed me Jim was playing with the Dixie Cats. I needed a great electric guitar man and that was Jimmy Clanton—the best young guitarist in southeast Louisiana." Undaunted, Holler asked Clanton to play with his band, the Nightrainers, when he was not working with the Dixie Cats. "So, we did a few gigs together at the Old State Capitol Building. Then in May of 1956, I was able to book a four-piece, four-night-a-week gig at the Wagon Wheel on Airline Highway in Baton Rouge.

"That engagement lasted three months and we slowly improved and in September of 1956, we began working at Club Carousel in Baton Rouge, the most important blues club in southeast Louisiana," Holler continues. "We played on Sunday afternoons and on Monday, Tuesday, and Wednesday nights, which left weekends open for casual gigs in other towns and states. The club changed our name to Dick Holler and the Carousel Rockets, but we shortened it to the Rockets."

Musicians who rotated in and out of the Rockets include

John Rebennack, Cyril Vetter and his brother Keith, Grady Caldwell, Bobby Lovless, Jack Bunn, Junior Bergeron, Ken Veca, Buck Rodriguez, Ed Hubbard, Lenny Capello, Johnny Holley, Glen Delatte, Kenneth Webb, Don Smith, Merlin Jones, and Bob Adams. By 1957 the Rockets were cutting demo tapes at Cosimo Matassa's studio on Governor Nicholls Street in New Orleans. "Coz [Matassa] is a great guy and the South's all-time top recording engineer and producer," Holler says. "He got us our first record deal."

Jimmy Clanton was initially reluctant to write any songs, but the advantage of creating original compositions soon became evident to both him and Holler. Beginning in 1957, when he started collaborating with Clanton, Holler wrote a string of hits that collectively have sold more than thirty-five million records. Holler, however, did not collaborate with Clanton in writing Clanton's first hit song *Just a Dream*. "I was in the same room, though, writing songs," he remembers. "We held several writing sessions at Jimmy's and my house."

Matassa called in the regular New Orleans session crew to play on *Just a Dream*. Soon after that, Clanton embarked on a solo career, while Holler continued to front the Rockets for two more years until he was signed by Herald/Ember Records in 1961. "They wanted a name change, so the Rockets became Dick Holler and the Holidays." The Holidays left Baton Rouge in August 1962 and performed and recorded until May of 1965 in and around Columbia, South Carolina. "Our records were selling there, so we went where the action was," he explains. "Our third single was *Double Shot of My Baby's Love*, written by Don Smith and Cyril Vetter." The song did not become a hit until 1966 and then by the Swingin' Medallions.

The future appeared bleak when Herald/Ember folded in 1964 following the payola investigation of 1959-1962. Holler disbanded the Holidays, and Phil Gernhard, his producer, returned to law school. Holler, however, was far from finished, and he has a popular comic strip to thank. In early 1966, cartoonist Charles Schultz introduced the Red Baron into the *Peanuts* comic strip. "Phil Gernhard jumped into action and rewrote one of my songs and *Snoopy vs. the Red Baron* was born," Holler says.[21]

A garage band from Ocala, Florida, calling itself the Royal Guardsmen entered a studio in 1966 to record an album for their label, Laurie Records. When they were finished, some studio time remained, so the band decided to record the novelty number cowritten by Holler and Gernhard. Laurie executives were so impressed with *Snoopy vs. the Red Baron* that they released it as the group's first single. The song was a local hit at first and then caught on across the U.S. during the Christmas season. By January 1967, it had peaked at number 2 in the U.S. and number 8 in the U.K., remaining on the charts for twelve weeks.[22] "We sold six million records of *Snoopy*," Holler states.

Then Dion DiMucci's version of Holler's composition *Abraham, Martin and John* made the top 5 and was covered by nearly twenty artists. *Abraham, Martin and John*, lamenting the violent deaths of Abraham Lincoln, Martin Luther King, Jr., and John and Robert Kennedy, was of such social significance that it was the first of twenty entries in *Songs Sung Red, White, and Blue: The Stories Behind America's Best-Loved Patriotic Songs,* a book by Ace Collins.

Dion and the Belmonts had broken up in the early 1960s because of Dion's heroin addiction. In early 1968 he and his wife moved to Miami, where, with help from his father-in-law, he managed to kick the habit just in time to record Holler's masterpiece. Dion's version reached number 4 in late 1968 and remained on the charts for fourteen weeks, earning a gold record.[23] Besides Dion's, four other versions made the *Billboard* Top 40, distinguishing it as the only song in history to make the *Billboard* Top 40 five times with five different artists. The other artists were Moms Mabley (number 6 in 1969), Tom Clay (number 8 in 1971), the Miracles (number 33 in 1969), and Marvin Gaye (number 9 in England in 1970 but never released as a single in the U.S.). *Abraham, Martin and John* also received the Broadcast Music, Inc. Four Million Airplay Award, making it one of the most prestigious songs of the last century. In 2001, it was ranked number 248 on the Recording Industry Association of America's Songs of the Century list.

Holler, who resides in Zurich, Switzerland, and Marietta, Georgia, calls the engineering Grammy for *Abraham, Martin and John* in 1969 "my proudest moment, although I'm sorry that events conspired that allowed me to write the song."[24]

Cayet Mangiaracina

In 1953, Cayet Mangiaracina, an eighteen-year-old seminary student at Loyola University of New Orleans, took time out to audition on piano for the Sparks, a five-member rock and roll band that played for a dollar an hour per member at CYO dances in the city. The band took him on as its piano player for a sorority dance even though he could not read music. Today, the Dominican priest is a vicar of Holy Ghost Church in Hammond, Louisiana, and still collects royalties as cowriter of the 1961 number 9 Ricky Nelson hit *Hello, Mary Lou, Goodbye Heart.*

Father Mangiaracina told Jackson, Mississippi, *Clarion Ledger* writer Peter Finney, Jr., that in 1954, he picked out a tune on his family's upright piano that he called *Merry, Merry Lou*. After Cayet left the Sparks to study for the Dominican priesthood, the group won a battle-of-the-bands contest in New Orleans. The prize was a recording session with Decca Records, and one of the songs the band chose for its record was *Merry, Merry Lou.* Bill Haley and the Comets and Sam Cooke liked the song so much they recorded it as well.

In late 1960 or early 1961, Ricky Nelson recorded *Hello, Mary Lou, Goodbye Heart.* In May 1961, the song peaked at number 9 on the *Billboard* Hot 100 and remained on the charts for fifteen weeks. The song's melody was identical to *Merry, Merry Lou,* and the Sparks' publisher filed suit against Nelson. The lawsuit was settled out of court, and Father

Mangiaracina was awarded co-authorship. Royalties were paid to his mother, who was designated as his agent. Since her death in 1988, royalty checks have been forwarded to the Southern Dominican Province. In 2006, his royalties on the song totaled thirty-five thousand dollars, and about three years before that, he got a check for ninety thousand dollars.[25]

Tony Haselden

A founding member of Louisiana's LeRoux, guitarist/vocalist Tony Haselden (September 19, 1945-) relocated to Nashville and soon established himself as a premier country songwriter. His songwriting credits include number 1 songs *That's My Story* (Colin Ray), *It Ain't Nothin'* (Keith Whitley), and *You Know Me Better Than That* (George Strait). Other than LeRoux, he has written for Shenandoah, Martina McBride, the Kinleys, Evangeline, Sawyer Brown, T. G. Sheppard, Sweethearts of the Rodeo, the Statler Brothers, Marie Osmond, Brusly's Amie Comeaux, Billy Ray Cyrus, Glen Campbell, Highway 101, Uriah Heep, Billy Dean, and Tracy Lawrence.

He also produced *Just Between You and Me* for the Kinleys on Epic Records and Shane Sutton's self-titled album on Polydor.[26]

Skip Scarborough

Born in Baton Rouge, Skip Scarborough (November 26, 1944-July 3, 2003) moved to Los Angeles where he worked as a songwriter, producer, arranger, and keyboardist. In 1988, he and cowriter Randy Holland won a Grammy for best R&B song with Anita Baker's *Giving You the Best That I Got.*

He wrote two number 1 R&B hits, *Love Ballad* by LTD, and *Ffun* by Con Funk Shun. *Love Ballad* was written in only twenty minutes but he had considerable difficulty getting anyone to record the song. Still another composition, *Can't Hide Love,* was a hit for Earth, Wind and Fire and Creative Source in 1976.

Scarborough also produced Patti LaBelle's 1979 hit

album *Music Is My Way of Life.* He died of cancer in Los Angeles.[27]

David Egan

After bouncing around for years, David Egan (March 20, 1954-) probably doubted success would ever find him. Leaving Shreveport in 1979, he wrote and sang jingles in Memphis before moving on to Nashville, where he drove a tour bus. All the while, he hawked demo tapes until he got a call to return to Shreveport to join the R&B group A Train. Two years with Jo-El Sonnier's band followed before Cajun accordionist Ward Lormand convinced Egan to join his Creole/Cajun band, Filé, in 1990.

Then, in 1992, his songwriting ship came in when Joe Cocker included Egan's composition *Please No More* on his *Night Calls* album. The album sold more than a million copies and suddenly Egan found a twenty-thousand-dollar royalty check in his mailbox. That breakthrough brought more songwriting success as top artists began seeking out his songs to record. Johnny Adams recorded *Even Now* on his final album, Percy Sledge cut *First You Cry,* and Irma Thomas, Tracy Nelson, and Marcia Ball included three of his songs on their critically acclaimed album *Sing It!*

By 2004, Egan and his wife had a new home in Lafayette and a three-year-old child. That same year soul singer Solomon Burke began work on a new album. *Make Do with What You Got* would included ten songs of such luminaries as Mick Jagger and Keith Richards, Hank Williams, Van Morrison, Bob Dylan, and Dr. John. Burke and his producer listened to about a thousand songs before narrowing the field. Heading the list of songs to include was Egan's *Fading Footsteps.* The song, Egan insists, was written with no particular artist in mind. Instead, he said he simply wrote what was in his heart and soul at the time and he was gratified when Burke picked it up for his album.

Egan was again honored when Irma Thomas not only included his composition *Underground Stream* for her album *Simply Grand*, but asked him to play piano on the song as well. Thomas's previous Grammy-winning album *After the Rain* also featured three of Egan's songs.

Egan, along with Benjy Davis, Maggie Lewis Warwick, and Tab Benoit, performed for a sold-out crowd at the Baton Rouge Shaw Center for the Arts in August 2008. The show, Louisiana Songwriters' Night, was produced by Johnny Palazzotto. Egan and Lil' Band o' Gold, a band that includes Warren Storm, Steve Riley, and C.C. Adcock, are regular performers at Lafayette's Festival International de Louisiane and the New Orleans Jazz and Heritage Festival.[28]

Margaret Lewis Warwick and Mira Smith

Margaret Warwick, née Lewis, and songwriting partner Mira Smith combined to write over a dozen songs for Jeanie C. Riley, Dolly Parton, and Johnny Adams. Warwick's husband's cousin Mira Smith owned and operated Ram Records and a recording studio in Shreveport. She also worked as a top session guitarist. Margaret Lewis, who made her debut on the *Louisiana Hayride* in 1957, scored her biggest success with *Reconsider Me,* with which Johnny Adams scored a hit (number 28 *Billboard* Hot 100 and number 12 R&B) in July of 1969.[29] Narvel Felts had a country hit when he covered the song in 1975.[30]

In September 2004, the Second Circuit Court of Appeals upheld a lower court ruling that awarded Lewis and her husband, Alton Warwick, a victory in a contentious legal battle over exclusive control of the "Louisiana Hayride" trademark.[31] In a case reminiscent of a 1970s dispute between competing California diaper services Tidee Didee and Tidy Didy, the Warwicks' litigation also hinged on variations of the "Louisiana Hayride" name.

Afterword

The golden era of Louisiana rock and roll has long since given way to musical tastes and trends that have evolved away from the guttural rhythm-and-blues of New Orleans and the rockabilly of north Louisiana. The *Louisiana Hayride* could not compete with *Marshall Dillon* and *Paladin* on Saturday nights and staged its last regular weekly show in August 1960 and eventually closed for good. The *Hayride* home, the magnificent old Municipal Auditorium, has since been relegated to the status of museum to commemorate what once was and never again shall be.

But even that is better than the ignoble fate of Cosimo Matassa's original New Orleans studio. Where Sun's first studio at 706 Union Avenue in Memphis remains a landmark tourist attraction complete with souvenir T-shirts, the old J&M Studio on North Rampart serves as an indistinguishable Laundromat. Located far from bustling Bourbon Street, it attracts little notice. Likewise, the Dew Drop Inn on LaSalle, which once served as a grand showcase for the greatest array of black musical talent this country had to offer in the postwar years, now sits boarded up, lonely, deserted, and desolate.

Just as the old radio stations, recording studios, and local independent record labels have disappeared, so too have many of the artists who led the way to the popular music promised land. They are fast fading from the scene as the years take their toll on men and women now in their sixties, seventies, and eighties. Without their influence, however, who can say if we would have ever even heard of the Rolling Stones, the Beatles, Aretha Franklin, or Otis Redding? We should always remember and be thankful that they paid their dues in the metaphorical darkness of the dives, honky-tonks, and roadhouses before emerging into the glaring spotlight of the national stage where restless teens waited impatiently for a different, exciting, and yes, sexual sound.

And let us never forget the role that Louisiana—literally every corner of the state—played in shaping the new sounds that came roaring out of the swamps, the prairies, the red clay hill country, and the "colored" night clubs of New Orleans where no white man could legally go. It was a revolution long before the Beatles, the Stones, Elvis, and the Animals were recording the songs of Little Richard, Larry Williams, Irma Thomas, Smiley Lewis, and Lead Belly.

But new life replaces old and even the alarming death rate of the older musicians and the demise of the studios and record labels cannot extinguish the eternal flame of the artistic creativity that has burned brightly in the Bayou State for more than six decades. Neither could three major hurricanes, Betsy, Katrina, and Rita. Louisiana is resilient and the music goes on with representatives like Kenny Wayne Shepherd, Marcia Ball, the Nevilles, Chris Thomas King, and too many Cajun and zydeco musicians to mention.

Don McLean notwithstanding, the music will never die in Louisiana.

Appendix

Artist	Title	Ranking		Year
		Hot 100	**R&B**	
Johnny Ace	*My Song*		#1	1952
	The Clock		#1	1953
	Cross My Heart		#3	1953
	Saving My Love for You		#2	1954
	Please Forgive Me		#6	1954
	Never Let Me Go		#9	1954
	Pledging My Love	#17	#1	1955
	Anymore		#7	1955
Johnny Adams	*A Losing Battle*		#27	1962
	Release Me	#82	#34	1968
	Reconsider Me	#28	#8	1969
	I Can't Be All Bad	#89	#45	1969
	I Won't Cry		#41	1970
	After All the Good Is Gone		#75	1978
Lee Allen	*Walkin' with Mr. Lee*	#54		1958
	Tic Toc	#92		1958
Louis Armstrong	*I Wonder*		#3	1945
	The Frim Fram Sauce		#4	1949
	Blueberry Hill	#29		1949
	Mack the Knife	#20		1956
	Now You Has Jazz	#88		1956
	I Still Get Jealous	#45		1964
	So Long Dearie	#56		1964
	Hello, Dolly!	#1		1964

	What a Wonderful World*	#1		1968
Gene Austin	*Too Late*	#75		1957
Joe Barry	*I'm a Fool to Care*	#24	#15	1961
	Teardrops in My Heart	#63		1961
Rod Bernard	*This Should Go on Forever*	#20	#12	1959
	One More Chance	#74		1959
Eddie Bo	*Hook and Sling: Part 1*	#73	#13	1969
James Booker	*Gonzo*	#43	#3	1960
Jivin' Gene Bourgeois	*Breaking Up Is Hard to Do*	#69		1959
Terry Bradshaw	*I'm So Lonesome I Could Cry*	#91		1976
Charles Brown	*Please Come Home for Christmas*	#76	#21	1961
Clarence "Gatemouth" Brown	*Mary Is Fine*		#8	1949
	My Time Is Expensive		#9	1949
Roy Brown	*Good Rockin' Tonight*		#11	1948
	Long About Midnight		#1	1948
	Rainy Weather Blues		#5	1949
	'Fore Day in the Morning		#6	1949
	Rockin' at Midnight		#2	1949
	Miss Fanny Brown		#8	1949
	Please Don't Go (Come Back Baby)		#9	1949
	Boogie at Midnight		#3	1949
	Hard Luck Blues		#1	1950
	Love Don't Love Nobody		#2	1950
	Cadillac Baby		#6	1950
	'Long About Sundown		#8	1950
	Big Town		#8	1951
	Bar Room Blues		#6	1951
	Let the Four Winds Blow	#29	#5	1957
	Party Doll	#89	#13	1957
Jimmy Buffett	*Come Monday*	#30		1974

	Margaritaville	#8		1977
	Changes in Latitudes,	#37		1977
	Changes in Attitudes			
	Livingston Saturday Night	#52		1978
	Mañana	#84		1978
Roy Byrd	*Bald Head*		#5	1950
(Professor Longhair)				
The Cadets	*Why Don't You Write Me?*		#3	1955
(with Will	*Stranded in the Jungle*	#15	#4	1956
"Dub" Jones)				
Johnny Cash	*I Walk the Line*	#17		1956
	Next in Line	#99		1957
	Home of the Blues	#88		1957
	I Just Thought You'd	#85		1958
	Like to Know			
	You're the Nearest Thing	#90		1958
	to Heaven			
	Ballad of a Teenage Queen	#14		1958
	Guess Things Happen that Way	#11		1958
	The Ways of a Woman in Love	#24		1958
	It's Just About Time	#47		1958
	All Over Again	#38		1958
	Big River	#90		1958
	What Do I Care	#52		1958
	Get Rhythm	#60		1959
	Frankie's Man Johnny	#57		1959
	Five Feet High and Rising	#76		1959
	Katy Too	#66		1959
	Little Drummer Boy	#63		1959
	I Got Stripes	#43		1959
	Don't Take Your Guns to Town	#32		1959
	Second Honeymoon	#79		1960
	Straight A's in Love	#84		1960
	Down the Street to 301	#85		1960
	Honky Tonk Girl	#92		1960
	Tennessee Flat-Top Box	#84		1961
	Oh, Lonesome Me	#93		1961
	Bonanza!	#94		1962
	Ring of Fire	#17		1963
	The Matador	#44		1963
	Understand Your Man	#35		1964

	It Ain't Me, Babe	#58		1964
	Orange Blossom Special	#80		1965
	The One on the Right is on the Left	#46		1966
	Everybody Loves a Nut	#96		1966
	Folsom Prison Blues	#32		1968
	Rosanna's Going Wild	#91		1968
	Daddy Sang Bass	#42		1969
	Blistered	#50		1969
	See Ruby Fall	#75		1969
	What is Truth	#19		1970
	If I Were a Carpenter	#36		1970
	Sunday Morning Coming Down	#46		1970
	Flesh and Blood	#54		1970
	Rock Island Line	#93		1970
	Man in Black	#58		1971
	Kate	#75		1972
	One Piece at a Time	#29		1976
Bobby Charles	*See You Later Alligator*		#14	1956
	Only Time Will Tell		#11	1956
Ray Charles	*It Should've Been Me*		#5	1954
	Don't You Know		#10	1954
	(Both recorded in Cosimo Matassa's J&M Studio)			
Alex Chilton	*The Letter*	#1	#30	1967
	Neon Rainbow	#24		1967
	Cry Like a Baby	#2		1968
	Choo Choo Train	#26		1968
	I Met Her in Church	#37		1968
	Soul Deep	#18		1969
	Sweet Cream Ladies, Forward March	#28		1969
	I Shall Be Released	#67		1969
	Turn on a Dream	#58		1969
	You Keep Tightening Up on Me	#92		1970
Ike Clanton	*Down the Aisle*	#91		1960
	Sugar Plum	#95		1962
Jimmy Clanton	*Just a Dream*	#4	#1	1958
	A Letter to an Angel	#25		1958

	A Part of Me	#38	#28	1958
	My Own True Love	#33		1959
	Go Jimmy Go	#5	#19	1960
	Another Sleepless Night	#22		1960
	Come Back	#63		1960
	Wait	#91		1960
	What Am I Gonna Do?	#50		1961
	Venus in Blue Jeans	#7		1962
	Darkest Street in Town	#77		1963
	Curly	#97		1969
The Coasters	*Down in Mexico*		#8	1956
(with Will	*Turtle Dovin'*		#8	1956
"Dub" Jones)	*One Kiss Led to Another*	#73	#11	1956
	Searchin'	#3	#1	1957
	Young Blood	#8	#1	1957
	Idol with the Golden Head	#64		1957
	Yakety Yak	#1	#1	1958
	Charlie Brown	#2	#2	1959
	Along Came Jones	#9	#14	1959
	Poison Ivy	#7	#1	1959
	I'm a Hog for You	#38		1959
	Run Red Run	#36	#29	1960
	What about Us	#47	#17	1960
	Wake Me, Shake Me	#51	#14	1960
	Besame Mucho	#70		1960
	Shoppin' for Clothes	#83		1960
	Little Egypt	#12	#16	1961
	Wait a Minute	#37		1961
	Girls Girls Girls	#96		1961
	Tain't Nothing to Me	#64	#64	1964
	Love Potion Number Nine	#76		1971
Sam Cooke	*Forever*	#60		1958
	I'll Come Running Back to You	#18	#1	1958
	(Both recorded in Cosimo Matassa's J&M Studio)			
Cookie and	*Mathilda*	#47		1959
the Cupcakes	*Got You on My Mind*	#94		1963
The Cowsills	*The Rain, the Park and Other Things*	#2		1967

	Indian Lake	#10		1968
	We Can Fly	#21		1968
	Poor Baby	#44		1968
	In Need of a Friend	#54		1968
	Hair	#2		1969
	Silver Threads and Golden Needles	#74		1969
	Prophecy of Daniel and John the Divine	#75		1969
Floyd Cramer	*Last Date*	#2	#3	1960
	On the Rebound	#4	#16	1961
	San Antonio Rose	#8		1961
	Your Last Goodbye	#63		1961
	Hang On	#95		1961
	Chattanooga Choo Choo	#36		1962
	Hot Pepper	#63		1962
	Lovesick Blues	#87		1962
	Let's Go	#96		1962
	Java	#49		1963
Dale and Grace	*I'm Leaving It All Up to You*	#1	#6	1963
	We've Got to Stop and Think It Over	#8		1964
	The Loneliest Night	#65		1964
Jimmie Davis	*You Are My Sunshine*†	N/A	N/A	1939
	There's a New Moon Over My Shoulder	#1		1944
Dixie Cups	*Chapel of Love*	#1	#1	1964
	People Say	#12	#12	1964
	You Should Have Seen the Way He Looked at Me	#39	#39	1964
	Little Bell	#51	#51	1965
	Iko-Iko	#20	#20	1965
Fats Domino	*The Fat Man*		#2	1949
	Every Night about This Time		#5	1950
	Rockin' Chair		#9	1951
	Goin' Home		#1	1952
	Poor, Poor Me		#10	1952
	How Long		#9	1952

Song			
Going to the River		#2	1953
Please Don't Leave Me		#3	1953
Rose Mary		#10	1953
Something's Wrong		#6	1953
You Done Me Wrong		#10	1954
Thinking of You		#14	1955
Don't You Know		#7	1955
Ain't That a Shame	#10	#1	1955
All By Myself		#1	1955
Poor Me		#1	1955
I Can't Go On		#6	1955
Don't Blame It on Me		#9	1956
I'm in Love Again	#3	#1	1956
My Blue Heaven	#19	#5	1956
When My Dreamboat Comes Home	#14	#2	1956
Blueberry Hill	#2	#1	1956
Bo Weevil	#35	#5	1956
So Long	#44	#5	1956
Honey Chile		#2	1956
What's the Reason I'm Not Pleasing You	#50	#12	1956
Blue Monday	#5	#1	1957
I'm Walkin'	#4	#1	1957
The Rooster Song		#13	1957
It's You I Love	#6	#2	1957
Valley of Tears	#8	#2	1957
Wait and See	#23	#7	1957
The Big Beat	#26	#15	1957
When I See You	#29	#14	1957
I Want You to Know	#32		1957
What Will I Tell My Heart?	#64	#12	1957
I Still Love You	#79		1957
Sick and Tired	#22	#14	1958
Little Mary	#48	#4	1958
Yes, My Darling	#55	#10	1958
No, No	#55	#14	1958
Young School Girl	#92	#15	1958
Coquette	#92	#26	1958
Whole Lotta Loving	#5	#2	1959
Be My Guest	#8	#2	1959
I Want to Walk You Home	#8	#1	1959
I'm Ready	#16	#7	1959

	I'm Gonna Be a Wheel Someday	#17	#22	1959
	I've Been Around	#33	#19	1959
	Telling Lies	#50	#13	1959
	When the Saints Go Marching In	#50		1959
	Margie	#51		1959
	Walkin' to New Orleans	#6	#2	1960
	My Girl Josephine	#14	#7	1960
	Three Nights a Week	#15	#8	1960
	Don't Come Knockin'	#21	#28	1960
	Country Boy	#25		1960
	Natural Born Lover	#38	#28	1960
	Tell Me That You Love Me	#51		1960
	Put Your Arms Around Me Honey	#58		1960
	Before I Grow Too Old	#84		1960
	If You Need Me	#98		1960
	Let the Four Winds Blow	#15	#2	1961
	What a Price	#22	#7	1961
	What a Party	#22		1961
	It Keeps Rainin'	#23	#18	1961
	Jambalaya (On the Bayou)	#30		1961
	Ain't That Just Like a Woman	#33	#19	1961
	I Hear You Knocking	#67		1961
	Rockin' Bicycle	#83		1961
	You Win Again	#22		1962
	My Real Name	#59	#22	1961
	Nothing New (Same Old Thing)	#77		1962
	Did You Ever See a Dream Walking?	#79		1962
	Ida Jane	#90		1962
	Dance with Mr. Domino	#98		1962
	Red Sails in the Sunset	#35	#24	1963
	There Goes (My Heart Again)	#59		1963
	Who Cares?	#63	#63	1964
	Lazy Lady	#86	#86	1964
	Sally Was a Good Old Girl	#99	#99	1964
	Heartbreak Hill	#99	#99	1964
	Lady Madonna	#100		1968
Lee Dorsey	*Ya Ya*	#7	#1	1961
	Do-Re-Mi	#27	#22	1962
	Ride Your Pony	#28	#7	1965
	Working in the Coal Mine	#8	#5	1966
	Holy Cow	#23	#10	1966
	Get Out of My Life, Woman	#44	#5	1966

	Go-Go Girl	#62	#31	1967
	My Old Car	#97		1967
	Everything I Do Gonna Be Funky	#95	#33	1969
	Yes We Can (Part 1)		#46	1970
	Night People		#93	1978
Dr. John	Iko-Iko	#71		1972
	Right Place, Wrong Time	#9	#19	1973
	Such a Night	#42	#76	1973
	(Everybody Wanna Get Rich) Rite Away	#92		1974
	Jet Set		#80	1984
Jimmy Elledge	Funny How Time Slips Away	#22		1961
Freddy Fender	Before the Next Teardrop Falls*	#1		1975
	Wasted Days and Wasted Nights*	#8		1975
	Secret Love	#20		1975
	Since I Met You Baby	#45		1975
	You'll Lose a Good Thing	#32		1976
	Vaya con Dios	#59		1976
	Living It Down	#72		1976
King Floyd	Groove Me	#6	#1	1971
	Baby Let Me Kiss You	#29	#5	1971
	Got to Have Your Love		#35	1971
	Woman, Don't Go Astray	#53	#3	1972
	Think about It		#49	1973
	I Feel Like Dynamite		#35	1974
	So Much Confusion		#95	1974
	We Can Love		#76	1975
	Body English		#25	1976
	Don't Cry No More		#96	1976
John Fogerty (solo)	Rockin' All Over the World	#27		1975
	Almost Saturday Night	#78		1975
	You Got the Magic	#87		1976
	Centerfield	#44		1985
John Fogerty (Creedence Clearwater Revival)	Suzy-Q (Part One)	#11		1968
	I Put a Spell on You	#58		1968
	Proud Mary*	#2		1969
	Bad Moon Rising*	#2		1969
	Green River	#2		1969

	Down on the Corner	#3*		1969
	Fortunate Son	#14		1969
	Commotion	#30		1969
	Lodi	#52		1969
	Up Around the Bend	#4*		1970
	*Travelin' Band**	#2		1970
	*Lookin' out My Back Door**	#2		1970
	Who'll Stop the Rain	#13		1970
	Run Through the Jungle	#48		1970
	Long as I Can See the Light	#57		1970
	Sweet Hitch-Hiker	#6		1971
	*Have You Ever Seen the Rain**	#8		1971
	Hey Tonight	#90		1971
	Someday Never Comes	#25		1972
	I Heard it Through the Grapevine	#30		1976
Frankie Ford	*Sea Cruise*	#14	#11	1959
	Alimony	#97		1959
	Time after Time	#75		1960
	You Talk Too Much	#87		1960
	Seventeen	#72		1961
Pete Fountain	*A Closer Walk*	#93		1960
	Yes Indeed	#69		1962
John Fred	*Shirley*	#82		1959
	*Judy in Disguise (With Glasses)**	#1		1968
	Hey, Hey Bunny	#57		1968
Paul Gayten	*Since I Fell for You*		#3	1947
	True		#5	1947
	Cuttin' Out		#6	1949
	I'll Never Be Free		#4	1950
	Goodnight Irene		#6	1950
	Nervous Boogie		#68	1957
	Windy		#78	1958
	The Hunch		#68	1959
Barbara George	*I Know* *(You Don't Love Me No More)*	#3	#1	1962
	You Talk about Love	#46		1962
	Send for Me *(If You Need Some Lovin')*	#96		1962

Mickey Gilley	*Room Full of Roses*	#50		1974
Guitar Slim	*The Things That I Used to Do*		#1	1954
Dale Hawkins	*Suzy-Q‡*	#27	#7	1957
	La-Do-Dada	#32		1958
	A House, a Car and a Wedding Ring	#88		1958
	Class Cutter (Yeah Yeah)	#52		1959
Roy Head	*Treat Her Right*	#2	#2	1965
	Apple of My Eye	#32		1965
	Just a Little Bit	#39		1965
	Get Back	#88		1966
	To Make a Big Man Cry	#95		1966
	My Babe	#99		1966
	Puff of Smoke	#96		1971
Clarence "Frogman" Henry	*Ain't Got No Home*	#20	#3	1957
	(I Don't Know Why) But I Do	#4	#9	1961
	You Always Hurt the One You Love	#12	#11	1961
	Lonely Street	#57	#19	1961
	On Bended Knees	#64		1961
	A Little Too Much	#77		1962
Jessie Hill	*Ooh Poo Pah Doo (Part II)*	#28	#3	1960
	Whip It on Me	#91		1960
Al Hirt	*Java*	#4		1964
	Cotton Candy	#15		1964
	Sugar Lips	#30		1964
	Fancy Pants	#47		1964
	Up Above My Head	#85		1964
	Al's Place	#57		1965
	The Silence	#96		1965
	Keep the Ball Rollin'	#100		1968
Johnny Horton	*The Battle of New Orleans**	#1	#3	1959
	Johnny Reb	#54		1959
	Sal's Got a Sugar Lip	#81		1959
	Sink the Bismark	#3		1960
	North to Alaska	#4	#10	1960
	Johnny Freedom	#69		1960
	Sleepy-Eyed John	#54		1961

	Honky-Tonk Man	#96		1962
David Houston	*Almost Persuaded*	#24		1966
	You Mean the World to Me	#75		1967
	My Elusive Dreams	#89		1967
	Have A Little Faith	#98		1968
T.K. Hulin	*I'm Not a Fool Anymore*	#92		1963
Ivory Joe Hunter	*Blues at Sunrise*		#3	1945
	Pretty Mama Blues		#1	1948
	Don't Fall in Love with Me		#8	1948
	What Did You Do to Me		#9	1948
	I Like It		#14	1948
	Waiting in Vain		#5	1949
	Blues At Midnight		#10	1949
	Guess Who		#2	1949
	Landlord Blues		#6	1949
	Jealous Heart		#2	1949
	I Almost Lost My Mind		#1	1950
	I Quit My Pretty Mama		#4	1950
	S.P. Blues		#9	1950
	I Need You So		#1	1950
	It's a Sin		#10	1950
	It May Sound Silly		#14	1955
	A Tear Fell		#15	1956
	Since I Met You Baby	#12	#1	1956
	Empty Arms	#43	#2	1957
	Love's a Hurting Game		#7	1957
	Yes I Want You	#94	#13	1958
	City Lights	#92		1959
Mahalia Jackson	*He's Got the Whole World in His Hands*	#69		1958
	Silent Night, Holy Night	#99		1962
Alonzo "Lonnie" Johnson	*Tomorrow Night*		#1	1948
	Pleasing You (As Long As I Live)		#2	1948
	So Tired		#9	1949
	Confused		#11	1950
Joe Jones	*You Talk Too Much*	#3	#9	1960
	California Sun	#89		1961
Janis Joplin	*Piece of My Heart*	#12		1968

	Coo Coo	#84		1968
	Kozmic Blues	#41		1969
	Me and Bobby McGee	#1		1971
	Cry Baby	#42		1971
	Get it While You Can	#78		1971
	Down on Me	#43		1972
Margie Joseph	*Your Sweet Lovin'*		#46	1970
	Stop! In the Name of Love	#96	#38	1971
	Let's Stay Together		#43	1973
	Come Lay Some Lovin' on Me		#32	1973
	My Love	#69	#10	1974
	Words (Are Impossible)	#91	#27	1975
	Stay Still		#34	1975
	What's Come Over Me		#11	1975
	Hear the Words, Feel the Feeling		#18	1976
	Don't Turn the Lights Off		#46	1976
	Come on Back to Me Lover		#85	1978
	I Feel His Love Getting Stronger		#94	1978
	Knockout		#12	1982
	Ready for the Night		#69	1984
Bill Justis	*Raunchy*	#2	#1	1957
	College Man	#42		1958
Ernie K-Doe	*Mother-in-Law*	#1	#1	1961
	Te-Ta-Te-Ta-Ta	#53	#21	1961
	I Cried My Last Tear	#69		1961
	A Certain Girl	#71		1961
	Popeye Joe	#99		1962
	Later for Tomorrow		#37	1967
	It Will Have to Do		#48	1967
Chris Kenner	*Sick and Tired*		#13	1957
	I Like It Like That	#2	#2	1961
	Land of 1,000 Dances	#77		1963
Casey Kelly	*Poor Boy*	#52		1972
Doug Kershaw	*Louisiana Man*	#9		1961
Chris Thomas King	*O Brother Where Art Thou* (album)**	#1		2001
Claude King	*Big River, Big Man*	#82		1961

	The Comancheros	#71		1961
	Wolverton Mountain	#6		1962
	The Burning of Atlanta	#53		1962
Earl King	*Those Lonely, Lonely Nights*		#7	1955
	Always a First Time		#17	1962
	Trick Bag		#17	1962
Jean Knight	*Mr. Big Stuff*	#2	#1	1971
	You Think You're Hot Stuff	#57	#19	1971
	Carry On		#44	1972
	You Got the Papers (But I Got the Man)		#56	1981
	My Toot Toot	#50	#59	1985
Kris Kristofferson	*Loving Her Was Easier (Than Anything I'll Ever Do Again)*	#26		1971
	Josie	#63		1972
	Jesus Was a Capricorn	#91		1972
	Why Me*	#16		1973
	A Song I'd Like to Sing	#49		1973
	Loving Arms	#86		1974
LeRoux (Louisiana's LeRoux)	*New Orleans Ladies*	#59		1978
Jerry Lee Lewis	*Whole Lotta Shakin' Goin' On‡*	#3	#1	1957
	Great Balls of Fire‡	#2	#3	1957
	Breathless	#7	#3	1958
	High School Confidential	#21	#5	1958
	Fools Like Me		#11	1958
	Break-Up	#52		1958
	I'll Make It All up to You	#85		1958
	You Win Again	#95		1958
	I'll Sail My Ship Alone	#93		1959
	What'd I Say	#30	#26	1961
	Sweet Little Sixteen	#95		1962
	High Heel Sneakers	#91		1964
	I'm on Fire	#98		1964
	What's Made Milwaukee Famous (Has Made a Loser Out of Me)	#94		1968
	Another Place, Another Time	#97		1968

	Me and Bobby McGee	#40		1971
	Chantilly Lace	#43		1972
	Turn on Your Love Light	#95		1972
	Drinking Wine Spo-Dee O'Dee	#41		1973
	Middle Aged Crazy	#7		1977
	Rockin' My Life Away	#18		1979
	I Wish I Was 18 Again	#18		1979
	Thirty-Nine and Holding	#4		1981
	I'd Do It All Again	#52		1982
Smiley Lewis	*The Bells Are Ringing*		#10	1952
	I Hear You Knocking		#2	1955
	One Night		#11	1956
	Please Listen to Me		#9	1956
Lightnin' Slim	*Rooster Blues*		#23	1959
Little Richard	*Tutti Frutti*	#17	#2	1956
	Long Tall Sally	#6	#1	1956
	Rip It Up	#17	#1	1956
	Slippin' and Slidin'	#33	#2	1956
	Ready Teddy	#44	#8	1956
	Heeby Jeebies		#7	1956
	She's Got It		#9	1956
	All Around the World		#13	1956
	The Girl Can't Help It	#49	#7	1956
	Keep a Knockin'	#8	#2	1957
	Jenny, Jenny	#10	#2	1957
	Lucille	#21	#1	1957
	Send Me Some Lovin'	#54	#3	1957
	Miss Ann	#56	#6	1957
	Good Golly, Miss Molly	#10	#4	1958
	Ooh! My Soul	#31	#15	1958
	Baby Face	#41	#12	1958
	True, Fine Mama	#68	#15	1958
	Kansas City	#95		1959
	Bama Lama Bama Loo	#82	#82	1964
	I Don't Know What You've Got But It's Got Me (Part 1)	#92	#12	1965
	Poor Dog (Who Can't Wag His Own Tail)		#41	1966
	Freedom Blues	#47	#28	1970
	Greenwood, Mississippi	#85		1970

402   LOUISIANA ROCKS!

	In the Middle of the Night		#71	1973
Bob Luman	*Let's Think about Living*	#7	#14	1960
Joe Lutcher	*Rockin' Boogie*		#14	1948
	Shuffle Woogie		#10	1948
	Mardi Gras		#13	1949
Nellie Lutcher	*Hurry on Down*		#2	1947
	He's a Real Gone Guy		#2	1947
	The Song Is Ended		#3	1948
	(But the Melody Lingers On)			
	Do You or Don't You Love Me?		#9	1948
	Fine Brown Frame		#2	1948
	Come and Get It, Honey		#6	1948
	Cool Water		#7	1948
	Lake Charles Boogie		#13	1948
	Alexander's Ragtime Band		#13	1948
	Wish I Was in Walla Walla		#13	1949
	For You My Love		#8	1950
	(with Nat King Cole)			
Barbara Lynn	*You'll Lose a Good Thing*	#8	#1	1962
	Second Fiddle Girl	#63		1962
	You're Gonna Need Me	#65	#13	1962
	(I Cried At) Laura's Wedding	#68		1963
	Don't Be Cruel	#93		1963
	Oh! Baby (We Got a	#69	#69	1964
	Good Thing Going)			
	Don't Spread It Around	#93	#93	1964
	It's Better to Have It	#95	#26	1965
	You Left the Water Running		#42	1966
	This Is the Thanks I Get	#65	#39	1968
	(Until Then) I'll Suffer		#31	1971
Bobby Marchan	*There's Something on Your Mind*	#31	#1	1960
	Shake Your Tambourine		#14	1966
Percy Mayfield	*Please Send Me Someone to Love*		#1	1950
	Strange Things Happening		#7	1951
	Lost Love		#2	1951
	What a Fool I Was		#8	1951
	Prayin' for Your Return		#9	1951

	Cry Baby		#9	1952
	The Big Question		#6	1952
	River's Invitation	#99	#25	1963
	To Live the Past		#41	1970
	I Don't Want to Be the President		#64	1974
Tommy McLain	*Sweet Dreams*	#15		1966
The Meters	*Cissy Strut*	#23	#4	1969
	Sophisticated Cissy	#34	#7	1969
	Ease Back	#61	#20	1969
	Dry Spell		#39	1969
	Chicken Strut	#50	#11	1970
	Look-Ka Py Py	#56	#11	1970
	Hand Clapping Song	#89	#26	1970
	A Message from the Meters		#21	1970
	Stretch Your Rubber Band		#42	1971
	The World Is a Bit Under the Weather		#47	1971
	Hey Pocky A-Way	#31	#31	1974
	People Say	#52	#52	1974
	Disco Is the Thing Today	#87	#87	1976
	Be My Lady	#78	#78	1977
Bobby Mitchell	*Try Rock and Roll*		#14	1956
Aaron Neville	*Over You*		#21	1960
	Tell It Like It Is	#2	#1	1967
	She Took You for a Ride	#92		1967
	Use Me		#93	1995
Neville Brothers	*Sister Rosa*		#75	1989
The Newbeats	*Bread and Butter*	#2		1964
	Everything's Alright	#16		1964
	Run, Baby, Run (Back into My Arms)	#12		1965
	Break Away (From That Boy)	#40		1965
	(The Bees Are for the Birds) The Birds Are for the Bees	#50		1965
	Shake Hands (And Come out Crying)	#92		1966
	Groovin' (Out on Life)	#82		1969

Jimmy C. Newman	*A Fallen Star*	#23	#7	1957
Randy Newman	*Short People**	#2		1978
Robert Parker	*Barefootin'*	#7	#2	1966
	Tip Toe	#83	#48	1967
Phil Phillips	*Sea of Love*	#2	#1	1959
Webb Pierce	*Bye Bye Love*	#73		1957
	I Ain't Never	#24		1959
	No Love Have I	#54		1960
	Is It Wrong (For Loving You)	#69		1960
	(Doin' the) Lovers Leap	#93		1960
	Fallen Angel	#99		1960
Shirley Pixley	*Shame, Shame, Shame*	#12	#1	1975
(Shirley & Co.)	*Cry, Cry, Cry*	#91	#38	1975
	I Like to Dance		#91	1976

Elvis Presley (In the interest of space, only those hits during the five-year period from 1956 to 1960 are included here. The list begins near the end of his tenure with the *Louisiana Hayride* and concludes the same year that the show, declining in popularity and influence, held its last regular weekly performance.)

	*Heartbreak Hotel**	#1	#3	1956
	*Hound Dog**	#1	#1	1956
	*Don't be Cruel**	#1	#1	1956
	*Love Me Tender**	#1	#3	1956
	I Want You, I Need You, I Love You	#1	#3	1956
	Love Me	#2	#7	1956
	I Was the One	#19		1956
	When My Blue Moon Turns to Gold Again	#19		1956
	Blue Suede Shoes	#20		1956
	Anyway You Want Me (That's How I Will Be)	#20	#12	1956
	Poor Boy	#24		1956
	My Baby Left Me	#31		1956
	Old Shep	#47		1956
	Blue Moon	#55		1956
	Paralyzed	#59		1956
	I Don't Care if the Sun Don't Shine	#74		1956

	Money Honey	#76		1956
	My Baby Left Me	#31		1956
	All Shook Up	#1	#1	1957
	Jailhouse Rock	#1	#1	1957
	(Let Me Be Your) Teddy Bear	#1	#1	1957
	Too Much	#1	#3	1957
	Treat Me Nice	#18	#7	1957
	Loving You	#20		1957
	Peace in the Valley (for Me)	#25		1957
	That's When Your Heartaches Begin	#58		1957
	Don't	#1	#4	1958
	Hard Headed Woman*	#1	#2	1958
	Wear My Ring Around Your Neck	#2	#1	1958
	One Night	#4	#10	1958
	I Got Stung	#8		1958
	I Beg of You	#8	#5	1958
	Doncha' Think It's Time	#15	#10	1958
	A Big Hunk O' Love	#1	#10	1959
	(Now and Then There's) A Fool Such as I	#2	#16	1959
	I Need Your Love Tonight	#4		1959
	My Wish Came True	#12	#15	1959
	Are You Lonesome Tonight?	#1	#3	1960
	It's Now or Never	#1	#7	1960
	Stuck on You	#1	#6	1960
	Fame and Fortune	#17		1960
	I Gotta Know	#20		1960
	A Mess of Blues	#32		1960
Lloyd Price	Lawdy Miss Clawdy		#1	1952
	Oooh, Oooh, Oooh		#4	1952
	Restless Heart		#5	1952
	Ain't It a Shame		#4	1953
	Tell Me Pretty Baby		#8	1953
	Just Because	#29	#3	1957
	Lonely Chair	#88		1957
	Stagger Lee	#1	#1	1959
	Personality	#2	#1	1959
	I'm Gonna Get Married	#3	#1	1959
	Three Little Pigs		#15	1959
	Come into My Heart	#20	#2	1959
	Where Were You (On Our Wedding Day)	#23	#4	1959

	Won't'cha Come Home?	#43	#6	1959
	Lady Luck	#14	#3	1960
	Never Let Me Go	#82	#26	1960
	Question	#19	#5	1960
	No Ifs—No Ands	#40	#16	1960
	For Love	#43		1960
	Just Call Me (And I'll Understand)	#79		1960
	(You Better) Know What You're Doing	#90		1960
	Misty	#21	#11	1963
	Billie Baby	#84	#84	1964
	Bad Conditions		#21	1969
	Trying to Slip (Away)		#32	1973
	What Did You Do with My Love		#99	1976
Louis Prima	*I'll Walk Alone*		#9	1944
	The White Cliffs of Dover		#9	1944
	Robin Hood		#10	1945
	Jump, Jive, and Wail	#44		1958
	That Old Black Magic	#18	#28	1958
	Bei Mir Bist Du Schon	#69		1959
	Wonderland by Night	#15		1961
	I've Got You Under My Skin	#95		1995
Jim Reeves	*Four Walls*	#11		1957
	Blue Boy	#45		1958
	Anna Marie	#93		1958
	Billy Bayou	#95		1958
	He'll Have to Go	#2	#13	1960
	Am I Losing You	#31		1960
	I'm Gettin' Better	#37		1960
	I Missed Me	#44		1960
	I Know One	#82		1960
	The Blizzard	#62		1961
	What Would You Do?	#73		1961
	Losing Your Love	#89		1961
	(How Can I Write on Paper) What I Feel in My Heart	#92		1961
	Adios, Amigo	#90		1962
	I'm Gonna Change Everything	#95		1962
	Guilty	#91		1963
	I Guess I'm Crazy	#82		1964
	I Won't Forget You	#93		1964

	Is It Really Over?	#79		1965
	This Is It	#88		1965
	Distant Drums	#45		1966
	Blue Side of Lonesome	#59		1966
	Snow Flake	#66		1966
Johnny Rivers	*Memphis*	#2		1964
	Mountain of Love	#9		1964
	Maybeline	#12		1964
	Seventh Son	#7		1965
	Midnight Special	#20		1965
	Where Have All the Flowers Gone?	#26		1965
	Cupid	#76		1965
	Poor Side of Town	#1		1966
	Secret Agent Man	#3		1966
	(I Washed My Hands) In Muddy Water	#19		1966
	Under Your Spell Again	#35		1966
	Baby, I Need Your Lovin'	#3		1967
	The Tracks of My Tears	#10		1967
	Summer Rain	#14		1967
	Look to Your Soul	#49		1968
	Right Relations	#61		1968
	Muddy River	#41		1969
	These Are Not My People	#55		1969
	One Woman	#89		1969
	Into the Mystic	#51		1970
	Fire And Rain	#94		1970
	Think His Name	#65		1971
	Sea Cruise	#84		1971
	*Rockin' Pneumonia & the Boogie-Woogie Flu**	#6		1972
	Blue Suede Shoes	#38		1973
	Help Me, Rhonda	#22		1975
	*Swayin' to the Music (Slow Dancin')**	#10		1977
	Ashes and Sand	#96		1977
	Curious Mind	#41		1978
Tommy Sands	*Teen-Age Crush*	#2	#10	1957
	Goin' Steady	#16		1957
	Ring-a-Ding-a-Ding	#50		1957
	My Love Song	#62		1957

	Ring My Phone	#95		1957
	Sing, Boy, Sing	#24		1958
	Blue Ribbon Baby	#50		1958
	Teen-Age Doll	#81		1958
	I'll Be Seeing You	#51		1959
	The Worryin' Kind	#69		1959
	The Old Oaken Bucket	#73		1960
Shirley and Lee	*I'm Gone*		#2	1952
	Feel So Good		#2	1955
	Let the Good Times Roll	#20	#1	1956
	I Feel Good	#38	#3	1957
	When I Saw You		#14	1957
	Let the Good Times Roll (Remake)	#48		1960
	I've Been Loved Before	#88		1960
	Well-A, Well-A	#77		1961
Rockin' Sidney	*My Toot Toot*	#98		1984
Joe Simon	*Let's Do It Over*		#13	1965
	Teenager's Prayer	#66	#11	1966
	Nine Pound Steel	#70	#19	1967
	My Special Prayer	#87	#17	1967
	Put Your Trust in Me (Depend on Me)		#47	1967
	(You Keep Me) Hangin' On	#25	#11	1968
	No Sad Songs	#49	#22	1968
	Message from Maria	#75	#31	1968
	Looking Back	#70	#42	1968
	I Worry about You	#98		1968
	*The Chokin' Kind**	#13	#1	1969
	Baby, Don't Be Looking in My Mind	#72	#16	1969
	San Francisco Is a Lonely Town	#79	#29	1969
	It's Hard to Get Along	#87	#26	1969
	Moon Walk (Part 1)	#54	#11	1970
	Farther on Down the Road	#56	#7	1970
	Yours Love	#78	#10	1970
	That's the Way I Want Our Love	#93	#27	1970
	Your Time to Cry	#40	#3	1971
	Help Me Make It Through the Night	#69	#13	1971
	You're the One for Me	#71	#12	1971
	Georgia Blues		#19	1971
	All My Hard Times	#93	#26	1971

Power of Love*	#11	#1	1972
Drowning in the Sea of Love*	#11	#3	1972
Pool of Bad Luck	#42	#13	1972
Trouble in My Home	#50	#5	1972
I Found My Dad	#74	#15	1972
Misty Blue	#91	#47	1972
Theme from Cleopatra Jones	#18	#3	1973
Step by Step	#37	#6	1973
River	#62	#6	1973
Carry Me	#12	#12	1974
The Best Times of My Life	#15	#15	1974
Get Down, Get Down (Get on the Floor)		#1	1975
Music in My Bones		#7	1975
I Need You, You Need Me		#5	1976
Come Get to This		#22	1976
Easy to Love		#12	1976
You Didn't Have to Play No Games		#62	1977
One Step at a Time		#28	1977
For Your Love, Love, Love		#27	1978
I.O.U.		#71	1978
Love Vibration		#15	1978
Going Through These Changes		#78	1979
I Wanna Taste Your Love		#87	1979
Baby, When Love Is in Your Heart (It's in Your Eyes)	#60	1980	
Glad You Came My Way		#43	1980
Are We Breaking Up?		#52	1981
Paul Simon Kodachrome	#2		1973
Percy Sledge When a Man Loves a Woman*	#1	#1	1966
Warm and Tender Love	17	#5	1966
It Tears Me Up	#20	#7	1966
Love Me Tender	#40	#35	1967
Cover Me	#42	#39	1967
Out of Left Field	#59	#25	1967
Just out of Reach (Of My Two Empty Arms)	#66		1967
Baby, Help Me	#87	#44	1967
What Am I Living For?	#91		1967
Take Time to Know Her	#11	#6	1968
Sudden Stop	#63	#41	1968

	Any Day Now	#86	#35	1969
	My Special Prayer	#93	#44	1969
	Sunshine	#89	#89	1973
	I'll Be Your Everything	#62	#15	1974
Slim Harpo	*Rainin' in My Heart*	#34	#17	1961
	Baby, Scratch My Back	#16	#1	1966
	Tip on In (Part 1)		#37	1967
	Te-Ni-Nee-Ni-Nu		#36	1968
Huey "Piano" Smith and His Clowns	*Rockin' Pneumonia and the Boogie-Woogie Flu*	#52	#5	1957
	Don't You Just Know It	#9	#4	1958
	Don't You Know Yockamo	#56		1959
	Pop-Eye	#51		1962
O.C. Smith	*The Son of Hickory Holler's Tramp*	#40	#32	1968
	*Little Green Apples**	#2	#2	1968
	Isn't It Lonely Together?	#63	#40	1968
	Honey (I Miss You)	#44	#44	1969
	Daddy's Little Man	#34	#9	1969
	Friend, Lover, Woman, Wife	#47	#25	1969
	Me and You		#38	1969
	Baby, I Need Your Loving	#52	#30	1970
	Primrose Lane	#86		1970
	Help Me Make It through the Night	#91	#38	1971
	La La Peace Song	#62	#27	1974
	Together		#62	1976
	Love to Burn		#34	1978
	Dreams Come True		#92	1980
	Love Changes		#68	1982
	What'cha Gonna Do?		#53	1986
	You're the First, the Last, My Everything		#52	1986
	Brenda		#58	1987
Benny Spellman	*Lipstick Traces (On a Cigarette)*	#80	#28	1962
The Spiders	*I Didn't Want to Do It*		#3	1954
	You're the One		#8	1954
	I'm Slippin' In		#6	1954
	21		#9	1955
	Witchcraft		#5	1955

Joe Stampley	*Soul Song*	#37		1973
Joe Stampley	*Not Too Long Ago*	#66		1965
and the Uniques	*All These Things*	#97		1966
Stephen Stills	*Love the One You're With*	#14		1971
(solo hits)	*Sit Yourself Down*	#37		1971
	Marianne	#42		1971
	Change Partners	#43		1971
	It Doesn't Matter	#61		1972
	Rock and Roll Crazies	#92		1972
	Isn't It about Time?	#56		1973
	Turn Back the Pages	#84		1975
Warren Storm	*Prisoner's Song*	#81		1958
Joe Tex	*Hold What You've Got*	#5	#2	1965
	I Want To (Do Everything for You)	#23	#1	1965
	You Better Get It	#46	#15	1965
	You Got What It Takes	#51	#10	1965
	A Woman Can Change a Man	#56	#12	1965
	One Monkey Don't Stop No Show	#65	#20	1965
	Don't Let Your Left Hand Know	#95		1965
	A Sweet Woman Like You	#29	#1	1966
	S.Y.S.L.J.F.M. (The Letter Song)	#39	#9	1966
	The Love You Save (May Be Your Own)	#56	#2	1966
	I've Got to Do a Little Bit Better	#64	#20	1966
	I Believe I'm Gonna Make It	#67	#8	1966
	*Skinny Legs and All**	#10	#2	1967
	Show Me	#35	#24	1967
	Papa Was Too	#44	#15	1967
	Woman Like That, Yeah	#54	#24	1967
	A Woman's Hands	#63	#24	1967
	Men Are Gettin' Scarce	#33	#7	1968
	Keep the One You Got	#52	#13	1968
	I'll Never Do You Wrong	#59	#26	1968
	You Need Me, Baby	#81	#29	1968
	Buying a Book	#47	#10	1969
	That's Your Baby	#88		1969
	That's the Way	#94	#46	1969
	Give the Baby Anything the Baby Wants		#20	1971

	*I Gotcha**	#2	#1	1972
	A Mother's Prayer		#41	1972
	You Said a Bad Word	#41	#12	1972
	Woman Stealer		#41	1973
	Under Your Powerful Love		#27	1975
	Have You Ever?		#74	1976
	*Ain't Gonna Bump No More (With No Big Fat Woman)**		#7	1977
	Hungry for Your Love		#84	1977
	Rub Down		#70	1978
	Loose Caboose		#48	1978
Irma Thomas	*You Can Have My Husband (But Don't Mess with My Man)*		#22	1960
	I Wish Someone Would Care	#17	#17	1964
	Anyone Who Knows What Love Is (Will Understand)	#52	#52	1964
	Times Have Changed	#98	#98	1964
	He's My Guy	#63	#63	1965
	Good to Me		#42	1968
Willie Tee Turbinton	Teasin' You	#97	#12	1965
Big Joe Turner	*S.K. Blues (Part 1)*		#3	1946
	My Gal's a Jockey		#6	1946
	Still in the Dark		#9	1950
	Chains of Love		#2	1951
	The Chill Is On		#3	1951
	Sweet Sixteen		#3	1952
	Don't You Cry		#5	1952
	Honey Hush		#1	1953
	TV Mama		#6	1954
	Shake, Rattle and Roll		#1	1954
	Well All Right		#9	1954
	Flip, Flop and Fly		#2	1955
	Hide and Seek		#3	1955
	The Chicken and the Hawk (Up, Up and Away)		#7	1956
	Morning, Noon and Night		#8	1956
	Corrine, Corrina	#41	#2	1956
	Lipstick, Powder and Paint		#8	1956
	Rock a While		#12	1956

	Love Roller Coaster		#12	1957
	Jump for Joy		#15	1958
	Honey Hush (Remake)	#53		1960
Conway Twitty	*I Need Your Lovin'*	#93		1957
	It's Only Make Believe	#1	#12	1958
	Danny Boy	#10	#18	1959
	The Story of My Love	#28		1959
	Mona Lisa	#29		1959
	Hey Little Lucy!	#87		1959
	(Don'tcha Put No Lipstick On)			
	Lonely Blue Boy	#6	#27	1960
	Is a Blue Bird Blue	#35		1960
	Whole Lotta Shakin' Goin' On	#55		1960
Tony Joe White	*Polk Salad Annie*	#8		1969
	Roosevelt and Ira Lee	#44		1969
	Save Your Sugar for Me	#94		1970
Hank Williams, Jr.	*Long Gone Lonesome Blues*	#67		1964
	Endless Sleep	#90		1964
	*Family Tradition***	#6		1979
Larry Williams	*Just Because*		#11	1957
	Short Fat Fannie	#5	#1	1957
	Bony Maronie	#14	#4	1957
	You Bug Me, Baby	#45		1957
	High School Dance	#90		1957
	Dizzy Miss Lizzy	#69		1958
	Mercy, Mercy, Mercy	#96	#23	1967
	Nobody		#40	1968
Little Walter	*Juke*		#1	1952
	Sad Hours		#2	1952
	Mean Old World		#6	1953
	Off the Wall		#8	1953
	Tell Me Mama		#10	1953
	Blues with a Feeling		#2	1953
	You're So Fine		#2	1954
	Oh, Baby		#8	1954
	You'd Better Watch Yourself		#8	1954
	Last Night		#6	1954
	My Babe		#1	1955

	Roller Coaster	#6	1955
	Who	#7	1956
	Key to the Highway	#6	1958
	Everything Gonna be Alright	#25	1959
Faron Young	*The Shrine of St. Cecilia*	#96	1957
	Alone with You	#51	1958
	Riverboat	#83	1960
	Hello Walls	#12	1961
	Backtrack	#89	1961
	It's Four in the Morning	#92	1972

*Million sellers as certified by the Recording Industry Association of America
**Grammy Award-winning
†Grammy Hall of Fame Award winner and one of the Songs of the Century as named by the Recording Industry Association of America; Louisiana's State Song
‡Included in the Rock and Roll Hall of Fame's list of 500 Songs That Shaped Rock and Roll

Notes

Introduction

1. "Fats Domino: The Fat Man," Jazz.com, http://www.jazz.com/music/2009/8/5/fats-domino-the-fat-man; Rick Koster, *Louisiana Music* (Cambridge, MA: Da Capo Press, 2002), 89.

2. Horace Logan and Bill Sloan, *Louisiana Hayride Years: Making Musical History in Country's Golden Age*, originally published as *Elvis, Hank and Me: Making Musical History on the Louisiana Hayride* (New York: St. Martin's Press, 1998; reprint New York: St. Martin's Griffin, 1999), 41.

3. Jeff Hannusch, *I Hear You Knockin'* (Ville Platte, LA: Swallow Publications, 1985), 74-75.

4. "1958 Grammy Awards," Information Please Database, http://www.infoplease.com/ipa/A0150535.html; "Grammy Retrospective: The Beginning," Vintage Vinyl News, February 6, 2007, http://winkscollectibles.blogspot.com/2007_02_01_archive.html.

5. Joel Whitburn, *Top R&B Singles, 1942-1995* (Menomonee Falls, WI: Record Research, Inc., 1996), 74, 94, 119, 270, 357, 408.

6. Logan and Sloan, *Louisiana Hayride Years,* 97-99, 258-61.

Chapter One

1. "101 Reasons Why Cosimo Matassa, Who Engineered the Sound of Rhythm & Blues and Rock n Roll, Should Be in the Rock n Roll Hall of Fame," Louisiana Music Commission, web page since removed.

2. "Cosimo Matassa's New Orleans Studio Awarded Landmark Status," *Blues Access Online* 41 (spring 2000), www.bluesaccess.com/No_41/access.html.

3. Cosimo Matassa, interview with author, 2006.

4. "A Chronology of Rock Music: The 1950s," Piero Scaruffi's

online music database, www.scaruffi.com/music/chrono50.html.

5. Cosimo Matassa, interview with author, 2006.

Chapter Two

1. Billy Altman, liner notes to *Leadbelly, Alabama Bound*, RCA records; Michael Mueller, "Leadbelly Biography," Musician Biographies database, www.musicianguide.com/biographies/1608000918/Leadbelly.html; Petri Liukkonen, "Leadbelly (1888-1949)," Authors' Calendar, www.kirjasto.sci.fi/ledbelly.htm; Charles Wolf and Kip Lornell, *The Life and Legend of Leadbelly* (New York: HarperCollins, 1992).

2. Koster, *Louisiana Music,* 132-33.

3. Liukkonen, "Leadbelly."

4. Ibid.

5. "500 Songs That Shaped Rock and Roll," Rock and Roll Hall of Fame, www.rockhall.com/exhibithighlights/500-songs/; Koster, *Louisiana Music.*

6. David Conrads, "Piano Man," review of *Jelly's Blues: The Life, Music, and Redemption of Jelly Roll Morton*, by Howard Reich and William Gaines, *World and I* 19 (March 2004).

7. "Ferdinand 'Jelly Roll' Morton," Red Hot Jazz Archive, http://www.redhotjazz.com/jellyroll.html.

8. "Alfonzo 'Lonnie' Johnson," Red Hot Jazz Archive, http://www.redhotjazz.com/ljohnson.html.

9. Deborah Evans Price, "Singing Governor Jimmie Davis Dies, Wrote Classic Hit You Are My Sunshine," *Billboard*, November 18, 2000.

10. Jason Berry, "Dirges for the Singing Governor," *New Orleans Magazine,* January 1, 2001.

11. "Jimmie Davis: A Long Story," *Louisiana Life* (Winter 2000/2001).

12. John Bush, "Jimmie Davis Biography," All Music Guide, available from CMT, http://www.cmt.com/artists/az/davis_jimmie/bio.jhtml.

13. ArtsEdge, "Louis Armstrong: The Man, the Musician, the Celebrity," John F. Kennedy Center for the Performing Arts, http://artsedge.kennedy-center.org/exploring/louis/scrapbook/bio/bio_detail.html.

14. "Louis 'Satchmo' Armstrong," Red Hot Jazz Archive, http://www.redhotjazz.com/louie.html.

15. "Inductee List," Rock and Roll Hall of Fame, www.rockhall.com/inductees/inductee-list/.

16. Joel Whitburn, *Top Pop Artists and Singles, 1955-1978*

(Menomonee Falls, WI: Record Research, Inc., 1979), 19.

17. Women in History, "Mahalia Jackson," Lakewood Public Library, http://www.lkwdpl.org/wihohio/jack-mah.htm.

18. Isaac Rosen, "Mahalia Jackson Biography," Musician Biographies database, http://www.musicianguide.com/biographies/1608001002/Mahalia-Jackson.html.

Chapter Three

1. Rick Coleman, *Blue Monday: Fats Domino and the Lost Dawn of Rock 'n' Roll* (Cambridge, MA: Da Capo Press, 2006).

2. Jeff Hannusch, "The South's Swankiest Night Spot: The Legend of the Dew Drop Inn," Louisiana Music Archive, http://www.satchmo.com/ikoiko/dewdropinn.html.

3. Jeff Hannusch, *The Soul of New Orleans: A Legacy of Rhythm and Blues* (Ville Platte, LA: Swallow Publications, 2001), 130.

4. Deacon John Moore, interview with author, February 2007.

5. Hannusch, *The Soul of New Orleans,* 132.

6. Deacon John Moore interview.

7. Hannusch, *The Soul of New Orleans,* 133-34.

8. Deacon John Moore interview.

9. Jason Ankeny, "Tuts Washington Biography," All Music Guide, available form Artist Direct, http://www.artistdirect.com/nad/music/artist/bio/0,,507618,00.html.

10. Joel Whitburn, *Top R&B Singles, 1942-1995* (Menomonee Falls, WI: Record Research, Inc., 1996), 126.

11. Rick Koster, *Louisiana Music* (Cambridge, MA: Da Capo Press, 2002), 134.

12. Greg Johnson, "Champion Jack Dupree," Cascade Blues Association, http://www.cascadeblues.org/History/ChampionJack.htm.

13. David Fricke, "Professor Longhair," *Rolling Stone,* May 19, 2005.

14. Hannusch, *I Hear You Knockin',* 16.

15. Koster, *Louisiana Music,* 79.

16. Grant Morris, "Biography," Professor Longhair.com: The Official Professor Longhair Website and Resource Guide, http://www.professorlonghair.com/archive/bios/gmorris.html.

17. Ibid.

18. Chris Morris, "Professor Longhair Enters Hall of Fame," *Billboard,* June 14, 1997.

19. Hannusch, *I Hear You Knockin',* 71.

20. Ibid., 74.

21. Whitburn, *Top R&B Singles,* 53.

22. Hannusch, *I Hear You Knockin'*, 78-79.

23. Ibid., 81-82.

24. Jessica Robertson, "Fats Domino Missing," *Rolling Stone*, September 1, 2005; Roger Friedman, "'Fats' Domino Missing in New Orleans," Fox News.com, posted September 1, 2005, http://www.foxnews.com/story/0%2C2933%2C168122%2C00.html.

25. "Fats Domino Found OK in New Orleans," CNN.com, posted September 1, 2005, http://www.cnn.com/2005/SHOWBIZ/Music/09/01/katrina.fats.domino/index.html.

26. Joel Whitburn, *Top Pop Artists and Singles, 1955-1978* (Menomonee Falls, WI: Record Research, Inc., 1979).

27. "Fats Domino," Rolling Stone, http://www.rollingstone.com/artists/fatsdomino/biography.

28. Elizabeth Thomas, "Fats Domino Biography," Musician Biographies database, http://www.musicianguide.com/biographies/1608000534/Fats-Domino.html.

29. Marv Goldberg, "Fats Domino: The Imperial Years," Marv Goldberg's R&B Notebooks, http://home.att.net/~uncamarvy/Fats/fats.html.

30. Kathryn Slusher, "Fats Domino and Dave Bartholomew," *Prairie Home Companion*, March 26, 2004, http://prairiehome.publicradio.org/features/aatm/2004/03/.

31. Coleman, *Blue Monday,* 72.

32. Whitburn, *Top Pop Artists and Singles,* 125-26.

33. Ibid., 124-25.

34. Dr. John [Malcolm Rebennack], "The Immortals—The Greatest Artists of All Time: 25) Fats Domino," *Rolling Stone*, April 15, 2004.

35. Roy Hayes, interview with author, 2006; "Fats Domino," The History of Rock 'n' Roll: The Golden Decade, 1954-1963, http://www.history-of-rock.com/domino.htm; "Bobby Charles," All About Jazz, http://www.allaboutjazz.com/php/musician.php?id=5645.

36. Coleman, *Blue Monday*, 206.

37. Ibid., 106, 140.

38. Jon Pareles, "Fats Domino and Friends on Cable," *New York Times,* July 31, 1986.

39. Coleman, *Blue Monday*, 280.

40. Rick Coleman, "Seven Decades of Fats Domino," Offbeat.com, http://offbeat.com/artman/publish/printer_674.shtml.

41. Coleman, *Blue Monday,* 292.

42. Recording Industry Association of America and National Endowment for the Arts, "The Recording Industry Association of America Top 365 Songs of the Twentieth Century,"

Association Admiration Aggregation, http://www.theassociation. net/txt-music5.html; "The 40 Greatest Jukebox Hits of All Time," Wurlitzer, http://www.gibson.com/Products/Wurlitzer/ Jukebox%20Museum/All%20Time%20Jukebox%20Hits/.

43. Kevin Krolicki and Nichola Groom, "Fats Domino Returns Home," *New Orleans Times-Picayune,* October 16, 2005.

44. Ibid.

45. Lynne Jensen, "Fats Domino's Pianos to Symbolize Storm Damage," *New Orleans Times-Picayune,* March 14, 2006.

46. Keith Spera, "Fats Domino Bows out of Jazzfest," *New Orleans Times-Picayune,* May 8, 2006.

47. Stacey Plaisance, "Fats Domino Returns to New Orleans Stage," *USA Today,* May 20, 2007.

48. "Fats Domino Named 'American Music Legend' by RIAA," posted August 18, 2007, on MOG Music Network, http://mog.com/ Mackenzie_P/blog/103728.

49. "Fats Domino Receives Gold Record Replacements in New Orleans," Associated Press, August 14, 2007.

50. Ibid.

51. *Goin' Home: A Tribute to Fats Domino,* various artists, Vanguard Records, 2007.

52. Bill Dahl, "Big Joe Turner Biography," All Music Guide, available from Artist Direct, http://www.artistdirect.com/nad/ music/artist/bio/0,,503750,00.html.

53. Steve Jones, "Atlantic Records Founder Ertegun Dead at 83," *USA Today,* December 15, 2006.

54. Cosimo Matassa, interview with author, 2006.

55. Whitburn, *Top R&B Singles,* 453.

56. Whitburn, *Top Pop Artists and Singles,* 185.

57. "Shake Rattle and Roll," The History of Rock 'n' Roll: The Golden Decade, 1954-1963, http://www.history-of-rock.com/ shake_rattle_and_roll.htm.

58. Terry Currier, "Big Joe Turner," *BluesNotes* (January/February 1997), http://www.cascadeblues.org/History/BigJoeTurner.htm.

59. Koster, *Louisiana Music*, 110.

60. "Elvis (1968 TV Special)," Wikipedia: The Free Encyclopedia, http://en.wikipedia.org/wiki/Elvis_Presley's_'68_ Comeback_Special.

61. Bill Dahl, "Lloyd Price: Biography," African Genesis Presents the Soul Music Center, http://afgen.com/lloyd_price.html.

62. Coleman, *Blue Monday,* 72-73.

63. Whitburn, *Top R&B Singles,* 357.

64. Ibid.

65. Whitburn, *Top Pop Artists and Singles,* 333.

66. Koster, *Louisiana Music,* 110; Whitburn, *Top R&B Singles,* 357.

67. Koster, *Louisiana Music,* 110-11.

68. Bill Dahl, "Lloyd Price: Biography."

69. John Broven, *Rhythm & Blues in New Orleans* (Gretna, LA: Pelican Publishing Co., 1974), 50-51; Greg Johnson, "Guitar Slim," Cascade Blues Association, http://www.cascadeblues.org/History/GuitarSlim.htm.

70. Greg Johnson, "Guitar Slim."

71. Hannusch, *I Hear You Knockin',* 177.

72. Ibid., 180-81.

73. Cosimo Matassa interview.

74. Hannusch, *I Hear You Knockin',* 182; Whitburn, *Top R&B Singles,* 178.

75. Hannusch, *The Soul of New Orleans,* 61; Cosimo Matassa interview.

76. Hannusch, *I Hear You Knockin',* 184-87.

77. Don Walter, "Ray Charles: Six Decades of Hits," *Billboard,* June 22, 2002; "The Immortals: The First Fifty," *Rolling Stone* 946 (April 15, 2004).

78. "Legends of American Music History: Ray Charles," Swing Music Net, http://www.swingmusic.net/Ray_Charles_Biography.html.

79. Broven, *Rhythm & Blues in New Orleans,* 49.

80. Hannusch, *The Soul of New Orleans,* 60-61; Cosimo Matassa interview.

81. "Ray Charles," The History of Rock 'n' Roll: The Golden Decade, 1954-1963, http://www.history-of-rock.com/ray_charles.htm; Cosimo Matassa interview.

82. Hannusch, *The Soul of New Orleans,* 60.

83. Ibid., 61.

84. Larry McKinley, interview with author, 2007.

85. Hannusch, *The Soul of New Orleans,* 62.

86. Ibid., 63.

87. "Legends of American Music History: Ray Charles."

88. Ray Charles Foundation, http://www.raycharles.com/the_man_ray_reflects_rock.html, page no longer available.

89. Cosimo Matassa interview.

90. "Inductee List," Rock and Roll Hall of Fame, http://www.rockhall.com/inductees/inductee-list/; "500 Songs That Shaped Rock and Roll," Rock and Roll Hall of Fame, http://www.rockhall.com/exhibithighlights/500-songs/.

91. Koster, *Louisiana Music,* 118; Whitburn, *Top R&B Singles,* 414.

92. Keith Spera, "Spiders Sing Chuck Carbo, 1926-2008," *New Orleans Times-Picayune,* July 14, 2008.

93. Whitburn, *Top Pop Artists and Singles,* 378.

94. Tom Simon, "Shirley and Lee," Tom Simon Home Page, www.tsimon.com/shirley.htm.

95. Ibid., 217.

96. Whitburn, *Top R&B Singles,* 398; Whitburn, *Top Pop Artists and Singles,* 378.

97. Jason Ankeny, "Sugar Boy Crawford," All Music Guide, available from Answes.com, http://www.answers.com/topic/sugar-boy-crawford.

98. Hannusch, *I Hear You Knockin',* 262-63.

99. Ibid., 265.

100. James Miller, *Flowers in the Dustbin* (New York: Fireside, 2000), 108-9.

101. Cosimo Matassa interview.

102. Broven, *Rhythm & Blues in New Orleans,* 103.

103. Hannusch, *I Hear You Knockin',* 222.

104. Cosimo Matassa interview.

105. Whitburn, *Top R&B Singles,* 270.

106. Cosimo Matassa interview.

107. Lauren Oliver, "A Wop Bop a Lou Mop a Lap Bam Boom," *TV Guide,* February 19-25, 2000.

108. Parke Puterbaugh, "Little Richard," *Rolling Stone,* October 15, 1992.

109. "Little Richard," Songwriters Hall of Fame, http://www.songwritershalloffame.org/exhibit_home_page.asp?exhibitId=334.

110. "Little Richard," Rock and Roll Hall of Fame, http://www.rockhall.com/hof/inductee.asp?id=179.

111. Hannusch, *I Hear You Knockin',* 246-53; Whitburn, *Top R&B Singles,* 119, 266.

112. Whitburn, *Top Pop Artists and Singles,* 403; Hannusch, *I Hear You Knockin',* 256.

113. Coleman, *Blue Monday,* 239; Hannusch, *I Hear You Knockin',* 256-57.

114. "1987 Award & Induction Ceremony: Sam Cooke," Songwriters Hall of Fame, http://www.songwritershalloffame.org/ceremony/entry/C3116/117.

115. "Sam Cooke," The History of Rock 'n' Roll: The Golden Decade, 1954-1963, http://www.history-of-rock.com/cooke.htm; Whitburn, *Top Pop Artists and Singles,* 96; Whitburn, *Top R&B Singles,* 94.

116. Whitburn, *Top Pop Artists and Singles,* 96; Whitburn, *Top R&B Singles,* 94.

117. Gene Santoro, "Sam Cooke," *The Nation,* March 13, 1995.

118. Interview with Ed Henderson, Barbara Cooke's former attorney, 2008.

119. "Inductee List," Rock and Roll Hall of Fame, http://www.rockhall.com/inductees/inductee-list/.

120. Greg Johnson, "Earl King," *BluesNotes* (October 2003), http://www.cascadeblues.org/History/king_earl.htm.

121. Hannusch, *I Hear You Knockin'*, 193.

122. Johnson, "Earl King."

123. Whitburn, *Top R&B Singles,* 247.

124. Hannusch, *I Hear You Knockin'*, 201.

125. Johnson, "Earl King."

126. Bruce Elder, "Bobby Mitchell," All Music Guide, available from Answers.com, http://www.answers.com/topic/bobby-mitchell.

127. Hannusch, *I Hear You Knockin'*, 286; Elder, "Bobby Mitchell."

128. John Wirt, "Huey 'Piano' Smith Gets R&B Honor,' *Baton Rouge Advocate,* September 22, 2000.

129. Hannusch, *I Hear You Knockin'*, 36; Steve Huey, "Huey 'Piano' Smith," All Music Guide, available from Artist Direct, http://www.artistsdirect.com/nad/music/artist/bio/0,,494593,00.html; Whitburn, *Top Pop Artists and Singles,* 350, 387; Whitburn, *Top R&B Singles,* 408.

130. Wirt, *"Huey 'Piano' Smith"*; Whitburn, *Top R&B Singles,* 157.

131. Letter from Huey Smith to author, January 20, 2006.

132. Wirt, *"Huey 'Piano' Smith."*

133. Jeff Hannusch, "Bobby Marchan, 69, Noted N.O. R&B Artist Dies," *New Orleans Times-Picayune*, December 6, 1999.

134. Ibid.

135. Ibid.

136. Stephen Thomas Erlewine, "Larry Williams," All Music Guide, available from Yahoo! Music, http://music.yahoo.com/ar-269508-bio--Larry-Williams.

137. Whitburn, *Top Pop Artists and Singles,* 451; Whitburn, *Top R&B Singles,* 483.

138. Erlewine, "Larry Williams."

139. Ibid.

140. Hannusch, *The Soul of New Orleans,* 77.

141. Whitburn, *Top R&B Singles,* 190; Whitburn, *Top Pop Artists and Singles,* 195.

142. Whitburn, *Top Pop Artists and Singles,* 195.

143. Hannusch, *The Soul of New Orleans,* 80-83.

144. Johnny Powers, "Clarence 'Frogman' Henry: An R&B

Legend!" Rockabilly Hall of Fame, www.rockabillyhall.com/Frogman.html.

145. Whitburn, *Top Pop Artists and Singles,* 228.

146. "Bill Justis," Space Age Musicmaker, http://www.spaceagepop.com/justis.htm.

147. Jason Ankeny, "Bill Justis Biography," All Music Guide, available from AOL Music, http://music.aol.com/artist/bill-justis/18601/biography.

148. Colin Escott and Martin Hawkins, *Sun Records: The Brief History of the Legendary Record Label* (New York: Omnibus Press, 1975), 125.

149. Ankeny, "Bill Justis Biography."

150. Jason Ankeny, "Edgar Myles Biography," All Music Guide, http://www.allmusic.com/cg/amg.dll?p=amg&sql=11:3cfwxqugld 0e~T1.

151. Hannusch, *I Hear You Knockin',* 307-14.

152. Ibid., 45, 48-51.

153. Dr. John [Malcolm Rebennack], *Under a Hoodoo Moon* (New York: St. Martin's Press, 1994), 207.

154. Hannusch, *I Hear You Knockin',* 52-54.

155. Irma Thomas, interview with author, March 2007.

156. Hannusch, *I Hear You Knockin',* 225-28.

157. Irma Thomas interview; Hannusch, *The Soul of New Orleans,* 225-27.

158. John Sinclair, "An Audience with Irma Thomas," *Blues Access* 41 (Spring 2000), http://www.bluesaccess.com/No_41/irma.html.

159. Ibid.

160. "Irma Thomas and the Professionals: Biography," Concerted Efforts, http://www.concertedefforts.com/artists_irma.html.

161. Hannusch, *The Soul of New Orleans,* 227-28.

162. Dan Phillips, "Let's Play It a Little Dissonant," Home of the Groove audioblog, posted May 19, 2006.

163. "Noted Singer Johnny Adams Passes Away," Louisiana Music Archives and Artist Directory, http://www.satchmo.com/nolavl/johnny.html.

164. Cosimo Matassa interview.

165. Hannusch, *I Hear You Knockin',* 272-73.

166. Whitburn, *Top R&B Singles,* 5; Whitburn, *Top Pop Artists and Singles,* 10.

167. "Noted Singer Johnny Adams Passes Away," http://www.satchmo.com/nolavl/johnny.html.

168. Andrew Hamilton, "Roosevelt Nettles," All Music

Guide, available from SwapaCD, http://secure.swapacd.com/cd/artist/480419-roosevelt+nettles.

169. Broven, *Rhythm & Blues in New Orleans,* 141-42; Whitburn, *Top Pop Artists and Singles,* 226); Whitburn, *Top R&B Singles,* 233.

170. Associated Press, "R&B Singer Joe Jones Dies at 79," December 3, 2005.

171. Broven, *Rhythm & Blues in New Orleans*, 142-44.

172. Cosimo Matassa interview.

173. Hannusch, *I Hear You Knockin'*, 317.

174. Jason Ankeny, "Jessie Hill Biography," All Music Guide, http://www.allmusic.com/cg/amg.dll?p=amg&sql=11:gnfoxqt5ldse~T1.

175. Hannusch, *I Hear You Knockin'*, 319-20.

176. Ankeny, "Jessie Hill Biography."

177. Ibid.

178. Jason Ankeny, "Prince La La," All Music Guide, available from Answers.com, http://www.answers.com/topic/prince-la-la-1.

179. Ibid.

180. Ibid.; Whitburn, *Top R&B Singles,* 359.

181. Janet McConnaughey, "Oliver 'Who Shot the La La' Morgan's Funeral in 9th Ward," Associated Press, August 8, 2007.

182. "Al's Bio: It's Carnival Time and Everybody's Havin' Fun," The Official Al "Carnival Time" Johnson web page, http://www.alcarnivaltimejohnson.com/bio.htm.

183. Hannusch, *The Soul of New Orleans,* 84-85.

184. Jason Ankeny, "Barbara George," All Music Guide, http://www.allmusic.com/cg/amg.dll?p=amg&sql=11:hiftxqe5ldke~T1.

185. Broven, *Rhythm & Blues in New Orleans,* 161-62.

186. Ibid.

187. Naomi King, "Remembering: Barbara George," *Houma (LA) Daily Courier*, August 17, 2007.

188. Whitburn, *Top Pop Artists and Singles,* 230.

189. Larry McKinley interview.

190. Irma Thomas and Larry McKinley, interview with author, 2007.

191. Hannusch, *I Hear You Knockin'*, 147.

192. S.J. Montalbano, interview with author, 2006.

193. Whitburn, *Top Pop Artists and Singles,* 230.

194. Neil Strauss, "Ernie K-Doe, 65, Who Sang 'Mother-in-Law' Is Dead," *New York Times,* July 7, 2001.

195. "Land of 1,000 Dances," Song Facts, http://www.songfacts.com/detail.php?id=293.

196. Hannusch, *I Hear You Knockin'*, 291-97.

197. Steve Huey, "Lee Dorsey," African Genesis Presents the Soul Music Center, http://afgen.com/lee_dorsey.html; Broven, *Rhythm & Blues in New Orleans,* 168.

198. Whitburn, *Top Pop Artists and Singles,* 129.

199. Cosimo Matassa interview.

200. Huey, "Lee Dorsey."

201. Dominic Turner, "Benny Spellman," Rockabilly Music Association, http://www.rockabillyeurope.com/mainframe. htm?references/references.htm.

202. Whitburn, *Top Pop Artists and Singles,* 393.

203. Jason Ankeny, "Willie Tee," All Music Guide, available from VH1, http://www.vh1.com/artists/az/tee_willie/bio.jhtml.

204. Ibid.

205. Keith Spera, "Funeral Services Set for Wilson 'Willie Tee' Turbinton," *New Orleans Times-Picayune*, September 11, 2007.

206. "Aaron Neville," Verve Music Group, http://www. vervemusicgroup.com/artist/default.aspx?aid=5868.

207. Whitburn, *Top Pop Artists and Singles,* 430.

208. Jason Berry, "It Takes a Cool Cat," *New Orleans Magazine* (January 1997).

209. "The Cyril Neville Band," Jam Base, http://www.jambase. com/search.asp?bandID=28824&display=bio.

210. Berry, "It Takes a Cool Cat."

211. Hannusch, *The Soul of New Orleans,* 298.

212. Aaron Neville web page, http://www.aaronneville.com.

213. Joe Edwards, "After Katrina, Neville Finds His Soul in Nashville," Associated Press, September 8, 2006.

214. "Stars Offer Heartfelt Performances in Benefit," Associated Press, September 5, 2005.

215. Edwards, "After Katrina, Neville Finds His Soul in Nashville."

216. "Biography," The Dixie Cups, http://lpintop.tripod.com/ thedixiecups/id1.html.

217. Whitburn, *Top Pop Artists and Singles,* 123; Whitburn, *Top R&B Singles,* 116.

218. "500 Songs That Shaped Rock and Roll," Rock and Roll Hall of Fame, http://www.rockhall.com/exhibithighlights/500-songs/.

219. Whitburn, *Top Pop Artists and Singles,* 407-8.

220. "Dixie Cups," Lyrics Vault, http://www.lyricsvault.net.

221. "Red Bird Records," Answers.com, http://www.answers. com/topic/red-bird-records.

222. Hannusch, *The Soul of New Orleans,* 236-38.

223. Ibid.

224. Whitburn, *Top Pop Artists and Singles,* 315; Whitburn,

Top R&B Singles, 340; Hannusch, *The Soul of New Orleans,* 239.

225. Larry McKinley interview.

226. Jason Ankeny, "Margie Joseph Biography," All Music Guide, available from Yahoo! Music, http://new.music.yahoo.com/margie-joseph/biography/.

227. Margie Joseph official web page, http://www.margiejoseph.com/site.html.

228. Scott Montgomery, Gary Norris, and Kevin Walsh, 'The Invisible Randy Newman: The Formative Years: New Orleans," *Goldmine,* 21, no. 8 (September 1, 1995), http://www.randynewman.info/biography/neworleans.html.

229. Timothy White, "Randy Newman's Portrait of America," *Billboard,* December 9, 2000; Sean Elder, "Randy Newman," Salon.com, http://www.salon.com/people/bc/1999/08/24/newman/.

230. L. Rob Hubb, "Cold Turkey: Randy Newman," Music Snob blog, posted October 12, 2006, http://mimezinemusicsnob.blogspot.com/2006/10/cold-turkey-randy-newman.html.

231. Montgomery, "The Invisible Randy Newman"; "500 Songs That Shaped Rock and Roll," Rock and Roll Hall of Fame, http://www.rockhall.com/exhibithighlights/500-songs/.

232. Jason Ankeny, "King Floyd," All Music Guide, available from MP3.com, http://www.mp3.com/king-floyd/artists/28616/biography.html.

233. Hannusch, *I Hear You Knockin',* 325; "King Floyd," Malaco Music Group, http://malaco.com/Catalog/Blues-R-B/King-Floyd/list.php.

234. Ankeny, "King Floyd."

235. Hannusch, *I Hear You Knockin',* 326.

236. "King Floyd," Malaco Music Group.

237. Ankeny, "King Floyd."

238. Hannusch, *The Soul of New Orleans,* 260-61.

239. Ibid.

240. Whitburn, *Top R&B Singles,* 252; Whitburn, *Top Pop Artists and Singles,* 238.

241. Hannusch, *The Soul of New Orleans,* 262.

242. Steve Huey, "Jean Knight," All Music Guide, available from Answers.com, http://www.answers.com/topic/jean-knight.

243. "Biography for Dr. John," Internet Movie Database, http://www.imdb.com/name/nm0236566/bio; Hannusch, *The Soul of New Orleans,* 177-83.

244. Dr. John, *Under a Hoodoo Moon,* 112-14.

245. Hannusch, *The Soul of New Orleans,* 183-84; Richie Unterberger, "Dr. John Biography," All Music Guide, available

from The Copyright Society of the USA, http://www.csusa.org/pdf/
Dr_John_Bio.pdf; Dr. John: The Unofficial Website of Dr. John,
http://drjohn.waiting-forthe-sun.net/Pages/Bio.html.

246. "500 Songs That Shaped Rock," Rock and Roll Hall of Fame,
http://www.rockhall.com/exhibithighlights/500-songs/; Whitburn,
Top Pop Artists and Singles, 124; Whitburn, *Top R&B Singles,* 118;
Hannusch, *The Soul of New Orleans,* 186-87.

Chapter Four

1. Bruce Eder, "Jimmy Clanton," All Music Guide, available from
VH1, http://www.vh1.com/artists/az/clanton_jimmy/bio.jhtml.

2. Dick Holler, correspondence with author, 2006.

3. Whitburn, *Top Pop Artists and Singles,* 84; Whitburn, *Top
R&B Singles,* 81.

4. Eder, "Jimmy Clanton."

5. "Singing Star's Body Due Here Today," *Lubbock Avalanche-
Journal* archives, posted February 23, 2000, http://www.
buddyhollyarchives.com/crash2.shtml.

6. S.J. Montalbano, interview with author, 2006.

7. Obituary notice, *Clark County Democrat*, June 17, 2004.

8. Whitburn, *Top Pop Artists and Singles,* 84.

9. Obituary notice, *Clark County Democrat*.

10. "One-Hit Wonders: John Fred & His Playboy Band,"
Epinions, http://www.Epinions.com/content_4202864772.

11. "John Fred," Museum of the Gulf Coast, http://www.
museumofthegulfcoast.org/personalities-music-legends-john-
fred.html.

12. Jason Ankeny, "John Fred," All Music Guide, available
from Answers.com http://www.answers.com/topic/john-fred.

13. Phil Davies, "John Fred," Black Cat Rockabilly, http://www.
rockabilly.nl/references/messages/john_fred.htm.

14. "One-Hit Wonders, Epinions."

15. Davies, "John Fred."

16. John Wirt, "John Fred Dies," *Baton Rouge Advocate*, April
16, 2005.

17. Whitburn, *Top Pop Artists and Singles,* 166.

18. "John Fred," Louisiana's Music, http://www.louisianasmusic.
com/Retail/john_fred%20bio.htm; Davies, "John Fred."

19. Ankeny, "John Fred."

20. Wirt, "John Fred Dies"; John Andrew Prime, "Singer Who
Had Big Hit *Judy in Disguise* on Local Label Dies," *Shreveport
Times*, April 16, 2005.

21. Angus Lind, "On the Comeback Trail," *New Orleans*

Times-Picayune, March 27, 2006.

22. Jay Chevalier, interview with author, 2006; Jason Berry, "Jay Chevalier's Louisiana Legacy," *New Orleans Magazine* (January 2003).

23. Tony Wilkinson, "Jay Chevalier," Black Cat Rockabilly, http://www.rockabilly.nl/references/messages/jay_chevalier.htm

24. Berry, "Jay Chevalier's Louisiana Legacy."

25. Dale Houston and Grace Broussard, interviews with author, 2006.

26. "Dale and Grace," ClassicBands.com, http://www.classicbands.com/DaleGrace.html.

27. Grace Broussard interview.

28. S.J. Montalbano interview.

29. Dale Houston interview.

30. Grace Broussard interview.

31. Dale Houston interview.

32. Grace Broussard interview.

33. Ibid.

34. Tom Simon, "Dale & Grace," Tom Simon web site, http://www.tsimon.com/dale.htm.

35. Dale Houston interview.

36. Linda Seida, "Van Broussard," All Music Guide, available from Answers.com, http://www.answers.com/topic/van-broussard.

37. Van Broussard, interview with author, 2006.

38. John Wirt, "Saxophonist Bobby Lovless Dead at 65," *Baton Rouge Advocate,* September 21, 2005.

39. "Biography," Johnny Rivers, http://www.johnnyrivers.com/jr/biography.html.

40. John Wirt, "Johnny Rivers Had Right Songs, Right Time, Right Sound," *Baton Rouge Advocate*, July 29, 2005.

41. Dick Holler, interview with author, 2006; Wirt, "Johnny Rivers Had Right Songs."

42. "Biography," Johnny Rivers.

43. Whitburn, *Top Pop Artists and Singles,* 30.

44. Ibid.

45. "Johnny Rivers," Kelly Productions, http://www.kellypro.com/Showtime/JohnnyRivers.htm.

46. "'I Gotcha,' Joe Tex, Dial 1010," Super Seventies RockSite, http://www.superseventies.com/1972_5singles.html.

47. Ibid.

48. Whitburn, *Top Pop Artists and Singles,* 417; Whitburn, *Top R&B Singles,* 440.

49. "'I Gotcha,'" Super Seventies RockSite.

50. Colin Larkin, *The Encyclopedia of Popular Music,* 4th ed. (New York: Oxford University Press, 2006).

51. Whitburn, *Top Pop Artists and Singles,* 380-81; Larkin, "Joe Simon Biography."

52. Percy Sledge, interview with author, 2006.

53. "Percy Sledge: 1993 Inductee," Alabama Music Hall of Fame, http://www.alamhof.org/percysledge.html.

54. "Percy Sledge," Rock and Roll Hall of Fame, http://www. rockhall.com/inductee/percy-sledge.

55. Chris Morris, "Sledge Looks for Comeback with Virgin's 'Blue Night,'" *Billboard,* April 25, 1995.

56. "Percy Sledge," Rock and Roll Hall of Fame.

57. Holly George-Warren, Patricia Romanski, and Jon Pareles, "Percy Sledge," *The Rolling Stone Encyclopedia of Rock and Roll,* 3rd ed. (New York: Simon & Schuster, 2001), http://www. rollingstone.com/artists/percysledge/biography.

58. Stephen Thomas Erlewine, "Percy Sledge Biography," All Music Guide, available from Answers.com, http://www.answers. com/topic/percy-sledge; "Percy Sledge," Museum of the Gulf Coast, http://www.museumofthegulfcoast.org/personalities-music-legends-percy-sledge.html.

59. "Percy Sledge," Rock and Roll Hall of Fame.

60. "500 Songs That Shaped Rock and Roll," Rock and Roll Hall of Fame, http://www.rockhall.com/exhibithighlights/500-songs/.

61. "Biography," LeRoux, http://www.laleroux.com/HTMLPages/ biography.html.

62. Koster, *Louisiana Music,* 236-37.

63. "Biography," LeRoux.

64. Whitburn, *Top Pop Artists and Singles,* 257.

65. Koster, *Louisiana Music,* 236; "Biography," LeRoux.

66. "Biography," LeRoux.

67. "Leon Medica," LeRoux, http://www.laleroux.comHTMLPages/ leon.html.

68. Leon Medica, interview with author, 2006.

69. Ibid.

70. "Leon Medica," LeRoux.

71. Ibid.

72. Leon Medica interview.

73. "Leon Medica," LeRoux.

74. Ibid.

75. "Duke Bardwell," Louisiana's Music, http://www.louisianas music.com/Retail/Duke%20bio.htm.

76. Duke Bardwell, interview with Arjan Deelen, The Original

Elvis Tribute 2010, http://www.elvisnews.dk/interviews/duke-bardwell/duke-bardwell.htm.

77. "Casey Kelly: Biography," Casey Kelly: Himownself, http://www.caseykelly.net/biography.html.

78. "Duke Bardwell," Baton Rouge Blues Society, http://www.batonrougeblues.org/Musicians%20biographies/duke_bardwell.htm.

79. "Casey Kelly," It's About Music.com, http://www.itsaboutmusic.com/caseykelly.html.

Chapter Five

1. John Fuhrmann, "Slim Harpo," The BluesHarp Page, www.bluesharp.ca/legends/sharpo.html.

2. Glenn Weiser, Slim Harpo biography from *Masters of the Blues Harp: Note-for-Note Transcriptions from Classic Recorded Performances* (Hal Leonard Corp., 2001), www.celticguitarmusic.com/harmslimharpo.htm.

3. Ibid.

3. Cub Koda, "Slim Harpo," All Music Guide, available from MOG Music Network, http://mog.com/music/Slim_Harpo/bio.

4. Whitburn, *Top R&B Singles,* 182; Whitburn, *Top Pop Artists and Singles,* 189.

5. "500 Songs That Shaped Rock," Rock and Roll Hall of Fame, http://www.rockhall.com/exhibithighlights/500-songs/.

6. Jimmy Beyer, *A Guide to the Baton Rouge Bluesmen and Their Music* (Baton Rouge, LA: Arts and Humanities Council of Greater Baton Rouge, 1980); Whitburn, *Top R&B Singles,* 182.

7. Beyer, *A Guide to the Baton Rouge Bluesmen.*

8. "Slim Harpo," Rolling Stone, http://www.rollingstone.com/artists/slimharpo/biography.

9. "Lightnin' Slim: Blues Guitarist, Vocalist," All About Jazz, http://www.allaboutjazz.com/php/musician.php?id=8759

10. Cub Koda, "Lightnin' Slim Biography," All Music Guide, Available from MOG Music Network, http://mog.com/music/Lightnin'_Slim/bio.

11. "Silas Hogan Biography," The Blues Daily, posted March 21, 2009, http://thebluesdaily.com/2009/03/21/3443/.

12. "Silas Hogan," All Music Guide, available from Answers.com, http://www.answers.com/topic/silas-hogan.

13. "Silas Hogan Biography," All Music Guide, available from Artist Direct, http://www.artistdirect.com/nad/music/artist/bio/0,,444764.html; "Slim Harpo," Baton Rouge Blues Foundation, http://brbluesfoundation.org/slimharpoawards.html.

14. Bill Dahl, "Whispering Smith," All Music Guide, http://

www.allmusic.com/cg/amg.dll.

15. Andy Cornett, "Henry's Bio," Henry Gray and the Cats, www.henrygray.com/bio.htm.

16. Lucky Cat Productions, "Henry Gray," Henry Gray and the Cats, http://www.henrygray.com/HG_EPK%20352%20KB1.pdf.

17. Cornett, "Henry's Bio."

18. "At 80, 'Gatemouth' Has Grown Beyond Blues," *USA Today,* November 29, 2004.

19. James Sullivan, "Gatemouth Brown Dies," *Rolling Stone,* September 12, 2005, http://www.rollingstone.com/news/story/7626739/gatemouth_brown_dies.

20. Ben Ratliff, "Guitarist Clarence Gatemouth Brown Dies at 81," *New York Times,* September 12, 2005, http://www.nytimes.com/2005/09/12/arts/music/12brown.html.

21. Whitburn, *Top R&B Singles,* 49; "Clarence Gatemouth Brown," Verve Music Group, http://www.vervemusicgroup.com/artist.aspx?aid=2780.

22. "Gate's Biography," Gatemouth Brown web page since removed, http://www.gatemouth.com/bio.htm.

23. Hannusch, *I Hear You Knockin',* 83-84.

24. Koster, *Louisiana Music,* 119.

25. Jason Ankeny, *Mr. Google Eyes,* All Music Guide, http://www.allmusic.com/cg/amg.dll?p=amg&sql=11:wbfoxqqjld6e~T1.

26. Tabby Thomas and Joylyn Wright, "Ernest J. 'Tabby' Thomas: Blues Artist," East Baton Rouge Parish Library, http://www.ebr.lib.la.us/reference/ourafamlegacy/oaal_peopleandplaces/people/TabbyThomas.htm.

27. Ron Wynn and Stephen Thomas Erlewine, "Rockin' Tabby Thomas," All Music Guide, available from Artist Direct, http://www.artistdirect.com/nad/music/artist/bio/0,,501349,00.html.

28. Thomas and Wright, "Ernest J. "Tabby" Thomas: Blues Artist."

29. Ibid.

30. Tabby Thomas, performance at Phil Brady's, April 2006.

31. "Bio & Photos," Tab Benoit, http://www.tabbenoit.com/biophoto.html.

32. Ibid; Richard Skelly and Al Campbell, "Tab Benoit Biography," All Music Guide, available from Starpulse Entertainment News Blog, http://www.starpulse.com/Music/Benoit,_Tab/Biography/.

33. "Tab Benoit Biography," Concord Music Group, http://www.concordmusicgroup.com/assets/documents01/Artists/Tab-Benoit/83674/Night-Train-To-Nashville-Biography.pdf.

34. "Raful Neal," Baton Rouge Blues Society, http://www.

batonrougeblues.org/Musicians%20biographies/raful_neal.htm.

35. "Kenny Neal Biography," Kenny Neal, http://www.kennyneal.net/kennybio.html.

36. "Kenny Neal," Alligator Records, http://www.alligator.com/index.cfm?section=artists&artistid=18.

37. Tim Holek, "Kenny Neal: *Let Life Flow,*" review of *Let Life Flow,* by Kenny Neal, Chicago Blues Guide, http://www.chicagobluesguide.com/reviews/cd-reviews/kenny-neal-cd/kenny-neal-cd-page.html; "Kenny Neal," Intrepid Artists, http://www.intrepidartists.com/kennyneal.html.

38. "The Bio," Lil Ray Neal Blues Band, http://www.lilraynealbluesband.com/1521420.html.

39. "Lil' Ray Neal Blues Band Brings Home Blues Award for Baton Rouge Blues Society," February 20, 2008 press release, Baton Rouge Blues Society, http://www.prlog.org/10052326-lil-ray-neal-blues-band-brings-home-blues-award-for-baton-rouge-blues-society.html.

40. "Lil' Ray Neal," Baton Rouge Blues Society, http://www.batonrougeblues.org/Musicians%20biographies/lil_ray_neal.htm.

41. "2008 Slim Harpo Awards Recipients Announced," Baton Rouge Blues Foundation, http://brbluesfoundation.org/slimharpoawards/foundationawards2008.html.

42. "Larry Garner," Baton Rouge Blues Society, http://www.batonrougeblues.org/musicians%20bios.htm.

43. Ibid.

44. Joel M. Snow, "Little Walter: Biography," Blues Online, http://physics.lunet.edu/blues/Little_Walter.html.

45. "Little Walter 'Fun Facts,'" Little Walter.net, http://www.littlewalter.net/funfacts.html.

46. Whitburn, *Top R&B Singles,* 270-71; Bill Dahl, "Little Walter Biography," All Music Guide, available from Yahoo! Music, http://music.yahoo.com/ar-254601-bio--Little-Walter.

47. "Lonnie Brooks," Alligator Records, http://www.alligator.com/index.cfm?section=artists&artistid=6.

48. Rich Cohen, "Buddy Guy: The Kingpin," *Rolling Stone,* February 23, 2006, http://www.rollingstone.com/artists/buddyguy/articles/story/9257392/buddy_guy_the_kingpin.

49. A.S., "The King of Chicago on His Early Days," *Rolling Stone*, September 18, 2003.

50. Buddy Guy, Hall of Legends, http://www.fenderplayersclub.com/artists_lounge/hall_of_legends/guy.htm.

51. Cohen, "Buddy Guy: The Kingpin."

52. Ibid.

53. Tim Parsons, "Buddy Guy Is the Blues," *Tahoe Daily Tribune*, May 11, 2007, http://www.batonrougeblues.org/Articles/buddy_guy_is_the_blues.htm.

54. Ibid.

55. Stephanie Zacharek, "Shine a Light," movie review of *Shine a Light,* by Martin Scorsese and the Rolling Stones, Salon.com, posted April 4, 2008, http://www.salon.com/ent/movies/review/2008/04/04/shine_a_light/; Donald Liebenson, "Buddy Guy's Play-Acting, Not Playing, in 'Electric Mist,'" *Chicago Tribune*, March 29, 2009, http://archives.chicagotribune.com/2009/mar/29/entertainment/chi-0329-buddy-guymar29.

56. "Buddy Guy," All Experts, http://en.allexperts.com/e/b/bu/buddy-guy.htm.

57. Linda Seida, "Marva Wright Biography," All Music Guide, available from Artist Direct, http://www.artistdirect.com/nad/nusic/artist/bio/0,,511895,00.html.

58. "About Marva," Marva Wright, http://www.marvawright.com/bio.htm.

59. Karl Bremer, "Snooks Eaglin: On the Trail of the Most Elusive Guitar Player in New Orleans," Blues Access 38 (summer 1999), http://www.bluesaccess.com/No_38/snooks.html.

60. David Fricke, "Out There," *Rolling Stone,* October 6, 2005.

61. Hannusch, *The Soul of New Orleans,* 279; Bremer, "Snooks Eaglin."

62. Broven, *Rhythm & Blues in New Orleans,* 177.

63. Koster, *Louisiana Music,* 139.

64. Ibid., 139-40.

65. Hannusch, *The Soul of New Orleans,* 280; Keith Spera, "New Orleans Guitarist Snooks Eaglin Dies at 72," *New Orleans Times-Picayune,* February 19, 2009.

66. Bill Dahl, "Etta James Biography," All Music Guide, available from Starpulse Entertainment News Blog, http://www.starpulse.com/Music/James,_Etta/Biography/.

67. Ibid.

68. "500 Songs That Shaped Rock and Roll," Rock and Roll Hall of Fame, http://www.rockhall.com/exhibithighlights/500-songs/.

69. Sonya Shelton, "Memphis Minnie Biography," Musician Biographies database, http://www.musicianguide.com/biographies/1608002338/Memphis-Minnie.html.

70. Ibid.

71. Barry Lee Pearson, "Memphis Minnie," Answers.com, http://www.answers.com/topic/memphis-minnie.

72. Shelton, "Memphis Minnie Biography."

73. Pearson, "Memphis Minnie."

74. Shelton, "Memphis Minnie Biography."

75. Amelia Feathers, "An R&B Comeback, More Than Three Decades in the Making," Blues Music Now blues blog, www.bluesmusicnow.com/lynn.html.

76. Steve Huey, "Barbara Lynn," All Music Guide, Answers.com, http://www.answers.com/topic/barbara-lynn-1.

77. Christopher Gray, "Still a Good Thing," *Austin Chronicle,* October 27, 2000.

78. "Janis Joplin," Famous Texans, www.famoustexans.com/janisjoplin.htm.

79. Richard B. Hughes, "Joplin, Janis Lyn," The Online Handbook of Texas, http://www.tshaonline.org/handbook/online/articles/JJ/fjo69.html.

80. Holly George-Warren, Patricia Romanski, and Jon Pareles, "Janis Joplin," *Rolling Stone Encyclopedia of Rock & Roll,* 3rd ed. (New York: Simon & Schuster, 2001).

81. Margaret Moser, "Janis Joplin Biography," Hot Shot Digital's Legends of Rock, http://www.hotshotdigital.com/WellAlwaysRemember.2/JanisJoplinBio.html.

82. Chester Rosson, "Janis Joplin," Texas Music Source, *Texas Monthly,* July 1997.

83. Laura Joplin, *Love Janis* (New York: Villard Books, 1992).

84. Richard Skelly and Al Campbell, "Marcia Ball Biography," All Music Guide, available from Yahoo! Music, http://new.music.yahoo.com/marcia-ball/biography/.

85. "Marcia Ball," Jam Base, http://www.jambase.com/Artists/10066/Marcia-Ball/Bio.

86. Ibid.

87. Chris Morris, "Thomas, Rounder women join on 'Sing It!'," *Billboard,* December 20, 1997.

88. Skelly and Campbell, "Marcia Ball Biography."

89. Hackberry Ramblers web site, http://www.hackberryramblers.com/; The Rosebud Agency, *Presumed Innocent* CD press release, http://www.rosebudus.com/ball/PresumedInnocent.html.

90. "Marcia Ball," *New Orleans Magazine,* April 1, 2001; B. Kimberly Taylor and Ken Burke, "Marcia Ball Biography," Muscian Biographies database, www.musicianguide.com/biographies/160800 4137/Marcia-Ball.html.

91. "Luther Kent," All About Jazz, http://www.allaboutjazz.com/php/musician.php?id=18372.

92. "Biography of Luther Kent," Luther Kent, http://www.lutherkent.com/info/luther.html.

93. "Luther Kent," All About Jazz.

94. "Biography of Luther Kent," Luther Kent.

95. Liner notes to *Spanish Town Mardi Gras,* Kenny Acosta, Bluzman Records, http://cdbaby.com/cd/kacosta.

96. John Wirt, "King Became Storm Evacuee, Hopes to Help Other Musicians," *Baton Rouge Advocate*, September 15, 2005.

97. Nate Guidry, "Chris Thomas King's New Album Recalls Triumph over Tragedy of Katrina," Block News Alliance, December 17, 2006; Wes Orshonski, "Chris King Builds on *O Brother*," *Billboard*, September 22, 2001.

98. "Chris Thomas King Biography," Musician Biographies database, http://www.musicianguide.com/biographies/1608003726/Chris-Thomas-King.html; "Chris Thomas King: Biography," Net Glimse, http://www.netglimse.com/celebs/pages/chris_thomas_king/index.shtml.

99. "Kenny Wayne's World," *Rolling Stone,* April 16, 1998.

100. Ibid.

101. Steve Huey and Richard Skelly, "Kenny Wayne Shepherd Biography," All Music Guide, available from Starpulse Entertainment News Blog, http://www.starpulse.com/Music/Shepherd,_Kenny_Wayne/Biography.

102. "Kenny Wayne Shepherd's 'Ten Days Out: Blues From the Backroads' Nominated for Two Grammys," Starpulse Entertainment News Blog, posted January 15, 2008, http://www.starpulse.com/news/index.php/2008/01/15/kenny_wayne_shepherd_s_ten_days_out_blue.

103. "Henry Butler Biography," Henry Butler: New Orleans Piano Legend, http://www.henrybutler.com/bio_01.html.

104. "Henry Butler," All About Jazz, http://www.allaboutjazz.com/php/musician.php?id=5501.

105. "Spencer Bohren," Spencer Bohren, http://www.spencerbohren.com/bio/.

Chapter Six

1. Barry Jean Ancelet, *Cajun Music: Its Origins and Development* (Lafayette: The Center for Louisiana Studies, University of Southwestern Louisiana, 1989); David Simpson, "A Brief History of Cajun, Creole, and Zydeco Music," www.lsue.edu/acadgate/music/history.htm.

2. Ancelet, *Cajun Music.*

3. Broven, *South to Louisiana* (Gretna, LA: Pelican Publishing Company, 1974), 101.

4. Simpson, "A Brief History."

5. Herman Fuselier, "Grammys Add Cajun/Zydeco Category," *Lafayette Daily Advertiser,* June 9, 2007.

6. Terrance Simien, interview with author, 2008; Herman Fuselier, "And the Grammy Goes to . . . Terrance Simien," *Lafayette Daily Advertiser,* February 11, 2008.

7. Broven, *South to Louisiana,* 22; "Hackberry Ramblers: Making Music Since 1933," CNN, November 11, 1997.

8. John Bush, "Hackberry Ramblers," All Music Guide, available from MOG Music Network, http://mog.com/music/Hackberry_Ramblers/bio.

9. Shane K. Bernard, "Hackberry Ramblers," Cajun Culture, www.cajunculture.com/People/hackberry.htm, page since removed; Bush, "Hackberry Ramblers."

10. "The Hackberry Ramblers," Official Website of the Hackberry Ramblers and the Hot Biscuits Recording Company, http://www.hackberryramblers.com/bio.html; Bush, "Hackberry Ramblers."

11. "News," Official website of the Hackberry Ramblers and the Hot Biscuits Recording Company, http://www.hackberryramblers.com/index.html.

12. Edward Darbone, interview with author, November, 2008; Keith Spera, "The Hackberry Ramblers' Luderin Darbone, 1913-2008," *New Orleans Times-Picayune*, November 26, 2008.

13. Craig Harris, "Leo Soileau," http://music.barnesandnoble.com/search/artistbio.asp?CTR=241211.

14. John Bush, "Nathan Abshire," All Music Guide, http://www.allmusic.com/cg/amg.dll.

15. Broven, *South to Louisiana,* 102.

16. "Amédé Ardoin," Last.fm, http://www.last.fm/music/Am%C3%A9d%C3%A9+Ardoin.

17. Ibid.

18. "Dennis McGee: Composer, Fiddler, and Vocalist," People of Interest, City of Eunice, http://www.eunice-la.com/dennismcgee.html.

19. Craig Harris, "Dennis McGee Biography," All Music Guide, available from Artist Direct, http://www.artistdirect.com/nad/music/artist/bio/0,,465921,00.html.

20. "Dennis McGee: Composer, Fiddler, and Vocalist," People of Interest, City of Eunice.

21. Jason Ankeny, "John Delafose," All Music Guide, available from Answers.com, http://www.answers.com/topic/john-delafose.

22. Melissa Block, "Geno Delafose, Keeping Zydeco in the Family," *All Things Considered,* National Public Radio, June 12, 2003.

23. Craig Harris, "Geno Delafose," All Music Guide, available from SwapaCD, http://secure.swapacd.com/cd/artist/68380-geno+delafose.

24. Geno Delafose and French Rockin' Boogie, http://genodelafose.net/GenoHome/GenoHome.htm.

25. Ibid; Harris, "Geno Delafose."

26. Wes Orshoski, "Zydeco Hero Chavis Mourned," *Billboard,* May 19, 2001.

27. Kevin O'Sullivan, "Boozoo Chavis Biography," Musician Biographies database, http://www.musicianguide.com/biographies/1608003333/Boozoo-Chavis.html.

28. K. Manning, "New Series Honors Local Heroes," *Rolling Stone,* June 13, 1991.

29. Larry Benicewicz, "Remembering Boozoo Chavis," Blues World,

30. Fuller, Reese, "The Record Man," *The Independent,* January 4, 2006.

31. Craig Harris, "Boozoo Chavis Biography," All Music Guide, available from MOG Music Network, http://mog.com/music/Boozoo_Chavis/bio.

32. Ibid.

33. Orshoski, "Zydeco Hero Chavis Mourned."

34. Sullivan, "Boozoo Chavis Biography."

35. Craig Harris, "Canray Fontenot: Biography," All Music Guide, http://www.allmusic.com/cg/amg.dll?p=amg&sql=11:gzfoxq95ldfe~T1.

36. Craig Harris, "Doug Kershaw: Biography," All Music Guide, available from Yahoo! Music, http://shopping.yahoo.com/p:Doug%20Kershaw:1927000572:page=biography.

37. Biography for Doug Kershaw, http://2009.SXSW.com/music/shows/schedule/?a=shows&s=91695.

38. Harris, "Doug Kershaw."

39. Ibid.

40. Ibid.

41. Mark Miller, interview with author, 2007.

42. Doug Kershaw biography, http://www.dougkershaw.com/Biography/biography.html, page since removed.

43. Elizabeth Wenning, "Clifton Chenier Biography," Musicians Biography database, http://www.musicianguide.com/biographies/1608000335/Clifton-Chenier.html.

44. Ibid.

45. Jim Bradshaw, "Clifton Chenier Put Zydeco Music on the Map," *Lafayette Daily Advertiser,* December 29, 1998.

46. Craig Harris, "Clifton Chenier," All Music Guide, available

from Answers.com, http://www.answers.com/topic/clifton-chenier.

47. "Lil' Buck Sinegal: Bio," NYNO Records, http://www.nynorecords.com/buck.shtml.

48. Andy Cornett, "Lil' Buck Senegal," www.tempoblues.com/%20Blues%20Eng/Lil%20Buck%20Sinegal%20Eng.html.

49. Ibid.

50. "Lil Buck Sinegal: Bio," NYNO Records: The Indigenous Music of New Orleans, http://www.nynorecords.com/buck.shtml.

51. Jason Ankeny, "Buckwheat Zydeco," All Music Guide, available from Billboard.com, http://www.billboard.com/bbcom/bio/index.jsp?pid=1561.

52. Ted Fox, liner notes for *The Buckwheat Zydeco Story: A 20-Year Party,* Tomorrow Records.

53. Ankeny, "Buckwheat Zydeco."

54. Ibid.

55. Fox, liner notes.

56. "Zachary Richard Biography," Zachary Richard: American Singer/Songwriter, http://zachary.waiting-forthe-sun.net/Pages/Biography.html.

57. Ibid.

58. Sarah Spell-Johnson, "Zachary Richard," *Louisiana Life,* Spring 1998.

59. Richard Skelly, "Sonny Landreth: Biography," All Music Guide, available from Yahoo! Shopping, http://shopping.yahoo.com/p:Sonny%20Landreth:1927028195:page=biography.

60. C. Michael Bailey, review of *All About Jazz,* by Grant Street, February 12, 2005.

61. Skelly, "Sonny Landreth biography."

62. Koster, *Louisiana Music,* 196.

63. Sandra Brennan, "Rockin' Dopsie," All Music Guide, available from Artist Direct, http://www.artistdirect.com/nad/music/artist/bio/0,,424525,00html.

64. Koster, *Louisiana Music,* 197

65. John Swenson, "Rockin' Dopsie," *Rolling Stone,* October 14, 1993; "About . . .," Rockin' Dopsie, Jr., and the Zydeco Twisters, http://www.rockindopsie.com/about.htm.

66. Jason Ankeny, "Rockin' Sidney," All Music Guide, available from Answers.com, http://www.answers.com/topic/rockin-sidney.

67. Koster, *Louisiana Music,* 200.

68. Ankeny, "Rockin' Sidney."

69. Ibid.

70. Ibid.

71. "Rockin' Sidney," Lala music catalog, http://www.lala. com/#artist/Rockin'_Sidney/bio.

72. Ibid.

73. Ibid.

74. Ankeny, "Rockin' Sidney."

75. "Wayne Toups: Biography," Wayango, http://www.wayango. com/wayne-toups/bio/.

76. Mark Miller, interview with author, 2007.

77. "Wayne's Bio," Wayne Toups & Zydecajun, http://www. waynetoups.net/bio.asp.

78. "Wayne Toups: Biography," Wayango.

79. Home page, Jo-El Sonnier, http://www.jo-elsonnier.com/.

80. Jo-El Sonnier biography, http://music.aol.com/artist/jo-el-sonnier/1812/biography.

81. "Jo-El Sonnier," Museum of the Gulf Coast, www. museumofthegulfcoast.org/Content/Personalities/Music_Legends/Jo-El_Sonnier.

82. Home page, Jo-El Sonnier.

83. Koster, *Louisiana Music,* 284.

84. Home page, Jo-El Sonnier.

85. David Simpson, "Joe Hall," Archive Files of Cajun, Creole, and Zydeco Musicians, http://www.lsue.edu/acadgate/music/hall.htm.

86. Pine Leaf Boys: Rockin' Cajun Music from Louisiana, www. pineleafboys.com/.

87. Herman Fuselier, "The Pine Leaf Boys: Real Cajun," *Sing Out! The Folk Song Magazine* (Fall 2006); Alex Rawls, "Pine Leaf Boys Reinvigorate Cajun Tradition," *San Diego Union-Tribune,* October 16, 2008.

88. "Grammy Winners Beausoleil avec Michael Doucet Perform March 24 at the Clark," Sterling and Francine Clark Art Institute, March 2, 2007 press release, http://www.clarkart.edu/visit/press/content.cfm?ID=705.

89. "BeauSoleil: Band History," Wayango, http://www.wayango. com/beausoleil/bio/.

90. Gordon Masson, "New Orleans Showcase Set to Become the 02's First Festival," *Music Week,* September 19, 2008.

Chapter Seven

1. Jeff Hannusch, "Swamp Pop," Tabasco PepperFest, http://www. tabasco.com/music_stage/music_band/swamp_pop.cfm.

2. Shane K. Bernard, *Swamp Pop: Cajun and Creole Rhythm and Blues* (Jackson: University Press of Mississippi, 1996), 55-57, 60-62.

3. Ibid., 6-7; Hannusch, "Swamp Pop."

4. Broven, *South to Louisiana,* 197.

5. Bernard, *Swamp Pop,* 145.

6. Broven, *South to Louisiana,* 200-1.

7. Ibid., 203.

8. Bernard, *Swamp Pop,* 149.

9. Rod Bernard, interview with author, 2008.

10. "Johnnie Allan," Museum of the Gulf Coast, http://www.museumofthegulfcoast.org/personalities-music-legends-johnnie-allan.html.

11. Louisiana Folklife Center, "Johnnie Allan: Louisiana Swamp Pop Musician," Northwestern State University, http://louisianafolklife.nsula.edu/artist-biographies/profiles/5.

12. Ibid.

13. Bernard, *Swamp Pop,* 156; "Johnnie Allan," Museum of the Gulf Coast.

14. Bernard, *Swamp Pop,* 138-39.

15. Broven, *South to Louisiana*, 248.

16. Ibid., 250.

17. "Autobiography of Willie 'Tee,'" Willie Tee: Louisiana Swamp-Pop Artist, http://www.willietee.com/bio.htm.

18. Whitburn, *Top Pop Artists and Singles,* 97.

19. "Cookie and the Cupcakes," Ace Records, www.acerecords.co.uk/content.php?page_id=59&release=430.

20. Whitburn, *Top Pop Artists and Singles,* 97.

21. Bernard, *Swamp Pop,* 116-19.

22. Ibid., 120.

23. Ibid., 122-23.

24. Joe Nick Patoski, "Huey P. Meaux: The Crazy Cajun," *Texas Monthly,* May 1996.

25. Ibid.

26. Whitburn, *Top Pop Artists and Singles,* 221.

27. Larry Benicewicz, "Lil' Alfred: Front and Center," *Blues World*, undated.

28. Whitburn, *Top R&B Singles,* 348; Whitburn, *Top Pop Artists and Singles,* 322.

29. Andrew Hamilton, "Phil Phillips Biography," All Music Guide, available from Artist Direct, http://www.artistdirect.com/nad/music/artist/bio/0,,733396,00.html.

30. Ibid.

31. Broven, *South to Louisiana,* 189-90.

32. Ibid., 190.

33. "Phil Phillips," Ponderosa Stomp Foundation, http://www.ponderosastomp.com/music_more.php/67/Phil+Phillips.

34. Ibid.

35. Southern Folklife Collection, "Goldband Records: Phil Phillips," University of North Carolina at Chapel Hill, http://www.lib.unc.edu/mss/sfc1/goldband/artists/phil_phillips/.

36. "Phil Phillips," Ponderosa Stomp Foundation.

37. Bernard, *Swamp Pop*; Whitburn, *Top Pop Artists and Singles,* 28; Whitburn, *Top R&B Singles,* 23.

38. David Fricke, "Joe Barry," *Rolling Stone,* October 30, 2003.

39. Bernard, *Swamp Pop,* 219-20.

40. Liner notes, *I'm a Fool to Care,* Joe Berry, Smash Records.

41. Broven, *South to Louisiana,* 221.

42. Ibid; Liner notes, *I'm a Fool to Care.*

43. Liner notes, *I'm a Fool to Care.*

44. Bernard, *Swamp Pop,* 166.

45. Whitburn, *Top Pop Artists and Singles,* 28; Bernard, *Swamp Pop,* 167.

46. Broven, *South to Louisiana,* 225.

47. Koster, *Louisiana Music,* 260.

48. "Boogie Kings," Museum of the Gulf Coast, http://www.museumofthegulfcoast.org/personalities-music-legends-boogie-kings.html.

49. Ned Theall, "The Fabulous Boogie Kings: Creation of a Legend," Berman Music Foundation feature article, spring 2002.

50. Nead Theall, "Clint West," chapter four in *The Boogie Kings,* http://www.boogiekings.com/Chapter4.html.

51. Ibid.

52. Ned Theall, interview with author, 2008.

53. Ibid.

54. Whitburn, *Top Pop Artists and Singles,* 88, 279; "Tommy McClain Bio," Tommy McLain, http://www.angelfire.com/la/tommymclain/index3.html; "Tommy McLain," Museum of the Gulf Coast, http://www.museumofthegulfcoast.org/personalities-music-legends-tommy-mclain.html.

55. Woody Anders, "Biography for Tommy McLain," Internet Movie Database, http://uk.imdb.com/name/nm0572165/bio.

56. Broven, *South to Louisiana,* 228-29.

57. Ibid., 229-30.

58. Ibid., 230.

59. Anders, "Biography for Tommy McLain."

60. Gary Edwards, review of *You Can Never Keep A Good Man Down,* by G.G. Shinn, Sounds of New Orleans Records, www.soundofneworleans.com/1051~CD.htm.

61. Jason Ankeny, "T.K. Hulin Biography," All Music Guide,

available from Artist Direct, http://www.artistdirect.com/nad/music/artist/bio/0,,616305,00.html.

62. "T.K. Hulin," Museum of the Gulf Coast, http://www.museumofthegulfcoast.org/personalities-music-legends-tk-hulin.html.

63. Ibid.; Whitburn, *Top Pop Artists and Singles,* 204.

64. T.K. Hulin, interview with author, 2007.

65. Patoski, "Huey P. Meaux: The Crazy Cajun."

66. Whitburn, *Top Pop Artists and Singles,* 193.

67. Michael Hall, "The Songs Remain the Same," *Texas Monthly,* March 2007.

68. Margaret Moser, "Roy Head and Gene Kurtz Still 'Treat Her Right," *Austin Chronicle,* August 31, 2007.

69. Brian Mansfield, "For 'Sundance' Head, It's in the Blood," *USA Today*, February 27, 2007.

70. Mark Williams, "The Return of Roy Head," *The Bulletin Online*.

71. Brian Mansfield, "Freddy Fender Found Fame across Genres," *USA Today*, October 16, 2006.

72. Webster & Associates Public Relations, "Freddy Fender: Keeping the Tortillas Hot," La Onda Network, http://www.ondanet.com/tejano/artists/Freddy.Fender/Bio.html.

73. Ibid.

74. Ibid.

75. John Morthland, "Wasted Days," *Texas Monthly*, October 1995.

76. Webster & Associates, *Freddy Fender: Keeping the Tortillas Hot*, http://www.ondanet.com/tejano/artists/Freddy.Fender/Bio.html.

77. Associated Press, "Freddy Fender has incurable cancer," *USA Today*, August 2, 2006.

78. Mansfield, "Freddy Fender Found Fame across Genres."

79. Steve Huey, "Lucinda Williams Biography," All Music Guide, available from CMT, http://www.cmt.com/artists/az/williams_lucinda/bio.jhtml.

80. Holly George-Warren, Patricia Romanski, and Jon Pareles, "Lucinda Williams," *Rolling Stone Encyclopedia of Rock & Roll*, 3rd ed. (New York: Simon & Schuster, 2001).

Chapter Eight

1. Horace Logan and Bill Sloan, *Louisiana Hayride Years: Making Musical History in Country's Golden Age,* originally published as *Elvis, Hank and Me: Making Musical History on the Louisiana Hayride* (New York: St. Martin's Press, 1998; reprint New York: St. Martin's Griffin, 1999), 231-33.

2. Joey Kent, interview with Fabris Giovanni Luca for the Rocabilly Hall of Fame, http://rockabillyhall.com/ElvisJoeKent.html.

3. Ibid.

4. Ibid.

5. Logan and Sloan, *Louisiana Hayride Years*.

6. Don Walker, "Louisiana Hayride Legend Horace Logan Has Died," *Shreveport Times,* October 14, 2002.

7. Michael Luster, "Rockin' the Country, North Louisiana Style," *Louisiana Folklife Festival* booklet, 1995.

8. "The Legendary Tillman Franks," Tillman Franks, www.tillmanfranks.com/biography.htm.

9. Myrna Oliver, Horace Lee Logan obituary notice, *Shreveport Times,* October 13, 2002.

10. John Andrew Prime, "Tributes to Late Music Pioneer Franks Roll In," *Shreveport Times,* October 26, 2006.

11. Logan and Sloan, *Louisiana Hayride Years,* 28-32.

12. Colin Escott, "Hank Williams," American Masters on PBS, http://www.pbs.org/wnet/americanmasters/database/williams_h.html.

13. Logan and Sloan, *Louisiana Hayride Years,* 65.

14. Ibid., 83.

15. Ibid., 52, 77, 80.

16. Stephen Thomas Erlewine, "Webb Pierce Biography," All Music Guide, available from CMT, www.cmt.com/artists/az/pierce_webb/bio.jhtml.

17. Logan and Sloan, *Louisiana Hayride Years*, 101-2; Eric W. Penman, "Webb Pierce: Pillar of Honkytonk," Classic Country Music Pages, http://hammer.prohosting.com/~coollz/webb.htm.

18. Penman, "Webb Pierce."

19. Erlewine, "Webb Pierce Biography."

20. Logan and Sloan, *Louisiana Hayride Years,* 9, 140.

21. Frank Page, "Elvis at the Louisiana Hayride," Rockabilly Hall of Fame, http://www.rockabillyhall.com/ElvisHayride1.html.

22. Logan and Sloan, *Louisiana Hayride Years,* 1-3.

23. Ibid, 135.

24. Peter Guralnick, *Last Train to Memphis: The Rise of Elvis Presley* (Boston: Little, Brown & Co., 1994), 137, 142.

25. Logan and Sloan, *Louisiana Hayride Years,* 137-42.

26. Ibid., 155, 157.

27. Ibid., 171-75.

28. Page, "Elvis at the Louisiana Hayride."

29. Ibid.; Logan and Sloan, *Louisiana Hayride Years,* 183.

30. Peter Guralnick, "Scotty Moore and D.J. Fontana," Rockabilly Hall of Fame, http://www.rockabillyhall.com/Scotty&DJ1.html.

31. Stephen Thomas Erlewine, "Faron Young Biography," All Music Guide, available from CMT, http://www.cmt.com/artists/az/young_faron/bio.jhtml.

32. Bill Koon, *Hank Williams, So Lonesome* (Hattiesburg: University Press of Mississippi, 2002), 68; Chet Flippo, "Hell-Raising Chart-Topper Young Dies," *Billboard,* December 21, 1996.

33. Erlewine, "Faron Young Biography."

34. Wade Jessen, "Country Corner," *Billboard,* December 21, 1996; Ace Collins, "Hello Walls, by Willie Nelson," in *The Stories Behind Country Music's All-Time Greatest,* available from StillIsStillMoving.com, http://stillisstillmoving.com/WillieNelson/hello-walls-by-Willie-Nelson/.

35. Erlewine, "Faron Young Biography."

36. Flippo, "Hell-Raising Chart-Topper Young Dies."

37. Logan and Sloan, *Louisiana Hayride Years,* 211-13.

38. Ibid., 214; "500 Songs That Shaped Rock and Roll," Rock and Roll Hall of Fame, http://www.rockhall.com/exhibithigh lights/500-songs/.

39. Logan and Sloan, *Louisiana Hayride Years,* 215.

40. "Music's Man in Black," American Academy of Achievement, http://www.achievement.org/autodoc/page/cas0bio-1.

41. Whitburn, *Top Pop Artists and Singles,* 70.

42. "Music's Man in Black," American Academy of Achievement.

43. "Johnny Cash," Rockabilly Hall of Fame, http://www.rockabillyhall.com/JohnnyCash.html.

44. Stephen Holden, "Johnny Cash, Country Music Bedrock, Dies at 71," *New York Times,* September 13, 2003.

45. Brad Schmitt and Peter Cooper, "Country Icon Merle Kilgore Dies at Age 70," *Nashville Tennessean,* February 7, 2005; "Merle Kilgore," Nashville Songwriters Hall of Fame Foundation, http://www.nashvillesongwritersfoundation.com/h-k/merle-kilgore.aspx.

46. "Merle Kilgore," Nashville Songwriters Hall of Fame Foundation.

47. Ibid.

48. "Cashin' In," *Rolling Stone,* March 18, 2004.

49. Brad Schmitt and Peter Cooper, "Country Music Figure Steals the Show after Day of Medical Tests," *Nashville Tennessean,* 2004.

50. Schmitt and Cooper, "Country Icon Merle Kilgore Dies at Age 70."

51. Ray Waddell, "Merle Kilgore, 70, Dies," *Billboard,* February 19, 2005.

52. Ed Dettenheim, interview with author, 2006.

53. Ibid.; "Tommy Blake," Rockabilly Hall of Fame, http://www.rockabillyhall.com/TommyBlake1.html.

54. Obituary for Thomas L. Givens (Tommy Blake), *Shreveport Times,* December 29, 1985.

55. John Andrew Prime, interview with author, 2006.

56. Dale Hawkins, interview with author, 2005.

57. Colin Escott, *Tattooed on Their Tongues* (New York: Schirmer Books, 1996), 32-33.

58. Liner notes, *We Wanna Boogie,* Randy McNutt.

59. Dale Hawkins interview.

60. Escott, *Tattooed on Their Tongues,* 33.

61. Dale Hawkins Web Site, http://www.dalehawkinsmusic.com/

62. "500 Songs That Shaped Rock and Roll," Rock and Roll Hall of Fame, http://www.rockhall.com/exhibithighlights/500-songs/.

63. Whitburn, *Top Pop Artists and Singles,* 191; Whitburn, *Top R&B Singles,* 185.

64. Interview with Dale Hawkins, 2005; http://www.dalehawkinsmusic.com/.

65. Logan and Sloan, *Louisiana Hayride Years,* 116-19.

66. "Jim Reeves Biography," Sing 365.com, http://www.sing365.com/music/lyric.nsf/Jim-Reeves-Biography/E3E09C861DB3FAEE48256DCF000C203A; Whitburn, *Top Pop Artists and Singles,* 344-45.

67. Ibid.

68. Logan and Sloan, *Louisiana Hayride Years,* 120-21.

69. Whitburn, *Top Pop Artists and Singles,* 344-45.

70. Logan and Sloan, *Louisiana Hayride Years,* 190-91); Stephen Thomas Erlewine, "Johnny Horton Biography," All Music Guide, available from CMT, http://www.cmt.com/artists/az/horton_johnny/bio.jhtml.

71. Escott, *Tattooed on Their Tongues,* 117.

72. Logan and Sloan, *Louisiana Hayride Years,* 190, 203-4; Whitburn, *Top Pop Artists and Singles,* 191); Whitburn, *Top R&B Singles,* 202.

73. Colin Larkin, "Claude King," *The Encyclopedia of Popular Music,* 4th ed. (New York: Oxford University Press, 2006).

74. Ibid.

75. Claude King biography, http//claudeki.dot5hosting.com/page3.html.

76. Ibid.

77. Shaun Mather and Phil Davies, "Let's Think about Luman," Rockabilly Hall of Fame, http://www.rockabillyhall.com/

BobLuman.html.

78. Ibid.

79. Ibid.

80. Whitburn, *Top Pop Artists and Singles,* 259; Sandra Brennan, "Bob Luman Biography," All Music Guide, http://www.cmt.com/artists/az/luman_bob/bio.jhtml.

81. Mather and Davies, "Let's Think about Luman."

82. Whitburn, *Top Pop Artists and Singles,* 234.

83. Ibid.

84. "David Houston Biography," Sing365.com http://www.sing365.com/music/lyric.nsf/David-Houston-Biography/8D4918D3FC43D0B048256E2A00127AAB.

Chapter Nine

1. Ken Burke, "Ivory Joe Hunter Biography," Musician Biographies database, http://www.musicianguide.com/biographies/1608004446/Ivory-Joe-Hunter.html

2. Brittany Edwards, interview with author, 2008.

3. Tom Simon, "Ivory Joe Hunter," Tom Simon web page, www.tsimon.com/hunter.htm.

4. Whitburn, *Top R&B Singles,* 202-3; Whitburn, *Top Pop Artists and Singles,* 50-51, 76-77.

5. Simon, "Ivory Joe Hunter."

6. Colin Larkin, "Ivory Joe Hunter," *The Encyclopedia of Popular Music,* 4th ed. (New York: Oxford University Press, 2006).

7. Whitburn, *Top Pop Artists and Singles,* 250; Colin Escott and Martin Hawkins, *Good Rockin' Tonight: Sun Records and the Birth of Rock 'n' Roll* (New York: St. Martin's Press, 1992), 189-201; "Jerry Lee Lewis," Rock and Roll Hall of Fame, http://www.rockhall.com/hof/inductee.asp?id=144.

8. Nick Tosches, *Hellfire* (New York: Grove Press, 1982), 57-58.

9. Charles M. Young, "The Killer Reloaded," *Rolling Stone,* October 19, 2006; "Jerry Lee Lewis: Yes, He Really Married His Cousin," The Rare Exception, www.rareexception.com/Garden/Rock/Jerry.php; Tony Papard, "Jerry Lee Lewis (a.k.a. The Killer) and Family," The Unorthodox Website Blog, http://www.btinternet.com/~Tony.Papard/JERRYLEELEWIS.HTM.

10. "Jerry Lee Lewis, a.k.a. the Killer," LivinBlues, www.livinblues.com/bluesrooms/jerryleelewis.asp; Undated appearance on *The Tonight Show* with Johnny Carson.

11. Colin Escott and Martin Hawkins, *Sun Records: The Brief History of the Legendary Record Label* (New York: Omnibus Press, 1975), 104.

12. Ibid; "Jerry Lee Lewis," ClassicBands.com, www.classicbands.com/jerrylee.html; Cub Koda, "Jerry Lee Lewis: Biography," All Music, http://www.allmusic.com/cg/amg.dll?p=amg&sql=11:giftxqe5ldde~T1.

13. Jerry Lee Lewis, http://www.thesixtyone.com/JerryLeeLewis/.

14. Tosches, *Hellfire,* 76-77.

15. Koda, "Jerry Lee Lewis: Biography."

16. Logan and Sloan, *Louisiana Hayride Years,* 105-6.

17. Tosches, *Hellfire,* 101-4.

18. Ibid., 109-10, 192.

19. Ibid., 115-17.

20. Koda, "Jerry Lee Lewis: Biography."

21. Escott and Hawkins, *Sun Records,* 195.

22. Escott and Hawkins, *Good Rockin' Tonight:* 195; "Jerry Lee Lewis," ClassicBands.com.

23. Escott and Hawkins, *Good Rockin' Tonight,* 195; Whitburn, *Top R&B Singles,* 265; Whitburn, *Top Pop Artists and Singles,* 250.

24. Patrick Wall, "The Killer: Jerry Lee Lewis," Rockabilly Hall of Fame, http://www.rockabillyhall.com/JLL.html.

25. "Jerry Lee Lewis," ClassicBands.com.

26. Escott and Hawkins, *Good Rockin' Tonight,* 198.

27. Whitburn, *Top Pop Artists and Singles,* 250; Whitburn, *Top R&B Singles,* 265.

28. Escott and Hawkins, Sun Records, 72.

29. "Jerry Lee Lewis," Rock and Roll Hall of Fame.

30. Tosches, *Hellfire,* 139-40.

31. Wall, "The Killer: Jerry Lee Lewis"; Robert Fontenot, "Jerry Lee Lewis," http://oldies.about.com/od/rockabill1/p/jerryleelewis.htm.

32. Linda Gail Lewis (Jerry Lee Lewis's sister), interview on BBC, February 19, 2005.
Jerry Lee Lewis: I Am What I Am, 1989, Hallway Productions documentary; Papard, "Jerry Lee Lewis (a.k.a. The Killer)."

33. "Jerry Lee Lewis," Rock and Roll Hall of Fame; Koda, "Jerry Lee Lewis: Biography."

34. Audrey Winters, "The Killer Tracks His Southern Roots," Kyle Esplin.com, http://www.kyleesplin.com/jllsb/JLLSBDIR/pages/65page.htm.

35. Bruce Eder, review of *Southern Roots/Boogie Woogie Country Man,* by Jerry Lee Lewis, All Music Guide, available from Answers.com, http://www.answers.com/topic/southern-roots-boogie-woogie-country-man.

36. "Jerry Lee Lewis," ClassicBands.com; Koda, "Jerry Lee Lewis: Biography."

37. Tosches, *Hellfire,* 253; Edna Gunderson, "Once More with Feeling: The Lewis Years," *USA Today,* September 26, 2006.

38. Holly George-Warren, Patricia Romanski, and Jon Pareles, "Jerry Lee Lewis," *The Rolling Stone Encyclopedia of Rock and Roll,* 3rd ed. (New York: Simon & Schuster, 2001); "Jerry Lee Lewis: 'The Killer'," RockSite, http://www.rocksite.info/r-lewis-jerry-lee.htm.

39. Koda, "Jerry Lee Lewis: Biography."

40. Chuck Miller, "Collectormania," *Goldmine,* January 1998, www.8trackheaven.com/goldmine.html.

41. Koda, "Jerry Lee Lewis: Biography"; "Jerry Lee Lewis," Rock and Roll Hall of Fame.

42. Stephen Thomas Erlewine, review of *Last Man Standing,* by Jerry Lee Lewis, http://www.answers.com/topic/jerry-lee-lewis.

43. Cathi Cox, "Gilley, Lewis and Swaggart Join Delta Music Hall of Fame," CMT News, http://www.cmt.com/news/country-music/1452735/gilley-lewis-and-swaggart-join-delta-music-hall-of-fame.jhtml.

44. Wall, "The Killer Influences Everybody, Man," Rockabilly Hall of Fame, http://www.rockabillyhall.com/JLL.html.

45. Papard, "Jerry Lee Lewis (a.k.a. The Killer)"; "Jerry Lee Lewis," ClassicBands.com.

46. "Tommy Sands," Rockabilly Hall of Fame, http://www.rockabillyhall.com/TommySands.html.

47. Ibid.

48. "Biography for Tommy Sands," Internet Movie Database, http://www.imdb.com/name/nm0762378/bio.

49. "Conway Twitty: Biography," CMT, www.cmt.com/artists/az/twitty_conway/bio.jhtml.

50. Mark Coleman and Don McLeese, "Tribute," *Rolling Stone,* August 5, 1993.

51. "Artist Biography: Conway Twitty," Countrypolitan, www.countrypolitan.com/bio-conway-twitty.php.

52. *The Conway Twitty Story,* Country Music Hall of Fame and Museum, http://www.countrymusichalloffame.com/site/inductees.aspx?cid=194.

53. "Conway Twitty," Delta Music Museum Hall of Fame, http://www.sos.louisiana.gov/Home/Museums/DeltaMusicMuseum/Exhibits/HallofFame/ConwayTwitty/tabid/723/Default.aspx.

54. "Conway Twitty," Country Music Hall of Fame and Museum, http://www.countrymusichalloffame.com/site/inductees.aspx?cid=194.

55. Stephen Thomas Erlewine, "Conway Twitty: Biography," All

Music Guide, available from http://www.answers.com/topic/conway-twitty; "Conway Twitty," Country Music Hall of Fame and Museum.

56. Erlewine, "Conway Twitty: Biography."

57. Whitburn, *Top Pop Artists and Singles,* 428-29.

58. Erlewine, "Conway Twitty: Biography."

59. Whitburn, *Top Pop Artists and Singles,* 428-29.

60. Erlewine, "Conway Twitty: Biography."

61. Coleman and McLeese, "Tribute."

62. Whitburn, *Top Pop Artists and Singles,* 140.

63. "Jimmy Elledge," Ponderosa Stomp Foundation, http://www.ponderosastomp.com/music_more.php/145/Jimmy+Elledge; "Westbank Musicians Hall of Fame, Inc. Inductees 2004," Westbank Musicians Hall of Fame, http://westbankmusicianshalloffame.uuuq.com/2004%20inductees.html.

64. Karen Gray, Elledge cousin, e-mail to author, January 6, 2006.

65. Pat McCabe, Elledge cousin, e-mail to author, January 6, 2006.

66. "Biography," Hank, Jr., www.hankjr.com/newbio.htm.

67. "Hank Williams, Jr.," Alabama Music Hall of Fame, http://www.alamhof.org/willhjr.htm.

68. Stephen Thomas Erlewine, "Hank Williams, Jr.: Biography," All Music Guide, http://www.allmusic.com/cg/amg.dll?p=amg&sql=11:3zfexqugldje~T1.

69. "Hank Williams, Jr.," Alabama Music Hall of Fame, http://www.alamhof.org/willhjr.htm; "Guide to Louisiana Music at the Grammys," Louisiana Music Archives and Artist Directory, http://www.satchmo.com/nolavl/grammy.html.

70. "Biography," Hank, Jr..

71. Jason Ankeny, "The Newbeats Biography," All Music Guide, available from Artist Direct, http://www.artistdirect.com/artist/bio/newbeats/473034.

72. Tony Rounce and Harry Young, "The Newbeats: Groovin' Out on Life," www.geocities.com/corkino/newbeats.htm; Whitburn, *Top Pop Artists and Singles,* 300.

73. Ibid.

74. "Biography," Larry Henley: The Official Website, http://www.larryhenley.com/biowindow.html; Whitburn, *Top Pop Artists and Singles*, 569.

75. Dale Kawashima, "Jeff Silbar: Writing the Classic *Wind Beneath My Wings,*" *Songwriter Universe Magazine*, http://www.songwriteruniverse.com/wind.html.

76. Richie Unterberger, "The Uniques," All Music Guide, available from Answers.com, http://www.answers.com/topic/the-Uniques.

77. Ibid.

78. Joe Stampley, interview with author, 2005.

79. Ibid.

80. "Joe Stampley: Biography," Official Joe Stampley Website, http://www.joestampley.com/Bio.htm.

81. Ibid.

82. Fannie Moore, "The Uniques to Perform in Springhill on Reunion Tour," *Minden Press-Herald*, August 17, 2005.

83. "O.C. Smith, Entertainer and Minister," African American Registry, http://www.aaregistry.com/detail.php?id=1600.

84. Tom Simon, "O.C. Smith," Tom Simon web page, http://www.tsimon.com/ocsmith.htm.

85. Whitburn, *Top Pop Artists and Singles,* 388.

86. "O.C. Smith, Entertainer and Minister," African American Registry.

87. Whitburn, *Top Pop Artists and Singles,* 448,

88. Cary Baker, "Tony Joe White," Cary Baker's Conqueroo, http://www.conqueroo.com/tonyjoewhitebio.html.

89. John Bush, "Tony Joe White Biography," All Music Guide, available from CMT, http://www.cmt.com/artists/az/white_tony_joe/bio.jhtml.

90. Jim Bessman, "Tony Joe's Campfire Songs," *Billboard,* September 25, 2004; Baker, "Tony Joe White."

91. Kenny Bill Stinson, interview with author, 2007.

92. The River of Song Project, "Kenny Bill Stinson," Filmmakers Collaborative and the Smithsonian Institution, www.pbs.org/riverofsong/artists/e4-kenny.html.

93. Lennon Piano, http://web.mac.com/caroline.true/lennonpiano/home.html; "John Lennon's 'Imagine' Piano gets Photo Op in N.O.," NOLA Entertainment Blog, posted May 31, 2007, http://blog.nola.com/entertainment/2007/05/john_lennons_imagine_piano_get.html.

94. Kenny Bill Stinson interview.

95. Ibid.

96. "Kris Kristofferson," Tribute Entertainment Media Group, http://www.tribute.ca/people/Kris+Kristofferson/1564/.

97. "Kris Kristofferson: Biography," CMT, http://www.cmt.com/artists/az/kristofferson_kris/bio.jhtml.

98. Alan Case, "Kris Kristofferson," Casenet, http://www.casenet.com/people/kriskristofferson.htm.

99. John Sacksteder, "Biography for Kris Kristofferson," Internet Movie Database, http://www.imdb.com/name/nm0001434/bio.

100. Andy Langer, "Q&A: Kris Kristofferson," *Esquire Magazine,* March 2006; Kris Kristofferson, interview with Mike

Lawson, August 15, 1995, http://www.mikelawson.com/module-ContentExpress-display-ceid-14.html.

101. "Biography of Kris Kristofferson," Astrotheme, http://www.astrotheme.com/portraits/aFAAaPf5pN32.htm; "Kris Kristofferson," PoemHunter.com, http://www.poemhunter.com/lyrics/kris-kristofferson/biography; Whitburn, *Top Pop Artists and Singles,* 333, 388, 227.

102. Kris Kristofferson interview; Whitburn, *Top Pop Artists and Singles,* 70; Joshua Lyon, "Kris Kristofferson & James Mangold," *Variety,* January 9, 2006;

103. Biography of Kris Kristofferson," Astrotheme; "BMI Legends Kris Kristofferson, Waylon Jennings Inducted into Hollywood RockWalk," Broadcast Music, Inc., www.bmi.com/news/entry/334889; Melinda Newman, "RockWalk for Kristofferson," *Billboard,* June 24, 2006. "Johnny Mercer Award: Kris Kristofferson," Songwriters Hall of Fame, http://www.songwritershalloffame.org/ceremony/awards/C3001; "Inductees List," Hollywood's RockWalk, http://www.rockwalk.com/inductees/.

104. "Jimmy Buffet," Booking Entertainment, http://www.bookingentertainment.com/artists/rock/booking-jimmy-buffett.php.

105. "Jimmy Buffett," ClassicBands.com, http://www.classicbands.com/buffett.html; "Jimmy Buffet," Booking Entertainment.

106. Ibid.

107. "Jimmy Buffett Biography," CMT, www.cmt.com/artists/az/buffett_jimmy/bio.jhtml.

108. "Jimmy Buffett," Answers.com, www.answers.com/topic/jimmy-buffett.

109. Inscription on wall of Margaritaville Café in New Orleans.

110. Whitburn, *Top Pop Artists and Singles,* 100.

111. Jason Ankeny, "The Cowsills," All Music Guide, available from Ask.com, http://www.ask.com/music/artist/the-Cowsills/3976 .

112. Rob Sheffield, "Alex Chilton," *The New Rolling Stone Album Guide,* 2004, http://www.rollingstone.com/artists/alex chilton.biography; Whitburn, *Top Pop Artists and Singles,* 48.

113. Ibid.; "Alex Chilton," Last Call Records, http://www.lastcallrecords.com/biographies/alexchilton.html.

114. "Biography for Stephen Stills," Internet Movie Database, http://www.imdb.com/name/nm0830317/bio.

115. "Stephen Stills Professional Biography," SuiteLorraine.com (Crosby, Stills, and Nash fan site), http://www.suitelorraine.com/suitelorraine/Pages/stillsbio.html; Whitburn, *Top Pop Artists and Singles,* 58.

116. Bruce Pilato, "Crosby, Stills and Nash See the Changes," *Crawdaddy!*, June 6, 2007, http://crawdaddy.wolfgangsvault. com/Article/Crosby-Stills-and-Nash-See-the-Changes.html; Whitburn, *Top Pop Artists and Singles*, 104.

117. "Stephen Stills Professional Biography," SuiteLorraine.com.

118. "Kimball, Bobby," Toto, http://www.toto99.com/features/ encyclopedia/kimball.shtml.

119. "Bobby Kimball," CorporateArtists.com, http://www. corporateartists.com/bobby_kimball_toto.html.

120. James Brady, "In Step with Randy Jackson," *Parade Magazine,* January 6, 2008.

121. Paula J. K. Morris, "Randy Jackson," Answers.com, http:// www.answers.com/topic/randy-jackson.

122. Eugene Chadbourne, "Will 'Dub' Jones," All Music Guide, http://www.allmusic.com/cg/amg.dll?p=amg&sql=11:djfqxql5ldde ~T1; Whitburn, *Top Pop Artists and Singles,* 88-89, 425.

123. Colin J. Hulin, liner notes for *The Best of Zebra in Black and White,* by Zebra, Mayhem, 1998.

Chapter Ten

1. Irma Thomas, interview with author, 2007.

2. Douglas Wolk, "Domino Dave: The Bartholomew behind the Fats,"*BostonPhoenix,* April 11-18, 2002, http://www.bostonphoenix. com/boston/music/other_stories/documents/02223802.htm.

3. "1998 Award and Induction Ceremony: Dave Bartholomew," Songwriters Hall of Fame, http://www.songwritershalloffame.org/ ceremony/entry/C3110/108.

4. "Dave Bartholomew," Rock and Roll Hall of Fame, http:// www.rockhall.com/inductee/dave-bartholomew; Rick Coleman, *Blue Monday: Fats Domino and the Lost Dawn of Rock 'n' Roll* (Cambridge, MA: Da Capo Press, 2006), 39.

5. Hannusch, *I Hear You Knockin'*, 98-100.

6. Wolk, "Domino Dave."

7. Whitburn, *Top Pop Artists and Singles,* 125-26.

8. Bruce Eder, "Roy Montrell," All Music Guide, available from VH1, http://www.vh1.com/artists/az/montrell_roy/artist.jhtml.

9. Hannusch, *The Soul of New Orleans,* 23.

10. Ibid., 25-26.

11. Ibid., 26.

12. "The Tommy Ridgley Biography," Tommy Ridgley, http:// www.tomyridgley.com/bio.htm.

13. Jonny Whiteside, "Earl Palmer, Rock & Roll's Heavy Hitter," *Louisiana Weekly*, July 23-29, 1999.

14. "2005 Inductees," Rock and Roll Hall of Fame, http://www.rockhall.com/inductee/earl-palmer.

15. Bill Dahl, "Earl Palmer Biography," All Music Guide, available from MP3.com, http://www.mp3.com/earl-palmer/artists/91775/biography.html.

16. "2005 Inductees," Rock and Roll Hall of Fame.

17. Keith Spera, "New Orleans Drum Legend Earl Palmer Dies in L.A. at 83," *New Orleans Times-Picayune*, September 20, 2008; "Earl Palmer, 84, a Jazz Session Drummer, Dies," *New York Times*, September 22, 2008.

18. Coleman, *Blue Monday,* 100-1, 294.

19. Jason Ankeny, "Herbert Hardesty," All Music Guide, available from Barnes and Noble, http://music.barnesandnoble.com/search/artistbio.asp?&z=y&CTR=132312.

20. Bruce Eder, "Lee Allen," All Music Guide, available from AOL Music, http://music.aol.com/artist/lee-allen/biography/1002949.

21. Broven, *Rhythm & Blues in New Orleans,* 91.

22. "AFO Musicians: Alvin 'Red' Tyler," AFO Foundation, http://www.afofoundation.org/musicians.

23. Ibid.

24. "AFO Musicians: Peter 'Chuck' Badie," AFO Foundation, http://www.afofoundation.org/musicians.

25. Coleman, *Blue Monday,* 150-51.

26. "Cornelius Coleman," BlackCat Rockabilly Europe, http://www.rockabilly.nl/references/messages/cornelius_coleman.htm.

27. Steve Huey, "Eddie Bo," All Music Guide, available from SwapaCD.com, http://secure.swapacd.com/cd/artist/3724-eddie+bo.

28. Ibid.

29. "Eddie Bo's Blurbs: About Me," Eddie Bo's MySpace page, http://www.myspace.com/eddiebosound.

30. James Johnson, interview with author, 2006; John Wirt, "James Johnson," Baton Rouge Blues Society, http://www.batonrougeblues.org/Musicians%20biographies/james_johnson.htm.

31. John Wirt, "Blues Man Lazy Lester Finding New Fame," *Baton Rouge Advocate*, April 20, 2006.

32. "AFO Musicians: John Boudreaux," AFO Foundation, www.afofoundation.org/musicians.

33. "AFO Musicians: Melvin Lastie," AFO Foundation, www.afofoundation.org/musicians.

34. Jason Berry, "Rhythm with a Spirit," *New Orleans Magazine,* September 2000.

35. Ibid.

36. Eugene Chadbourne, "Wardell Quezergue," All Music Guide,

available from Barnes and Noble, http://music.barnesandnoble.com/search/artistbio.asp?CTR=161125.

37. *Legends of New Orleans*, prod. Michael Murphy Productions and The New Orleans Jazz & Heritage Foundation, dir. by Michael Murphy and Ron Yager, 2001, DVD.

38. Steve Huey, "Allen Toussaint," All Music Guide, available from Verve Music Group, http://www.vervemusicgroup.com/artist/default.aspx?aid=6938.

39. Ibid.

40. Hannusch, *I Hear You Knockin'*, 62; Larry McKinley, interview with author, 2007; Cosimo Matassa, interview with author, 2006; "Allen Toussaint: Biography," Last.fm, http://www.last.fm/music/Allen+Toussaint/+wiki.

41. "Allen Toussaint," New Orleans Talent, http://www.epluri.com/NOTfolder/Acts/AllenTousiant.html; "Allen Toussaint: Fast Facts," Mahalo, http://www.mahalo.com/Allen_Toussaint.

42. "Allen Toussaint," New Orleans Talent.

43. Bill Holland, "Allen Toussaint," *Billboard*, September 24, 2005.

44. "A Forward 'River in Reverse,'" *USA Today*, June 21, 2006.

45. Gerald James McGee, interview with author, 2008.

46. "Gerry McGee," Rockabilly Hall of Fame, http://www.rockabillyhall.com/GerryMcGee1.html.

47. Ibid.

48. Gerald James McGee interview.

49. Dan Gilbert, Deacon John Interview for *Where Y'at Magazine*, http://www.ponderosastomp.com/music_more.php/141/Deacon+John.

50. Bob Putignano, "Jazz Sides: Deacon John Moore," *Goldmine*, March 2003; Hannusch, *The Soul of New Orleans*, 213.

51. Gilbert, Deacon John Interview; Deacon John Moore, interview with author, 2007.

52 Gilbert, Deacon John Interview.

53. Ibid.

54. Putignano, "Jazz Sides."

55. Gilbert, Deacon John Interview.

56. Mike Shepherd, Louisiana Music Hall of Fame director, interview with author, 2007.

57. Deacon John Moore, interview with author, 2007; Todd Smith, "Deacon John's Jump Blues," All About Jazz, http://www.allaboutjazz.com/php/article.php?id=461.

58. Colin Kilgour, "D.J. Fontana," Black Cat Rockabilly Europe, http://www.rockabilly.nl/references/messages/d_j_fontana.htm.

59. Stephen Koch, "Floyd Cramer's Country Keys," *Arkansas*

Times, May 3, 2007, http://www.arktimes.com/Articles/ArticleViewer. aspx?ArticleID=4281eb97-df2f-4cd6-9bf1-98af23c80b8a; Logan and Sloan, *Louisiana Hayride Years,* 105; "Floyd Cramer," Rock and Roll Hall of Fame, http://www.rockhall.com/hof/inductee. asp?id=2028.

60. Colin Escott, "Floyd Cramer," Country Music Hall of Fame, http://www.countrymusichalloffame.com/site/inductees.aspx?cid=110.

61. "Floyd Cramer," Rock and Roll Hall of Fame.

62. Escott, "Floyd Cramer."

63. Whitburn, *Top Pop Artists and Singles,* 100-1.

64. Don Rhodes, "Cramer Played Piano for Legends of Music," *Augusta (GA) Chronicle,* January 9, 1998.

65. Chet Flippo, "Nashville Vet Floyd Cramer, 64, Dies," *Billboard,* January 17, 1998; Jon Wiederhorn, "Floyd Cramer: 1933-1997," *Rolling Stone,* February 19, 1998.

66. Ed Dettenheim, interview with author, 2007.

67. Shane Hughes, "Mr. Hoody: The Tragedy of Tommy Blake," Rockabilly Hall of Fame, http://www.rockabillyhall.com/rarerockabilly04.html.

68. Ibid.

69. Ibid.

70. Ed Dettenheim interview.

71. Dale Hawkins, interview with author, 2007; Dale Hawkins, follow-up e-mail to author, May 25, 2007.

72. Hughes, "Mr. Hoody."

73. Ibid.

74. "Catfish Festival: Featuring a Tribute to Winnsboro's Own Fred Carter, Jr.," *Franklin (LA) Sun,* April 10, 2002; Whitburn, *Top Pop Artists and Singles,* 381-82, 177, 355, 134; Fred Carter, Jr., interview with author, 2007.

75. Fred Carter, Jr., interview.

76. Tapio Vaisanen, "Maylon Humphries," Black Cat Rockabilly, http://www.rockabillyeurope.com/?references/references.htm.

77. Lee Cotton, "Drummer Men," *Rock & Blues News,* February-March 2001.

78. Ibid.

79. Charles Conner, interview with author, 2006.

80. Ibid.

81. Ibid.

82. Cotton, "Drummer Men."

83. Charles Conner interview.

84. Ibid.

85. Jack Conrad, "Review: Lakland Joe Osborn(e) Signature

Series Bass," *Music Biz Magazine,* June 2001.

86. Ed Hogan, "Joe Osborne: Biography," All Music Guide, available from Answers.com, http://www.answers.com/topic/joe-osborne.

87. Ibid.

88. "James Burton," Spiritus Temporis Web Ring Community, http://www.spiritus-temporis.com/james-burton/.

89. "Biography," The Official James Burton Website, http://www.james-burton.net/portal/index.php?option=com_content&task=view&id=26.

90. "James Burton," Rock and Roll Hall of Fame, http://www.rockhall.com/inductee/james-burton.

91. Ibid.

92. "James Burton," Rockabilly Hall of Fame, http://www.rockabillyhall.com/JamesBurton.html.

93. James Burton, interview with Arjan Deelen, 1999, http://www.james-burton.net/interview.html.

94. Ibid.

95. "James Burton," Rock and Roll Hall of Fame.

96. "Biography," The Official James Burton Website; "James Burton," Rock and Roll Hall of Fame.

97. Allen Harris, interview with author, 2008; "Allen 'Puddler' Harris," Wapedia: Mobile Encyclopedia, http://wapedia.mobi/en/Allen_%22Puddler%22_Harris; "Allen 'Puddler' Harris," Delta Music Museum Hall of Fame, http://www.sos.louisiana.gov/Home/Museums/DeltaMusicMuseum/Exhibits/HallofFame/AllenPuddlerHarris/tabid/735/Default.aspx.

98. Jon R. Smith, interview with author, 2008; "Jon R. Smith," Strokeland Records, http://www.strokeland.com/StrokelandJazz/JonRSmith/JonRSmithCD/JonRSmithCD.htm; "News and Info," Jon Smith, http://www.jonrsmith.com/.

99. "Discography," Jon Smith, http://www.jonrsmith.com/discography.html.

100. Jon R. Smith, interview with author, 2008; Ned Theall, interview with author, 2008.

Chapter Eleven

1. Whitburn, *Top Pop Artists and Singles,* 87, 122, 261, 287, 465; Dick Holler, interview with author, 2006.

2. Roy Hayes. Interview with author, 2006.

3. "Inductee Exhibits," Songwriters Hall of Fame, http://www.songwritershalloffame.org/exhibits/era.

4. "Hall of Fame Members," Nashville Songwriters Hall of Fame, http://www.nashvillesongwritersfoundation.com/hall-of-fame.aspx?pages=A-C.

5. Jason Ankeny, "Dorothy Labostrie," All Music Guide, available from Answers.com, www.answers.com/topic/dorothy-labostrie.

6. Broven, *South to Louisiana,* 183.

7. Scott Jordan, "Searching for Bobby Charles," *Gambit Weekly,* October 26, 2004.

8. Whitburn, *Top R&B Singles,* 73, 185.

9. Jordan, "Searching for Bobby Charles."

10. Steve Huey, "Bobby Charles," All Music Guide, available from Artist Direct, http://www.artistdirect.com/nad/music/artist/bio/0,,413905,00.html.

11. Jordan, "Searching for Bobby Charles."

12. Ibid.

13. Roy Hayes interview.

14. Whitburn, *Top Pop Artists and Singles,* 125-26); Roy Hayes interview.

15. Amazon.com, www.amazon.com.

16. Roy Hayes interview.

17. J.C. Marion, "Strange Things Happen: Percy Mayfield," http://home.earthlink.net`v1tiger/percy.html; Bill Dahl, "Percy Mayfield: Biography," African Genesis Presents the Gift of Soul, www.afgen.com/percy_mayfield.html.

18. Marion, "Strange Things Happen: Percy Mayfield."

19. Whitburn, *Top Pop Artists and Singles,* 76-77.

20. Marion, "Strange Things Happen: Percy Mayfield."

21. Dick Holler, e-mail correspondence with author, 2006; Dick Holler, interview with author, 2007.

22. "The Royal Guardsmen," ClassicBands.com, www.classicbands.com/royalguardsmen.html; Whitburn, *Top Pop Artists and Singles,* 361; Dick Holler e-mail correspondence.

23. Whitburn, *Top Pop Artists and Singles,* 87, 122, 261, 287, 465; Dick Holler interview; Ace Collins, *Songs Sung Red White, and Blue: The Stories Behind America's Best-Loved Patriotic Songs* (New York: HarperCollins, 2003).

24. Dick Holler e-mail correspondence.

25. Peter Finney, Jr., "Song from '50s Still Paying off for Dominican Priest Who Co-Wrote It," *National Catholic Reporter,* November 9, 2007; Paula Day, "Dominican Shares Musical Gifts with Holy Cross," *Georgia Bulletin,* April 20, 1989.

26. "Tony Haselden," LeRoux, http://www.laleroux.com/HTMLPages/tony.html.

27. John Michael, "Local Songwriter Dies in California," *Port Allen Riverside Leader,* July 10, 2003; Ed Hogan, "Skip Scarborough," All Music Guide, available from Answers.com, http://www.answers.com/topic/skip-scarborough.

28. John Wirt, "Louisiana Music Vet, Egan, Mainly Known for Songwriting," *Baton Rouge Advocate*, August 1, 2008; David Egan, e-mail correspondence with author, 2008; Robert Fontenot, "Quote," Southern Artistry, http://www.southernartistry.org/biography.cfm?id=2043.

29. Margaret Lewis Warwick, e-mail correspondence with author, 2008; Brian Nevill, *Shreveport High Steppers,* Ace Records, September, 2001; Whitburn, *Top Pop Artists and Singles,* 10; Whitburn, *Top R&B Singles,* 4, 5.

30. Phil Davies, "Margaret Lewis," Black Cat Rockabilly, http://www.rockabilly.nl/references/messages/margaret_lewis.htm.

31. Ruling of Second Circuit Court of Appeal, September 22, 2004.

Index